The Track of Man

THE
Track of Man

ADVENTURES

OF AN

ANTHROPOLOGIST

by Henry Field

GREENWOOD PRESS, PUBLISHERS
NEW YORK

TO JULIE

Acknowledgments

This book was begun at Acapulco in March 1946. The original manuscript has twice been bisected. Much extraneous material to my career as an anthropologist and archaeologist has been deleted.

However, I must express my deep gratitude to my family, friends and acquaintances, scientific colleagues, particularly at Field Museum and in the Peabody Museum at Harvard, and government officials at home and abroad—all of whom contributed to the final results.

To my three tutors, Mr. Henry Balfour, Dr. R. R. Marett, and Dr. L. H. Dudley Buxton, and to my scientific advisers, Sir Arthur Keith, Sir Henry Wellcome, Dr. Berthold Laufer, Dr. Earnest Hooton, go especial thanks for constant guidance and encouragement.

To those who have contributed funds for my travels, expeditions, research work, my two Exhibition Halls in Chicago, and publications, mere words are far from adequate.

To Miss Evelyn Wells, who assisted in rearranging and editing the final draft, goes my admiration for patience and skill.

Millions enjoy hunting, so do I, but fox hunting in Leicestershire, grouse shooting in Scotland, partridge and pheasant shooting in England, quail and turkey hunting in Georgia, wild boar hunting in Iraq—none can compare to the thrill of being on the greatest hunt of all—THE TRACK OF MAN.

Coconut Grove
Florida
July 23, 1953.

List of Illustrations

FOLLOWING PAGE 96

1. *Skeleton guarding Sumerian tomb.*

2. *Excavating four-wheeled chariot.*

3. *Four-wheeled chariot with copper nails around rim.*

4. *Reconstruction of Sumerian four-wheeled chariot.*

5. *Copper rein-ring excavated at Kish.*

6. *View over "Y" Trench at Kish with diagram of strata.*

7. *Arabs lunching on bread and dates.*

8. *Payday at Kish camp.*

9. *Mound "W" where cuneiform tablets were excavated.*

10. *Northwestern entrance to Nabonidus temple.*

11. *Fragment of primitive pottery vessel.*

12. *Aurignacian "Venus of Willendorf."*

13. *Dr. Hugo Obermaier, the author, and Abbé Henri Breuil outside Altamira Cave.*

14. *Limestone caves in southern Spain.*

15. *Neanderthal family.*

FOLLOWING PAGE 256

16. *Aurignacian artist.*

17. *Bronze statue of Shilluk warrior.*

18. *Dancing girl of the Sara tribe.*

19. *Skulls from tomb in southwestern Sinai.*

20. *Author measuring skulls.*

21. *Bedouin being measured by author.*

22. *Nabataean inscription from Roman period.*

23. *Excavated brick pavement and drain, Kish.*

24. *Bedouin and camel with members of U.C. African expedition.*

25. *Yezidi tombs at Sheikh Adi.*

26. *Hedgehog and toy model excavated at Kish.*

27. *Standing copper support for ceremonial bowl.*

28. *Modern lawn coaster.*

The Track of Man

OXFORD was foggy that November of 1925. The towers of New College Chapel and the old city wall were shrouded in mist. Guy Fawkes Day had slipped by with the occasional whang of a firecracker breaking the hazy silence. Now all that was left were these dreary gray days before Christmas vacation; days good for study and little else.

I was lying on the sofa reading a book about the Cambrian deposits in the British Isles. The flames from the fireplace pushed heat and shadows into the room. There was a knock and the landlord brought in a letter postmarked San Francisco.

A letter from my favorite grand-uncle Barbour Lathrop was always a welcome diversion. It is almost impossible to give a clear picture of Uncle Barbour, although many have tried, and one of the best was as an "Unforgettable Character" by Marjory Stoneman Douglas in the *Reader's Digest*. He had traveled around the world many times and was a great believer in the educational advantages of travel, and his letters beginning "Dear Old Digger" invariably expressed his displeasure that I was spending so much time listening to lectures and learning what others had done and thought. His admonition, that if I wanted to be an anthropologist I should start digging, had been urged upon me since my twelfth year.

This time, he wrote, he was bolstering his advice with a check; under no circumstances was I to spend it on more books or study. He would require a full accounting, and on the strength of that he would know whether he should help finance my scientific career.

As I shook the envelope a check fluttered to the floor, face down. Fortunately I sat down on the couch as I picked it up or I probably would have crashed to the floor. The check was for one thousand dollars.

The fog swirling against the window was no hazier than my thoughts. Through my mind swirled a jumble of skulls and pyramids, Arabs with bare toes curled in the sand, the Nile, the Tigris, the Euphrates, and beyond all these Kish, in Mesopotamia, the "first city built after the Flood," undergoing excavation in those misty areas that held the secrets of man's past. All I had wished to see, to discover, to learn, was empowered in that moment by that magic paper. I knew instantly where that check would carry me. I was going to Kish.

I do not know how long Kish had been the El Dorado of my dreams. Nor am I quite able to determine the exact moment when I chose to become a student of man and a hunter along the track of his mysterious past. It seems to me the choice was always mine, yet there was little in my early environment to point out this long, sometimes lonely, and often hazardous way.

I remember being pushed in a carriage beside Lake Michigan in Chicago, where I was born in a brownstone house on Elm Street on December 15, 1902; running away in Washington from Madame Touvenant, my French governess, who chased me with an umbrella across Dupont Circle; falling off a horse on a gravel road at York Harbor, Maine; watching a drunk staggering along Beacon Street in Boston with his umbrella blown inside out; being permitted to clang the foot bell of a trolley on a swaying ride to Portsmouth, New Hampshire; boarding an ocean liner bound for England . . . then Christmas at Brooksby, England, with my cousins, David and Ethel Beatty; walks in fog and rain with striding Madame Touvenant wrapped in waterproofs and jabbering French; the meet of the Quorn Hounds on the grass in front of Baggrave Hall in Leicestershire on a perfect sunny morning with Mother in a check habit on a beautiful horse as my center of attraction; and Captain Algernon Burnaby, owner of Baggrave, with his eyes on the same attraction.

On July 18, 1908, at York Harbor, Maine, Mother, who had divorced my father several years before, married Algy Burnaby. As the blessing was pronounced, my life changed.

When we drove up to Baggrave the second time, this was to be home. We came through the gate where tiny American and British flags were flying, and up the winding drive to an ancient and charming stone country house, home of the Burnabys for many generations, set in about two thousand acres of glorious English countryside.

In Chicago I would have been reared on stories of the exploits of the many Fields in America, the building of fortunes, the store that bears my great-uncle's name, Field Museum of Natural History, the story of Cyrus and the cable, and other family legends. But a small Yankee had changed worlds, and while I took with me a determination to return someday to Chicago, it was Baggrave and its history that held my growing years. To this old English country house and its surroundings I may owe the curiosity that led to the study of archaeology and anthropology and geology in an attempt to unravel the secrets of our past two million years, and was to carry me, on a rough estimate, some half a million miles on the exciting hunt for the Story of Man.

The life at Baggrave certainly appears to be gone forever. Leicestershire was the fox hunter's paradise, and here came the sporting rich for a few months each winter to gallop at racing pace over the grassy fields. Our lives were geared to this sport. Summers might be spent riding, playing golf and tennis, in trips to Scotland or Maine or the Continent, but winters at Baggrave centered around fox hunting. Conversations ranged on few other topics. Horses were schooled and exercised, hounds bred and trained, foxes protected the year round in preparation. I was "blooded" by George Leaf outside Gaddesby Spinney at the age of six—a terrifying ordeal. From then on I was a junior member of the Quorn Hunt.

In this new life Mother was the central figure. She took the keenest interest in being the wife of the Joint Master of the Quorn Hunt, in helping with the Hunt's many problems as well as looking after the Baggrave tenants and their wives and children. She always rode the finest horses and picked the highest place in the fence. Baggrave was the center of the best parties and there was no grander hostess.

My stepfather was the finest type of English gentleman. Algy Burnaby enjoyed life and made everyone around him gayer. He loved to hunt, fish, play golf and tennis, and did everything well. He was lucky at all games, the best field master of his day, and took his jobs as Master of Fox Hounds, churchwarden, justice of the peace on the Melton Mowbray Bench, and other County duties very seriously. Many sporting books have paid tribute to him, and the Duke of Windsor has written about him in what to me are touching words in *A King's Story*. He and my stepfather were great friends. Once at dinner at Baggrave, H.R.H. said to him, "Algy, if you were Prime Minister, with your brains and wit, and I were King, we would be unbeatable."

To have had Algy Burnaby for a stepfather was the luckiest event of my life. As I sit at his desk, in his chair, I wish that my pen could do justice to my feelings. His good influence still touches those who came under his spell.

We three had a wonderful time, always doing everything together. I cannot say more.

I remember glimpses: A typical Friday meet at Baggrave, the grooms coming up the drive leading the hunters, the Whips turning the hounds through the front gate and onto the sloping grass before the old house. The Virginia creeper is bronze-red and gold-flame on the stone walls. The big windows shine like crystal.

Down the steps come the Master and his lady to welcome the members of the Hunt, and in the wake of Mother and my stepfather is Langford, the butler, and a footman, carrying a silver tray with a decanter and many small glasses and pieces of fruitcake.

Then the riders, in their gay costumes, exercise their horses on the grass: Mother, beautifully turned out and sitting straight as a ramrod on Rapidan, one of the best mares ever to follow the Quorn; my stepfather mounting his blaze-faced chestnut favorite, Cherry Bob; I on my beloved Bum Bay, who knew far more about fox hunting than I would ever know; among the best riders, Teddy Brooks, Philip Hubbersty, the "Wombat" Johnsons and cousin-in-law David Beatty; among lovelies who went superbly across country, the Duchess of Westminster, Monica Sherriff, Sandra Crawford, and Clare Tennyson; in a special category must be mentioned Lexie Wilson, who rode astride. Also Dorothy Sitwell, whose knowledge and "eye to the country" were unexcelled.

The most glamorous members of the Quorn Hunt naturally

were the four princes, with the Prince of Wales especially attracting every eye.

All this was colorful pageantry, and it is gone; but it was part of my childhood and youth and young manhood, and it was Baggrave.

Baggrave had a thousand fascinations for a growing boy. The old house was lit by candlelight when we first went there, and warmed only by open fireplaces. I was fascinated by a story that gave the origin of the name. Hundreds of years before, a cook had been opportuned by a woman begging a bowl of broth and bread. As "she" sat before the fire, the cook saw trouser legs showing below "her" skirt. "This'll warm ye," said the cook, approaching with the broth in one hand and the bread knife in the other, and plunged the knife between the robber's shoulders. The body was tumbled into a bag and buried in the woods, hence the name "Bag-grave."

In proof of this story, an early artist had painted the cook peeling potatoes on wood. This plank hung outside the kitchen door, and had hung there for centuries.

It was during the summer holidays of 1913 that I became actively interested in the history of Baggrave. I was eleven years old. My favorite source of information was Nichol's *History and Antiquities of the Town and County of Leicester*, which stood in a small glass cabinet beside my stepfather's desk. From this I learned that Baggrave had been inhabited in Anglo-Saxon times. I was fascinated by the many Anglo-Saxon relics in the Leicester Museum. The horse, which played so large a role in our fox hunting, was well represented, for there were fragments of trappings and chariot wheels, bronze parts of a bridle, and a bronze terret, or rein ring, as well as one of the most important of Bronze Age objects, the Mountsorrel bucket, with its ring ornament of oxheads. I was drawn to the romance of the past, trying to reconstruct in my mind the way of life of the Anglo-Saxons and, before them, the Romans, for there are many Roman ruins in Leicestershire.

I discussed this with my stepfather, who to my surprise told me that about fifty years before, while a tree was being planted, Saxon relics had been found at Baggrave. A spear (*framea*), an

17

iron umbo or boss from the center of a shield, and a string of glass beads had been found in an Anglo-Saxon grave and sent to the Ashmolean Museum at Oxford.

He showed me the outlines of a Saxon village, clearly discernible on either side of a stream on the grounds. A huge chestnut tree dominated the bank; I liked to think that planting this tree had led to the discovery of the Saxon finds.

I spent hours under it, studying the earth outlines and wondering what lay below the grass.

When I was asked what I wanted for my twelfth birthday, my answer was ready: "A day's work from Harry Hunt and Herbert Payne." These men were the two best posthole diggers on the estate.

Right after breakfast that gray morning of December 15, we three walked across the lawn to the Saxon village site and I pointed out the exact spot I wanted excavated. Within an hour we had uncovered a cobblestone pavement and a hearth. All that long day they dug through the heavy blue clay. We found ancient postholes with traces of wood still in them and a rectangular cobbled area, probably where the Saxons had kept their animals.

Only a handful of small objects were found, but no discoveries since have equaled these, for they were my first. When identified later by the authorities of the British Museum, the finds proved to be a spindle whorl or bead, Saxon or possibly Roman, a flaked flint, a metal coin or token, possibly monastic, and a few animal teeth.

Pumpelly at Anau, Schliemann at Troy, Evans at Knossos, De Morgan at Susa, Howard Carter at Luxor could not have been more thrilled than I at Baggrave that wintry night of my twelfth birthday. No day spent hunting with the Quorn had been more exciting. I knew now what I wanted to be—I would be an archaeologist. It was the start of the long hunt that would last through a lifetime.

That night, I remember, I was too excited to go to sleep.

My first break with Baggrave had come when I was eight, when Mother and my stepfather drove me to Sunningdale School near Ascot one gloomy afternoon, and left me there. This was the low point of life so far. It was hard to fall asleep that night; no new boy dared to cry except silently into his hard pillow. A clanging bell, reminding me of poor Oliver Twist and his troubles, awoke us at seven-thirty. A scurry into the bathroom where each boy had to plunge into an ice-cold tub, then breakfast, and the locker room, where a larger boy grabbed me by the hair and told me to tie up his shoelace. I hit him an uppercut as Pat, Mother's groom, had taught me, and he went backward to the floor.

From that moment I was branded a fighting "Yank" and often paid the consequences, which consisted of pummelings on the floor. The taunting query, "What is the other Yellow Race?" always started me off on a small riot.

Fortunately I won the School Handicap the first summer. Emphasis was placed on sportsmanship in games, notably cricket and soccer, but at the same time the scholastic standard was high.

The trials of being the only Yank at Sunningdale subsided after the first three years, and when the end of the fifth and last term came I found it sad to part with old friends and familiar places.

By this time World War I had started. Major Algy Burnaby was with his regiment "somewhere in the Mediterranean." We heard no word for weeks, for they were at Suvla Bay on Gallipoli, one of the greatest hellholes of the war, with the Turks entrenched on the hilltops and the British clinging to a narrow beachhead below.

Finally the order was given to evacuate. My stepfather was the last officer to leave. One hour before, a million pounds of food and supplies had been set on fire and Suvla Bay was bright as day with the flames. After all were aboard, the great battleship *Queen Elizabeth* moved silently downstream. Not a shot was fired on either side.

We rejoiced when my stepfather was invalided out of the army and we could be at Baggrave together for the last two years of the war.

During this time, in December 1915, Mother and I went to Rome to visit my grandparents. My step-grandfather, Thomas Nelson Page, was our ambassador to Italy and that was the first of several Roman visits, an exciting experience, especially in wartime.

It was drizzling upon our arrival, and a red carpet had been spread beside the Paris–Rome Express to keep the ambassadorial feet dry. I found this innovation fascinating and fancied all my future travels would be conducted on the same scale.

Grandpa encouraged my interest in the ancient city and Mr. Moses Ezekiel, a charming, white-haired American sculptor, took us sight-seeing. With him we toured the Forum, Colosseum, Vatican, Baths of Caracalla, Hadrian's Villa, the Catacombs, and many other glories of ancient Rome. During these weeks my interest in archaeology was truly awakened.

One day I went alone to the Baths of Caracalla and by tipping the guide became the possessor of a fragment of white Carrara marble. I wanted to put this in my "museum," where I kept my Saxon finds. In another room, when no one was watching, I exchanged it for a carved piece of similar size. My grandfather inquired how I had obtained such a fine carving. I told him. Quietly he gave me my orders.

"After lunch Ford will drive you to the Baths of Caracalla. You will find the guide and tell him of your wicked deed. You will replace this piece of marble exactly where you stole it. No object must ever be taken from a National Monument." That was an ignominious trip indeed.

Then, for my birthday and at my request, Grandpa arranged a strange gift: a private audience for Mother and me with the Pope. In the Vatican Pope Benedict XV was impressive, dressed in white, wearing his miter. For some time he talked with Mother in French, while I grew restless. This audience was my birthday present and I was being ignored. I had learned, and rehearsed many times, a long sentence in Italian, which expressed my interest in Rome and Italy and particularly the glories of ancient Rome. It took almost a full minute to recite.

At last the Pope turned to me, still speaking French: "And how do you like Rome, my child?"

In grammatically flawless Italian I plunged into my breath-taking sentence. I could see that His Holiness was astonished by a young foreigner who could speak Italian so fluently! He stood patting my shoulder while speaking very rapidly—in Italian—of his interest in meeting a boy interested in archaeology at such an early age. I got the drift of his talk and kept repeating, "Sì, Sua Santità," but I was very nervous and did not understand half of what he said.

A few nights later my grandparents were giving a large dinner party in the Palazzo del Drago and I was sent to bed early. I awoke to find Grandpa by my bed. He wanted me to meet someone.

I put on my slippers and dressing gown and followed him into the corridor. A handsome Italian officer stood there, his face clean-shaven, his hair thin, and on his chest five rows of medals, more than I had ever seen worn by anyone except David Beatty.

Grandpa said to the officer, "Please tell my grandson something he will remember all his life."

The young officer spoke to me impressively.

"You know the ancient wall of Rome, how thick and high it is? Well, on your twenty-first birthday you will be able to see through that wall."

Even then the young officer-genius, Marconi, was working on television.

On Christmas Eve in the Quirinal, in a marble-columned hall, we were received by the King and Queen and their beautiful children. The enormous tree towered to the ceiling, and we youngsters stood looking at it and feeling a little awkward, since Umberto and Mafalda knew little English and my Italian was limited to my sentence on the Roman glories and a couple of decidedly inappropriate phrases such as "Cuanta costa cuesta?"

Mafalda, who was standing beside me, solved our problem. She spoke simple Italian phrases very slowly and I replied as slowly in English. However, our whispering was discouraged by a queenly frown. There was complete silence, then, quietly, on rubber-tired wheels, a number of chairs containing wounded soldiers were wheeled into the hall to form a circle around the great tree, for one wing of the Quirinal was being used as an army hospital. Near us was a "basket case," a young boy with no arms, no legs. The Queen spent several minutes with him and as she turned from his chair I saw her eyes fill with tears.

Later in the evening Grandma told the Queen of my interest in archaeology and the Queen invited us to the opening of a royal tomb now being excavated at Ostia, the port of ancient Rome. For several nights I could not sleep for excitement, and then, the evening before we were to drive to Ostia, a messenger came from the Queen with the news that a troop train filled with wounded had arrived from the front and she could not leave them.

I was bitterly disappointed but, back at Sunningdale, my schoolmates took a flattering interest in my vacation experiences. I was invited to give an illustrated lecture on the "Glories of Ancient Rome." About thirty colored lantern slides of the Holy City were assembled and one stormy night, while the rain drummed on the roof, I stood on the platform before the entire school and lectured doggedly on Rome. Never again would I dare tackle such a subject. Nevertheless, this remains my most successful lecture. My schoolmate assistant had never run a magic lantern before and most of the slides were shown upside down to the wild delight of everyone; it was a great success.

A few months later I was looking out of the window during study hall when a black limousine cruised silently past the window and around to the headmaster's entrance. I was summoned to the headmaster's study—always a terrifying ordeal.

Waiting there was a grim-faced Italian who bowed low as he handed me a package bound with vivid green ribbon held with red sealing wax. Inside was a note from the Queen of Italy to Grandma, saying that she was sending her grandson some objects from the royal tomb group at Ostia to make up for his disappointment.

I unwrapped the box with shaking hands. There were a narrow-necked vase ornamented with a painted frieze of three dark red bulls; two lachrymatories, or small vases for catching tears, one of dull pottery and one of dark green glass; and a bronze spoon.

Here was a real archaeological treasure. This small collection from Ostia and the handful of objects I found on the site of the Saxon Village are the only archaeological objects I have kept. These, with a piece of Hitler's bathtub from Berchtesgaden, form my sole collection. Everything else that I have found or purchased or been given, including all ethnological specimens from

22

Southwestern Asia, is now in Field Museum of Natural History in Chicago.

Everyone warned me that Eton would be quite different from prep school. Another mental adjustment must be made. From being an Old Boy and center forward on the soccer team, I must start again at the bottom of the ladder and face, not sixty, but more than a thousand boys, the majority of whom were older and superior in every way.

In the autumn of 1916 I arrived at Eton College, on the opposite side of the Thames from Windsor. The wheezing taxi crawled out of Windsor Station and past the flickering lights of the somber castle, over the bridge, down the main street lined with the school shops and connecting Windsor and Eton, and drew up at the small door of Todd's House in Common Lane. Around in the twilight stood the grouped buildings of Eton, and covering acres beyond were the famous playing fields. . . .

The janitor, or odd man as we called him, whispered loudly, "All new boys please come this way." We shuffled with downcast eyes down well-worn stairs to the study—a room whose dread we never outgrew. Here was Leonard Todd, our shortish, clean-shaven, and genial housemaster, to be referred to forever after as M'Tutor. He welcomed us graciously as new boys and made a little speech, concluding with his pet slogan: "Go hard, go straight, play the game, and think of others."

This first night he concluded by patting my shoulder.

"You're the first American in my House," he said, rather in the tone of a zookeeper referring to his first kiwi. The words sounded ominous, for they recalled my early sufferings at Sunningdale School. Now I was a Yank at Eton, following in the tradition of my two Field cousins, Marshall and Henry, who had been at Booker's.

I was to learn that it is a rare privilege to be an Old Etonian. No matter where you travel, or how far, you will be unlucky indeed if there is no O.E. to welcome you. Within the territory under British sway Old Etonians hold many key positions in government. In each case the bond that is Eton overcomes age differences and even the normal barriers of nationality.

This was to be of the greatest benefit to me in my work, particularly in Asia and Africa.

Life at Eton was severe during my years there, 1916–21, in the full impact and aftermath of World War I. But the system was rugged under any circumstances.

At M'Tutor's we were dominated by "fagging" and fear of our "fag-master." Each new boy is assigned to a senior, who may have one or more fags, depending on his position in the House. The highest in rank, the Captain of the House and the Captain of the Games, might have as many as four fags apiece.

I was my fag-master's only slave. My duties were to keep his room neat and tidy, light the fire, prepare his tea, make hot buttered toast, run inside errands, and go downtown to buy things or carry messages. In addition, each fag had to leave his door partly open, so that he could hear the roar of "Boy" from any of the fag-masters. At this every fag had to race to the call, the last becoming the errand boy.

On some evenings there would be as many as fifteen to twenty runs, hardly conducive to excellent homework.

Our feeling toward older boys was one of complete humility, for after all we were but "scugs"—an onomatopoeic word for small fry. Imagine our surprise when one of our group, with eyes shining, came into M'Tutor's saying rather casually: "Spoke to a fellow in Fifth Form just now." It came out that the conversation was one-sided and consisted of: "Get out of my way, you little bastard."

School punishments were of an entirely different system and progressive order of magnitude.

Birching was administered only by the headmaster. It was always the result of a very serious offense and never taken lightly in any sense. The miscreant knelt on the famous wooden block while his shirttails were duly upheld by two Collegers. To add insult to injury, the cost of the birch was charged to the boy's school bill under the heading of "Medical Care."

During the Michaelmas half, a burly policeman from Slough Police Station asked to see me. When I appeared, chaperoned by M'Tutor, he asked if I was an alien. Thinking this must be another word for German spy, I denied it vigorously and said that I hated the Germans. M'Tutor smiled kindly and explained that I was an American and therefore an alien under British laws.

The next afternoon, instead of playing football, I had to walk alone the two miles to Slough Police Station where the desk sergeant wrote my name, age, nationality, and residence in a huge book labeled "Alien Register." Every thirty days, from then on, I had to call at a police station for my Alien Permit to be endorsed.

This was before our entry into the war and Americans were not being looked upon with much favor; in fact snide remarks quoting President Wilson, such as "You're too proud to fight," were commonplace. The air of superiority was almost intolerable, and the police supervision placed me in a category apart. I was called "spy" and "traitor," the latter always calling for a battle but against superior odds.

This taunting was hard to bear.

When America did enter the war I received many apologies and we were all friends again, at least outwardly.

To be different at school is always hard and calls for a strengthening of character. This is all to the good, provided permanent hatred does not result. My friends stood loyally by me through the worst places and defended my cause.

We worked under the excellent tutorial system in which each boy has an opportunity to discuss problems with his various tutors. For example, I had three: M'Tutor for school, House, and personal problems; G. J. Chitty for classics; and M. D. ("Piggy") Hill for science.

Hill was our biology teacher. Short and full of vitality, his eyes twinkled incessantly and an untamed mustache gave him a puckish look. He had a keen sense of humor and was utterly charming, and it was impossible not to learn in his courses. Above his desk, in his classroom, he had painted:

Science is organized common sense.—T. H. Huxley

and on the opposite side of the wall:

Blessings on Science when the Earth was young
And taught a language to its lisping tongue.

In his natural history courses Piggy Hill was bright and amusing, and he aroused my interest in archaeology, especially when he began to lecture on early man and his cultures. The excitement and curiosity I had known with my first dig in the Saxon mounds was reborn in Hill's classroom. Since I was the only boy in the entire school—out of more than a thousand boys—who was interested in geology, I asked for extracurricular reading in that subject. Hill gave me private lessons and directed my reading.

I was privileged to work as an "assistant assistant" in the school museum, and here I learned about cataloguing and classifying geological specimens.

It was Hill who told me: "Prizes mean little. It is real knowledge that counts." And he encouraged me to begin reading about the history of Sumer and Akkad in ancient Mesopotamia. Later I was grateful for this preparatory study. His influence upon me was great, and we are still good friends. I stopped by to see him on his Ledbury farm in 1950.

Sunday Qs, or Bible questions, were a bore, but we absorbed a good working knowledge of the Bible and the Commentaries, a knowledge which was to prove of service to me in passing "Divvers" (Divinity) at Oxford and, much later, in my excavations in the Bible lands.

For some extraordinary, barbaric reason best known to the school authorities, the evening service on Sundays was the occasion for the reading of the names of those who had been killed in the war. I remember one ghastly night when it was raining hard outside and all of us were feeling depressed and gloomy inside. The Germans seemed to be winning the war; they were sweeping forward across France toward Paris, and our food and heat supplies were shrinking in proportion to the advance. The provost, Montagu Rhodes James, was absent that night and the master who read the lessons gave us absolutely no lift. Then the headmaster stepped forward to read the list of those killed in action during the preceding week. Every now and then, as the name of a boy's father or brother was read out, there would be a muffled or choking sound. Other boys stood stiffly at attention, their faces white. These boys had been notified in advance of their loss.

When the headmaster came to the Ms he gave the name of

M—— C——, and our friend and school companion, hearing his father's name read then for the first time, pitched over on his face in the aisle. The telegram bearing the news had not reached him before.

In that First World War, of the 5687 Etonians who served, 1160 were killed in action or died of wounds, and 1467 were wounded. Thirteen won the Victoria Cross.

Piggy Hill's class and private tutoring aroused my interest in the geology of Leicestershire, and this interest went hand in hand with that of the history of the county. Vacations at Baggrave were not all recreation; I was studying, in my own fashion and along my own lines, in the direction I now knew to be mine.

Riding through the glades of Charnwood Forest was a delight, for the flowering shrubs and ferns form picturesque patterns under the ancient oaks. But more than this, the Archaean or Pre-Cambrian rocks of the Forest are of the greatest geological interest, for they are among the earliest types found in Britain.

Charnwood Forest is part of the backbone of England, with the Blackbrook grits and hornstones, formed of volcanic dust laid down in water, as the base of the complete section. Above lie Carboniferous limestone, Millstone Grit, the Coal Measures, Permian, Trias (Bunter, Keuper sandstones and marls), Lias, Oölites, glacial drift, and Post-Pleistocene alluvium.

The surface of Leicestershire is covered with a thick mantle of boulder clay and large boulders are scattered around the country. To me one of the most fascinating was our "Weatherstone" at Baggrave, a slab marker brought by glacial action, which is listed in Domesday Book. Mother had this stone moved to the water garden at the bottom of Gypsy Field, and its removal required a sled, two cart horses, and three men with crowbars. There are many other outliers of local interest.

Neolithic remains are widely scattered; these include celts, ax-heads, and hammerstones.

The greater part of Leicestershire, I learned, was once covered with forest where roamed such animals as reindeer, red deer, bison or aurochs, the straight-tusked elephant, and the wild boar.

Here, too, roamed Man, their ancient enemy.

It may be presumed, according to the testimony of the stones, that the men of the Old Stone Age camped on the highest points overlooking the broad grass-covered valleys. Such points as Whadborough Hill near Tilton, Burrough Hill, Life Hill near Billesdon Coplow, and the high ground at Somerby and Belvoir, must have served as excellent lookouts for spying game and hostile bands.

Slowly a picture of early man in Leicestershire took form in my mind and stimulated my eagerness to go on with the hunt.

The more I glimpsed of the past Story of Man, the greater became my eagerness to pursue the study. Eton had served to whet my archaeological interests and now the years at Eton were drawing to a close, and I was faced with the problem—after Eton, what?

It was now that Uncle Barbour Lathrop stepped into the breach, as he was to do so often in my life, and with telling effect. He wrote me at length from the Bohemian Club in San Francisco, which was his only pied-à-terre, telling me that he was too far away to guide me in my selection of a university, but that he was asking his old friend Dr. Henry S. Wellcome, of Burroughs, Wellcome & Company, to act in his behalf, and he further counseled me to see him soon and to follow his advice.

Accordingly, during the "long vac" I called on Sir Henry by appointment in his Historical Medical Museum in Wigmore Street, London.

I walked through groups of life-size African witch doctors, fortunately in plaster, past horrifying yet fascinating exhibits of primitive medicine, and into a large exhibition hall filled with graying plaster casts of the great in medical history. An attendant brought two small straight-backed chairs and placed them without a word between the stern plaster presences of Jenner and Pasteur. Almost immediately a short, white-haired gentleman with bright, twinkling eyes appeared from behind Pasteur with the words:

"I am Dr. Wellcome, your Uncle Barbour's friend. He has written me about you. I will be delighted to help you in any way."

Only a teen-age schoolboy, such as I was then, would have

'dared to beard such a fabulous character as Dr. Wellcome. He was one of the most amazing men then living and was almost unknown, as an individual, to the public. He had a genuine passion for anonymity. Through the years I was to learn that he was born in 1850 in a small Wisconsin town. At the age of four he found his first Indian arrowhead and began his museum, which later became the $50,000,000 Wellcome Foundation in London.

As a young man he migrated to Canada to become an apprentice in a chemist's shop. The children hated the bitter pills he sold, and one day, pitying a small customer, young Wellcome rolled them in sugar.

Thus, in a tiny back room in Canada, was born the sugar-coated pill, beginning of the Wellcome millions. Soon after this, Burroughs, Wellcome was founded in London.

I have been told that on his first archaeological expedition he ran out of funds for digging and cabled London for a draft, and the answer rushed back, "Burrow and welcome!"

He was, after William Randolph Hearst, the greatest collector of this century. After his death his will revealed three large warehouses full of unopened packing cases of collections. Prior to this, no one had known of their existence.

Sir Henry's staff lived in dread of his rapid footfall. They were well paid, loyal, and terrified. But this despot I faced was Uncle Barbour's friend, and his eyes twinkled. In about five minutes I had outlined my interest in archaeology and anthropology; the Saxon excavations at Baggrave, the visits to Rome and Grandpa's encouragement; the objects from Ostia sent me by the Queen of Italy; Piggy Hill's courses and private tutorials at Eton; and where, I wanted to know, should I turn now?

There was quiet for a moment. Then Sir Henry looked me straight in the eye; his twinkle was gone.

"You will never make a fortune being an archaeologist or an anthropologist," he warned me. "In fact, even with private means, you will find it hard to persevere. You will have to work long hours, not like the average businessman. You must learn to study, pay attention to detail, know how to keep accounts, handle men, take good photographs, speak several languages—in fact, every qualification you can develop will prove an asset.

"However, the inner reward amply repays the effort. Expeditions are the great compensation. My own main interest has always been in the history of medicine. In this museum I am collecting material from all over the world. After all, primitive medicine is linked closely to folklore, and that's anthropology. Well, how may I help you?"

I was listening, wide-eyed. I said: "I am now working with Mr. Hill at Eton. He has stimulated my interest in geology and ancient man. Where can I get the best education along these lines?"

Sir Henry did not hesitate.

"At Oxford, under Balfour, Marett, and Buxton. To be specific, I recommend that you visit Mr. Henry Balfour, Keeper of the Pitt-Rivers Museum at Oxford. There you will receive the best possible training."

He wound up emphatically. "There is one thing I can always do for you. I can arrange for you to meet anyone in Europe, provided you have a question he alone can answer. That should give you confidence."

This was a strange offer to make a boy of fifteen.

Sir Henry stood up and patted me on the head with a final admonition. "Go out and learn everything of something and something of everything." I have never been given better advice.

As for Uncle Barbour, I wrote him directly after my visit to Sir Henry, knowing he would be pleased with its success, and thanking him for his help. He wrote back:

Dear Old Digger,

I am delighted. Hurry up with your education. I want you to begin to dig. May your pickaxe always find the treasure you are seeking!

And this, too, was fine advice and perhaps the best I have ever received. Now I was filled with impatience to be through Eton and Oxford and start digging!

Oxford in the fall of 1921 was a gay and exciting place. Probably never in five centuries had the old buildings and quads resounded with so much constant gaiety. For here were hundreds of undergraduates who had returned victorious from World War I. The majority had sampled the night life of gay Paree or a reasonable facsimile elsewhere, but were returning to Oxford to obtain their degrees. These young bloods, who had tasted freedom, soon livened up the far more law-abiding and timid freshmen straight from public school.

The mantle of academic learning under the shadow of Gothic spires and dignified walls covered us all. We new arrivals felt encircled and inspired by the intangibles. I was now nearly nineteen and determined to apply myself to all Oxford could offer.

After making my bare rooms more homelike with knickknacks, photographs of the family, and a leather desk set from Rome, it was time for Hall.

Down the stone stairs were thundering heavy footsteps amid chatter. I followed, feeling very lonely, this time a Yank at Oxford, across the quad along gravel paths, over flagstones, and up some well-worn modern stairs.

The great oaken beams and mullioned windows gave a cathedral-like sanctity to the Hall. However, at the long tables running almost the length of the room were seated about two hundred undergraduates, most of whom had plenty to talk about. At the center of a raised table sat a tiny, white-haired old gentleman almost bent double over his soup. I recognized him from photographs as Warden Spooner, the albino with the pinkest of pink eyes, world-famous for his "Spoonerisms."

I met the "old Spoo" the next morning when, wearing my new short, black gown purchased from Adamson's right after breakfast, I entered a large room overlooking the main quad. Warden Spooner motioned me to a seat and in a high-pitched, quaking voice said: "Well, let me see, Mr. Field, you're going to read theology, aren't you? As a doctor of divinity I welcome you to New College. I will follow with interest your progress in this subject so close to my heart." I replied: "I am afraid that is not quite correct, Warden. You see, I'm going to read geology and anthropology." He held a sheet of paper less than one inch from his right eye and chuckled: "Oh yes, I was reading the wrong line!"

Within a few days my program was outlined after conferences with my three tutors as well as with Henry Balfour, R. R. Marett, and L. H. Dudley Buxton—all of the anthropology staff. However, since I wanted to read for honors—the old New College tradition—I could not read my main interest, for the university gave only a Diploma in Anthropology. Hence I decided to do the first two years of pre-med school with chemistry, physics, botany, and zoology, then the final honor school in geology at the end of four years and then for the fifth year the Diploma in Anthropology.

This was an ambitious undertaking with five long university years ahead. However, Dr. Marett whispered to me at our first meeting that this plan might lead to one of the highest degrees at Oxford—the Doctorate of Science; but I would not be eligible for this until sixteen years after matriculation. I must say that on that day in 1921 the summer of 1937 seemed far, far away.

This advice was re-emphasized by Henry Balfour when I called on him in the Pitt-Rivers Museum. During the first two years I spent much time with him there, in the curator's office. Later I would study cultural anthropology with him. These quiet talks were always stimulating. He also talked to me of a long-range program, of the pre-med course, of an honors degree in geology, of the Diploma in Anthropology, of training in Germany, of courses at Harvard under Hooton, of museum experience, of expeditions, of writing and publishing monographs, and of the Doctor of Science degree for which I would be eligible "to supplicate" in 1937.

Such was the plan upon which I embarked.

In the years to come I grew very fond of Balfour, Marett, and Buxton and shall always remember their wise counsel and friendly encouragement. To them, to Piggy Hill, to Julian Huxley, to Professor William J. Sollas, and in later years to Sir Arthur Keith, to the Abbé Breuil, and to Dr. Ernest Hooton I owe more than cold words in print could ever express.

During the first two years I struggled with chemistry and physics, the latter proving exceptionally difficult. My tutor, A. F. ("Fanny") Walden, was always helpful, generous with his patience, and most anxious for each of us to pass the examination.

Botany was taught by Sir Frederick Keeble, who always lectured wearing a blue suit. As he talked he rubbed his handkerchief over his spotless glasses, which dangled from a broad black ribbon. Since he was married to a former stage star, we were full of admiration. The lab course was tedious, xylotomy difficult, and the technical names hard to remember. Fortunately the examination was easy.

Julian Huxley, then sporting a reddish beard, taught zoology in an unusual manner. His lectures were divided into two parts: (a) for the pre-med students and (b) for the advanced students.

Huxley, during one zoology lesson, gave what I consider the best example to the often asked question: Can animals reason? Ants have organized colonies. Dogs often seem almost human. But Huxley's prize example was based upon the actions of Sally, a chimpanzee.

Sally belonged to two elderly maiden ladies who lived in a London suburb. She occupied the third place at the table at every meal, ate with a knife and fork, used a napkin, and behaved in a decorous manner. Every night after dinner the elder Miss Jones opened the door into the garden. Sally shuffled out, banged on the door a few minutes later, re-entered, and jumped on the lap of the younger woman. One evening there had been a light shower, and when Sally entered the younger woman said—though she never had before, "No, Sally, your feet are wet."

Sally crossed the room, returned with a copy of the *Times*, spread it over the silk-clad lap, and then, smiling broadly, jumped up to her usual place.

That, said Julian Huxley, was a true example of reason.

Most of us did not appreciate the half dozen undergraduettes who attended Huxley's pre-med courses. They were deathly serious students. They wrote reams in their notebooks. They always sat in the center of the front row. When a demonstration was given they crowded around the microscope. We felt instinctively that none of them would become a distinguished zoologist—and we were right.

Julian Huxley, on one occasion at the beginning of a lab session shouted: "Do all of you have your own spermatozoa?" Two of the girls put up their hands modestly.

33

In 1923, after I had passed the pre-med course in chemistry and physics, zoology and botany, Henry Balfour encouraged me to read for honors in geology, since there was no final honor school in anthropology.

He indicated with a twinkle in his eye that the three-year course could be completed in two years "by serious application" and that he had discussed my case with W. J. Sollas, professor of geology.

As the author of *Ancient Hunters*, still a standard reference work on ancient man and his cultures and their modern parallels, Sollas gave me special attention when I told him of my desire to study geology in relation to man. He would require archaeological reading and would give me special questions in the examinations, since the rest of the small class planned to be geologists. Here I could easily recognize the delicate touch of Henry Balfour.

The following two years were tedious: lectures on structural geology, mineralogy (a hateful subject for the average poor mathematician), learning hundreds of index fossils, lab work, and the eternal piles of textbook reading.

The only relieving features, as far as I was concerned, were the field trips and my assignments in Pleistocene geology with special emphasis on prehistoric man. The latter was fascinating to anyone interested in the Cradle of Man and his development on every continent during the last million years or more.

Sollas' lectures on ancient man were all-absorbing and encouraged me to read ever more widely.

We were a small class, deeply serious in our work. Dr. A. J. Douglas, an expert on index fossils (especially nummulites) relative to oil in the Middle East, was intolerant of errors, unsympathetic to lack of knowledge, and encouraging throughout the courses although shy with words of praise.

Sollas, true to his word, gave me two out of three special questions to answer in the finals. One was on dinosaurs, a special interest, later to involve me with Sinclair Oil advertising; the other two on prehistoric man. During the reply to the former, my arm became cramped with writing, so I put in a frivolous detail which amused the professor, as he told me during the Oral some weeks later. In talking with the keeper of the elephant house at

34

the London Zoo, I had found out the quantity of food consumed daily by a large bull. By rough calculation "a large dinosaur would have to eat for twenty-three hours out of the twenty-four, which did not allow much time for entertainment and relaxation."

All of us passed. A sigh of relief could be heard from Land's End to John o' Groats. We each had our Bachelor of Arts degree.

Now at last, after four Oxford years, I could begin to study for the Diploma in Anthropology.

At his opening lecture on social anthropology, the infinitely wise Dr. R. R. Marett, with a gay flicker in his eye, gave us Malinowski's definition of the subject:

"Anthropology is the study of Man, embracing Woman."

So my fifth year at Oxford began.

I became such a regular attendant of the Oxford University Anthropological Society that Dorothy Garrod proposed me as honorary secretary. Dorothy's father, Sir Archibald Garrod, was Regius Professor of medicine at Oxford, and Dorothy was later to become the first woman professor at Cambridge University, where she lectured on prehistory until she retired in 1952. My honorary activities entailed the usual bookkeeping, including the figures of the society's perennially precarious financial position, arranging the three lecture courses, and keeping the members informed. Since local postage would have placed the society in the red, I delivered most of the mail by bicycle, even in pelting rain.

Hearing discussions about the meetings of certain learned societies in London gave me the desire to attend some of them, a privilege reserved to duly sponsored and elected Fellows. In 1921 Henry Balfour nominated me for the Royal Anthropological Institute of Great Britain and Ireland and for the Royal Geographical Society; Julian Huxley for the Zoological Society of London. I went up to London to attend some of the meetings. The first time I visited the Anthropological Institute was at a five o'clock session. I crept into the room, which seemed to be full of aged and bearded men and a few short-haired, firm-jawed women. As I sat down a kindly old gentleman whispered:

"Young man, this is the Anthropological Institute. The billiard rooms are next door."

At the Zoological Society I always felt awed in the presence of so many distinguished-looking Fellows, usually dressed in black. The Duke of Bedford was so tall, the lectures on such a high plane. One of the most interesting meetings was that at which white-bearded Sir Arthur Smith-Woodward addressed the society on the newly found Rhodesian skull from Broken Hill, which lay on the table beside the shining carafe of water and the glass. We listened eagerly while Sir Arthur described in detail the discovery and the anatomical details, laying particular stress on the massive brow ridges and corresponding sulcus, and its probable great antiquity.

This skull was found by workmen in the Broken Hill diamond mine, South Africa. Viewed from the front and side, its appearance seemed to be Neanderthal, but the well-filled and rounded vault and occiput (back of head) were of modern type. The discussion regarding its antiquity had resulted in mixed opinions.

After the lecture the Fellows surrounded Sir Arthur Smith-Woodward to congratulate him on his presentation and to examine the skull. On the left side a round pencil-sized hole caused some comment. One fresh newspaperman, to whom the geological evidence had been mere gobbledegook, pointed to the hole: "I say, Sir Arthur, did you find the bullet?"

I had a question but did not dare to ask it. The next afternoon during a tutorial with Julian Huxley I questioned him. Could the Rhodesian skull be a case of acromegaly?

Julian replied that he did not know. He said, "I suggest that you ask Sir Arthur Keith. I will give you an introduction to him."

A few days later I met for the first time the greatest living anthropologist, who was to become a lifelong friend. He was then conservator of the Royal College of Surgeons. He talked to me in his gentle Scotch burr as he showed me around. Here was the world's finest collection of acromegalic casts of faces, hands, and feet, and here, if anywhere, lay the answer to my question.

Homo rhodesiensis had some characteristics which appeared acromegalic and which had led me to suspect that the ancient possessor of the skull had been a victim of the overfunctioning of the pituitary gland. If this occurs before puberty, giantism results; after puberty, it is called acromegaly. The frontal bone grows forward, the chin grows downward, the hands and feet become huge. The pituitary gland, normally the size of a large green pea, expands until it presses on the optic nerve and finally death results. In most cases an acromegalic dies before he reaches thirty years of age.

But Sir Arthur would have none of my theory concerning the Rhodesian skull. "Dear boy, it is not a case of acromegaly. Unless you are a specialist on hyperpituitarism, I cannot explain the details. Just take my word for it. However, it's a good question."

He guided me from exhibit to exhibit. Here were the dwarfs, their casts and skeletons, including that of tiny Madame Crachmani, the Sicilian dwarf, 19.8 inches tall. And beyond her, at the opposite extreme of endocrine disorder, we came to the giants, where, towering in his case with a metal ring through his cranium, hung the bony remains of O'Brien, the Dublin giant, who stood 7 feet 7 inches in life.

The College had come by this famous skeleton in a curious way. Many years before a surgeon had offered the then living O'Brien five pounds in advance for his body after death for dissection, his skeleton for study. The giant, being in need of cash, agreed. Then the idea began to prey on O'Brien's mind. He hired a rowboat, bound himself with heavy ropes and stone weights, and dropped overboard in a lake. But the surgeon dredged the lake by night and dragged up the body. O'Brien's skeleton remains an outstanding exhibit in the Royal College of Surgeons.

All this time the longing grew to go on an expedition and perhaps make discoveries of my own. Studying physical anthropology with Dr. L. H. Dudley Buxton stimulated this longing.

Buxton was a tall, brilliant, retiring man, exceptionally correct in all his actions. He had written an excellent book, *Peoples of Asia,* as well as a book on college etiquette and propriety. His dozen students found him an excellent teacher. He was known to us informally as "Bones," and his enthusiasm for the study of man radiated to us.

A few months before I joined his class one of his students had sent him a present from South Africa. The Oxford postal authorities were dubious about permitting him to take the foul-smelling carton, but Buxton persisted, realizing this might be a treasure for the university museum. On the way home, under a street lamp, he could not resist peeking into the carton. Staring up at him was the grisly head of a Bushman from the Kalahari Desert, with protruding lips and peppercorn hair. As he stared back, fascinated, heavy footsteps sounded a few paces away. Buxton did not want to explain his possession of a recently severed human head to the patrolman so, like a rabbit on home ground, he flew around the corner and dove under some bushes. The very proper Oxford don and authority on Oxford etiquette squatted on his haunches in the bushes, clutching the putrid head, while a suspicious cop streaked around the corner, searching in vain.

Even so, I stood in awe of him and it would have surprised us both to learn he was shortly to be my companion in my first great adventure. Fired by Buxton's scholarly leadership, both in class and in tutorials, I read with avidity every scrap of news concerning digs and discoveries around the world. The opening of Tutankhamen's tomb was making headlines. With special interest I pored over the pamphlets sent me each month from Field Museum in Chicago, an institution that claimed my interest for family as well as scientific reasons. Near Babylon in Iraq, formerly Mesopotamia, the Field Museum-Oxford University Joint Expedition was excavating Kish, onetime capital of the world. The workmen there were uncovering skeletons thousands of years old. There could be no better place in which to start tracing the mystery of the past, and the longing grew to go to Kish and see for myself how the secrets of the ancients were being brought from the dusty earth. Studies were fascinating, but how much more fascinating if it were possible to do what Uncle Barbour was always advising: be done with books and lectures and start digging on one's own!

And so, on that foggy November day at Oxford in 1925, when Uncle Barbour's check for one thousand dollars fluttered before my dazzled eyes, I knew exactly what that money meant to me. I was going to Kish. In another moment I knew I would not go alone. I did not know enough as yet to dig alone; I would need

38

a companion on this greatest of adventures. Not any companion, but Buxton, formal in manner but the wisest of teachers, who would know exactly how to excavate and study and classify the bones I dreamed of finding at Kish. What a privilege it would be if Buxton would go with me on my first "dig"!

The next morning after classes I cycled down the "Corn" with Uncle Barbour's check in my pocket, and after a visit to Cook's, where travel folders and facts and figures were pressed upon me, I raced along the Woodstock road. Buxton led me into his library, lit his pipe, and regarded me searchingly through his thick glasses.

"Well, what's on your mind?"

I told him. Christmas vacation was coming. If we went second class, on Uncle Barbour's check, we could both go to Kish during that six weeks. I was certain the Expedition would let us study their methods of excavation first hand, especially if we were paying guests. "A thousand-dollar check—Uncle Barbour—do something——"

Buxton cut in with dignity. "I'll have to talk it over with my wife and the university authorities."

I tried to absorb a little of his patience and calm. But when, the next morning, he called to tell me that he could go, these were thrust aside by exuberance.

I called Mother for her permisson and to say I hated to miss Christmas at Baggrave. I received enthusiastic encouragement from home.

At last school ended and the great day came. Buxton and I boarded the train in Oxford and were off to Baghdad.

Buxton was still formal, calm and sitting up very straight in the train seat. By the time we reached Paddington he had his feet up on the opposite seat and was relaxed in enjoyment. My qualms concerning the professor-student relationship ebbed with every click of the wheels.

By the time we reached Cairo we were boon companions on holiday. As the train chugged across the warm Nile Delta we tried to plan our three days in Egypt, and everything Buxton mentioned I wanted to see.

Bright sunlight was reflected a thousandfold from the white stucco buildings of Cairo as we drove in a cab to our hotel. I wanted to start seeing things. We changed into light clothes, hired a car, and headed for the Pyramids. I wanted to climb to the top. Buxton hesitated. As we toiled up the three-foot steps that had been built to cover the body of Cheops, I better understood Buxton's reluctance. This pharaoh had ordered some 2,300,000 blocks of diorite to be lugged 400 miles to cover nearly thirteen acres for his tomb.

We felt nearly as tired as his slaves must have when we reached the top, but the view was adequate compensation. The sun was setting and the crimson glow filled the entire sky to the west. The palm trees' green foliage glinted red. The dusty streets of the city to the north sprinkled an orange haze over the white outlines of the square houses. Below us, and even more mysterious in the fading light, lay the sculptured outlines of the Sphinx.

I have no idea why I was seized by a terrific urge to drive a golf ball from the top of the Great Pyramid. Like so many ideas, this was unfeasible, and I had to be content with reading years later that the Prince of Wales, moved by the same curious impulse, had hit a screamer from the top of this giant tee.

By the time we returned to Cairo it was dark. The blazing 200-watt light bulbs with no shades lit the narrow, dirty streets. Mangy dogs barked; victrolas bawled discord into the night; merchants hunched over grimy fruit and vegetable stands jabbered their wares; beggars begged for baksheesh; dirty little urchins tried to sell their sisters, dirty little sisters tried to sell their brothers. Cairo crawled with the smell of thousands of humid, sweat-stinking years, pounded into the dirt by thousands of muddy feet. We could not stomach the goulash at our own hotel, so we went to Shepheard's, world-famous crossroads caravansary, and extended the budget and our waistlines. The food was delicious, the conglomeration of epicures fascinating. At one table sat Russell Pasha, chief of police of Egypt, whose name for almost two generations would strike fear into every opium peddler, smuggler, and thief in the region of the Nile. At another table a group from the Riviera sat with their jewels reflecting the light from the great crystal chandeliers. Here were handsome Arabs in fine cotton robes, and businessmen, army officers, explorers, and adventurers of many nationalities. Adventuresses, too—at the table next to us, an extremely beautiful Frenchwoman, dressed in a white, close-fitting dress that left little to the imagination, tossed the waiter a sultry smile. He almost dropped the bowl of soup. I glanced at Buxton. He was studying her too, and not with the detached air of an Oxford don. I was sorry that Buxton and I could not use our calipers on her that night. A magnificent specimen . . .

Shepheard's was always glamorous to me, and I hate to think of it gone, burned by incendiaries during the rioting of 1952.

The next morning we visited the Cairo Museum. The objects which we had most hoped to see, those from the treasure tomb of "King Tut," irreverently called "King Toot-and-come-in," were not as yet in the Cairo Museum. Above all, I longed to see the gold coffin of the boy king.

We returned to our hotel for lunch and found Professor James H. Breasted of the University of Chicago waiting for us. A quiet, white-haired man, one of the greatest of Egyptologists, Breasted was the man who had proposed the theory that the Nile, Tigris, and Euphrates region had formed one cultural unit at the dawn of the historical period. He had coined the expression "Fertile Crescent" for the narrow strip that skirts the desert wastes of Arabia, runs in a giant semicircle from Palestine to Iran, and is separated from the Nile Delta only by Sinai. In the decade to come I was to hear him describe his greatest dream—that of the Oriental Institute of the University of Chicago, for the study of ancient man and his cultures in the Fertile Crescent.

In his obituary I wrote: "So long as the Nile flows past Luxor will the name of Breasted be revered by those who seek the truths of ancient times."

A burning intensity came over him when he talked to us of Egypt. Our stay was far too short, he said, but it was important that we see the Valley of the Kings at Luxor. Among other discoveries, the Tutankhamen finds were there.

That night we slept on a train and woke up beside the Nile at Luxor. The air was heavy with the scent of citrus groves. I had never seen an orange tree before. The symphony of my first trip across the Nile was the dip of our oars in the water and the faint blended chant of four men pulling a *diahbeah* downstream.

Three snoozing donkeys waited on the opposite bank. In their sleep they plodded us to the Valley of the Kings. Mine was appropriately christened Columbus. The tombs of Seti I and Tutankhamen were gaping holes in the dusty hillside. Guards were posted at the gate of a high wire fence. We sent our visiting cards by our Arab guide, Aboudi. Buxton and I waited on dust-covered boulders near the entrance, trying to appear nonchalant. Howard Carter, in charge of this excavation, had the reputation of tearing into shreds the cards of would-be visitors.

But Mr. Carter was friendly. He was smiling as he led the way into the most publicized tomb in history. He talked of the discoveries and excavations and Buxton listened with fascinated attention, but my mind was on one subject only.

"Young man," Carter said suddenly, "you seem to be restless. What is it you want?"

I blurted out the truth. "To see the gold coffin of Tutankhamen."

He smiled. "Lift that sheet by your right foot."

The sheet was dirty. I lifted it and stared with dazzled eyes at the blindingly beautiful carved mass of gold that had held the mummy of the young king. The oil lamp placed on a rock in the tomb diffused a brilliant light over the stylized beard, face, and headdress in the coffin—the mask of solid gold. I was to see this again, years later, in the Cairo Museum, but it would never again seem so magnificent as in that moment, in the ill-lit shaft cut into the hillside of the Valley of the Kings.

Then Howard Carter led us down a winding path into the tomb. Passing through several rooms, now empty, he stopped before a wall in which an irregular hole had been made at eye level. A flashlight beam swept around the room that had held undisturbed the presence of death for more than three thousand years. A light film of dust covered the furniture—chairs, tables, and wooden headrests—but their richness shone through.

This great discovery had also made news because of the superstition that calamity would befall those who dared break into the gold-filled tomb of Tutankhamen. Buxton and I were struck by the inscription over the door: "Death to those who enter . . ."

In the years to come the more lurid newspapers carried many stories describing the power of this curse. First Lord Carnarvon, the financier of the expedition, died, then Howard Carter. Then, one by one, according to the newspapers, many of the people who had worked in the tomb's area or taken any part in its discovery died, and it was invariably pointed out that their deaths were the results of the ancient Egyptian curse.

This I most emphatically do not believe. However, I do believe that there is much in existence that cannot be explained by any means known to us now. History is filled with strange happenings, coincidences—call them what you will—that remain strange. The owners of the Hope Diamond, for example, seem to have met with more than their normal share of ill luck.

Archaeology is ridden with legends, old and new. There is a story about Sir Bruce Ingram, long-time editor of the *Illustrated London News,* who was given a mummy's hand as a paperweight. The wrist was still bound with a copper bracelet set with a scarab. The hieroglyphs on the scarab, translated, proved to be, "Cursed be he who moves my body. To him shall come fire, water, and pestilence."

Several months later the editor's beautiful country house burned to the ground. It was rebuilt and a flood promptly swept through its ground floors. Sir Bruce did not wait for the pestilence. He sent the mummy's hand back to the Valley of the Kings.

To call this superstition combined with coincidence is the easiest and also the most scientific way out. Nevertheless, there have been many times when I have hesitated before the locked and sealed doors of the past. Something grips the imagination then and holds one back. It is not a pleasant sensation. That day at Luxor, in King Tutankhamen's tomb, I knew it for the first time, and never more powerfully.

Now we were more eager than ever to reach Kish, but we were going to see as much of interest on our way as our time and funds would allow. Two days later we were in Jerusalem, where we found rooms in the Hotel King David, left cards at Government

House, and drove to the museum. Here we met some of the staff and saw many interesting flint implements from the Stone Age of Palestine, excavated from caves and rock shelters not far from the fringe of the Mediterranean.

We walked to Bethlehem. I was deeply shocked to find men with fixed bayonets guarding the historical birthplace of Our Lord. That evening we climbed the Mount of Olives and sat under olive trees, watching the sun sink over Jerusalem. Here on the Mount were no words, just thoughts. In this hour of darkness and almost-stillness it was hard to believe the events of the past two thousand years.

At four o'clock the next afternoon a 1919 touring Cadillac appeared at the door of the King David Hotel. At the wheel sat Ernie Worrell, one of the crack transdesert drivers of the Nairn Overland Desert Mail. We climbed in, Buxton and I and Professor Stephen Langdon, director of the Field Museum-Oxford University Expedition at Kish, who was to accompany us on this last part of our journey. Then we were off at last on the trail of prehistoric man, the long hunt that was never to end for me.

We crawled past Jericho, the Dead Sea, the river Jordan. An iron bridge led over the Jordan's muddy water strip to the other side. This was Transjordan, today the Hashemite Kingdom of the Jordan.

As we wound, more slowly, up steep mountainous slopes toward the village of Es Salt, we saw Bedouins living in a small rock shelter, just as their ancestors lived thousands of years before. Every now and then we met a shiny new American car filled with Arabs in flowing robes. Once a motorcycle sped past us in the dust, bearing an Arab wearing a white flowing headdress.

The old and new—the new and old.

Supper was at Amman, capital of Transjordan. This was the ancient city of Philadelphia, built as a Roman outpost, and signs of Roman occupation were apparent, with fallen columns on every hand. We ate in a tent near the Royal Air Force Camp, behind which stood the palace of the Emir Abdullah, King of Transjordan and brother of King Faisal of Iraq.

44

After supper Ernie said we would leave almost immediately. The rest of the convoy joined us: two Buicks with nets over the hood and running boards that held a thousand pounds of mail for Baghdad and India. Ernie drove all night, Langdon beside him, Buxton and I in the rear. We passed the few twinkling lights of Qasr el Azraq, one of the chain of outposts of the Roman Empire, now inhabited by Druze. In the crystal-clear desert night, with thousands of stars overhead, we crossed the fifty-mile stretch of lava bed of the great Harrat ar Rajil. It took us an hour to cover eight miles; the going was so rough, we had to hold to the sides and top of the car. The great basalt boulders, scattered as if by giants, make this one of the most desolate parts of the Near East.

It was seven o'clock next morning when we reached a large mud flat surrounded by low hills. The convoy halted beside a shallow lake. Ernie collected camel's-thorn for a blazing fire. Buxton and I were wandering around, looking for anything of interest on the ground. Since I was studying geology, I searched for wind-faceted pebbles, known as *Dreikanter*. Suddenly Buxton shouted, "Come here, I've found one." I ran over to him, and sure enough he had picked up the first flint flake chipped by ancient man found in that part of the world. Up to this time no evidence of prehistoric man had been found east of the great lava bed we had passed; in fact the North Arabian Desert was believed to have been a barrier to migration. In general terms, the next links of evidence for prehistoric human habitation were the Caucasus to the northeast and India, many, many miles to the east. This was indeed an exciting moment.

Buxton and I began to collect more of these flakes as rapidly as possible; in a short time we had about twenty.

The Cadillac horn honked that breakfast was ready. Here was my first conflict between science and the inner man; this time the latter won. We hated to leave this mud flat, known as RAF Landing Ground "H" on the air line from Cairo to Baghdad. We continued all through that day at about thirty miles an hour over hard sand, often covered with gravel or flint-strewn. Buxton and I watched longingly, eager to stop and search. Sometimes the track led through shallow wadis (dry stream beds) ever eastward over the rolling flint-covered hills. In this *hamad*, or stony desert, there are no great sand dunes like those in the Sahara; this is really wilderness or steppe, not a true desert. The principal vegetation is camel's-thorn, low, prickly bushes that grow in clumps. We saw no animals, only a few birds. No human being seemed to live here, although Ernie told us that actually there were hundreds of Bedouins with their camels near by.

About one o'clock we stopped to eat some canned food which tasted delicious. Buxton and I continued our search for flint flakes chipped by man. We found several more and were delighted that our discoveries on Landing Ground "H" had not been the only ones in this region. It now looked as though man in several prehistoric phases of culture had passed over that section of the world, the crossroad between the three continents of Asia, Africa, and Europe.

As we continued, one car after another had tire trouble. We searched for flakes and rejoiced in the delays. By nightfall we had a small collection which to us was certain indication that we were on the track of ancient man.

We stopped at eight o'clock for supper. Now it was my turn to ride beside Ernie. His eyes were bloodshot and he looked very tired. He had been at the wheel about twenty-four hours under constant strain because of scattered boulders and deep sand.

Dawn found me at the wheel, with Ernie asleep, his head resting like a baby's on my shoulder. In the back seat Buxton and Langdon slept while their heads bobbed to the bumps. We all looked dirty and our unshaven faces made us look more than a little like convicts. I glanced in the back again and wondered who could have recognized two distinguished Oxford dons.

The desert was illuminated by the red glow of the rising sun and I saw dust to the east. I woke Ernie. The dust rose as we passed our first caravan of about . fifty camels led by three Bedouins.

Beyond, rosy-towered in the dawn, lay Baghdad.

The name of Baghdad conjures up the very essence of romance. However, the city was a bitter disappointment to me. There was little of the mystery of the past and the present was far from

46

attractive. On the banks of the muddy Tigris dust-covered palms waved over drab-colored buildings. An occasional dome or minaret shone like gold in the sun. Again, as in Cairo, the blaring of victrolas conflicted with the medley of street noises—a cacophony of four-wheeled *arabana* bells, a beating of hoofs. This was an Arab town and for the first time I saw women with veils or thin wire latticework frames over their faces. The light caught the glinting of brown or black eyes and I liked to imagine the covered faces were beautiful.

Fortunately for us, we were invited to stay at White Lodge, the home of Mr. and Mrs. R. S. Cooke. Mr. Cooke proved to be a middle-aged Scot and a genial host, with a great knowledge of Iraq. In addition to his duties in the Waqf, he was keenly interested in the Iraq Museum in Baghdad, founded by Miss Gertrude Bell, whose name was legendary in this part of the world.

After a bath and a nap we were far more presentable, but our bloodshot eyes still smarted from dust and sand. After tea Mr. Cooke showed us some fine rugs and Sumerian and Babylonian pottery figurines. I am not by nature covetous and in fact do not care to collect things for my own, but I remember very well a series of small Babylonian stone weights, each in the shape of a duck, which adorned his mantelpiece. If I recall correctly, the smallest were of hematite, the largest (about three inches long) of gray limestone. On the base of each the weight was carved in cuneiform.

I really coveted those duck weights.

Just as we started upstairs to dress for dinner, Mr. Cooke took me aside.

"Gertrude Bell is coming for dinner," he said, and added, "I hope that everything will go all right. You know she is the Director of Antiquities."

This remark came as a surprise. I was delighted to meet the fabulous Gertrude Bell on my first night in Baghdad, but why was my host afraid things might not go well?

I finally decided they all thought I was going to behave in some extraordinary manner, but exactly how they thought I was going to do this in front of an assembled company, mainly strangers, I had no idea.

Downstairs we found three other guests, British residents of Baghdad.

We were standing around talking when in swept a tall majestic creature who moved with the authority of a queen. Gertrude Bell was then fifty-seven. Her keen blue-gray eyes flashed imperiously under white upswept hair, cowing our little group. Her close-fitting black dress with long lace sleeves and high lace collar accentuated her paleness. She was very lovely, very feminine, and very haughty.

Mr. and Mrs. Cooke leaped forward to shake her hand and present the guests. I was the last to be presented.

Miss Bell fixed me with an eye as cold as a steel bayonet.

"So you are Henry Field! Young man, I want to talk to you."

She was charming, as only a charming woman can be. At dinner she insisted that I sit on her right.

She was an excellent raconteuse with an inexhaustible fund of stories about her life in the desert. She radiated a quiet determination and it was not difficult to visualize her riding with a small group of Bedouins over the desert as she had so many times. I felt it would be extremely hard to prevent her doing anything she really wanted to do.

With considerable enthusiasm I told of our discovery of prehistoric flint implements in the high desert. She was fascinated. This, she said, was the first evidence ever found of prehistoric man in Iraq. Suddenly she said, "Where are those flints?" We spread them on a table covered with newspapers and Miss Bell asked question after question and made us show on a map where the discoveries were made. Until far into the night Miss Bell kept us talking about prehistoric man in that part of the world, and asked me to come and see her in her garden the next day.

That night I dreamed of prehistoric men. I saw them wandering across the high desert, hunting wolves and gazelles, and looking very ferocious, chasing me down a steep wadi. I woke with a start and was glad to find myself safe in bed in Baghdad.

The morning brought an upsetting thought. Buxton, during our discussion over the flint implements, had stated that, while they indicated the existence of prehistoric man in the barren wilderness in which we had found them, the evidence of these

48

few man-made flakes would not serve to convince the skeptics. But I felt certain that more evidence was lying on the surface of this desert around us, and I woke with a burning desire to obtain permission to search for it in the areas where the first flakes had been found.

Buxton agreed with me. We had to start for Kish almost at once, but there was no reason why he and I should not go hunting in the extremely inaccessible desert on our way back, provided we could find a way.

A few hours later, after a delightful visit to Miss Bell in her garden, I entered the office of the Air Vice-Marshal, where I was met by Sir John Higgins. Sir John offered me a cup of strong Lipton's tea and buttered bread thinner than any slices I had ever cut in the botany lab. As I sat on the edge of my chair balancing the tea, Sir John came out with a booming "What can I do for you?"

All I wanted, I explained, was his permission to accompany his armored car patrol so that we might have one full day searching for flint implements around Landing Ground H.

Sir John threw back his head and roared with laughter. Never in all his experience, he said, had such a strange request been made; a civilian, a foreigner, asking permission for an armored car patrol to search for traces of prehistoric man in the desert! Then, stopping as suddenly, furrowing his brows, he told me that, "weather permitting," the armored cars would be outside the Maude Hotel at 1:30 P.M. on January 10.

I went out, walking on air, to thank Gertrude Bell. I knew now that a word from her was the greatest asset one could possibly have in Iraq.

The next afternoon found Langdon, Buxton, and me jouncing over the dirt road leading from Baghdad in the direction of Kish, in an aged Model T Ford that managed about thirty-five miles an hour. Hilla, sixty-five miles away, appeared beautiful because clean palm trees lined both sides of the Euphrates and the water ran relatively clear under the bridge we crossed to enter the town. As we drove into Hilla we were greeted by an enormously fat man, perhaps four hundred pounds, wearing a long gray garment over a white cotton shirt. He welcomed

49

Professor Langdon like a long-lost brother. He, it seemed, was the Hilla barber and, typically, the center of all gossip; he was to be my friend and ally, though I did not know it then, through the years to come. Langdon called on the *Muttasarrif*, governor of Hilla Liwa (Province) and also the chief of police, and told him that we were proceeding to Kish. The *muttasarrif* seemed but mildly interested, and I realized that if everything went well with us he would not derive much benefit, but if anything went wrong he would be responsible to the authorities in Baghdad.

Recrossing the Euphrates, we followed a rough and hilly track until at last we reached the main canal and then, far off, I saw a high mound dominating the plain. I knew it at once and shall rarely know again the excitement I felt at my first glimpse of the ziggurat—this was Tell el Uhaimir, "The Red Mound."

Kish lay before us.

Here in the middle of Mesopotamia, between the Euphrates and Tigris rivers, the large Expedition was encamped on the site of Kish. On this spot man had lived continuously for six millennia —since the dawn of history. Here had centered the intelligentsia of Mesopotamia—like Egypt then, a great civilization. Here had flourished one of the great centers of learning of the ancient world. Semitic-speaking peoples had lived and died in this place and its sands had known the proud footprints of Nebuchadnezzar.

Around us, beneath the sands of Mesopotamia, lay buried the Biblical past. The Garden of Eden had not been far from Kish. Abraham came from Ur of the Chaldees, about 150 airline miles to the south. The Tower of Babel had stood within twenty miles of us, and the sun, vanishing now over the desert, was sinking behind all that remained of the Hanging Gardens of Babylon, eight miles from Kish.

I looked with awe at this historic earth, but with no idea of the hold Kish was to take upon my life.

Ernest Mackay, the field director, wearing gray flannels and a blue turtle-neck sweater, stood waving in the courtyard of the encampment as our Ford wheezed to a stop, and Buxton, Langdon, and I, a little groggily, stepped down upon the ancient site of Kish.

50

M<small>Y</small> ONE-ROOM hut was a ten-foot cube. Its flat roof was lined with reed mats; another mat formed the door, and others covered the mud floor. Dust storms, I knew, and the inevitable night cold would find easy entry to my sanctuary, and rains would turn my floor to porridge. A row of nails on the wall was the only wardrobe.

A hole in the wall had been filled with empty bottles sealed in mud. This was the window, but little light came through. The cavelike place was lit by a sputtering oil lamp.

But the washbasin was a handsome hand-hammered copper bowl and the water jug a beautifully spouted copper ewer and what matter that both stood on the floor, for was I not at Kish?

I spread my bedroll over the iron bed frame and hoped for the best. Over it, with the help of two of the camp boys, I draped a mosquito net and within an hour my little mud home in Mesopotamia seemed very desert-shape.

I went out of doors. Two fierce-looking brigands were wandering about the camp, armed with rifles and large daggers in bright silver scabbards. These, I discovered, were our camp guards, Mahdi and Juad. I soon learned that their fierceness was purely external and at any mention of robbers I am sure both would have run so fast a dust storm would have been raised at their heels. They had an assistant camp guardian a friendly mongrel dog with the classical name of Samsiluna. He and I were to become fast friends.

Just outside the courtyard stood a large white tent, used for the sorting, classification, numbering, and preliminary cleaning of specimens.

The dining room was partly underground. Its flat roof protruded about five feet from the ground. It had been built this way under Mr. Mackay's directions in the hope of gaining a little relief from the oppressive desert heat during the midday meals. The cookhouse, another mud hut, was a hundred feet away. This smelly sanctum was presided over by an Armenian named Shemu, who shaved about every ninth day and who wore perched on his shaggy hair a Russian caracul hat which never left his head night or day. The only English words he knew were swear words, and he summoned us to seven o'clock dinner with a stream of short Anglo-Saxon expletives, exploding through smiles, that would have shocked Elizabethan England. It was quite obvious he had no idea what he was saying, but hoped to please.

Mackay, Langdon, and Buxton came from their mud quarters and we descended the eight steps into the dining room. Lukewarm soup, the grease thick upon it, congealed in plates on the large plain table. Shemu's language was more palatable than the food he served. The next course was a piece of very tough meat and a boiled potato with some canned beans. The bread was the locally made *chupatties*, the flat unleavened Arab cakes which, unless crisp and dry, taste like old wet waffles. Some of Mr. Bartlett's most delicious pears were our dessert.

I must say I have had to think hard to remember the food served at this meal. Discomforts of any sort meant little to me. I remember the excitement and eagerness I felt at being a budding anthropologist with three great experts, and at hearing Mackay's description of the work already done in the excavations, and all they hoped to do. A large, beaked coffeepot stood in the center of the table, and beside it on a blue and white saucer rested a can of Nestlé's sweetened condensed milk. After supper we sat a long time over coffee and in all my life I have known no finer talk and no better time.

Blue clouds of smoke curled lazily toward the palm roof beams. We were all smoking pipes, Mackay his king-size pipe, and Langdon the treasured new one that had been given him by his bride just before he left Oxford a few weeks before. Mackay was eagerly awaiting his approval of the excavation plans, and I was bursting with questions.

I wanted to know why anyone would plan an expedition to

Mesopotamia—"The Land between the Two Rivers"—why tens of thousands of dollars would be raised and spent to excavate these old mounds buried for millennia beneath sand, and why professors and their assistants would risk permanent injury to their health—all for the advancement of knowledge about the cultures and peoples of ancient "Mespot," as it is called irreverently.

Why Mesopotamia, I demanded, and above all, why Kish?

Langdon, leaning back in his chair and puffing on his hot pipe, was the first to answer.

For one hundred years, he explained, archaeologists had known that Mesopotamia was one of the cradles of civilization. It stands at the focal point between Asia, Africa, and Europe. For this reason the cultural links with the Nile Valley to the west, with Anatolia to the northwest, with the Caucasus to the northeast, with Iran, Afghanistan, and the Indus Valley to the east, and finally with Arabia to the southwest, are of paramount importance to the student of history.

The first European traveler to visit and write a description of the ruins at Kish was J. S. Buckingham, who, toward the end of July 1816, accompanied by Mr. Bellino, secretary to the British Residency in Baghdad, left that city to visit Babylon. Following the exaggerated description of the extent of the city of Babylon as given by Herodotus, they continued in an easterly direction until they reached the temple tower, or ziggurat, of Tell el Uhaimir, which they imagined to be part of the city of Babylon.

Jules Oppert, the Assyriologist, led an official expedition to Babylon in the year 1852, and conducted some minor excavations on the site of the city of Kish. He reported the discovery of important objects, which unfortunately were lost on a raft that sank in the Tigris River. Then for more than fifty years Kish remained untouched by explorers and almost unmentioned by scholars.

The Abbé H. de Genouillac excavated there in 1912 for a few months near the smaller of the two temple towers.

In the spring of 1922, Mr. Herbert Weld expressed a desire to excavate some ancient Babylonian site, and he chose the ruins of Kish as offering the most important site for excavation. With the co-operation of Field Museum of Natural History, a joint expedition with Oxford University was formed, with Langdon as director. Permission to excavate was granted under the local antiquities law by Gertrude Bell. From November to March every year since 1923, the Expedition had continued work on a large scale.

Langdon's explanation covered my first question. I had another, and curiously enough it was one which was to be asked of me, in various ways, in lecture rooms and after radio and TV talks and in letters, for the next twenty-seven years.

"How do you know where to dig?"

Mackay answered. He had been in charge of excavating Kish since the beginning and the latest methods were employed.

He said, "It may seem like magic, but actually it is not so difficult. You see, Kish was a very large city, five miles long and two miles wide. The surface of its flat, alluvial plain is covered with mounds. We asked the Royal Air Force to make an aerial mosaic of the city from about five thousand feet."

The photograph, covering the ten square miles, was taken in the early morning when the shadows cast by the mounds were long. Enlarged and studied carefully under a magnifying glass, it showed clearly the lines of the long-buried outer walls, with guardhouses set at the city's corners and at intervals along the walls.

According to the map, ancient Kish was divided into two sections by the former channel of the Euphrates River. Western Kish was dominated by the highest mound, Tell el Uhaimir. In Eastern Kish stood a complex of mounds, the largest being Tell Inghara. Lying between these two tells was a smaller but extensive mound which Mackay called Mound "W."

This was the general ground plan as visible from the air.

I interrupted with another question, and this also was to be asked frequently of me in years to come.

"How do these mounds develop? Are they the result of blown sand?"

No, my panel of experts assured me, pouring more coffee, puffing at their pipes. The shadow-marked mounds on the air maps held the alluvia of the past. The builders in ancient Mesopotamia used sun-dried bricks for buildings and walls. In Nebuchadnezzar's time the bricks were large and flat and each bore the imprint of his own personal seal, beginning: "I, Nebuchadnezzar,

54

King of Kish, King of Babylon . . ." This seal impression was stamped on each brick before drying. Wherever fragments bearing this inscription are found, it is known that the brick was made during the time of Nebuchadnezzar, some twenty-five hundred years ago, about 550 B.C.

When a town was sacked or destroyed, or, to use a phrase we were to find so frequently in the Kish texts, "The city was smitten with weapons," the conquerors destroyed the buildings, leveled the ground, and rebuilt on the surface. Since the walls were often twelve feet in height and three feet thick, when they were flattened the level of the ground rose. On top of this the new buildings were erected, several feet higher than the previous floor level. During five or six thousand years the accumulation grew and the mounds that marked the site of Kish were the result.

Geological agents, such as wind and rain, the severe frosts at night and the intense heat during the day, had served to disintegrate the bricks and return them to Mother Earth.

The next step, Mackay explained, was to examine foot by foot the surface of the largest mounds, because these would almost certainly contain buildings, objects, including tablets or inscriptions, and skeletons.

The low mounds around the periphery of an ancient city are naturally the guardhouses. Soldiers, then as now, would be apt to leave little of archaeological value.

Mackay summed up the plan by saying, "The choice of the area to excavate is usually done by selection and elimination."

I told Mackay that during a lecture at Oxford an archaeologist had been asked what method he employed in selecting the place to dig, and he had answered that the simplest and most practical method and the one that had given him the greatest yield was to blindfold himself, spin around with a weight flying at the end of a string, let the weight fly, and start digging wherever it fell.

"However," I added hastily, "your more scientific theory appeals to me, even if it is not so romantic."

Buxton looked at me reproachfully over his pipe.

Mackay and Langdon, by turns, told the rest of the story of the Kish excavations. Mackay had worked alone at the start, in 1923, until Langdon joined him in the fall. He had begun the principal excavation, that of the temple area at Uhaimir, and started work under the ziggurat and in the southern part of the *temenos*, or outside platform.

The first ground work had been the collecting of broken pottery and other archaeological fragments from the surface of each of the mounds. Then a rough sketch was made of each mound or group of mounds. It is comparatively easy to identify Arab, Babylonian, or Sumerian pottery from the fragments called potsherds. In the Kish area most of the mounds were covered with Arab pottery and glass and unpainted Babylonian ware. The Sumerian pottery, being about five thousand years old, would naturally tend to lie far below the surface.

Searching for the earlier cultures was a vastly more complex procedure, but from previous experience in other sites it was known that a site sacred in Babylonian times had also been sacred hundreds, if not thousands, of years before. The procedure, therefore, was to locate the Babylonian temple and palace, with the adjoining rooms for the priests, and the cemetery. During and after excavation a series of photographs was taken to complement the detailed ground plan. Then these buildings were removed, and below were the earlier cultural levels. This method was followed from just below the top of the mound, which was probably Arab, down to virgin soil.

They had found Babylonian sherds in profusion on the slopes of all five mounds, they said.

"There was a teaser," Langdon said. "How could we make the wisest selection for our first trial trenches? Well, we know from other excavations in Mesopotamia, particularly at Babylon only eight miles to the west, that the richest finds always lie near the temple, the most hallowed area. It was then a matter of elimination. Fortunately Nebuchadnezzar and his immediate successors built their temples in the same proportion. Knowing this and that they were all oriented in the same direction, we eliminated three out of the five mounds. Of the other two, we selected the one which would have the best view of the river.

"That was how I selected Tell el Uhaimir for the first trial trenches and subsequent excavations. After two seasons we have found very little. So tomorrow morning we start to attack Tell

56

Inghara and the adjoining complex of mounds. I am glad you are here to see this because my hunch is that we shall find some wonderful things.

"Now as to objectives. What are we looking for? Well, these can be divided arbitrarily into two categories: research material, such as plans of buildings, tablets, and inscriptions, and all data and photographs to be published; and specimens for museum exhibits.

"The latter are always extremely important from the point of view of fund raising.

"Any sponsor can appreciate a golden necklace. With explanation he or she can understand the significance of a painted pottery vessel linking the early cultures of Mesopotamia, Iran, and the Indus Valley.

"There are numerous objectives in this type of excavation. We want to determine the history of the city from its earliest occupation down to the twentieth century. By history we mean not only the chronology of the main events which occurred here during the past six thousand years, but also the cultural sequences and the physical and racial characters of the inhabitants.

"Naturally, we are especially interested in the origins of Mesopotamian culture and the earliest racial type or types. These data would give us clues as to cultural and racial links with adjoining territories.

"To illustrate the variety of practical objectives right around this table: Mackay is interested in the plans of buildings and monuments. I would rather find tablets or inscriptions than eat. You and Buxton are interested in bones. Field Museum wants objects to exhibit in a Kish Hall. Both Oxford University and Field Museum plan a series of scientific publications. The academic world will quote and requote our results. The excavations at Kish will really add a page or two to the long historical record. . . ."

Buxton and I had the same thoughts. Mackay had summed up our presence at Kish as being due to our interest in bones, but the story behind that interest was as long as the tale of civilization. Our purpose at Kish was part of that story. We were here because we hoped to collect a series of human skeletons and skulls so that

57

we could help determine the racial types that had lived at Kish since the dawn of history, about 4000 B.C., and add in any way we could to the collection of data concerning the ancient and modern dwellers in central Mesopotamia.

There were basic questions to be solved.

Who were the first dwellers in central Mesopotamia? Were they longheaded or roundheaded? Where did they come from? By what route did they come? What were the physical characteristics of the main waves of invaders of Kish? Many times the cuneiform texts found at Kish had recorded its being "smitten with weapons"; who were the smiters?

These questions belonged to Buxton and to me. We had three weeks in which to find some answers.

Mackay's pipe was out. Langdon yawned. We all stood up. I thanked each of them before returning to my mud hut and my first night at Kish. I might not have slept so soundly had I known I was to spend the next twenty-eight years attempting to answer some of the questions I had asked that night.

At six o'clock I was awakened by our Arab servant Ali, with hot water and a friendly sputtering of Arabic. Mackay, Langdon, and Buxton were in the downstairs dining room where a solid, if not delectable, breakfast was provided for us by Shemu, still wearing his fine caracul hat. Mackay told us to be ready to start for the excavations directly after breakfast, as work began at seven.

My heart began to pound, but I covered my excitement with what I hoped was undergraduate nonchalance.

An Arab driver, whose head and face were muffled in a spotted kerchief, started us off in the Ford, to the cheers of Mahdi, Juad, and Shemu and the earnest barking of Samsiluna. The car sputtered and snorted in the cold morning air, and the red foxes playing outside their earth at the southern tip of Tell el Uhaimir paused to cast wary looks in our direction. The ancient desert silence was broken by the roars of our tin Lizzie as we bounded over the rickety bridge. Buxton and I were clinging for our lives, but our interest was caught by the low mounds we jounced between,

58

which were temptingly covered with pieces of broken pottery and Arab glass.

About midway between Eastern and Western Kish we crossed the dry bed of the Euphrates River, which in Sumerian and early Babylonian times had watered Kish.

Shortly after crossing this rough section of the track we passed Mound "W," the Babylonian area, and for the first time I saw the cleft earth, revealing an ancient civilization. We waved to the workmen, who raised their picks and shovels in the air as a sign of welcome to Professor Langdon, the returning "big boss."

The Arab driver seemed to regain some control over the bounding Ford as it reached the south end of the great mound of Tell Inghara, which rose fifty feet above the level of the plain. As we came into sight 150 Arab workmen were standing or squatting in groups awaiting the order to begin work. When the car, groaning with its load of "Brain Trust," approached them these Arabs, who were friends of Professor Langdon and had not seen him for a year, began to shout and cheer. They waved their cloaks and jumped in the air and shouted many greetings, in the most friendly manner. The Arabs did not understand what they were supposed to be doing, or the great purpose behind it, since none of them had ever heard of a museum or had any conception of other parts of the world. But Langdon was a good friend of theirs and well they knew it, and the work was a source of revenue, which could be used to buy wives and other luxuries.

The *rais*, or foreman, Hassan Jedur, came forward to greet Professor Langdon. He was dressed in a long black coat of Prince Albert type, which had seen many years of service in Europe before it reached Iraq in a bale of secondhand clothes. Hassan had a fine, strong, deeply lined face. On his head a black and white speckled kerchief was held in place by a black camel's-hair coil, called an *agal*. His dark brown eyes were kindly yet uncompromising.

The *rais* is responsible for the control of the men, their good behavior, and their honesty.

Hassan Jedur was an expert *rais* because he had been employed by Koldewey during part of his eighteen years of excavation by the German Expedition at Babylon.

59

Several leaders of the working gangs, known as *jokhas*, came up to shake the professor warmly by the hand and welcome him back in their midst. These were the pickmen, each in charge of a small gang for whose work they were responsible; many of them became my good friends.

The greetings over, Mackay explained to us that he proposed to attack the southern end of the great temple complex, dominated by the summit of Tell Inghara. (Later it was discovered that this area was known as Harsagkalemma, dedicated to the Earth Goddess.)

Mackay was like a trained pointer at work. With string and pegs he marked out on the ground the position for each "trial trench." The center of the attack was directed at the middle of the mound lying just west of the ziggurat. Hassan Jedur placed a *jokha* about thirty feet behind each tent peg at intervals of about fifty feet. The front over which the eighteen *jokhas* were to operate was nearly three hundred yards in length and the distance from the point where the mound rose from the plain was about a hundred feet. Each gang consisted of a pickman, two men with broad-headed hoes, and six basket-boys—these were actually children, seven to twelve years of age, who removed the earth and carried it back to the dump. Mackay marked on the ground with another staked rope the position at which the dump must begin; this was about fifty feet behind each of the gangs. Deciding that there would probably not be any objects of value here, he felt relatively confident that this earth, once placed on top of the ground, would not have to be moved again in order to recover further antiquities. In any excavation this is an important decision because each time the earth is moved the expense naturally increases. On the other hand, to carry the earth to a dump unnecessarily far back is also a waste of time, money, and effort. Here is where a careful study of the terrain combined with practical experience counts.

The gangs went to their positions. Mackay raised both his arms as a signal.

The excavation of Eastern Kish began.

Mackay lighted his pipe. He pointed toward the line of workers and explained the importance of maintaining a relatively straight front because some of the less conscientious workers tended to try to race ahead in order to find objects, and thus obtain baksheesh. However, Mackay said that if one of his best pickmen seemed to be progressing faster than his colleagues on each side he would not object, because it was always better to have a good pickman in front. Only an expert could recognize a sun-baked brick wall, now long disintegrated.

As soon as there was any question of striking the face of a wall, work stopped and there was a consultation. Hassan Jedur borrowed a pick, balanced it very carefully between thumb and forefinger, and struck the earth. If it was a brick, it had a certain quality of resistance which Hassan Jedur, because of his many years of practical experience, could recognize. Then, with extra care, they looked for the facing of the wall.

They continued down until the wall was some seven or eight feet in height, and fanned out in both directions until the entire wall was exposed.

It should be fairly easy to imagine the scene: in each of these little narrow trenches there was a pickman working carefully ahead. Behind him two men with hoes scraped the dirt into baskets. The six basket-boys in relays, in a never ending chain, came into the trench and threw their baskets on the ground, to be filled with earth by the two men. Then the boys carried the baskets up to the dump, an ever growing pile. It was surprising how many cubic feet of earth could be moved by this simple system in a few hours.

Buxton and I went down into some of the trenches and talked to the men as best we could. We found them throwing up pieces of pottery, fragments of stone, and other objects, but little of any archaeological value. We longed for a glimpse of a human bone.

Langdon had gone to Mound "W," where he hoped to find during this season a horde of cuneiform tablets—a philologist's dream!

Buxton and I wandered over Tell Inghara and the adjacent mounds, trying to imagine what secrets lay beneath us—probably fifty or sixty feet down to virgin soil.

The sun dazzled my eyes and the broken lines of the desert seemed to run in waves before me, but the sense of excitement

61

held. At long last I was in Kish. I had started on the long backward journey that was the history of mankind. I thought of Kish as it had been fifty-five hundred years before—of Kish five thousand years before—of Kish twenty-five hundred years before. The periods ran like motion pictures through my mind and I longed to grasp them and make them real. How I wished I might have lived through them all! I wanted to see a Sumerian goldsmith bending over his work in some long-vanished courtyard, the crowds in the streets, the building of the Great Temple, the covered markets with their purely Oriental sounds of street vendors and tinsmiths and coppersmiths hammering on their metals, and the greenness of wheat fields that must have surrounded Kish in those early centuries. I would have liked to look into one of the ancient laboratories where the astronomers were at work making their calculations—a far cry, those star studiers of thousands of years past, from those who watch nightly through the 200-inch reflector telescope on Mount Palomar in California. And I thought how exciting it would be to visit the library at Mound "W" as it had been then, and see the librarian poring over the clay tablets and the tablet repairer hard at work. . . .

One hundred generations ago Kish had been a teeming city set in green surroundings, divided by the flowing waters of the Euphrates. History does not give the identity of the brilliant enemy engineer who succeeded in diverting the river's course from its main channel midway between Tell el Uhaimir and Tell Inghara. The populace was panic-stricken as the sparkling waters suddenly began to lessen. Then Kish was "smitten with weapons" for the last time, and on a tremendous scale.

The terrified citizens fled from their waterless, uninhabitable city and migrated westward to a site eight miles away where the refreshing waters of the Euphrates were now flowing in another channel. Here Nebuchadnezzar founded the city called Babylon. Kish became an outpost of the new city, maintained for research, mostly in mathematics and astronomy. Nebuchadnezzar would have come often to Kish.

Then I imagined him as he might have been in the days of his glory, visiting Kish's streets in a chariot drawn by gaily bedecked bulls. He was standing in this primitive flatcar vehicle, with his royal robes flowing in the desert wind, with trumpeters in advance and a train of bearers following. Around him musicians played on curious instruments as dancing girls moved their sinuous forms. Flowers were strewn in the pathway of the great king. He waved solemnly, majestically, and I, watching him from the far vistas of my imagination, remembered the story of this man who had "thrown himself on the floor and had eaten grass." I recalled suddenly that it was not grass Nebuchadnezzar had eaten, but that he was probably a sufferer from epilepsy, who had thrown himself on the floor and torn with his teeth at the rush mats. I imagined his haughty patronizing stare as he rode through Kish, making me realize that Kish, in his time, was no longer the center of this part of the world. Babylon had become the center. At Babylon were this great king's Hanging Gardens, his large buildings, his swarms of dancing girls, with all the revelry and merrymaking that were part of Nebuchadnezzar's day—twenty-five hundred years ago. Kish was outpost then, part of Babylon.

But Kish was also, in those days, the astronomical center of the world, the research laboratory of its time.

A shout jerked me back to the dusty Kish of 1925. Mackay, hands high above his head, was shouting, *"Bydos!"* This was the signal for noon recess, and there was much wild excitement and cheering from the Arab workers. The adults and children immediately seated themselves in groups and began eating their dates and unleavened bread.

Now it was quite hot on the desert and a relief to get back into the comparative coolness of our underground dining room where Shemu had luncheon waiting. It was an almost silent meal, for each man had his own thoughts. Mackay's were wrapped in the problems confronting him at Tell Inghara. Langdon was excitedly confident of finding some cuneiform tablets very soon. Only Buxton and I were morose. We saw little hope of any human skeletons coming to light.

By one o'clock we were back at the excavations and the signal started work at both sites. Langdon, Buxton, and I went to Mound "W," where the Babylonian level was being uncovered. Workmen were advancing steadily but slowly into the center of the low mound which stood about twelve feet above plain level.

Langdon introduced me to the young *rais* and to several of the workmen, who shook hands with me, and I again found it pleasant to see how good were Langdon's relations with the Arab workmen.

We were now standing, Langdon told us, on a mound that had been buried since the time of King Nebuchadnezzar, about 550 B.C. Here they had been finding pottery, human skeletons in a fairly good state of preservation, and also cuneiform tablets with their records of land purchase and the buying and selling of wheat and other commodities. Langdon's principal and personal interest was in these written documents, so the excavation of Mound "W" was a search for a series of cuneiform tablets that could be shipped to Oxford and studied and published by him, thus revealing the historical and documentary record of Kish some twenty-five centuries ago.

He was disappointed when the *rais* told him that only a few fragments of tablets had been found and removed to the camp museum. He asked the workmen to work very slowly and carefully, and to raise the signal of "*Maktub* [tablet]" if one found so much as a fragment. Then he explained to us that tablets are far harder to recognize even than the bricks, as each tablet is only about three inches long, two wide, and less than one inch thick. The clay, carefully selected by the Babylonian "bookmen," was inscribed with a stylus, then hardened by baking in the sun. The tablets were almost identical in color with the earth in which they lay. However, they were of a different consistency, being sun-baked. Since the tablets were extremely hard to find and great prizes, the Arabs were watching for them like hawks.

As we stood looking down into the trench, a cluster of large, unpainted pots was uncovered. Langdon explained that a room was being unearthed and the vessels were part of the household equipment. We watched while thousands of fragments of pottery were removed. Where there were sherds, Buxton said, we were almost certain to find graves. But a grave was difficult to determine in that tightly packed earth. Then suddenly, in gray relief against the reddish dirt, we sighted bones.

Immediately Buxton jumped into the trench. I was right after him. The workmen fell back. Buxton unpacked the small kit he had carried so hopefully to Kish. He took out scalpels and paint-brushes, and as we knelt side by side in the trench he delicately brushed away the earth and fine dust from the long bones of a human leg. I was fascinated. I had never before seen this work done, although I had read so often in the textbooks that "the greatest care must be employed while removing bones or delicate objects from the ground." This was the pedantic sort of advice that made Uncle Barbour turn purple with rage. Now I knew why—I was savoring the full experience of the hunt and he had been right in saying that the only way to learn was through experience.

The bones were poorly preserved. Buxtom worked slowly and cautiously, but all that was found was the central part of a right femur and part of a right tibia. However, the *rais* assured us that human skeletons had been found in Mound "W" and that from now on, as soon as any were found, Buxton would be notified and all work stopped in that section so that he might excavate at leisure.

But no more bones came to light, although we watched eagerly through the long hot afternoon, while the nine *jokhas* toiled patiently and steadily, relieving the monotony of their work by singing a refrain many times repeated.

That refrain would become familiar to me in the years to come. "May the scorpion sting the pickman!" our Kish workmen chanted in Arabic in the monotonous hope that a scorpion might bite their leader's foot so they would not have to work so hard. By the shadow of a stick in the sand they calculated the time quite accurately, so about five minutes before closing time, at noon or evening, their chant would turn to an urgent "Look at your watch! Look at your watch, Sahib," lest we in our zeal for digging should let them work a second overtime.

Buxton and I walked over to Tell Inghara, about half a mile distant. We found that under the watchful eyes of Hassan Jedur the men had progressed far into the plain; it was now possible to see the outer section of a wall, and Mackay's selection of a digging spot was well vindicated. Before long, we hoped, some exciting discoveries would come to light. Then Mackay again called "*Bydos*"; it was four o'clock and time to stop work. There was an immediate stampede, particularly among the children, who raced in a swarm along the road toward the camp, for their homes lay in the village a couple of miles to the west.

Back at camp, a cup of Shemu's hot, strong tea was most welcome, for the mounds were dusty and I had inhaled pounds of ancient Kish that day.

Mackay then opened the heavy padlock on the mud hut which served as the temporary museum. Two walls were lined with rough wooden shelves; these, and a long center table, were covered with neatly labeled objects—potsherds and bits of stone and copper objects, unbroken, unpainted pots, a few stone vessels, and some copper tools. Over one table group was a card labeled Mound "W," and here, with their lower jaws resting unnaturally beside them, stood five human skulls.

Buxton and I forgot all else but the precious skulls. He pointed out to me that they were longheaded, or dolichocephalic, and that they had the characteristic parietal bosses which are so typical of the Kish area. All five seemed to be of the same racial type, and according to their labels, they were of approximately the same date, the Nebuchadnezzar period (550 B.C.).

It was of great importance, Buxton told me, that we obtain a series of skulls from Mound "W" so that we could study the basic type and variations. He also explained the significance of obtaining human skeletal remains from the lower levels of Tell Inghara, especially just above virgin soil.

We went to bed shortly after dinner because we were all tired. My first day at the excavation of the ancient city of Kish had been one of the most exciting of my life. No field hunting was ever more thrilling than that first glimpse of bone in the dust of Nebuchadnezzar's city. I tried to stay awake and savor over and over that high moment, but the first I knew, the sun was striking wanly through my bottle-set window, and it was time to get up and breakfast and return to the dig.

Mackay left us at Mound "W" and went on to Tell Inghara, promising to let us know if he found any skeletons there, no matter how fragmentary. Buxton and I took our positions by the dust-filled trench and prayerfully watched the workmen. Not more than fifteen minutes later, the cry of "Bones" came from the dusty pit. Only they did not shout, "Bones," but "*Adham*," which is Arabic for Adam, meaning "man." Not knowing whether the bones were male or female, the Arabs simply shouted "man," to let us know bones had been found.

Buxton and I scrambled down. There lay a human femur. Buxton's experience and skill were now needed. I watched while he supervised the pickman's removal of the heavy overload of earth. Then the pickman took his carved dagger from his belt and scraped away the earth with this weapon, which also served as a tool. After about an hour the earth had been removed to a depth of about two feet so that the bones rested on a kind of earthen shelf. Now Buxton went to work; borrowing the Arab's dagger, and using his own scalpels and knives, he scraped the earth very carefully and delicately, stopping now and then to remove dust and fine earth with the different-sized paintbrushes from his kit. At times he knelt to blow the dust from the bones. Slowly the leg bones came to view, showing that the skeleton lay flexed and on its right side, then the ankle and toe bones; from the other side, Buxton worked carefully toward the place where the skull should appear. The vertebrae were scattered out of position but he managed to unearth most of them. The entire skeleton was just beginning to show when the shout of "*Bydos*" called us from our trance and sent us back to the camp for lunch.

We were back as soon as the Ford could carry us. Buxton said that it was important to get the skeleton out that day and avoid the danger of its being disturbed during the night. Jackals prowled around Kish and were apt to dig in freshly turned earth; occasionally a fine specimen had been lost that way.

Buxton continued to dig and brush and blow in the place where the head should be; none was there. He worked on. The sun beat into the trench and the dust was hot in our eyes and throats but we did not notice. A tooth was found, then another. The skull should be about here, Buxton said, grimly digging on, but it was two hours before the fragile cranium was bared.

Now the whole skeleton lay exposed on the earth, and I photographed it with the 3¼ x 4¼ Graflex. Buxton decided to remove the find at once. We had taken the precaution of bringing from camp two Standard Oil wooden boxes, a pile of old newspapers,

67

and a roll of cheap cotton wool. The papers he spread on the ground beside the bones and as each was lifted from the earth it was brushed and blown upon and placed reverently on the papers, wrapped, and laid away in the wooden box.

Up to this time I had done absolutely nothing. I had not even been permitted to use my breath to blow the dust from the bones! Buxton had ruled that I must watch every move at least three times before being permitted to work on specimens. So I watched wistfully as the bones disappeared into the boxes—first the leg and foot bones; then the pelvic girdle; then the vertebral column; and last the calvarium and mandible.

The skull Buxton wrapped with cotton and placed with great care in a separate box. The skull, he explained to me, is not only delicate but it is always the most important racial criterion. Though the stature might be reconstructed on the basis of the leg bones, the long bones and particularly the vertebral column were of little value in the identification of the racial type, which was of such great interest to us. However, Buxton pointed out squatting facets on the tibia: small protrusions of bone which develop as a result of sitting constantly in a squatting position.

He was jubilant because he had been able to remove almost all of this well-preserved skeleton.

The lower jaw, with only three loose teeth, was found. Later it would be easy to cement these into the jaw; then we would have a good Babylonian skull for study.

Buxton identified the skeleton as that of a young man about twenty years of age. However, it is always more difficult to determine the sex of a skeleton when the individual is not fully adult; it is only in middle age or in later life that positive sex determination can be made. The main differences between the male and female skeleton are these: in the male, the places where the main muscles are attached are apt to be rough, the angle of the sacrosciatic notch is narrow and deep (in the female it is broad and shallow), the bones are generally heavier and more robust, and the upper margin of the orbit is round and smooth (it is sharp in the female).

There are a number of other criteria, but it takes years of experience and the handling of many skeletons to be able to identify and sex them even reasonably accurately. In a museum series it is generally possible to be correct about ninety per cent of the time; however, there is much less difference between a male and a female skeleton at the age of about twenty. For example, the muscular attachments on the skull of the male have not fully developed, and it therefore has the gracile quality which is usually associated with the female.

We rode back to camp in triumph with our prize. Langdon and Mackay were both very pleased that we had excavated a skeleton. Here was the beginning of our study of the ancient dwellers of Mesopotamia.

We hastily downed several cups of good strong tea and hurried to the tent outside the main courtyard of the camp, where, on a large table used for the cleaning and shellacking of specimens, we unwrapped from his newspaper cerements the skeleton of the youth who had probably seen Nebuchadnezzar walking in stately procession to the Temple of Kish or strolling through the Hanging Gardens of Babylon. . . .

We prepared him for his long journey to Chicago.

I say "we," but again it was Buxton who took sole charge of this delicate task. A careless movement might mean irreparable loss. Again the long bones and the small bones were cleaned of as much dust and dirt as remained, then they were treated with hot paraffin and wax and put into trays and numbered, then placed in a drawer for later wrapping.

Work now began on the skull. Darkness was setting in, so we had to bring two table lamps into the tent. It took Buxton about half an hour to remove the dirt from the inside, through the foramen magnum, the hole through which the spinal column enters the base of the skull. Some of the earth and mud clung tenaciously to the interior of the orbits and had to be removed with the greatest delicacy and care. Buxton explained that to remove any more might cause the whole thing to fall to pieces.

Then he brushed a thin coat of yellow shellac over the cranial sutures, on the inside of the orbits and the remains of the nose, and finally a thin coating was applied all over the skull. This was done to preserve the bones and harden the sutures. During the long period underground the gelatin had disappeared and unless replaced with shellac the cranial bones would come apart. Buxton told me it was important that the protective coat be put on as soon as possible after the bones were exposed to the air.

Half an hour later the mandible was clean. Buxton cleaned the three missing teeth, and with adhesive replaced each tooth in its correct socket. Finally a thin film of shellac was applied all over the jaw, and it was labeled and put onto the tray, where it would remain until time came for the final packing for shipment to Chicago.

It was quite clear to me that this was much more than a mechanical task. It was necessary to know the general shape of bones; to determine the probable position in which the skeleton was lying; and to ascertain from uncovering a few bones, or even fragments, the position of the skull. Then the delicate work of removal from the earth, transportation to camp, the skilled mechanical work, and the cataloguing, labeling, and packing for shipment. I had been itching to be allowed to help, but Buxton insisted that I should watch him for two more days before he would allow me to attempt the salvage of such valuable human material.

Supper, one of Shemu's worst, was nevertheless a festive affair. We had uncovered the first complete Babylonian skeleton found at Kish.

Mackay described the work at Tell Inghara during the day. The gangs of workmen had uncovered the top of a huge platform, the *temenos,* which always surrounded the base and the outer walls of a Babylonian temple tower. Since this platform might be twenty or thirty feet thick, Mackay was employing the entire group of workmen to clear and to demarcate the top of the platform. After uncovering the *temenos,* the workmen could begin trenches on the inner side in order to locate one or more outer walls which would still have to be uncovered. No objects of any kind had been found. No human bones had come to light. Our Babylonian lad remained the stellar find.

The next two days were spent on Mound "W," where Buxton uncovered several fragmentary human skeletons. By nightfall two days later, he had six skulls and two partial skeletons. Four large pottery vessels containing skeletons of babies had been unearthed. One of the pickmen had found these four vessels lying almost side by side in a straight line. Mackay told us that the Babylonians buried or sacrificed children alongside the outer wall of a new building to propitiate the gods.

EARLY the next morning Buxton and I were shivering on the top of Mound "W" when we saw the Ford raising a trail of dust across the plain. The driver brought a note from Mackay suggesting that we come over immediately: they had found a burial. We raced to Tell Inghara, where some human bones were lying beside one of the walls, just the other side of the *temenos*. Buxton was bitterly disappointed to find that the long bones crumbled to dust as soon as the air reached them. The damp earth at this spot ruined almost every chance of preservation. However, Buxton was hoping to find the skull more or less intact so that some deductions could be drawn from it. For example, was it long and narrow or short and broad?

Buxton was just beginning to uncover part of the skull when one of the workmen came over from Mound "W" with a message from the *rais* that a burial had been found there. Buxton turned to me. "There's your chance. Excavate that skeleton but don't remove it from the earth. I will come as soon as I possibly can."

With shining eyes, I ran across to Mound "W," carrying the knapsack with the excavating tools. At the bottom of the trench, nine feet below the surface, were some bones. They were small, but they were bones. Immediately I went to work in as professional a manner as I could muster. Proceeding with infinite caution, at the end of two hours I had uncovered the skeleton of a child. I was a little surprised at the position of the bones, which lay almost in a semicircle. This infant appeared to be about six months old. Using the scalpels and brushes, I had exposed most of the bones up toward the head when I heard Buxton coming up the trench behind me. He sat down on the ground beside me to watch, and I felt amateurish under the eagle eyes of the master. I stopped to ask him about the skull at Tell Inghara. He replied that it was broken into several pieces but it would be possible to restore it in the laboratory in Chicago. In any event it was a skull from a much earlier period than the Babylonian level at Mound "W," and every piece of evidence would help us to reconstruct the physical characters of the ancient dwellers at Kish.

Then he knelt beside me and began to chuckle. This seemed to me rather cruel since this was my maiden effort. He asked me to describe what I was excavating. I replied with dignity that this was a young child, flexed, lying on the left side. His only comment was, "Your baby seems to have a very long tail." It was rather horrifying, and I did not fully comprehend immediately what he meant. With a few deft strokes he uncovered the skull, which turned out to be about the size of a closed fist. What I had thought to be the vertebral column, flexed and bent into more or less an arc, turned out to be the tail of a small dog. I was completely humiliated.

However, Buxton was quite cheerful and said everyone had to make mistakes, adding: "I'm glad you made this one right at the beginning, because that will give you a practical lesson that you could not get out of a book. I am sure your Uncle Barbour would be very pleased if he were here now, not by your first failure, but to see you obtaining the practical experience he has advocated for so long."

While I was sitting, very humble and mortified, looking at the skeleton of the dog, one of the workmen about twelve paces away called out that he had found a human skull. Buxton said immediately, "There's your next chance. I won't watch you. Go to it and let me know when you have it uncovered."

I did not want to go back to camp for luncheon that day but Buxton insisted, and so it was not until midafternoon that I was ready for him to come down into the trench. This time I was sure it was not a dog—unless it was a dog with a human head—because this was a human skull, beyond any shadow of doubt. Buxton gave me a word of praise and several pointers which I was to follow in the future.

During the next few days I spent all my time excavating human fragments and transporting them back to the museum, where all objects were stored until the division at the end of the season. We

74

were busy because at Mound "W" there was a whole series of skeletons in a line. On the third day I found another small dog, but this time I recognized him or her; it was just as though it wagged its tail.

Friday was the weekly holiday, for our workmen were Moslems. We were the only Christians around, so Mackay felt that the religious majority should rule.

Thursday evening, therefore, was payday and workers of all ages came to camp. Mackay had set up a table in the courtyard. Beside him stood the foreman, Hassan Jedur, and the guards, Mahdi and Juad.

Each pickman led his *jokha* to receive their pay. The pickman received one rupee daily. The two hoemen received twelve annas apiece, the basket-boys eight annas. The two *rais* each received one and a half rupees daily. The total amount per week paid for the employment of about 225 workers was about 850 rupees ($270).

There was much confusion in the camp, as there always is, during pay time; this turmoil is sometimes heightened by the intervention of the camp sentries armed with sticks. A great deal of money exchanging went on as the men left the line with their pay. The members of each *jokha* paid a tax out of their earnings to the pickman who had chosen them to work on his gang. The small basket-boys had little left for their hard work after the pickman, and their relatives, had taken shares out of their ninety-six cents for a fifty-four-hour week. The children all seemed to owe one another money and as soon as one was paid he would be surrounded by small companions trying to get a share. The camp rang with shrill squabbles.

By the time the dying sun outlined the rim of the desert the excitement was over. The workers hurried off to their homes, and peace returned to the camp. In the distance the barking of the dogs signaled the arrival of the first of the children at their villages. The children usually outran the men, although they had done a day's work and had run most of the way to and from the excavations.

I had been standing behind Mackay as he paid the men and boys, and noticed that many had slips of paper with figures writ-

75

ten thereon. Later he explained this—the baksheesh system—to me.

The Arabs, he said, were like children in that they needed tangible rewards for good work. Each foreman whose *jokha* found archaeological objects during the day was given a baksheesh slip payable on the next payday, after Mackay had valued the find.

The main reason behind the baksheesh system was to encourage the workers to be honest. A small object, such as a cylinder seal, or a lapis-lazuli bead, could be readily hidden in the folds of a workman's flowing garments and sold later to Jewish merchants in Hilla, who would resell them to antique dealers in Baghdad for the export market. Twice the usual baksheesh was always paid for gold objects to discourage theft. Small objects were brought into camp each evening by the basket-boys, who received as baksheesh the smallest local coin, half an anna. Encouraged to bring everything, they were rewarded with this tiny coin.

If a workman was caught attempting to steal, word was sent to the chief of police in Hilla. Two mounted policemen handcuffed the thief to a stirrup and rode off with the poor devil between them. The next day members of his family would be in our camp, whimpering for mercy. Mahdi and Juad were sent out to handle them, for they felt personally ashamed that one of the workmen would act as a traitor to us.

With these stern methods, it is certain that few objects from Kish passed into the hands of antique dealers in Baghdad. However, some years later I was shown a fragment of Sasanian sculpture in New York which had undoubtedly been stolen from Kish.

The friendliest relationship existed between the foreigners and the local Arabs. Every evening a group of Arabs would be standing or sitting outside Mackay's mud hut, requiring first aid for a headache, or a cut finger, or even a cold or cough. Mackay would treat each case, pat the man on the back, and send him home with a kindly word.

The Arabs around us lived very like their ancestors of thousands of years ago. If Abraham had returned, he would not have been too astonished at what he saw except for such things as electricity, automobiles, and airplanes. The primitive methods of agriculture,

76

village and desert life, the social organization, and customs differed only a little from those of ancient Kish.

The December days raced by. By day we toiled, in the evening we gloated over our finds—our only time for talking or asking questions was at the end of supper—and at night we dreamed of finding more. The excitement of the hunt was on in full cry. Was there an outer world—London—Oxford—Chicago—Baggrave? We had forgotten. Our thoughts were always in the earth where fragment by fragment, seal by seal, tablet by tablet, and bone by bone we were fitting together the missing pages of a human story forgotten for thousands of years.

"*Sitta wa nuss, Sahib, mai harr* [Six-thirty, sir, your hot water]." This was my Christmas morning greeting from Ali as he shuffled into my mud hut.

Breakfast at seven in the cold underground room, then a cold drive across the wind-swept desert to the great temple complex dedicated to the Earth Goddess where two hundred and fifty Arabs awaited the starting signal, and the day spent among dark underground rooms five thousand years old—this was Christmas at Kish.

At sunset an Arab horsemen galloped into camp, bringing a cabled greeting to the Expedition staff from President Stanley Field in far-off Chicago.

After Shemu's "special" dinner we drank a standing toast to absent family and friends and soon left for our separate mud huts.

Over my head Miazan, the Big Dipper, looked finger-tip close. Our Arab guards paced over the cooling sands with an occasional "*Menu hadha* [Who goes there]?" Far away jackals barked eerily.

I stood there a moment under the stars, feeling very far from home and modern civilization, but very close somehow to the Wise Men who had followed a star over sands like these.

Buxton and I continued to find skeletons at Mound "W." Then, from Langdon's point of view, the mound became even more interesting because a few fragments of tablets were uncovered. As soon as the cry of "*Maktub, maktub!*" echoed from a trench,

Langdon would dash down, armed with scapels, brushes, pencil, and notebook, and unearth a Babylonian tablet which had laid in this mound for twenty-five hundred years. The tablets became more frequent and in better condition, until one day Langdon's excitement reached highest pitch as he delicately cleaned the dust from a whole series of tablets. Before our dust-reddened but shining eyes were uncovered several thousand, stacked on a shelf exactly as books in modern libraries are, except that these books were not paper but hardened clay and were marked with the cuneiform writings that held the ancient history of Kish. Now Langdon spent most of his time in the trench on his hands and knees, armed with scalpels and a small knife, and covered with dust, prying out his precious tablets one by one and taking them back reverently to the museum.

Meanwhile Mackay kept on directing the work at Tell Inghara. Slowly the outer walls of the base of a great temple were being uncovered. This was tedious work and resulted in nothing but a ground plan and photographs. Of all the treasure we had dreamed of finding in the temple, there came to light but five golden beads, which some hand had hidden in ancient times behind a brick in a high wall. What story lay behind them, of guilt or romance, we shall never know.

But the excavation of this great temple was typical of the tedious necessary work, with few tangible results. This is part of the chance one takes, that makes archaeology among the most exciting of experiences.

One evening Mackay brought into the dining room some painted potsherds of a very early type that had been brought to him by a Bedouin who had found them on a low mound far out in the desert.

He spread the sherds on the table and as Langdon examined them his eyes began to glitter.

"These look older than anything we have found at Kish," he said excitedly. "We'll have to try to find that place. It may be a new site. If it is small, perhaps we can sink some trial trenches."

The suggestion fascinated us all. Excavating a large city like Kish is difficult because of the tremendous overload of earth that must be removed before reaching the most interesting, the

78

earliest, cultures. But if we could find a surface site, occupied for a short period only in ancient times and then abandoned, we might achieve superlative results with a minimum of effort.

Soon after dawn several days later Mackay and a Bedouin guide drove off together in the Ford. That night he returned, exhausted but jubilant, to report that he had located the low mound. It was Jemdet Nasr, about eighteen miles northeast of Kish, toward the Tigris. Mackay had had considerable difficulty reaching the spot, and the area, when found, was extremely barren and totally waterless. But it was covered with thousands of monochrome and polychrome sherds, many ornamented, and he spread handfuls of fine examples on the table to prove his words.

This was too much for Langdon. I could see he was itching to get out to Jemdet Nasr, and so was I. You can imagine my feelings when he invited me to accompany Mackay and himself to the mound on the following day—a day to be written in red letters all my life—January 6, 1926.

After a solid breakfast by starlight, we three left camp just as the first glow of red appeared over Tell Inghara. With us were our driver and four of the best pickmen, armed with pick-axes and shovels. With shouts of encouragement we pushed the Ford, for the car was sleepy at that hour.

The poor old Model T set forth with groans and bumps on its exciting mission. The four pickmen clung to the running boards. On top of the red mound behind our camp the red foxes again stopped their play to watch us go.

Buxton waved good-by a little sadly from the courtyard, for someone had to remain in charge at Kish.

It was rough going and a crooked course over irrigation ditches and canals. The workmen, clinging to the sides of the car, were enjoying themselves. Every time we jolted over a ditch they gave forth cheers of sheer excitement. After an hour we left the ditches behind and faced a waterless, trackless stretch of some fifteen sandy miles.

In the distance we saw mounds, one called Tell Bargouthiat, "The Hill of the Little Flea." Then we nearly passed without seeing it a low mound not more than twenty feet high and perhaps one hundred and fifty yards in length. Immediately painted pottery fragments were visible everywhere and we knew this was Jemdet Nasr. Here on this small site was treasure trove, lying, not twenty-five or fifty feet underground as at Kish, but on the surface. And if so much lay above the centuries of ravaged outer earth, what might not lie below!

The Ford hurtled to a stop and the pickmen were off the running boards and at work in a matter of moments.

We three meandered over the low mound, collecting pieces of painted pottery and other fragments of this early Sumerian civilization—the Jemdet Nasr period as it would later be called in texbooks—which existed about 3500 B.C.

Not twenty minutes had passed before one of the workmen found a wall. He began to follow it, and as we watched he excavated a small room. The floor was only about three feet below the surface! Then we were exclaiming over and passing from hand to hand a spouted vessel that had lain hidden in a corner for nearly six thousand years. It was fourteen inches wide and eight inches high, with designs painted in red around it.

Here *in situ* lay the first complete painted pot of the Jemdet Nasr period.

We stopped for a picnic lunch at noon but were far too excited to eat. We walked around the mound, munching sandwiches and scanning the earth as if refusing to believe we could not see through to the treasure we were certain lay below. I was hoping beyond all else that a human skull would be found, for this would give us a clue to the racial type of the earliest inhabitants of Mesopotamia.

Langdon asked me to walk across to Tell Bargouthiat to take some photographs. He offered the car, but I refused, for in the strong clear light the tell seemed very close. Trudging on foot over the hard, hot sand seemed to send it ever farther away, but at last I reached it and, climbing to the top, took photos of the plain and the mounds from different angles. I found no painted pottery but thousands of plain sherds, samples of which I placed in my rucksack, and a small female figurine of Babylonian style.

On the other side of the tell, out of sight of Jemdet Nasr, I seemed to be very far from civilization. The white bones of a camel kept grim watch over the plain. In this dreary stretch of territory, midway between the Tigris and Euphrates rivers in the central part of Mesopotamia, I knew that Bedouins migrated back and forth, but I saw no one. There were a few birds, mainly sand grouse. A small lizard scurried past. The glare of the sun was intense, but the world around seemed dun-colored and dreary.

As I plodded back over the hot sand I tried to visualize the people who had lived in this place thousands of years before. Where had they come from? Why had they chosen this dreary site? How did they get their water supply? What did they look like? I asked these questions, little knowing that in the years to come we were to answer many of them.

I arrived back on Jemdet Nasr to find Langdon and Mackay wild with excitement. Several other complete painted vessels had been unearthed. Then, just as we were about to leave in order to be back in Kish before nightfall, one of the workmen clearing the floor of a small room found two tablets. In a flash Langdon was on his hands and knees. After he had cleaned the surfaces with a small brush he took out his pocket lens; then, squatting on the floor of that mud room, he let out a whoop of joy such as I had never thought to hear from the throat of any Oxford professor. As we gathered around him he was shouting: "This is the most dramatic of all our finds! This is the first pictographic tablet in linear script to be found in this part of the world. It is the earliest form of writing here! It is much older than the cuneiform tablets. It must be nearly six thousand years old—possibly earlier. . . ."

Right then and there in our jubilation we decided that, regardless of the risk and the difficulties involved, Jemdet Nasr must be excavated.

I could see in Langdon's eyes that he would never rest content until he had a number of those tablets in linear script. His mind was made up, and none of our wildly excited group riding back in the bouncing Ford could have guessed that the price of excavating Jemdet Nasr was to be his life.

I was the only one who harbored a trace of disappointment, for we had not found a skull, not even a trace of a historic bone I might have carried back on my knees.

Buxton was waiting as we bumped back into the encampment after dark. He had been anxious and had considered asking the local sheik to send men to hunt for us. Now we were back not only safe but with wonderful prizes and I saw him manfully concealing the disappointment he shared with me that no skull had been found to show us what racial types had lived at Jemdet Nasr and painted the beautiful pottery and written on the pictographic tablets.

However, it had been a wonderful day, and Langdon, before going to sleep, dictated the following night letter to be sent from Hilla to the Associated Press in London:

OXFORD AND FIELD MUSEUM EXPEDITION DISCOVERING QUANTITY PAINTED POTTERY FIVE THOUSAND FIVE HUNDRED YEARS OLD AND PICTOGRAPHIC TABLETS EIGHTEEN MILES FROM KISH FORMING FIRST COMPLETE SERIES FOUND IN MESOPOTAMIA ALSO UNBROKEN SUMERIAN PAINTED POTTERY AND OLDEST WRITING ON CLAY TABLETS. INFORM CHICAGO.

On that day, January 6, 1926, while cleaning out a painted jar at Jemdet Nasr, I found some seeds which were later sent to Field Museum for identification. They had been much blackened by the fire which destroyed the city during the fourth millennium before the Christian Era. Professor John Percival of Reading, England, an authority on wheat, was to report this to be *Triticum turgidum*, rivet or cone wheat. Langdon would add: "Thus, the statements of Herodotus, Strabo and Pliny concerning the astonishing productivity of Babylonian wheat are confirmed. We have at last a discovery from the Sumerian period contemporary with Predynastic Egypt. A good many samples have been found in Egypt for the same period, but these are all, I am told, emmer wheats and a less-developed product than the *Triticum turgidum* which was found at Jemdet Nasr. . . . Percival, who had also examined most of the cereals found by Petrie in Egypt, says that the Jemdet Nasr wheat is the first really ancient sample of *Triticum turgidum* which he had seen. The discovery confirms the theory long accepted by historical botanists that Mesopotamia is the original home of the breadmaking wheat."

It is significant that these ancient grains are apparently identical

82

with varieties now being grown, after a lapse of more than five thousand years. This wheat is now on exhibition in Field Museum.

I had another question. It had jogged back with me on the ride from Jemdet Nasr instead of the skull we had not found. It had followed me up the lonely slopes of Tell Bargouthiat. Perhaps all the time I had been in Kish it had pursued me and now, this night after the trip to the new mound, it kept me awake.

But I waited until morning when Buxton and I were standing in the deep trench at Mound "W." No skeletons were appearing so we were just watching the pickmen.

Then I said, "Supposing it were possible to bring to life the skeletons we have found here at Mound 'W' and at Tell Inghara—if we could bring back the dead who lived at Kish twenty-five hundred and even five thousand years ago, and if we dressed them in clothes similar to those worn by these Arab workmen who are digging them up, could you tell the difference between them?"

He looked at me intently. "You mean, is there any difference in the physical type of the ancient inhabitants of Mesopotamia and those of today?"

I waited.

"Not I, nor anyone else in the world today, including Sir Arthur Keith, could answer that question," he said finally. "We lack anthropometric data. For example, there are so few measurements, studies, or racial-type photographs of the Arabs of modern Iraq, and so few skeletons and skulls of the ancient inhabitants, that no valid deductions may be made. My own general impression is that, if data were available, they would prove that there is little difference physically between the ancient dwellers of Mesopotamia and the modern peoples of Iraq, particularly in the Kish area."

I stared at the bowed back of the good-looking young Arab pickman ahead of us and in imagination saw one of our ancient finds returned to life. . . .

"How can we prove it?" I demanded, as eagerly as if I knew that my whole future was balanced in that moment and on that question.

83

Buxton looked very serious.

"It is a fascinating question," he said carefully. "The only way to solve the riddle of ancient man in Mesopotamia is to measure, photograph, and study a series of skulls from various chronological levels and compare the results with similar data from other sites in Mesopotamia and adjoining regions. Thus, trends may be established.

"In order to study the changes or lack of change between the ancient and modern population we will have to pool all these Mesopotamian skeletal data in order to compare them with a large series of measurements on the living, particularly south of Baghdad.

"It would be necessary to record a series of anthropometric measurements on several thousand living persons. These would have to be worked out statistically and, on the basis of a careful anthropometric survey of Iraq, it would then be possible to determine the general relationship between the ancient and the modern peoples of this region.

"We would then have to compare the ancient and modern peoples of Mesopotamia and Iraq with those of the Nile Valley, Anatolia, Arabia, the Caucasus, Iran, Afghanistan, and the Indus Valley.

"Finally, the true racial position of the peoples of Mesopotamia in relation to the ancient and modern inhabitants of Asia, Africa, and Europe might then be determined."

I stared at the pickman's back through the dust and knew Buxton and I were sharing the same inspiration. Kish lay in one of the key areas of the world, in fact the "Garden of Eden" must have lain within a two-hundred-mile circle of where we were standing, and the problems as propounded by Buxton seemed some of the most important that could be solved in physical anthropology. My thoughts and ambitions concentrated on this problem. . . .

"Why not?" demanded Buxton, looking me squarely in the eyes. "Why not make this your special study? If you accumulate a lot of information and publish it, you should then be able to answer the question you have just asked me. I think this is probably the most useful piece of work you could do, particularly

84

if you correlate it not only with physical anthropology but also with an anthropogeographical study of Iraq and the adjoining areas. This would include work in the Caucasus, Iran, Saudi Arabia, and all the surrounding areas. However, it would be better if you began by concentrating on Iraq; later to do work in the adjoining areas. Then you may be able to correlate all available data and determine the general trends. You then will have an opportunity of knowing about the past and the present of the peoples of Iraq, which forms the hub of Southwestern Asia. This area is equidistant from the periphery of the land masses of Asia, Africa, and Europe. In other words, China, South Africa, and England are all approximately equidistant from Southwestern Asia. This is the focal point on the earth's surface, the surface of the Old World, where man seems to have developed. I think you could not select any area so little known or so important for a long-term project."

I managed one more question.

"How long do you think it will take?"

Buxton hazarded a guess of twenty-five years. This was his only miscalculation. My researches in Southwestern Asia, from the Suez Canal to the Caucasus Mountains, as outlined in that dusty trench in Mound "W," have taken me twenty-eight years and the work remains unfinished.

Suddenly I was in a fever to begin, and our stay at Kish was now so very short. Buxton solved this. "I think we should start today," he said. "Right now!"

During the noon rest period, with Mackay's enthusiastic cooperation, we made arrangements through Hassan Jedur to measure a series of our workmen. He explained that we would pay a small coin to each person who submitted to measurement and observation. We had brought with us from Oxford the special instruments required for anthropometric measurements.

At the end of the working day Buxton and I waited before one of the mud huts in the camp with our equipment set up, and a table and two chairs in readiness. As each man came Buxton measured first his stature in the anthropometer, then, in rapid sequence, the height from acromion to sole (shoulder to ground), sitting height, head length, head breadth, breadth of the forehead, breadth of the face, total length of the face, length of the upper part of the face, length of the nose, breadth of the nose, and length and width of the right ear. He called out each measurement number and I repeated it as I wrote it down, very much like a tailor measuring for a suit of clothes.

Each subject was then seated at the table opposite Buxton, who made notes on the form regarding eye color, hair form, color, and texture, and other observations, including an examination of the teeth, occlusion, and any other particular features. We regretted being unable to photograph them from front and profile because of the poor light; however, forty measurements and observations were recorded on each person.

Our good-natured Arabs were completely mystified but, since they suffered no ill effects and were paid for their patience, they submitted willingly.

After supper Buxton studied the results and said he was greatly pleased. His trained eye spotted several racial elements among the Arabs of the Kish area, hence a small series would throw but little light on the final result. However, he was glad to have this small sample. Buxton then suggested that we try to obtain a mixed series from Iraq for comparison with this localized group in the Hilla area. The ideal series would be obtained on Iraq soldiers quartered at Hilla Camp, because recruits would be representative of each of the areas in Iraq.

Consequently, the next morning we called on the local commandant, who granted permission for us to measure a series. They were lined up on the parade ground; in five hours we had data on 222 soldiers. We were extremely grateful for the opportunity to obtain these two series: a completely mixed sample and a local group from central Iraq.

Now only two days at Kish remained. Buxton and I had to leave, much against our wishes, on January 9 in order to be in Baghdad on the day we had arranged to leave for our search in the desert with the armored cars. However, it rained hard on January 8. My heart sank lower with each drop, for I was afraid of two ominous words of the Air Vice-Marshal's, "weather permitting." Armored cars do not attempt the desert in heavy rain.

I did not voice my fears in words but obviously Buxton had the same thoughts.

We spent the night before our departure packing the skulls and bones into wooden boxes for shipment to Chicago. Fortunately for us, the Department of Antiquities was not interested in collecting skeletal material.

I looked around the mud hut that was the Kish Museum and wondered how the division of all this treasure could possibly be made, and fairly. I asked Mackay how it was done.

Gertrude Bell, he explained, one of the most sporting characters who ever lived, had originated her own unique method for dividing the spoils at the end of the season. It was manifestly unfair, she argued, that a foreign expedition should spend at least twenty thousand dollars in one season and then have no opportunity to take away some of the finest objects. If the Director of Antiquities was permitted to make the first selection each time, the Iraq Government would always get the rarest finds. This would put the Expedition at a great disadvantage and do little to encourage its backers to continue their large donations.

On her own initiative she had evolved the following system:

When, in March, she drove into the Kish encampment, she would find all the specimens laid out on tables in the museum and in the tent; the tomb groups placed together, and the pottery, copper, bronze, stone, bone objects, and vessels in separate groups.

Standing erect before the table that held the best tomb group, the dignified Miss Bell, director of antiquities, watched the dignified Mr. Mackay, director of the Expedition, as he flipped a coin.

She always called heads.

If she won, she made the first choice for the Iraq Museum at Baghdad. If she lost, he chose. Thus, choosing alternately, they went through each group. At the next series they tossed again.

This was the division between the local Iraq Government and the foreign institutions. Those objects for Baghdad were packed in wooden cases and labeled. Now began the division between Oxford and Chicago. The arrangement was that every specimen bearing writing or an inscription belonged to Oxford, the remainder to Chicago. However, in order that the Ashmolean Museum might have a good exhibit, a representative series of pottery, copper tools, and miscellaneous objects was sent to Oxford. Thus, during a period of thirteen seasons at Kish, both foreign institutions were to obtain magnificent exhibition material.

Mackay admitted, with a pleased smile, that the toss had often been won by the Expedition director. Some of the finest objects excavated at Kish were to find their way to Field Museum of Natural History in Chicago and the Ashmolean Museum at Oxford.

This method of distribution was followed during Miss Bell's lifetime, and it satisfied everyone.

Before going to bed I gave Langdon a check to cover any possible cost Buxton and I might have been to the Expedition, for the understanding had been that we were there as paying guests. He was more than delighted with the check. He also thanked us for our assistance both at Kish and at Jemdet Nasr.

The next morning, as the Ford bounded westward toward Babylon, I looked back longingly over the dry broken earth to the rain-misted mounds of Tell el Uhaimir and Tell Inghara, and while I did not know then the length of the ties that held me to Kish, I knew they were strong. Uncle Barbour had been right and, thanks to him, I had learned more in the past three weeks at Kish than from the reading of many hundreds of books. However, none of the "book learning" had been a loss; in fact the historical background and special reading at Eton and Oxford had proved their value at Kish. I remembered Piggy Hill giving me the book to read on Sumer and Akkad and saying, "Here, digest this well. You are the only boy at Eton reading about the early history of Mesopotamia. I hope someday it will be of practical use."

I could be grateful now to Hill and to Buxton, bouncing beside me on the Ford's broken springs en route to Babylon.

And Babylon, like Kish, was mounds of sand.

At Babylon Nebuchadnezzar had directed the building of temples and palaces, the "Hanging Gardens"—one of the seven wonders of the world, which actually were magnificent garden terraces—and the Ishtar Gate, by the greatest craftsmen of his day.

The relentless sweep of history turned much to dust and slowly, across the centuries, Babylon followed Kish beneath the mounds.

Some twenty-five hundred years later Koldewey directed the excavations of a German expedition for about eighteen years at Babylon. There is no finer example of patience, fortitude, and devotion, as priceless objects were unearthed, cleaned, labeled, photographed, and shipped to Berlin for study, publication, and exhibition. From the Ishtar Gate large plaques with animals in white glaze on backgrounds of deep yellow or blue were removed from mud walls and shipped on rafts down the Euphrates to Basra and by steamer to Germany, where, after years of effort, they were installed in the Pergamon Museum in Berlin. I was to see this reconstruction later in Germany and be awed by the magnificence achieved thousands of years before.

One dark night in 1945 a fleet of one thousand bombers was to swoop off from England in precise formation. Despite anti-aircraft attack and fighters, Berlin was reached—the heart of Nazism. A young pilot, who knew but little of Nebuchadnezzar and history, shouted: "Bombs away." A scream; an explosion far, far below; the Pergamon was ruined. The work of Nebuchadnezzar's craftsmen was destroyed forever. No painstaking years of work can restore them now. This is the twentieth century with its great advances in civilization—electrical power, radio, movies, TV, bathtubs, intercontinental air travel, millions of automobiles. Now we have atomic power. . . .

Buxton and I climbed on what must have been the Hanging Gardens and sat on top of the mound. Only a thin line of trees marked the course of the Euphrates. Around us stretched "abomination and desolation," and the words of the Bible came to us vividly: "By the waters of Babylon . . . we sat down and wept."

We had found time while we were at Kish for a brief visit to Ur of the Chaldees. Since Ur was 150 miles each way, we traveled by train two nights to spend one day. After Sir Leonard Woolley had shown us around the excavations and taken us to the top of the famous temple tower, he led us down to a series of small rooms recently cleared by the Arab workmen. In a mud slab was preserved a naked footprint and Woolley, jokingly perhaps, said this was Abraham's. In any event it was contemporary with Abraham. This footprint now hangs in the University Museum in Philadelphia.

Some years later, when the royal tombs were unearthed at Ur, a sculpture in the round, colored with gold leaf, was among the precious objects found. It represented "a ram caught in a thicket" and probably illustrated the Bible passage (Genesis 22:13).

Wherever we hunted in Mesopotamia we were finding additional proof of the historical accuracy of the Bible.

We were delighted to find that little rain had fallen in Baghdad and that Gertrude Bell was waiting for us behind the tea table in her garden. She was very excited over our experiences, particularly by the new discoveries at Jemdet Nasr. I could see her metaphorically licking her chops over her share of the beautiful painted pottery that would come to the Iraq Museum. Several times she spoke of how she wished she were younger and did not have so many administrative duties. She seemed to crave a trip into the desert and I think she would have given much to accompany us on the armored car patrol.

She made me promise that sometime, if it were possible, I would visit the Roman fortress of Qasr el Burqu, the easternmost outpost of the Roman Empire, about a hundred miles northeast of Qasr el Azraq. She wanted me to visit the fort and take photographs and complete a ground plan she had begun in 1913.

I promised, but the opportunity did not come until two years later, and by that time my friend was dead.

I hated to leave Miss Bell that day. Listening at her feet was a great experience. She accompanied us to the door of her garden and shook hands very warmly in farewell. As long as I live I shall remember her framed in that Arab doorway in Baghdad . . . a great and gracious lady of many adventures and much wisdom.

We had no word from the Air Vice-Marshal regarding our trip to Landing Ground "H," but we began our rush preparations. Notebooks, pencils, pocket knives, desert maps, and boxes for collecting specimens—all had to be assembled for our hoped-for journey across the desert. Collecting bags was another matter; we needed plenty of those to contain all we hoped to find. Near the hotel was a *babu* (Hindu) tailor who said he could "run up" the required bags. We ordered fifty large and fifty small, each with a tab at the bottom on which could be written dates and numbers with indelible pencil, which is far easier than trying to write on a bulging bag. This trick we learned from a British geologist and it has spread widely.

The tailor sat cross-legged behind a whirring Singer sewing machine while a few feet away a large old-fashioned Victrola blared forth "Alexander's Ragtime Band." When we made ourselves heard over this fantastic noise we asked whether he enjoyed music; he said no, he hardly heard it. Such is the power of concentration in the East—and among our teen-agers.

We were packed and ready to leave right after lunch, although in my heart I wasn't at all sure our trip would materialize. Several Britishers were eying us as we waited in the dining room of the Maude Hotel, and these men I remembered as having been skeptical that any civilians, particularly an American such as I, would be permitted to accompany an armored car patrol into the desert. I think Buxton and I were both beginning to share their pessimism, when there was a commotion in the dining room.

An RAF officer came to our table. "Are you Mr. Henry Field? Armored cars 'Glengorm' and 'Glengarry.' All present, sir."

My last dazed impression of the Maude dining room was an expanse of faces, all with mouths half open.

In the street a milling crowd had gathered around the two Rolls-Royce armored cars, each weighing five tons, and the two-ton truck. Buxton and I followed our baggage aboard and took places on two boards facing each other in the back part of "Glengorm" just behind the big searchlight and the movable conning tower containing the machine gun. The flying officer raised his right hand and blew his whistle. The crowd waved. We waved back. The convoy moved off down the Baghdad main street and we were off across the Tigris River and into the Falluja Desert.

It was rough riding, but we were too excited to care. Even

91

Buxton seemed to be enjoying himself like a schoolboy. He kept saying, "I really never thought this was possible."

West of Ramadi the heavy cars had difficulty winding through the sand dunes. It was raining now and becoming colder; then to our astonishment we were bombarded with hailstones as we clung to the swaying car with hands that were almost numb with cold.

About ten miles west of Ramadi I took a standing position behind the conning tower as a change from the springless bench. We were plowing through the deep sand at about ten miles per hour. Visibility was poor through the rain of hailstones.

Suddenly, to the northwest, I saw a green Very light. This is a red, yellow, or green ball shot into the air as a distress signal. The RAF planes and some vehicles carried Very pistols.

I banged on the metal frame of the conning tower and the driver stopped. The other two cars pulled alongside. I told the group what I had seen. As I spoke, another green ball raced skyward and faded away. The officer shouted, "Battle positions." In a minute the machine guns were loaded, the bulletproof metal shields closed on the radiator front and over the windshield, leaving a narrow slit open. Buxton and I were bundled unceremoniously inside. A red flag was hoisted over each conning tower. A voice called out, "All ready for action, sir."

The officer took his place on "Glengorm" behind the manned machine gun and blew his whistle. The Rolls ground forward, every eye straining through the pelting rain.

We cruised up and down for an hour. Nothing was seen or heard. No tracks could be found, except our own. Finally we resumed our course to Rutba Fort, where a signal was sent by radio to RAF Headquarters, Baghdad, requesting all planes to keep watch west of Ramadi. Nothing was ever seen or reported.

I puzzled over this long and often. Almost twenty years later I was drinking coffee in a Damascus dive frequented by trans-desert drivers. From the next table I heard a grizzled veteran say, "Well, I saw the old green light on my way over." I could not resist the temptation. Introducing myself as an amateur old desert hand, the following conversation ensued.

"What light was that?"

"Oh, I mean the green Very light west of Ramadi. Everyone of us had seen it, most of us several times."

"What is it?"

"No one has any idea. We've all driven around looking for a car in distress or a plane crash, but there is nothing. Now we just wave to it and drive on." I was to tell of this, together with several other curious inexplicable incidents, to the Extra Sensory Perception class of Dr. J. B. Rhine at Duke University. There are things that cannot at present be explained, like flying saucers.

Rutba Wells, where we spent the night, consisted of a white tent, in which the chief of police lived, and some small shacks. While we were preparing camp a Bedouin, dressed in a white cotton nightshirt with a brown camel-hair garment over the top and wearing on his head a black and white speckled kerchief, led me to one side. Opening the folds of his white garment, he untied a knot containing shining pieces of metal. He put them in my hand; in the light of the setting sun they glinted like gold. He kept repeating the word "*Dhahab* [gold]."

The Bedouin said that about a day's ride on a camel to the northwest the entire desert looked like burnished gold. I gave him a large coin for the sample. That night I dreamed of a practical discovery—a part of the North Arabian Desert covered with gold. Unfortunately, when I got to Oxford and showed these in the Department of Geology the report was: "Nice samples of iron pyrites." However, I am sure the Bedouin continued to feel that he was going to be one of the richest men in the world.

In the morning we crossed the Wadi Hauran and continued westward over low, rolling, flint-covered hills.

Since Buxton and I were in the leading car, we had arranged with the flying officer that we could stop anywhere for ten minutes. In this way we made a small but very important collection of flint implements and flakes.

We passed the highest point, came over a ridge, and there below was Landing Ground "H" mud flat. We decided to camp on the western rim, at a sheltered spot where we thought prehistoric man would also have selected his campsite. Buxton and I collected flints until it was too dark to see.

The members of the RAF convoy naturally looked upon us as very strange people. Here we were, two civilians who had been able to commandeer three military cars to a landing ground far out in the desert, picking up small stones. However, since we seemed to be extremely keen on our hunt they became interested. One of the men picked up three flints and asked us if they were any good. Buxton rejected two and kept one that showed human flaking.

Buxton explained that certain flakes bear the "bulb of percussion," a swelling at the point where a flake has been struck. This differentiates man-made from the handiwork of nature. The man seemed to be so interested that I suggested to Buxton that he give a talk, illustrated with some of our specimens.

After dinner fifteen men with their flying officer sat around the blazing camel's-thorn fire on gasoline cans and empty wooden boxes.

Buxton described the purpose of our trip, which was to obtain evidence that prehistoric man had visited Landing Ground "H" mud flat many thousands of years ago. He demonstrated how flint is flaked either by hammerstone or by pressure flaking. Rejects, which resembled those made by man, and for contrast a flint scraper with a fine bulb of percussion, were passed around.

Buxton described the geographical position of Landing Ground "H" in relation to Asia, Europe, and Africa. At Oxford he had seen a map, in a book soon to be published, showing the words "Geographic Barrier" in large letters right across the area where we were now sitting around the campfire. In other words, prehistoric man was presumed not to have crossed the region between Palestine, Transjordan, and Syria on the west, and Iraq on the east, but to have followed the northern limits of Syria and Iraq, just south of the Turkish frontier. However, as a result of our discoveries these words would now be replaced by a double-headed arrow, indicating two-way migration. What type of man made these stone implements? Buxton said that they probably looked like the Bedouins but their weapons and tools were of stone, bone, and wood. The climate was different then. The

94

wadis flowed with water and were rarely dry. Now even the great Wadi Hauran, which we had crossed not so many hours before, was dry except after seasonal rains. He said that this part of the world was becoming drier as the years went by.

Different animals had roamed here in prehistoric times. Buxton reminded them that the last lion had been killed not many miles from where we were sitting, at Qasr el Azraq, at the beginning of the century. For thirty minutes Buxton held his audience spellbound. It was exciting for me to look at the faces of these men who had no knowledge of archaeology, and to see the tremendous interest his simple talk aroused. Two of them said it was unfortunate that it was dark now, because otherwise they were sure they could find some fine specimens. They asked a number of intelligent questions and, as Buxton often said, that was the keenest audience to whom he ever talked anywhere.

We went to bed, impatiently awaiting daylight. After a delicious breakfast of eggs and bacon and sausages before daylight, we began to search the mud flat for more flint implements. By nightfall we had a series of flakes and a few implements. Now we had a series to convince even skeptics. We felt confident we had established the fact that prehistoric man had migrated across this vast wilderness.

Our gratitude to the Air Vice-Marshal was unbounded. We wrote notes to thank him for his assistance. We also sent a note to Miss Bell, thanking her for her enthusiastic support of our mission and telling her that we had found some implements, part of which would find their way to Case No. 1 in the Iraq Museum. The remainder went to Field Museum.

As we left Landing Ground "H" I wondered if I would ever see it again. It still seemed strange to have been searching for prehistoric man in two Rolls-Royce armored cars mounted with machine guns—again a curious mixture of old and new.

Back in Jerusalem we called on Sir Ronald and Lady Storrs to give them an account of our experiences. They were greatly interested in our discoveries, particularly those in the North Arabian Desert.

Sir Ronald asked if we would take a letter to the editor of the

London *Times*. This letter accompanied an article he had just written on a Crusader buried outside the Church of the Holy Sepulchre in Jerusalem. He handed me a large envelope bearing the crest of the governor of Jerusalem and sealed with a blob of red sealing wax.

That night we left the Holy Land and continued by train to Alexandria, where we embarked on a Messageries Maritimes boat for Marseille. This sea passage gave us a chance to write up our notes and to think about the wonderful experiences we had crowded into those few weeks. When the steamer reached Marseille it was too late to disembark, although we were alongside. We were told that we would have to miss the night train to Paris and await the train the next morning. This was very tiresome as it meant we would be delayed in returning to Oxford, and we were already behind our schedule.

I suddenly thought of Sir Ronald Storrs's letter. The totally irrelevant but impressive document produced a near miracle. Buxton and I were bowed through customs and helped onto the train as it started to move. Changing trains, we crossed via Calais–Dover and up to London.

As the train left Paddington we sat thinking of our experiences during the past forty-three days. Buxton would not listen to my thanks for his company. He got out a sheet of paper and began a note of thanks to Uncle Barbour. I did the same and later wrote a long report on our trip, knowing he would be delighted with the results. From then on I knew I would dream and pray that someday I would go back to Kish.

The train stopped at the station. Oxford was still foggy.

. Skeleton guarding entrance to Sumerian
tomb with four-wheeled chariot excavated
at Kish in Iraq.

. Excavating four-wheeled chariot with Equid skeleton above lying in shafts.
The wheels are oval from the pressure of overlying forty feet of earth.

3. Four-wheeled chariot with copper nails around rim. Two wheels are encased in plaster for shipment to Field Museum of Natural History, Chicago.

4. Reconstruction of Sumerian four-wheeled chariot of 5000 years ago prepared in Field Museum of Natural History, now Chicago Natural History Museum.

5. Copper rein-ring, surmounted by an Equid, excavated at Kish by Field Museum-Oxford University Joint Expedition. This was found near
two-wheeled chariot.

6. View over "Y" Trench at Kish with the temple of Nabonidus in the upper section. Director Louis Charles Watelin and the author supervising excavations by Field Museum-Oxford University Joint Expedition during 1928 season.

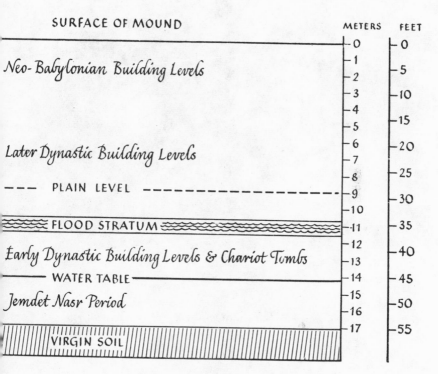

SURFACE OF MOUND

Neo-Babylonian Building Levels

Later Dynastic Building Levels

--- PLAIN LEVEL ---

FLOOD STRATUM

Early Dynastic Building Levels & Chariot Tombs

WATER TABLE

Jemdet Nasr Period

VIRGIN SOIL

METERS	FEET
0	0
1	
2	5
3	10
4	
5	15
6	20
7	
8	25
9	30
10	
11	35
12	40
13	
14	45
15	50
16	
17	55

Diagram of strata supplied from Chicago Natural History Museum.

7. Arabs eating bread and dates during noon recess at Kish excavations.

8. Payday at Kish camp. Every Friday the Arabs were paid wages and baksheesh for objects found by Field Museum-Oxford University Expedition.

9. Loading trucks at Mound "W" where the Babylonian library of cuneiform tablets was excavated
   at Kish.

10. Northwestern entrance to huge unfinished tem-
    ple constructed at Kish by Nabonidus about
    550 B.C.

© C. N. H. M.

11. Painted pottery vessel in primitive naturalistic style excavated at Jemdet Nasr, northeast of Kish, Iraq.

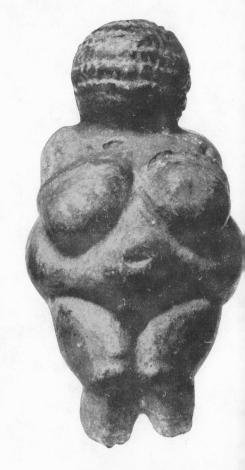

12. Aurignacian female figurine called the "Venus of Willendorf." This is one of the oldest sculptures in the round.

AFTER our return in January 1926, Buxton and I awaited eagerly the reports that reached Oxford from Kish. Shortly afterward Langdon started excavations at Jemdet Nasr, and in imagination I followed every swing of the pickaxes as they advanced through that fascinating mound. I continued to work for the Diploma in Anthropology. Books and lectures seemed less appealing after our adventures in Iraq.

At Oxford, in fact all through the Thames Valley, the end of winter always seems to drag on. The early spring days are quickly submerged by wind and rain. Bicycling to and from classes in miserably unpleasant weather makes staying well difficult, and nearly everyone has a cold. However, we survived the first days of spring and at last fine weather came and, with it, a letter from the Abbé Henri Breuil.

The Abbé was—and is—the world's leading authority on pre-history and prehistoric arts and cultures, and his is the last word on cave art. Some months before, an address by him had been the highlight of the winter series of the Oxford University Anthropological Society of which I was the Secretary.

Before the lecture Sir Archibald and Lady Garrod had given a dinner at their house for the Abbé to which I was invited. I had listened spellbound to the short, nearly bald Abbé, who had the brightest of dark eyes, a magnificent profile, and the most delicious sense of humor.

After the lecture I had driven him in my aging Morris-Cowley back to the Garrods'. I told him of my interest in prehistory and the journey to Kish, and he invited me to visit him sometime in Paris and see his Stone Age collections, notably the wall paintings of prehistoric animals he had copied in caves in France and Spain.

97

Now here was his handwritten letter in French. I raced by bicycle over to the Garrods' to see if Dorothy could decode this extraordinary manuscript. Dorothy not only could, she had a similar one. The squiggles invited us to accompany the Abbé to visit prehistoric caves and rock shelters in the south of Spain. Dorothy's family had encouraged her to accept.

I excitedly telephoned my family at Baggrave and asked permission to go to Spain for a month during the spring vacation. This meant I would not be home for Easter, and I had been at Kish for Christmas. Mother was bewildered but loyal, and said she would give me the trip as an Easter present.

So early April found me once again on a train as I sat up all the way to Algeciras, at the southerly tip of Spain.

In Algeciras the balmy air was filled with Spanish music. To the south from my window in the Reina Cristina Hotel could be seen the lights of Gibraltar with one or two flickering near the top; were these monkeys chasing their girls with flashlights, I wondered, or the lights of the British sentries guarding the Rock?

I had been told to meet the party the next morning at seven o'clock for breakfast. I found the Abbé pacing around the table like a caged lion. Dorothy Garrod had preceded me. With her was her friend Mrs. Milton, who was also to accompany us to the caves. The Abbé was trying to get breakfast, and it is just as difficult to get food in the early morning in Spain as it is to get dinner before ten o'clock at night. There was little conversation as we ate. Dorothy was very quiet. Mrs. Milton's friendly attempt to talk was silenced by a stern look from the Abbé, who seemed a pretty impatient sort of person, and I began to worry about how the expedition would work out.

I found out later that the main thing griping the Abbé was Mrs. Milton's insistence upon wearing riding breeches. Since so many prehistoric female figurines accentuate the breadth of the pelvic girdle, especially the "Venus of Willendorf," I was a little surprised at the Abbé's attitude. At any event, breakfast was an ominous meal.

At a quarter to eight the Abbé had us lined up before the hotel, waiting. At ten minutes to eight he was in a temper because the car was not there, and no one dared remind him that it was not supposed to be there until eight o'clock and that, after all, this was Spain where people cared little for punctuality and less for time.

About ten minutes after eight our chauffeur-driven Buick rolled unhurriedly around the corner. We were packed into the car in about eighty seconds flat and were off to the mountains.

Late that afternoon we turned off the main Algeciras–Cadiz road and bumped over a rough field to a stone farmhouse, Casa Retín. This was to be our headquarters. Nicola, the sixty-year-old proprietor, greeted us with a wide flourish of his aged black sombrero.

I spent an uninspiring couple of hours the next day at a peculiar kind of "homework." The Abbé had noticed that I had great difficulty in recognizing stone implements, since many quartzites are shaped by nature almost like those flaked by hand. In a sack he placed a fine example of a hand ax among fifteen unworked quartzites, and I kept feeling through the pile of stones until I could recognize the hand ax by touch.

At dawn with two guides we set out on horseback in a deluge of rain to the bold cries of "*Arre, mulo!*"

Our first stop was in a plowed field on the side of a low hill known as "Tapatanilla-Taivilla." This was a Chelleo-Acheulean open-air site where the furrows, and sometimes the ridges, contained many specimens. Here we spent an hour collecting quartzite implements—flakes, hammerstones, and a few hand axes, all flaked by human hands tens of thousands of years before. The Abbé naturally collected the largest pile but Dorothy also had some beauties. The human flaking was still very hard for me to recognize, and the Abbé became impatient because I kept bringing him what he called "rubbish." In any event I was not entirely useless because the final collection of worked quartzites must have weighed seventy pounds, and these I carried some distance back to the horses, the Abbé encouraging me merrily from the rear with shouts of "*Arre, burro!*" and "*Arre, mulo!*"

We continued toward the mountains, on the lookout now for caves. The scenery became more beautiful as the vegetation changed. No description or photographs can do full justice

99

to the mountains of southern Spain. They are of Eocene sandstone carved into fantastic shapes by aeolian action—incessant blowing of the wind. Chellean gravels overlie a Miocene argillaceous marl with clay and calcareous bands. A fertile imagination can picture the charm of riding slowly for hours among these mountains in search of caves painted by ancient man with so interesting and amusing a person as the Abbé Breuil; he was tireless in his search for prehistoric cave art, full of energy in the collection of beetles and plants, always ready to answer questions, and with a limitless repertoire of amusing stories and anecdotes—indeed a volatile and charming guide.

Despite my poor showing in the quartzite hunt, I was now feeling very happy about the entire adventure. The Abbé was undoubtedly a dominant character. The girls seemed to be getting on all right. Mrs. Milton really looked very well in those tight-fitting breeches; however, I could see that the Abbé preferred to ride in front of her.

We came to a village near Facinas where charcoal burners were at work and among them was a good-looking girl whose appearance surprised me, as she looked very much like an Arab; then I remembered that the Moors had occupied Spain not so many centuries before.

That night we spent in a small group of huts in the mountains. The villagers were glad to see us. It was extremely difficult for me to catch more than a word here and there, but the Abbé had no difficulty with the patois.

It was extraordinary how, after a few minutes, the entire village was crowded around the Abbé, hanging onto his every word. Wherever we went this happened. The Abbé had a faculty for getting on with everyone.

The next day we followed the mountain pass around the mountain, down a valley, up another mountain. Far above us we could see an outcrop of limestone where, the Abbé explained, lay our major objective, the rock shelter of Tajo de las Figuras. After many more hours of climbing the Abbé decided to look for Tajo de las Figuras without us, so we sat under a tree and waited.

There came a loud shout from far above. We climbed to find the Abbé waiting for us in a rock shelter facing south. On the walls he pointed out a series of marks, drawings, figurines, and stylized animals, the majority in red. Painted figures abounded on the right wall, and in the little chamber at the far end literally hundreds of figures covered the walls: men, women, stags, goats, birds and tectiforms, etc., in a schematic style of yellow, red, and white. Since red overlies yellow, and white overlies red, the yellow designs were the oldest.

We could but stare in amazement at the marvelous collection of Neolithic, or probably Aeneolithic, painted figures. The Abbé pointed out each minute detail, for he had spent three weeks in this shelter in 1919 while copying the paintings directly from the wall.

These were the first drawings by prehistoric man I had ever seen. Of course, from textbooks and particularly the Abbé's book on the Cueva d'Altamira, I had become familiar with their general style and effect on paper. But standing on this Spanish mountainside and seeing them fresh and vigorous was indeed a thrilling experience.

I decided then and there that no photograph or reproduction could ever do justice to the real thing.

How I wished for Uncle Barbour!

The Abbé pointed to a blank section of the wall in his most dramatic fashion. "There's a fine horse in Paleolithic style." Then, as we stared, he splashed the drab stone with water and the colors freshened and appeared to reveal a horse's head in naturalistic style—the first painting of a Prehistoric horse I had ever seen *in situ.*

There were five hundred figures or designs, among them many deer with long antlers. One painting was of a man armed with what appeared to have been a metal ax, thereby giving an approximate date to this series of paintings—a few millennia before the dawn of history.

As I studied the paintings I began to wonder about the ancient artists, their cultures, how they had lived. But when I asked the Abbé the main questions racing through my mind, he replied that in this area there were many unknown factors. He explained how he was able to determine the relative age of some of the wall drawings. For example, some designs were faded and partly covered with lichens; others were obviously superimposed on older drawings. To distinguish relative age and interpret the mass of designs requires patient study and what the French call "*l'œil*," or "the eye." Among those with the gift for seeing, the Abbé Breuil is the all-time master.

I was fully aware what a privilege it was to be with the Abbé and hear him explain the different drawings on these walls.

We ate a picnic lunch outside the rock shelter overlooking the great valley. Afterward we searched the cliff for other rock shelters, but the vegetation made this exceptionally difficult. At one point the Abbé asked me to climb up a sheer wall to a cleft in the limestone to see if any drawings were there. By removing my shoes I managed to get up but in so doing pulled down the only means of support, a small bush growing in a split in the rock wall. I found it difficult to climb down the last ten feet of sheer wall. Masses of thornbushes below did not encourage a jump.

The Abbé called up, "Use my head." Pressing his shining bald head against the rock and bracing his neck with both hands, he ordered, "*Venez, vite, vite.*"

It seemed prudent to obey orders. I could see his head apparently imbedded in the rock wall. Stepping down on it as lightly as possible, I bounded gratefully to the ground. When I thanked the Abbé for his "mental support" I added that I was sure this was the only time one of his students had ever stepped on him. This amused him greatly and years later, in Paris, he recalled the incident with great glee.

We spent that night in a thatched hut where Antonio, a charcoal burner, and his wife welcomed us. A charcoal fire smoldered in a small open pan on the floor; the roof was blackened by smoke. The furniture consisted of low, rudely made chairs and a small wooden table. The twin beds were of beams with interlaced branches. Cattle horns and wooden utensils hung from nails. The general atmosphere was reminiscent of a Neolithic community.

We passed a relatively pleasant night, except that I had about a hundred bites on my body next morning. It was Easter. Very early the Abbé galloped off to Mass, returning hungrier than ever. We sat around all day, resting and writing notes. The Baggrave pew in Hungarton Church seemed far, far away. The following afternoon we visited, among other caves, the Cueva del Arco, with its natural aeolian-formed arches upon which a few paintings are still visible.

The day was concluded by a visit to the Cueva de la Paja, where the Abbé had slept during his three weeks in that region years before. It is a very low and small rock shelter but, he assured us, quite comfortable.

We rode reluctantly back to the valley and to the farmhouse, Casa Retín, our base of supplies. Later we made several local excursions, always to hunt traces of ancient mural art. We were in an area where these were few and far between, and even the slightest daubs of paint aroused a thrill. On one of these trips Mrs. Milton, much to the amusement of the Abbé, slid feet-first down a rocky slope with a ripping, tearing noise, but fortunately her well-made pants withstood even this. The Abbé laughed uproariously.

That afternoon we passed through large herds being kept for bullfights. The Andalusian bulls are among the finest and fiercest in Spain. We rode through them without any trouble whatsoever; they ignored us. And still, as soon as one of these bulls enters the ring he charges straight for a horse.

This had already been a ten-hour day and it was still nearly four hours' ride back to Casa Retín, mainly in complete darkness.

But it was not a tiring trip. The Abbé collected some interesting beetles and some rare specimens of plants, belonging mainly to the iris and orchid families, which he carried stuffed in the sides of his boots. He was in splendid form and delighted us with stories and reminiscences.

The next day we returned to Gibraltar.

It was another fascinating experience to visit the Rock of Gibraltar with the Abbé, to look at Devil's Tower rock shelter where years before he had found Mousterian implements. The gray-blue Rock, towering some five hundred feet above the brilliant water against the equally blue sky, was majestic and almost literally overpowering. The Abbé and I scrambled several hundred feet up the scree slope and, owing to a peculiar optical illusion, I had the feeling all the time that the Rock was going to topple over on us.

We found a few flakes below Devil's Tower rock shelter. On this slope the Abbé had found worked flakes which indicated that the rock shelter above had been inhabited many thousands of years ago.

It was in the hope of confirming the Abbé's theory that next morning Dorothy began her excavations outside Devil's Tower rock shelter.

This rock shelter, which stands about a hundred feet above sea level, consists of a high, narrow fissure, like a chimney, extending twenty feet up into the limestone face of the otherwise sheer cliff.

One of the most fortunate details about working this site was that there was plenty of space below for "throwback"—a detail that might appear insignificant but is nevertheless of the greatest importance.

Dorothy employed four workmen who began that morning to clear away the debris from the platform in front of the rock shelter. Three hearths were found at different levels. Just above one hearth Dorothy found a worked piece of quartzite and the lower jaw of a wild boar (*Sus scrofa*) as well as a few limpet shells, which indicated humans had lived and dined in this cave.

These finds stimulated our hopes that Dorothy would excavate a Mousterian skeleton *in situ*. Forbes Quarry was only a quarter of a mile away and it was there that the famous Gibraltar skull, now in the Royal College of Surgeons in London, had been found without adequate data to establish its antiquity.

I certainly hated to leave this Mousterian site where at any moment another Neanderthal man might be found. I pictured myself at Oxford waiting prayerfully for the telegram that would bring the news from Gibraltar. We had planned in advance that Buxton was to receive the original for Oxford and I was to have a cast for Field Museum!

That day, although we did not know it, young "Abel" was sleeping his long sleep behind the steep face of the Rock, waiting to be found and taken on his long journey to Oxford. . . .

For it was only a few months later that the Abbé's earlier finds were confirmed when Dorothy uncovered in the Devil's Tower the skull of a Neanderthal child known to science as "Abel," and associated with a Mousterian culture. Gibraltar then is the most western location of Neanderthal man. It is indeed a far cry from Gibraltar to Teshik-Tash near Tashkent, where A. P. Okladnikov found some twenty years later a Neanderthaloid child. Between these two widely flung sites lies La Quina in the Charente, where Dr. Henri Martin also found a Neanderthal child.

But Abel's discovery waited in the future. The Abbé went back to Algeciras to arrange a new expedition, Dorothy kept on with her digging, and I toured Gibraltar.

Our next expedition, carefully planned by the Abbé, was to the cave of La Pileta near Ronda. Several days later we were threading our way through mountain passes beyond Benoajan. The Abbé and I were on foot, carrying our rucksacks. Dorothy, who had reluctantly torn herself away from the Devil's Tower for this trip, was on a mountain pony. Our guide led another pony that was burdened with our luggage, including ropes and ladders and other equipment for the cave. Mrs. Milton had not been able to join us, or perhaps she had had her fill of speleology for a time.

Since many bandits or brigands were reported to be in these mountains, we were handed on by the inhabitants from valley to valley. One guide led us up over the mountain and down the other side. As we started up the next slope another figure appeared on the sky line; we then rode up to meet our new guide. We spent the night in a small village near the famous cave of La Pileta.

Next morning we started for the cave. The rope ladder, acety-lene lamps, candles, and other cave-exploring equipment were entrusted to the wild-looking village men who came along as guides. We were ten when we set out, on horses, for La Pileta.

After about an hour's ride we came to the cave, which opens on the side of a large depression near the top of the sierra. In this section the Jurassic limestone is extremely broken and there are many outcrops on every hand. I changed into my rope-soled shoes before entering. What we would encounter inside I had no idea, as the Abbé gave us no special warning. But I carried another pair of shoes in my rucksack, together with candles, matches, and some chocolate, for which last we would all be grateful later on.

We entered the narrow fissure in single file, with the Abbé and one of the local guides in the lead. Behind trudged the other guides, carrying the caving equipment. It was cold and wet and rough going; in places we had to scramble on all fours. We were glad to have on thick sweaters. None of us said anything as we hurried along in single file with the Abbé always going a little too fast ahead.

After about an hour of strenuous effort the Abbé said we would rest for five minutes. The flickering light from the lamps showed that we had come into a rocky passage that was a good deal narrower than the entrance. A pool of water covered the rock floor over which we hung our feet as we sat on boulders to rest. The Abbé lit an evil-smelling Caporal cigarette.

I could not figure out why we were resting, for surely we must be close to that section of the cave decorated by prehistoric man. I tried to peer at the walls but could see nothing except a large rock that seemed to bar our way.

The guides were unwinding the rope ladder. They fastened one end around a boulder on the cave floor and began paying it out over the large rock.

My eyes opened wide as the ladder disappeared into the darkness. I had not known it was so long. I lay on the ground by the rock and turned my flashlight over the edge. I could not see the bottom, only a hazy gray-blue chasm falling far below. I dropped a small pebble and listened. "Eighty feet?" The Abbé nodded casually. Evident he was not in the mood for being questioned as to why we were going down into this abyss.

Dorothy sat quietly.

The men completed their preparations, and one of the guides disappeared over the edge of the rock. I lay on my stomach holding my flashlight as he climbed hand over hand down into the darkness; the beam could not follow him all the way down. A shout assured us he had reached bottom.

Another man went down, then the Abbé, with an agility that dismayed me. Then Dorothy rose from her rock seat, grasped the ladder, and lowered herself out of sight.

The guides at the ladder were now looking at me. I was looking at the rope ladder and the rock that anchored it—firmly, I could only hope—to the watery floor of the cave. I did not dare refuse. So, swinging in spider fashion in the dark, I felt my way gingerly down the slippery rungs and at last gratefully dropped from the last rung onto the muddy floor of a chasm lined with heavy blue clay.

I felt that after this effort we should be rewarded with the sight of superb drawings on the walls, although how prehistoric man would have dared to crawl down into this black abyss I had no idea.

But the Abbé did not glance at the dark walls. Instead he fell on his knees in a particularly dark and damp corner and began digging feverishly with his fingers. Dorothy and I stared at him in amazement in the dim light. Then, looking up, he handed to us and to each of the men small corked test tubes with a hasty, "Here, please try and catch some."

So this was why we had risked our lives climbing down into this cave below a cave! We were to look for beetles. The Abbé, grubbing away like an active mole, explained that he needed a series for a friend at the Musée de l'Histoire Naturelle in Paris.

He said that when he had been in La Pileta some years before he had collected a pair of these blind beetles and they had caused tremendous excitement in coleopterous circles. This new species was now called forever *breuili*. His friend said that if ever he got a chance to go back to La Pileta he must collect a good series. And here we were.

It was a weird sight—otherwise perfectly normal people rooting around in wet clay for blind beetles at the bottom of a dark cave in the mountains of southern Spain.

We spent half an hour grubbing feverishly in the clay, catching these very elusive, though blind, beetles. By this time we had about thirty specimens of *breuili*. The Abbé was enchanted. Dorothy and I were not. We had been first startled, then annoyed at finding ourselves in this ridiculous predicament. But in the "interests of science" we tried to overcome our lack of enthusiasm. The Abbé, seeing that we were inwardly fuming, thanked us very formally in Spanish, then in French, just as he might have done at the end of a presidential address in the well-lit lecture hall of some world capital.

The question now was how we were going to get back to the upper cave. As I looked up the steep side of the stone wall I could see high above two tiny pin points of lamplight glowing like stars.

The Abbé did not seem perturbed. He suggested that I go up first, Dorothy should follow me, and he would come next. The ladder did not quite reach the ground, so a loose rope had to be used for the ascent to the first rung. Clinging to the rope with wet, clay-covered fingers was difficult, and the clayey rope soles of my shoes slid off the slippery rungs as if they were greased. But as the Abbé was shaking the rope impatiently below, I fairly raced up the first fifty rungs. This was a mistake. I was soon out of breath and my feet shot from under me several times, so that only a desperate gripping with mud-covered fingers saved me. I was winded long before I reached the overhanging rock.

Above me the two guides standing on the rock rim turned their lamps over the protruding ledge, which seemed an impossible barrier. I could not get my fingers around the rope at this point because it was pressed so firmly against the rock by my weight. I had to reach high enough above the rock to grab a rung. With clay-slippery hands and feet, this was highly dangerous. I slipped twice before I was able to grab the rung above the ledge. With a great deal of grunting I arrived on the rock where the two Spaniards were waiting with anxious eyes. I knew then that this was the most difficult piece of climbing I had ever attempted.

My worry now was as to how Dorothy would make it, for she was very tired from the eighty-foot descent and the beetle hunt. I was sure her arms could never reach from the ladder under the ledge to the rock above.

I lay full length on the edge of the rock with the wan light of my flashlight beaming on her as she came up, slowly and carefully, resting every now and then. The worried guides put their lamps on the ground and prepared to help if possible. When she reached the jutting rock, which was ten feet below me, she was panting, and there above her was the five-foot gap. She was very tired and I could see she was close to tears. I did not see how she could stretch up to grasp the next usable rung. The feat had taken my last ounce of strength. While she rested, clinging to the ropes,

I decided the only thing to do was to let myself down to give her a hand. I tied a rope around my ankles with firm knots and explained to the men what I was going to do and that they must hold onto the rope or I would crash headfirst to my death. I could only hope they understood.

They gradually payed out the rope as I slid head down over the edge of the rock. I could see Dorothy's head a few feet below me and far down in the distance, which seemed a mile away, I could see the lamplit figure of the Abbé. He was shaking the rope and shouting what on earth was the delay. I slid down very precariously until I could grab one of Dorothy's wrists, then, calling to the men above in what I hoped was Spanish, I asked them to pull me up—slowly and steadily. They understood, and slowly I dragged Dorothy up over the dangerous ledge until I felt her left hand closing over a rung. I know we will both always remember this moment. Then I pulled up her other wrist. It, too, found a rung and clung. Dorothy was now swinging by her arms over the abyss. Again I pulled her upward slowly, by both wrists now, until I had lifted her almost bodily over the jutting edge of the rock. I felt utterly exhausted both from the danger and from fatigue. Dorothy lay down where she stood, which happened to be in a pool of shallow water, and closed her eyes.

We shouted down to the Abbé that all was now clear for his ascent. He jumped on the bottom rung and came up with amazing agility. The gap offered no challenge to him. He stretched, jumped, and caught hold with accomplished skill. He made the whole climb in record time and I doubt if any Olympic champion could have done better. He scrambled up over the rock to Dorothy, who was still lying full length in the puddle, and, whipping out a Caporal and panting only slightly from his physical exertion, he remarked, "*Venez vite, vite.*"

Dorothy opened one eye and said, "*Je ne bouge plus.*"

I think the Abbé was a little surprised, even shocked. This was probably the first time anyone had been so definite with him. However, it was very clear that she was exhausted, so muttering to himself, "*Toujours les femmes!*" he sat down and smoked three or four Caporals very impatiently. I also welcomed a chance to rest.

109

At last Dorothy stood up and started to walk back down the cave in the direction from which we had come, it seemed years before. The cave seemed almost smooth to us after all our climbing. However, the Abbé did not permit us to reach the entrance but steered us deftly into a cleft he had ignored when we passed it on our way into the cave.

We had now been underground for four hours. It was cold and damp and no one had suggested anything to eat. Our feet were wet and covered with mud, we were bedraggled-looking, and Dorothy and I at least were as miserable as we looked. But the Abbé marched us down the corridor and flashed his lantern through the water dripping from the roof and there on the cave wall was the section that had been ornamented by prehistoric man, the paintings that were our objective before we had been sidetracked by the blind beetles.

Dorothy and I stared at them drearily. Our enthusiasm had waned.

The Abbé, as enthusiastic and energetic as ever, pointed out in triumph the different techniques of art. I'm afraid Dorothy and I were two of his less apt pupils at that moment.

Then I remembered the chocolate bars in my rucksack. They made us feel a lot better. We were able to work up some enthusiasm for the paintings we had traveled so far to see, which were, in fact, the main objective of this trip to Spain.

They were all of animals, and of four different series: (a) the earliest in yellow similar to the early Aurignacian paintings of northern Spain; (b) those in red, which may be compared to the more developed red paintings of La Pasiega; (c) those in gray-black not unlike some of the early Magdalenian drawings in northern Spain, although this series might have been a late Aurignacian or Capsian development; and (d) a series in coal black comparable to the conventionalized Neolithic and later drawings found in rock shelters in large areas of Spain.

At La Pileta, according to Miles Burkitt, whom I have been quoting above, examples of these four series are often painted one above the other. This had enabled the Abbé to determine the relative ages of this series. Since the coal-black drawings always appear overlying examples of the other three series, they are the most modern.

The Abbé decided we had better leave, and we turned our weary feet and wearier bodies back toward the entrance. It seemed a very, very long way. The places where we had to go on all fours, scrambling over boulders, seemed far more difficult now, weary as we were.

Ninety minutes passed before we saw the gray light at the entrance, which looked extremely bright to us although it was late afternoon.

Outside I took some photographs which illustrated the "before and after" of speleology. We were exhausted and sopping wet and looked like sorry, muddy tramps.

We had spent six hours in the cave, with nothing to eat but a few squares of chocolate. But the late sun dried our clothes and cheered our spirits. The Abbé did not need cheering. He was in a delightful mood and whistled and hummed as we rode down the mountain trail. Never have I seen such boyish enthusiasm and such reserves of physical energy. He kept telling us how pleased his friend would be with the beetles.

Back at the village we washed as best we could in water heated in a kettle, changed our clothes, and had a good square meal cooked in the open. Next day we were at Ronda, and then it was time to return to England.

Dorothy went back to Gibraltar to resume her hunt for Abel. The Abbé and I said good-by. My muscles still ached, but I was able to thank him sincerely for a great experience. He was now one of my heroes, and so he has remained ever since.

I had spent three weeks in Spain. Despite the blind-beetle episode, Dorothy and I had been shown some of the earliest prehistoric art in Europe by the Abbé, the master interpreter of such art, and I would always be grateful that he had given me my first introduction to the underground galleries where the ancient hunters had drawn or engraved their pictures on the walls. I had made friends with the Abbé. He had invited me to visit with him the fabulous cave of Altamira in northern Spain and also the cave art of the Dordogne and the Pyrenees. I had also promised to visit him in Paris during the summer, when I hoped to tour the museums on the Continent.

We made many indefinite plans for the future before I climbed aboard the Madrid train and set my face toward England.

One last week was left of the Easter vacation. I spent it delightfully at Baggrave with the family before returning to Oxford.

Another ambition had been gratified. A year before I had played as a Reserve on the Oxford golf team, winning my singles match against Cambridge at Hoylake. This year I became a Golf Blue and was lucky enough to beat Leonard Crawley, later to become British amateur champion.

Several months later, in June of 1926, came the written and oral examinations for the Diploma in Anthropology. Our class of nine passed.

I was an anthropologist.

MY FIRST desire, after graduating from Oxford, was to work in a museum, and it had been my dream since childhood to return someday to Chicago. Both desire and dream were to be realized, for I received an appointment as assistant curator of physical anthropology at Field Museum of Natural History.

My work did not begin until October 1 . . . the summer of 1926 beckoned ahead, enchantingly empty. The family were to spend part of the summer at Le Touquet (Paris-Plage) on the Channel. I made other plans.

Years before, when Sir Henry Wellcome and Mr. Balfour had helped plan my studies, they had recommended some training in a German university. Accordingly I enrolled for a summer course at Heidelberg which I planned to follow with a tour of European museums.

After a couple of weeks at Baggrave I took the train to France, where I had the pleasure of visiting the Abbé Breuil at his country house at L'Isle-Adam. Here the Abbé has his retreat to which he retires mainly for week ends in the spring and autumn. In the garden are plants that he has collected in all parts of the world, a *mélange extraordinaire*, as he himself would call it. Each plant, carefully labeled, is a memory of his world-wide travels.

At Strasbourg I stopped to see the magnificent cathedral and its famous clock. A procession of figures marches sedately around the great face, striking the hours. I rarely pass through Strasbourg without stopping to pay my respects.

Since Hubertus de la Feld, a good brigand chief of the ninth century, and others of my ancestors came from this part of the world, I spent some time searching through the Strasbourg graveyard and was rewarded when the aged verger scraped moss from the stone of an early ancestor.

Late that afternoon the train crossed the Rhine. At Heidelberg the rain was pouring down, reminding me of Oxford, that other university city where I had just spent five pleasant years. I had arranged to stay at the home of Heinrich Münter, assistant professor in the Department of Anatomy, and that evening I found my German inadequate for ordinary dinner-table conversation. However, to stay with a family always seems to be the accepted way of learning a language efficiently and rapidly.

Within two weeks, thanks to my lessons and the fiendish homework and an occasional movie or concert, my German improved miraculously. I could now read a newspaper without too much difficulty and even say a few sentences.

At the university I was enrolled for a series of lectures, one a week on geology, one on anatomy, and some special work from Dr. Münter in physical anthropology. The latter was the reason I had come to Heidelberg, since I wanted to know how they catalogued, numbered, and arranged their specimens, and the general museum technique, which had been so highly developed in Germany.

The morning after my arrival I found myself in a lecture hall with twenty-five German students, all with crew haircuts and some of them sporting scars on their faces. One boy had a wide strip of adhesive tape holding cotton wool to his right zygomatic arch. Every eye was fixed on me, but in a relatively friendly manner. Later I found I was the first Allied student to attend the University of Heidelberg after World War I. This was eight years after the Armistice.

Münter showed me the laboratory work on which he was engaged. He was making a detailed study of a series of Coptic skulls which had been sent to him from Egypt. This monograph is now a standard reference work. He was deeply enthusiastic over his subject and explained the method and technique he employed. In general, the technique was the same as that taught by Buxton at Oxford with minor variations. For example, he took a great many more measurements and observations. This is a standard German technique. In Vienna I was to see an old bearded gentleman recording one thousand measurements and observations on each of eight skulls!

In the collection at Heidelberg were several thousand human skulls, arranged on shelves in dustproof cases. Münter explained that dust should be kept out because it causes bones to disintegrate.

He was very interested in the work at Kish and I described our series of skulls which were to be shipped from Iraq to Oxford and Chicago for study.

There was much to see and learn in and around Heidelberg. I visited museums there and in several nearby cities.

In the Geological Museum I had the great privilege of studying *Homo heidelbergensis*, the famous Heidelberg jaw which was found at Mauer. This is one of the oldest representatives of the human race in western Europe—about a hundred thousand years old. To hold the Mauer jaw was indeed an experience. Münter spent about an hour showing me its finer points. For comparison on the table were the mandibles of a gorilla, orangutan, chimpanzee, and a modern western European.

In Bonn, in the Provinzial Museum, Professor Lehner opened the case so that I could handle the skeletal fragments of the first Neanderthal man ever found. In 1858 Hermann Schaafhausen had found these bones in a rock shelter in the nearby Neander Valley. These human fragments caused Virchow, Huxley, and others to wrangle over their antiquity and their normal or pathological condition until evidence from other parts of Europe proved the existence of a Neanderthal race. To hold the original calvarium from the Neander Valley was also a great thrill.

The weeks slipped by and it was almost time for me to leave. By this time I had explored the woods and climbed the hills around Heidelberg and knew the city and university well. But there was one thing I still wished to do: attend a *Mensur* in the Hirschgasse where the duels took place.

Three days before I was to leave I was invited, in greatest secrecy, to a duel. My guide led me into a building on a hillside and into a large room where in platoon formation stood six groups or corps, each of twenty students, dressed in their colorful student uniforms. I was given a place of honor with a clear view. A doctor, dressed in a long white coat, carried his little black bag to a table, laid out his instruments, put on his rubber gloves, and beamed.

There were to be three duels. These were not duels of honor; in fact the duelers might be good friends. Each corps or fraternity had selected a representative by lot. The victor was he who drew blood twice.

The first two duelists wore metal masks and heavy leather jackets with padded shoulders. Their long narrow foils were protected with buttons so no thrust could penetrate. Their right hands were protected by heavy gauze metal gloves with wrist shields, their eyes by gauze metal goggles, giving them an inhuman appearance.

There was deathly silence in the room as the young men faced each other. Each right hand was raised; the foils crossed high. Naturally the taller had the advantage and was able to nick the head of his opponent almost immediately. The fight was stopped by the referee. The boy was led through the group to the medical table, where the doctor began to sew up his scalp. It was all very professional and businesslike.

No one but me cast even a casual glance toward the patient. All the students were looking with admiration at the tall, handsome blond who had drawn first blood.

Within a minute or two the boy was sewn up. The doctor led him back through the crowd, whose lines quickly re-formed around the ring. There was the clash of steel against steel, the rapid flashing of blades. Once again every eye was riveted on the scene with the "thirst for blood" look. I suddenly saw what was bound to happen. A small drop of blood was forming on the top of the smaller boy's head. This drop of blood grew larger. Amid all the flashing and crashing of steel, it began to move slowly forward down the boy's forehead. It disappeared in the black gauze glasses over his eyes. The smaller boy would be blinded by his own blood. At that moment the tall boy, who now looked to me like a giant, flicked his wrist; his blade very neatly cut the smaller boy's right jaw from ear to mouth. The bright red skin lay open below his chin; and his back teeth flashed white in a red pool. As I saw this gaping wound within a few feet of my eyes, I shut them in horror, and felt the crowd move back, presumably for the doctor, now with a real chance to do his stuff.

The next thing I remember was a German boy bending over me as I lay on a sofa in the next room. He was offering me beer. I had fainted! This was a most ignominious moment. I asked for water. While he was gone I staggered out into the fresh air. No one saw me, so no one stopped me. I staggered through the woods down to a bench overlooking the river and the town and I sat there in the sunlight. I tried to analyze my feelings. The main thing was that these two duelists were not settling a dispute. I think that if they had been trying to settle an affair of honor I would not have minded so much. The thing that really bothered me was that these two young men were so unevenly matched. The second was the lust for blood in the eyes of the watchers and the presence of the doctor. The third thing was that anyone could so steel himself that no matter when or where the blow came there was no involuntary flinching. It had been explained to me that these boys never twitched; that if they did they were disgraced for the rest of their lives. How anyone could train himself to that frame of mind seemed to me really remarkable. Such self-discipline often leads to sadism; it undoubtedly accounts for the horrors of Dachau.

But the real cause of my inward and outward revulsion was the look on the faces of the students. They were not watching in a casual way. I have never seen a more intense or more anxious group of faces. They were fully aware and appreciative of any skillful thrusts or parries. But this was really the background. What they really wanted to see was blood. He who could draw blood twice was the winner. The doctor rubbed salt into the wound to retard healing; often a small plug was inserted so there would be no chance of healing first on the outside. To enhance the scar, the stitches were not drawn. I had read of this sort of thing among "savages," but the fact that any so-called "civilized" group of young men would go to that extent of self-mutilation, primarily for the admiration of their women, seemed to me to be quite apart from anything I had ever witnessed before. I had discussed this with one German woman who had expressed in no uncertain terms her pride in her husband's scars.

117

As I sat on the bench above Heidelberg that morning these things surged through my mind. I was worried, deeply worried, for the future of Germany and these young men.

I left Heidelberg the next day and began the tour of the European museums my various scientific godfathers had advised. Since I was anxious to make as wide a sweep around central and northern Europe as possible, I decided the best procedure, with the limited funds at my disposal, was to eliminate hotel bills by spending each night sitting up on a train. ("Always carry a pillow and blanket; you never know when you'll need them," Uncle Barbour used to say.)

I spent the following eighteen out of twenty-one nights on trains. The days were nearly all spent in museums.

It was the sort of trip only youth could stand. But during it I was able to enjoy and study the finest museums in Europe, to hold in my hands the originals of the greatest finds of prehistory, and to meet their excavators and some of the leaders of thought and science of Munich, Vienna, Budapest, Zagreb, Brünn, Wisternitz, Prague, Dresden, Weimar, Berlin, Stockholm, Oslo, Copenhagen, Hamburg, Amsterdam, Haarlem, Brussels. Everywhere I was made welcome and display cases and files were thrown open to the young newcomer in the field of the study of man. I made acquaintanceships that would last and be of greatest help in the future.

The Museum für Vorgeschichte in Munich was fascinating, for it contained the eight-thousand-year-old Azilian skulls from Ofnet in Bavaria. Theodor Mollison allowed me to examine these skulls which had been found orientated toward the west. Gashes by flint knives on the atlas bones indicate decapitation. Around one child's skull a chaplet of deer's teeth had been placed by some loving hand perhaps ten thousand years ago.

In this museum Baron Dr. Egon von Eichstett showed me his reconstruction of the Neanderthal man of La Chapelle-aux-Saints. By modeling the soft parts and hair over a cast, he had achieved a good result. Later, in Chicago, this method would be used by Frederick Blaschke in reconstructing the figures in the Hall of the Stone Age of the Old World in Field Museum.

In Vienna I found Adolf Bayer examining his collection of

Paleolithic stone implements from Gaza in Palestine. In the study collection there were twelve thousand human skulls from all over the world. On exhibition were the two Crô-Magnon skulls from Lautsch and the Brüx calvarium, the latter with no label of any kind. Bayer led me into his office, opened the desk drawer, and handed me a dark red jewel box. Inside was the real "Venus of Willendorf." The famous prehistoric female figurine showed Negroid traits and was attributed to the Upper Aurignacian Period, about thirty thousand years ago. This figurine, three inches tall, was found by Szombathy at Willendorf in Austria during 1908. To our sense of artistic beauty in the Western world, as exemplified by "Miss America," this female form is a monstrosity. However, in 28,050 B.C., she was probably the reason why men left caves.

In Zagreb, formerly Agram, in Yugoslavia I called on Gorianovic-Kramberger, the discoverer in 1899 of Neanderthal man at Krapina in Croatia. He was about eighty, tall and dignified with a gray-white beard. He wore a black cap and slightly out-of-date clothes for this century, but his eyes were sharp and twinkling and his smile charming. He seemed to be very surprised that an American student would come all the way to pay respects to him and to see his Neanderthal skeletons. I explained to him that I was making this kind of pilgrimage around central and northern Europe because it seemed worth any effort to meet the excavators and handle the original specimens.

The old gentleman patted me on the shoulder as I left, and said, "You are the first in a long time to make a pilgrimage to the Neanderthalers of Krapina. You will probably be the last to see them in the hands of their discoverer." I was.

At Brünn (Brno) in Czechoslovakia I was shown, in the Moravske-Zemske Museum, two prehistoric skeletons, a male and female from Brünn, and the marvelous finds from Předmost, Wisternitz, and Pekarna which illustrated the culture and everyday tools of those ancient artists and hunters of Moravia.

These treasures, including the female figurine known as the "Venus of Wisternitz," were afterward removed to a schloss for safekeeping during World War II. According to the story, a

German SS major ordered gasoline poured down the staircase and set fire to the building as U.S. troops advanced.

I was allowed to take part in the excavations at Wisternitz. Above the trench towered a conical hill surmounted by a castle, below was a wide valley strung with shining rivers. I thought what a delightful picture this must have made in Aurignacian times, with mammoths, hyenas, cave lions, and cave bears roaming across the steppes. Our ancestors must have been the hunted rather than the hunters.

In Dresden, a bright and shining town with formal gardens, Dr. Heydrich showed me around the Museum für Völkerkunde, where in the zoological section we stopped to admire two cases of pheasants and ospreys. Two *Aepyornis* eggs lay nearby; Germany seems to have a corner on these rarities which make the zoölogist's mouth drool.

Berlin in the sunshine glistened and shone. Everything was extremely clean and well kept and there was the same feeling of arrogant efficiency I had felt in Heidelberg. Here again was the formal bowing of the men as they passed on the street; the clicking of heels as a man bowed to kiss the hand of a lady; the air of correctness and efficiency, coupled with a fierceness of expression.

These did not look to me like people just defeated in a world war. They were more like conquerors.

Next morning I walked down the Unter den Linden from the Adlon to the Staatlichen Museum. I wanted to pay my respects to the two most famous prehistoric skeletons in all of Germany, the Le Moustier and Combe-Capelle skeletons, the bones of two former dwellers in France. Le Moustier and his Neanderthal relatives roamed the Dordogne some five hundred centuries ago. Combe-Capelle was an Aurignacian who lived about thirty thousand years before Christ.

How did these French treasures reach Berlin? According to the French version of the story, a German excavator, Dr. O. Hauser, was given permission to excavate near Les Eyzies in the Dordogne region of France. Just before World War I broke out in August 1914, Hauser found the Combe-Capelle and Le Moustier skeletons. During the several days of confusion before hostilities actually began, Hauser received a secret order from

Germany to get them out of France. With "collaboration" he put these skeletons and a very fine representative series of stone implements into two new coffins with proper papers saying these were two Germans who were going to be buried in Germany. Hauser and his assistant accompanied the two coffins to the Franco-German border. Since the papers were in order no questions were asked.

However, that night there was a great feeling of tenseness in the air. World War I was just about to begin.

The train left the French side of the border and proceeded very slowly to the German side. A Frenchman aboard said he thought the coffins seemed very heavy. He tried to lift one of them and could not. The train was just pulling into the German station. Hauser stepped forward, struck the Frenchman in the face, and said, "We are now on German soil. Try to get these away from us if you can. They are on their way to Berlin, and you'll never get them—neither you nor your armies nor anyone else."

I visited some of the other museums and walked about the streets to try to get a different impression. But I could not like Berlin.

That night the train moved swiftly across Prussia to Warnemünde, across the Baltic by steamer and on to Stockholm, a clean, thriving city. Driving out to Frescati, about two miles out of town, I came to the State National Museum where Dr. Geijer showed me the geological exhibits, well arranged, not overcrowded, and well labeled, and I had the pleasure of meeting Drs. Arne, Hallström, Lindquist, and Linné. I was shown through the Stone Age collections, a magnificent series of northern European types with which I was unfamiliar.

As usual I spent that night wearily sitting up on the Stockholm–Oslo Express, which puffed westward through heavily wooded hills. By this time I was afraid that I would never be able to sleep normally again either in a bed or off a moving train.

That afternoon I wandered through the Norsk Folksmuseum in Oslo, beautifully laid out in a large park. The guides, dressed as peasants in their bright regional costumes, added to the attractiveness of this open-air museum.

As darkness fell, as if by instinct I climbed aboard the train bound for Malmö at the southern tip of Sweden. Museum cases, labels, exhibits whirled before my closed eyes.

In the morning the train pulled into Malmö and I took the first ferry across to Copenhagen. In the National Museum Dr. Friis Johansen showed me around the Bronze Age collection. Dr. Johannes Brøndsted showed me the best examples of Danish flint-work, including the famous Fünen dagger, the most beautiful piece of flint in Europe, almost paper-thin.

The most exciting moment of the trip was when we visited Haarlem to see the famous *Pithecanthropus erectus*, the Java Ape Man. This had been discovered by Dr. Eugène Dubois at Trinil in 1891. However, since that time he had guarded it very preciously; very few people had been allowed to see it—in fact for the past twenty-five years no one had been able to examine it. Because of the nature of the International Congress, then taking place, he was forced to give a public demonstration. I went to his lecture and there on the table by his right hand was the Java Ape Man, one of the oldest remains yet found. Dubois was a peculiar-looking individual who practically never took his eyes off the skull beside him. At the end of the lecture he received an ovation from the fifty people present and we were each allowed to handle the skull.

Finally, exhausted with museums, sight-seeing, and train seats, I arrived in Paris. . . .

After three weeks of nights spent sleeping on a train it was difficult to sleep with sheets and a pillow and without hearing the rumble of wheels.

This had been my third trip in less than a year—the journey to Kish, the second to Spain, and this last flying survey through the museums of central and northern Europe. These invaluable experiences were to serve me the rest of my life.

There were a few swift weeks of happy luxury—golf, tennis, and swimming with the family in France—and then England.

At Baggrave I packed for my fourth journey, to Chicago. Baggrave had never seemed more beautiful. I realized that its story was ended for me and my life there ended. Most of my years had been spent there—1908–26.

As the train raced toward London I thought of the life I was leaving for the city of my birth on Lake Michigan. I had never lived in a city. I did not know what Chicago, and Field Museum, would mean to me. I looked back to the first days at Baggrave, being blooded by George Leaf, jumping a big fence on the Bum Bay, shooting rabbits in the Prince of Wales's covert, playing tennis, working in the hayfield, learning to milk a cow and steer a plow, watching Sport retrieve a runner, listening to Pat's stories, riding to the Quorn with Mother and my stepfather.

Now I was joining the staff of Field Museum in Chicago and our lives would naturally grow apart. The times we could spend together henceforth would always be too short, always feeling the seconds flying by with never enough time.

LANDING in Boston, I spent several days with my aunt and uncle, the Thomas P. Lindsays, at their charming Lynbrook near Southboro'. Aunt Florence was to be my closest friend and relative from that day. Her children, Minna, Florence, and John, are a wonderful trio. Lynbrook, later the Gate House in Beverly Farms, was to be my second home.

On the last day in September I drove into Chicago. Turning right off Michigan Avenue, I circled the museum. The huge white Georgia marble building in classical Greek style looked cold and austere in the evening light. Looking up the steps, I read the legend:

"Field Museum of Natural History. Founded by Marshall Field, 1893."

I was to report for work there in the morning. I hoped Great-uncle Marshall would be pleased. Uncle Barbour had written that he was delighted with my appointment.

I drove up Michigan Avenue past the Art Institute. I waved to the lions, that famed pair modeled by Paul Kemeys and given by my grandmother in memory of my grandfather Henry Field. Turning on Elm Street, I stopped the car outside 1130 Lake Shore Drive almost next door to the house where I was born. I was greeted by "Aunt" Fran and "Uncle" Albert Sprague, my closest kin and friends in Chicago. My circle had been completed. Twenty-one years later, I had come home.

I reported the next morning to Mr. D. C. Davies, director of the museum, in his darkly paneled office overlooking Grant Park and Lake Michigan. He gave me my orders. An office was ready for me. Dr. Laufer had laid out my program. The president—Cousin Stanley Field—would see me at ten; he insisted upon punctuality. . . .

Dr. Berthold Laufer, chief curator of anthropology, entered. I looked at him with respect and some trepidation, for he was to be my chief. His eyes smiled as he extended his hand. "Well, my boy, I've been waiting for you for a long time."

I knew in that moment Dr. Laufer and I would be friends.

We walked down the concrete-floored corridor to my office. The sun was shining brightly this morning of October 1, 1926. Lightly stained office furniture shone against a dark blue carpet, bookcases lined the wall. Along the hall another storeroom, Room 59, was piled high with hundreds of cartons of human bones.

Dr. Laufer explained that this was the museum's collection of human skulls and skeletons from all over the world. This, he said, beaming, was to be my first job—to unpack, check, catalogue, and file away about one million human bones!

My official duties began with the arrival at my office door of a Swedish janitor carrying a vacuum cleaner and a gas mask. This was Olsen, and he was to be my assistant in the bone-dusting project.

We spent the better part of that year in "the boneyard," as Dr. Laufer playfully called Room 59. Olsen would open a carton, put on the gas mask, and dust off each bone in perfect silence. Almost three decades of Chicago grime lay thick on our treasures. All day long in that room, five and a half days a week, the vacuum groaned and whirred and I sorted and catalogued bones on the long tables. Someone cracked that I was "piling Olsen on ossa. . . ."

One evening while I was checking the numbers on a miscellaneous series of human long bones that lay on a table between two large steel cabinets, I heard the door open and a voice say, "Good night, Joe." The next night the same thing happened. On the third night I jumped up and ran around the case to see a man disappearing down the hall. Calling him back, I asked the reason for this nightly visit. "Oh, I wouldn't think of going home without saying good night to Joe. He was a janitor here for years," the man said, pointing to an articulated skeleton swinging from a metal ring through its skull.

Together Olsen and I sorted all the cartons of bones by con-

126

tinents, then alphabetically by states. The stacks of North and South American skulls and bones dominated the room. I checked every single number in ink on every single bone of more than three thousand skeletons and hundreds of skulls and long bones. I then wrote the five- or six-figure number in large figures on the side of each carton. By the end of the year we had every bone in its right drawer and catalogued so that any specimen could be found at any moment.

There is a theory that childhood scenes are always disappointing when we see them again. But Chicago did not let me down. Since the age of eight I had dreamed of someday coming back to live there and my birthplace held every charm I had imagined. Chicago was windy and cold after Leicestershire and the Thames Valley, but I found its air bracing. I never tired of watching the lake in its many moods. I liked the work I was doing, the fun I was having. Never was anyone given a better time by so many friends.

There was a seamier side to my natal city. Its beef barons had given way to the barterers in crime and human lives and the Gold Coast yielded to Cicero. Prohibition had brought Capone and his henchmen to power.

I remember very well during these years that everywhere I went—New England, Europe, or even the Near East—everyone looked with a certain admiration and astonishment at someone who "lived in Chicago." And people everywhere asked first if I knew Al Capone.

The city's reputation became so black that travelers avoided Chicago because they would have to change trains and were afraid of being hit by stray bullets.

Once I was driving my friend Marvin Breckinridge to the station to catch the train to California. She asked the usual question about gang warfare and I assured her it was mostly headlines and we rarely saw or heard of trouble. Whereupon we passed a man lying covered with blood in a gutter and a squad car raced up the street. After that, conversation palled until I put Marvin on the train, when she said, "Chicago must be a fine place to live!"

I said that it was indeed. And so it was!

Another time I had some English friends for lunch near the Lake Shore Athletic Club. One of them had just asked if the stories about gang warfare were true and if one was apt to be shot.

"Heavens, no," I said airily. "Nothing ever happens here, or if it does, it is always on the West Side, mainly in Cicero."

As I finished speaking there was a terrific explosion, the club-house shook and rocked, and through the windows we saw smoke pouring from the adjoining apartment building less than two hundred yards away. Police sirens wailed. Some gangster had tossed a pineapple into a rival gangster's room during his Sunday afternoon nap with a blonde.

Soon after my arrival in Chicago I was taken around town by John Drury of the Chicago *Daily News*. John knows Chicago by night as well as anyone can. I was interested in the various racial groupings of the city, and he took me on tour through each of the sections, from the Gold Coast to the Black Belt. We went to police headquarters to view the midnight line-up, and there I met Walter Storms, later to become deputy chief of detectives. This huge man, with the strongest wrists I have ever seen, some time afterward became the main single force in putting down gangster terrorism in Chicago and adjoining Cicero.

As a physical anthropologist I included in my interests a study of the faces of our Chicago gangsters. Is there such a thing as a criminal type? Years before, while an undergraduate at Oxford, I had obtained permission from the Home Secretary to visit Dartmoor to study the racial and facial types. In Iraq I made a survey of Arab criminals in prison.

At police headquarters I pored over the thousands of front and profile photographs of criminals on large cardboard sheets in steel files. The majority of these pictures of Chicago law-breakers showed them pudgy-faced and heavy-browed. "Scar-face" Al Capone's marred visage was typical. As a type he interested me greatly, and I tried to meet him, but never succeeded, though I sat ten feet away when he pleaded guilty to income tax evasion.

On two occasions I was invited to help the Police Department and Northwestern Crime Laboratory. A murder had been committed. The room gave evidence of a bitter struggle and the right hand of the victim clutched some hair identified as human by the Crime Laboratory. Further microscopic examination revealed that the hair was neither typical Negroid, Mongoloid, nor Caucasian. The murder had taken place near the small Arab quarter. Was this Arab hair? Deputy Chief of Detectives Storms telephoned to know if I had collected hair samples of Arabs in the Near East. Here was a practical test. I made up three samples, each of about a hundred hairs, from my collection of hundreds of hair samples. The Crime Laboratory reported to Storms that he had better look for an Arab. Within twelve hours a cordon had been thrown around the Arab quarter; an Arab confessed to the slaying.

The other occasion was after a human skeleton was found during a bulldozing job near the Des Plaines River. The Police Department had evidence that this might be the remains of a well-known missing gangster. Storms asked me if someone in the department could make a cast of the skull and reconstruct the face for possible identification. However, this proved impossible as my time and thoughts were absorbed in a new project, one that was to require complete dedication for years to come.

THE new museum project had started with a conversation in the boneyard.

I had toiled for a year in Room 59 and the last bone was dusted and filed in the steel cabinets. Olsen and his vacuum departed. Through the windows came the first scents and sounds of spring, of buds bursting around Lake Michigan and birds making their housing plans.

Dr. Laufer came into the room. He was beaming.

"You have done well with the bones, Henry. But you must have some other research projects, something to direct your work here. Have you any such ideas?"

I had indeed. Every specimen from Kish, seen in the clean light of the museum, aroused my longing to go back to a search uncompleted. And the anthropometric survey Buxton and I had started there had been but a beginning.

So I said, "I want to continue my research on the ancient and modern peoples of Southwestern Asia."

"That's fine," he said, "but I mean exhibits in the museum. A new idea we can work on here."

In that, too, I was ready for him. Ever since Hill had inspired me at Eton I had longed to see the complex history of mankind portrayed exactly as it had developed, link by link.

"I have two dreams," I told Dr. Laufer. "I would like to see the Story of Man portrayed in two adjoining exhibition halls, one dealing with prehistoric men of the Stone Age, and the other with all the races of mankind."

He showed the keenest reaction. "I've had an idea for an exhibit of physical anthropology since 1915," he said. "Write me a memo with your suggestions."

That night I sat up long past midnight writing pages and pages in longhand. In the morning I wrote and rewrote the memo and finished up with something along these lines:

I recommend two exhibition halls for the museum:
1. The HALL OF PREHISTORIC MAN with large dioramas ranging from the Chellean to the Lake Dwellers of Switzerland, 250,000–6000 B.C. Opposite would be scientific data from each period.
2. The HALL OF RACES OF MANKIND with a series of full-length figures, busts, and heads, representing the principal racial types of the world. A special section would illustrate the bases on which mankind may be divided and regular physical anthropology exhibits.
3. For both Halls the finest artists in the world must be found for these unusual techniques.
4. When completed, these two Halls will be the most popular, not only in the museum, but on any continent. For man is more interested in himself than anything else. The finest dramatic presentations will draw the greatest crowds for decades to come.

This brief memo on one single sheet was to change my life for the next six years. Dr. Laufer forwarded it to the director with a covering recommendation, and next afternoon President Stanley Field sent for us and together we urged the idea of the two Halls. He told us to prepare the plans and to list the material already available in the museum. This looked like a pale green light. Upstairs I began to assemble all the Stone Age materials from Europe, Asia, Africa, and Australia. The cultures of the Swiss Lake Dwellers were well represented among the gifts made to the Field Columbian Museum at the close of the World's Fair in 1893. There was a small series of hand axes and cleavers from the Somme gravels in northern France and some stone tools from Egypt, Somaliland (Seton-Kerr collection), South Africa, and India.

For the Hall of Races of Mankind we would have to start almost from scratch. There were, however, skulls showing artificial cranial deformation, fine examples of trepanning and trephining, and many photographs of racial types from all over the world.

132

Here at least was a nucleus from which to begin both Halls.

Dr. Laufer gave me the outline of the plan for an exhibit of physical anthropology he had made more than a decade before. This was along stereotyped lines, with cases illustrating hair color and form, eye color, nasal profile, head form, photographs of racial types, etc.

A week or two later the president invited me to lunch with Marshall Field and himself in a private dining room at the Chicago Club. With the last spoonful of vanilla ice cream, Marshall pushed back his plate. "Henry, what's this Stanley tells me about an idea you have for two exhibition halls?"

I talked for five minutes about the two Halls as graphically as I could. As he left, Marshall said he was extremely interested. The president ordered me to prepare two blueprints without regard to space, time, or cost.

The go-ahead light was becoming greener.

After a dusty, dirty day in the boneyard I used to go home, have a bath and supper, and cover yards of paper with diagrams and notes. Even part of the lunch hour was thus occupied. Ideas came in the middle of the night. For six years I was never without a pad and pencil to jot down ideas—even at night. Many of the best suggestions were stimulated by good music, especially the Thursday night symphonies with Frederick Stock conducting in Orchestra Hall.

Dr. Laufer suggested that I visit Balboa Park in San Diego to study the physical anthropological exhibit prepared some years before by Dr. Aleš Hrdlička, delightfully referred to as "Hard liquor" in *The New Yorker*. There I might pick up some valuable ideas, some of which could be duplicated in our proposed Hall. Since I had never been west of Chicago, this trip was most profitable. I stopped off in Denver and San Diego to see the museums. In Balboa Park I spent five days and finished up by hiring a local artist to copy many of the unique exhibits of physical anthropology, including charts of the racial variations in skin color, hair form, head type, etc. I made a detailed plan of every case. Some of these exhibits are at present on view in Field Museum, for this work of Hrdlička's was far and away the best of its kind at the time.

It was on this trip that a detour permitted a trip to the Grand Canyon. As I stood alone on the rim, lost in the vastness of space— one of the few sights in the world that cannot disappoint—I felt a nudge on my left arm. "Move over," a voice said, "I want to get the full view." I glanced from the miles-long panorama to the photographer. He was using a No. 1 Brownie.

As the train clicked on over the rails I worked on the list of racial types to be represented. By the time I reached Chicago, my total was 155 individuals. Dr. Laufer had his own list. We combined them for a total of 164, arranged according to racial importance with special emphasis on the primitive groups such as the Tamils, Sakais, Andamanese, Todas, Ituri Forest pygmies, the Bushmen of the Kalahari and Australia. Now we could begin to group them in alcoves by continent. The central motif would be a White, Black, and Yellow man supporting the world. This would symbolize the "Unity of Mankind," the basic concept of the Hall.

At this point I sent the list of the types selected to the leading physical anthropologists throughout the world, men such as Sir Arthur Keith, A. C. Haddon, Dudley Buxton, Davidson Black, Eugen Fischer, Egon von Eichstett, Eugène Pittard, and many others. An accompanying letter requested them to send comments and criticisms, especially regarding which types should be full-length figures designating racial importance.

We were now making definite headway on the plan.

I visited Dr. Hrdlička in the Smithsonian, Dr. Henry Fairfield Osborn and Dr. William K. Gregory at the American Museum of Natural History, and Dr. Earnest Hooton at Harvard in order to obtain their advice. Dr. Gregory told me about the Cap Blanc skeleton, which had been for sale for eleven years in New York. This was an almost complete Magdalenian skeleton. The story was as follows: Monsieur Grimaud, owner of the Cap Blanc rock shelter near Les Eyzies in the Dordogne district of France, had excavated the skeleton of a young girl below the famous frieze of horses carved in high relief on the limestone wall. The skeleton was said to have been smuggled out of France during World War I in a coffin as an American soldier with the necessary papers forged. In New York the skeleton was offered to

134

the American Museum of Natural History for the sum of ten thousand dollars and sent there. Since this price was considered excessive, no sale was made.

I wrote to the Abbé Breuil, who replied that the Cap Blanc skeleton was in New York and he had every reason to believe that it was still in the Museum of Natural History.

Here was a chance to fire the imagination of Chicago. I recommended to Dr. Laufer that, through Georges Robrieux, the representative of Marshall Field and Company in the Rue St. Georges, Paris, be sent to Monsieur Grimaud with twenty-five thousand-franc bills (the equivalent of a thousand dollars) in one hand and a receipt ready for signature in the other. Stanley Field decided to take this gamble. If the deal went through, he could determine whether Field Museum visitors really had any interest in a prehistoric girl.

Some days later a cable came from Paris saying that the Cap Blanc skeleton was ours. I hurried to New York and in the basement of the Museum of Natural History packed her very carefully in cotton wool and carried her in a suitcase to a compartment on the Twentieth Century. We had a very uneventful night together. In the museum I unpacked her. Almost every bone was complete. The skull was broken but the lower jaw and teeth were intact. An ivory harpoon point, described as having been found near her ventral cavity, lay in a small box.

A case was ordered for the installation. Armed with Gray's *Anatomy*, I laid her out full length on the floor of the case. The phalanges and small bones of the hands and feet were hard to separate. The pelvic girdle was definitely feminine. Her age was about eighteen.

Photographs of the frieze of horses at Cap Blanc were labeled and framed. The ivory point was given a prominent place. Finally we were ready to put the Magdalenian maiden on exhibition.

Early on a Saturday morning we wheeled the case into a prominent place in Stanley Field Hall just inside the main entrance to the museum. The evening and morning papers and the press services had carried the dramatic story of the arrival in Chicago on the Century of a twenty thousand-year-old Magdalenian girl —the "only prehistoric skeleton in the United States," which she

135

was at that time. This was front-page news. The story went all over the world.

There was much speculation. Why had she been buried beneath the frieze of horses? Was she killed by her lover's ivory lance point? Was it by another Crô-Magnon girl? Was her brother avenging the family's honor? Was she killed in battle? Why was she buried in the sanctuary? Was she the daughter of the sculptor-high priest?

There was no real evidence, except that death probably resulted from blood poisoning.

That Saturday 22,000 visitors came to the museum, most of them to see "Miss Crô-Magnon." At noon the crowd was so dense around her that the captain of the guard, Sergeant Abbey, notified the director that two guards must be placed there to keep the people moving and orderly. D. C. Davies could hardly believe his eyes—nothing like this had happened before in Field Museum. The press and photographers badgered Dr. Laufer, as chief curator, for interviews and pictures. This was the first exhibit in the new building to capture the public and press imagination. That night I went to bed very happy.

The furor continued again on Sunday and to a lesser extent on the following weekdays and paydays. I am sure that "Miss Crô-Magnon's" obvious popularity played a dominant role in deciding the president and trustees to look favorably on our proposed Hall of Prehistoric Man.

When the press stories concerning Miss Crô-Magnon reached Paris, Le Temps ran a vicious story under the heading, "Your grandfather and mine sold to the Americans." I was afraid the French government might try to recall Miss Crô-Magnon from her pleasant resting place beside the shore of Lake Michigan. I wrote a letter to Le Temps stating that, fond as I was of the French, I thought they merited some criticism when they said that a Magdalenian teen-age girl could be anyone's grandfather. The subject was dropped.

At this point another factor entered into our plan. Charles R. Knight, the world-famous mural painter of prehistoric animals, was under contract by the Department of Geology to do a series

136

of gigantic murals for Hall 38. At the recent end of the sequence were to be two large dioramas, *Mesohippus* (a five-toed horse) and a Neanderthal group. Regarding the latter, I was called into consultation by Dr. Oliver C. Farrington, chief curator of geology and an authority on meteorites.

Meanwhile Frederick C. Blaschke, the distinguished sculptor from Cold Spring on Hudson, New York, had been engaged to make these two dioramas. Dr. Farrington asked me if I could assist Blaschke with the Neanderthal group. Since I was going that November on a museum expedition to the Near East, I would be able to spend some weeks with him in Europe discussing the plans for the two Halls with Sir Arthur Keith, Dudley Buxton, the Abbé Breuil, and others.

I suggested to Dr. Farrington that we reconstruct a Neanderthal family at the entrance to Le Moustier, the type Neanderthal station in France.

When I told Blaschke of my plan his eyes lit up as he saw the great possibilities of a Hall of Prehistoric Man with eight large dioramas, one of them forty-two feet around the curve.

Many long evenings were spent with Blaschke going over the details. A scale model, one inch to a foot, of the case in Hall 38 was made. At my suggestion he made a rough one-third-life-size Neanderthal figure so that Sir Arthur Keith, Sir Grafton Elliot-Smith, and other specialists could direct his fingers in plastilene.

Blaschke and I sailed together from New York aboard the same ship, so we could work on the Neanderthal group. I had a suitcase full of reference books, a Graflex camera and film, many empty notebooks, and eight scale models for the dioramas in Hall C and one for Hall 38.

In London I took Blaschke into the study of my good friend Sir Arthur Keith, conservator of the Royal College of Surgeons. Since 1921, when I first met Sir Arthur in the Royal College of Surgeons, I had been under the spell of his charm and encyclopedic knowledge on anatomy and physical anthropology. For thirty-two years I have been encouraged by his sincere interest in my work. If I had to designate "the greatest living anthropologist" it would be Sir Arthur and most of my colleagues would concur.

Sir Arthur looked up from his desk and said, "Must be from

Central Europe, probably between Prague and Vienna." Blaschke of Bratislava was amazed.

The meeting was instantly sympathetic. The small plastilene figure on an armature was unwrapped. Sir Arthur directed Blaschke's skilled fingers in changing the angle of the head and neck on the shoulders, muscles were added here and there, the crude clay face achieved a human look under the heavy brow ridges. The hair was roughed in with a scalpel. Sir Arthur was deeply impressed with Blaschke's ability to transfer his ideas into modeling clay. Three days later Sir Arthur nodded satisfaction. Here was a perfect team: the knowledge of one man transmuted to clay through the super technical skill of an artist.

A cast of the Le Moustier skull was purchased from F. O. Barlow in London. Sir Arthur then guided the application of plastilene to replace the skin and the soft, fleshy parts, such as the nose and ears. At each significant point on the skull, the thickness of the plastilene was measured with a graduated needle. Sir Arthur and Blaschke worked head to head for many hours until both were satisfied. The dark brown eyes, graying brown hair, and skinlike composition added the final touches of realism.

In Paris we showed the reconstruction of "Monsieur Le Moustier" to the Abbé Breuil, who agreed that this was the best reconstruction ever made. It was good to see the Abbé again and to find him as lively and enthusiastic as always. He readily agreed to go with us in search of background material for the Hall of Prehistoric Man.

We discussed the reconstruction of Le Moustier. We needed motion and still photographs and color sketches for the background. The Abbé suggested his cousin, Pierre Gatier, who had a good sense of portraying the countryside, especially its various shades of green.

The next recruit was Henri Barrèyre, professional motion picture operator. He was ready to come to the Dordogne for a month with us. He would use my 35-mm. Cinex and the Graflex.

The cavalcade was ready. The Abbé Breuil, Gatier, Barrèyre, Blaschke, and I, accompanied by a mountain of equipment, took the train to Périgueux, where we hired a car and a truck to take us to the Hotel Delsaut at Les Eyzies some twenty miles away. Next morning we climbed up the steep escarpment to Le Moustier rock shelter overlooking the green valley of the Vézère. The scale model, boxes, and sacks were carried by three local farm hands. Blaschke began to measure and model the curious gray-blue limestone formation with its white or yellow infiltrations. I collected two wooden cases of debris, including hundreds of flint flakes and chips for the floor of the case in Hall 38. Gatier made a series of color sketches under the direction of the Abbé, reconstructing the valley from the exact angle which would have to be painted on the background by Charles Abel Corwin. The Abbé indicated the size of the Vézère and the type of vegetation existing on a spring morning some fifty thousand years before. We could not have obtained a more expert opinion.

Barrèyre took several reels of 35-mm. film and about a hundred stills. We talked, thought, and tried to recapture the picture of life during the Mousterian period in this now charming *petit coin* of France.

As we sat outside Le Moustier on a rock overlooking the green valley of the Vézère I read to Blaschke from Sir Arthur Keith's words about the discovery in 1908 within a few meters of where we were sitting:

"Further excavation was stopped until autumn, when, surrounded by a company of German anthropologists, in the heart of France, the skeleton was finally extracted from its ancient bed, with expert eyes looking on to bear witness to its authenticity and antiquity. The skeleton was that of a lad of perhaps sixteen years of age; his canine and third molars were not fully erupted; the growth lines of the long bones were unclosed. There could be no question; he had been deliberately buried. Near his right hand was a handaxe of the Acheulean culture, but typical implements of the Mousterian period were nearby. Charred remains of an ancient ox—the urus—were noted. The body had been laid on its right side, with the face turned down, and a pillow of stones placed under the head."

Study of a widespread series of Neanderthal skulls and fragmentary skeletons leads us to deduce that speech was little

139

developed, probably not more than clucks and grunts, the hands and feet were large, the great toe being separated from the rest of the foot.

The Neanderthal hunters found that a fire built near the entrance to Le Moustier protected them from cave lions, big bears, and savage hyenas. Neanderthal man was probably the first to begin family life. That was why we were reconstructing a family group at Le Moustier in Field Museum so many thousands of miles away.

The concentrated studies of Le Moustier were completed in a week. Now we were ready to tackle some of the scale models of the eight dioramas for the Hall of Prehistoric Man. We moved to nearby Cap Blanc, each of us collecting and recording data. Blaschke modeled the frieze to scale. Three wooden cases of debris were obtained for the floor of the group.

The Abbé and I discussed the purchase of collections of artifacts with Monsieur D. Peyrony, dean of prehistorians in this district. He gave us the names and addresses of the principal private excavators in the Dordogne and assured me that this would not in any way interfere with objects he might obtain for the Les Eyzies museum. The Abbé and I left Blaschke, Gatier, and Barrèyre at work, while we drove around buying collections for exhibition in Hall C. In almost every case the owner would refuse to sell selected pieces, so we were forced to buy the entire collection. However, I realized that in this way we would have an excellent study collection. The Abbé was very fair, encouraging me to pay about double the amount he would give if he were buying for the National Museum at St. Germain-en-Laye. That was natural. I was buying for a foreign museum with dollars, then at twenty-five francs to the dollar.

It was exciting driving from farmer to farmer, for here in the Dordogne they all knew the cash value of Palaeolithic tools and art objects. The bargaining was fun, my schoolboy French was improving of necessity. These were fine people, leading the good life of the French farmer, industrious, thrifty, and delightful company. I drank wine, kissed babies, told stories, and behaved like a politician in order to bargain with them. After the deal we clinked glasses, paid the cash, wrapped up the collection with labels and notes, and drove on our way.

The Abbé told me about some wonderful Magdalenian necklaces made of ivory beads from the tusk of a mammoth. These had been excavated at La Souquette near Sergeac by a farmer named Marcel Castanet. Here was an exhibit everyone could understand. I wanted these beads very badly indeed. However, there was a slight complication. Castanet was employed during the summer months by Professor George Grant MacCurdy, director of the American School of Prehistoric Research, who was excavating a rock shelter on his hillside at Sergeac. MacCurdy might want these necklaces either for the school or for Yale.

I asked him if he planned to buy the Castanet collection and/or the necklaces. MacCurdy said that he had wanted them, but the price was far too high and he had decided not to argue any further with Castanet.

After lunch the Abbé and I drove to the farmhouse, where Castanet greeted him like a long-lost brother. Four small, flat-topped glass cases were fitted with Magdalenian treasures—the four necklaces, bone spear points, beautiful flint scrapers, long blades, and a host of other flint tools. The necklaces caught my eye, both eyes. Two hours later, and after much pleasant bargaining, they were purchased.

Among MacCurdy's students was Mrs. Harper Kelley, who invited me to visit her husband, in bed with a cold. Armed with a sputtering candle, Alice led me upstairs to meet Pat, who was feeling miserable. This was my first meeting with a real friend who was to help me immeasurably in the buying and cataloguing of the huge collections I purchased in France. Pat has a fantastic memory. For example, years later he can recall all the details of any one special object out of many thousands. His knowledge and friendship have been mainstays during the long years.

After the data on Cap Blanc were complete, we all moved to Gargas in the Haute-Garonne, where similar work was done to reproduce the thirty thousand-year-old Aurignacian "frieze of hands," many with mutilated fingers believed to have resulted from their propitiatory rites. For example, during the nineteenth century the Kalahari Bushwomen of South Africa cut off their little fingers as a sign of deep mourning. On Tonga in the Pacific Captain Cook reported that a finger was sacrificed to propitiate the god Atoa.

Then southward to Mas d'Azil in the Ariège, where we planned a wild-boar-hunting scene with leashed dogs, the first evidence we have of the domestication of animals.

Returning to the Charente, we visited Le Roc with Dr. Henri Martin, discoverer and excavator of La Quina. With his generous permission we arranged to buy casts of the frieze of Solutrean animals, so Blaschke roughed them out on the model.

Across to northwestern France we trouped, to work at Carnac in Brittany. The great alignment of standing stones would make a perfect diorama.

Under the Abbé's guidance Blaschke made the scale model for No. 1 diorama in our series—a moonlit Chellean scene of two hundred and fifty thousand years ago on the Somme near Amiens.

Devil's Tower rock shelter at Gibraltar, which I had visited before with the Abbé and Dorothy Garrod, was selected as the setting for the other Neanderthal family scene and the model blocked out from photographs under our joint direction, as was the Lake Dweller scene on Lake Neuchâtel, because our collections already in Field Museum were from this site.

We had now completed the nine scale models and accumulated the necessary data for most of them, and had purchased splendid collections representing the major Palaeolithic periods in France.

Two important missing items were the glass eyes and the hair. The former could be bought in New York. The Folies-Bergères told me that the best wigs were made of human hair by Madame Duplessis. At a certain address Blaschke and I found this purveyor of ladies' tresses. A lovely, buxom young girl, her assistant, led us into a back room with a curious smell, the smell of human hair. From a cabinet was pulled a large, narrow tray on which a dozen hanks of long, gray-brown hair lay in neat rows. Blaschke took two skeins to the daylight and chose enough for the Neanderthal man, his wife and baby-in-arms, his mother-in-law, and a young boy.

142

Blaschke handed Madame the strands of hair with a courteous Old World gesture. She carried them into the front room to a pair of old-fashioned scales and began to list the prices hank by hank. For the best quality—and a Neanderthal family would resent anything less—Blaschke paid nearly four dollars an ounce.

He was now ready to return to his studio on the Hudson to make the life-size Neanderthal family. I was to join the Field Museum Expedition in the Near East. Many months later Blaschke brought his hairless figures to Chicago. Spaces had been left in the wooden flooring for setting the family in place. In a museum studio he applied the human hair by inserting it with a hot needle into his own special fleshlike composition. This was a tedious business, especially the hair on the man's legs.

Blaschke modeled the rock shelter over wire and lath and Corwin painted in the background. The cave debris from Le Moustier was spread on the floor. The finished figures were placed. A hidden mirror was hung to throw light and give life to Monsieur Le Moustier's eyes. The glass was set, the labels installed. The can of poison to kill all forms of insect life was hung behind the rock-shelter. The Neanderthal family of Le Moustier was ready to receive all comers.

Next morning being Saturday and the press having carried the story, thousands of visitors poured in to see the new arrivals of fifty thousand years ago. Once again two guards were assigned to keep the long, long queue moving. Miss Crô-Magnon sulked in her glass case.

Millions have seen this Neanderthal family, for Blaschke's realism captivates the imagination. This was the first life-size reconstruction of prehistoric man ever made in a museum. Some months later Madame Tussaud's in London did us the honor of attempting to copy Le Moustier.

The president, director, and Dr. Laufer were pleased with Blaschke's work of reconstructing the Le Moustier family in Hall 38 and with the excellence of the eight scale models for Hall C. I was instructed to draw up a contract. Stanley Field, by now our greatest enthusiast, raised the $110,000 for the dioramas, the greater part being a gift from Marshall Field. Other contributors were Silas H. Strawn, Frederick H. Rawson, and Samuel Insull. The contract was duly signed and sealed.

That night I went to bed tired but thrilled. Half of my dream would be realized.

At last the Hall of Prehistoric Man was under way.

AFTER Blaschke returned to Cold Spring on Hudson in the late summer of 1927 I continued eastward to Jerusalem. Dr. Laufer had suggested that after the buying and data-collecting work for the two Halls was concluded I should return to Kish for the winter to continue my North Arabian Desert archaeological survey, to record additional anthropometric work in Iraq, and to excavate all the skeletal material found that season at Kish. The triple assignment thrilled me.

I had wanted to continue the desert hunt for Stone Age man ever since Buxton had found the flint implements lying on the surface of the desert between Amman and Baghdad. They had left so many questions in my mind: who had used these implements, what did these men look like, had they migrated into this desert from Central Asia or India, or across Sinai from the Nile Valley?

Often at night in Chicago as the foghorn boomed across the lake, I had lain awake wondering and thinking. Half asleep, I could imagine picking up perfect Chellean hand axes, Mousterian and Aurignacian implements . . .

So it was wonderful to find myself, early in November, on a train puffing into Jerusalem, after the dusty year spent working in the boneyard. From this time on until the completion of the two Halls I alternated museum work with my annual summer pilgrimage to Europe to buy specimens for the Hall of Prehistoric Man and to select data for the Hall of Races of Mankind. Now research was to be carried out by a Field Museum Expedition of which I was leader. This was an independent archaeological unit bent on tracing the migrations of prehistoric man in that great, and now inhospitable, region between Baghdad and the Mediterranean.

145

Waiting beside the platform at Jerusalem stood a 1919 open touring Cadillac with a tall, husky Englishman at the wheel. This was S. W. ("Lofty") Quarrie, one of the crack Nairn Overland Desert Mail drivers.

On a hunch I selected Bayir Wells in Transjordan as our objective. Group Captain L. W. B. Rees of the RAF—one of the few Royal Air Force wearers of the Victoria Cross—warned me in their headquarters at Amman to tell no one where we were going. Flying Officer Silcox would accompany us as guide.

Next morning with Quarrie at the wheel the old Cadillac carried us over the gravelly plain. As we passed the ruined fort of Ziza I asked Quarrie to stop. We were crossing a narrow flint bank that extended to both horizons. I could not restrain a cheer. My two companions came running. I had found a deeply patined flint bearing the human hallmark, the bulb of percussion.

It was our first sign of prehistoric man.

That night, after the fine stew Quarrie cooked over the Primus, we stretched our bedrolls on the stone floor of the blockhouse at Al Qatrani, and with a native on guard and our firearms within reach, we slept restlessly.

The next morning, fifteen miles along the track, I found several more worked flints. These were again encouraging proof that Stone Age man had passed this way.

Now we had left behind us all traces of modern man. Around us was trackless wilderness.

There was not a bird or animal anywhere. We were surrounded by an awful silence. I stood alone on a low mound. This was my first real taste of loneliness since Tell Bargouthiat in central Mesopotamia. In every direction stretched the sandy, gravel-covered wilderness. Silence, perfect silence. At that moment I felt a true respect for the desert, a respect that has grown over the years. For here there were no human beings, no animals, no water, nothing but sand and gravel and low thornbushes. It would be easy to die of thirst here. I had read of the swollen tongue, the choking sensation, the mirages and painful death . . .

When prehistoric man lived here the wadis flowed with water, game must have been abundant. Transjordan was then a pleasant land.

146

Apart from the inhospitable nature of the terrain, we were in constant danger of attack from Bedouins. I had faith that Quarrie could repair any minor breakdown, but a broken half-axle shaft or a battery failure would leave us stranded. The group captain at Amman had promised to send aircraft to search for us if we did not send a telegram from Ma'an seventy-two hours after leaving Al Qatrani. But those might prove to be very long hours.

About fifty miles farther along Quarrie urged the old car up a narrow, winding trail used by gazelle and camels; once we sighted a herd of 150 gazelle! The Zeiss glasses picked out triple-peaked Thlathakhwat (The Three Sisters) far away to the northeast. They looked magnificent in their solitary grandeur.

I longed to search on the summits of the Three Sisters, but time did not permit. Crossing low, rolling, flint-covered hills, we saw directly ahead two circular limestone buildings near four wellheads. This was Bayir Wells.

Why I had chosen this place on the map I did not know. But as we halted beside the ruins of an old castle I remembered that Gertrude Bell had once told me to be sure to visit this place someday and make drawings. She had attributed this ruined castle to the eighth century. The walls were covered with graffiti and hammered camel brands (*wasms*) to mark the passing of Bedouin tribes. The water supply of the wells had long been a source of contention between the tribes.

As we rested on the wellhead, deeply scarred by centuries of bucket ropes, I remembered that Miss Bell had halted here back in her desert travel days just before World War I, and that Colonel T. E. Lawrence, a few years later, had many times passed by Bayir Wells.

From a depth of sixty-four feet we pulled up a bucket of evil-smelling water. The putrid body of a she-camel does not improve any water.

Nearby was the mound of a huge Bedouin grave. Above it pieces of red and white cloth fluttered from a rustic pole. This was the grave of Auda abu Tayi, according to Lawrence, "the greatest fighting man in northern Arabia."

It was Auda who, after Lawrence persuaded him to join the Allies, had rushed to crunch his false teeth on a rock because they had been made by a Turkish dentist, now one of the enemy. As a result Lawrence had to send for a British dentist by air from Cairo. Auda's good digestion was essential to the Allied cause.

No worked flints lay close to the *qasr* or the wells. I walked across to the plateau gravels exposed along a cliff. A glance revealed many rounded quartzite pebbles, indicating deposition by a once fast-flowing stream. With my geological hammer, which bore scars from Cumnor and other key points near Oxford, I began to dislodge some of these pebbles from the cliff. Behind a large pebble appeared a quartzite hand ax. My heart skipped a beat. A shout brought Quarrie and Silcox on the double; they thought I had been bitten by a horned viper.

"Here's a Lower Palaeolithic hand ax, the first one found *in situ* east of Petra."

"A what?"

"An Upper Acheulean hand ax, made by a prehistoric hunter possibly a hundred thousand years ago. This is our first real proof of the antiquity of man in this area. This is worth the whole trip!"

The great Charles M. Doughty, author of *Arabia Deserta*, was the first to find surface traces of Stone Age man in this area. But now we had found a hand ax deep in a gravel deposit!

We had been warned not to remain near Bayir Wells after sundown, for armed Bedouins wander around. While Quarrie repacked the car I walked to the top of the low cliff. Here we were, amid perfectly lifeless silence, far from civilization, far from Baggrave, far from the marble museum beside Lake Michigan. What stories those wells could relate! The surrounding silent country began to grow black as the light faded. The Three Sisters glowed pink in the west. To the east lay the Wadi Sirhan in Saudi Arabia, a place I longed to visit. To the south lay the holy cities of Medina and Mecca, two places I never expected to see. My heart sang, for we had located a chain of new prehistoric surface stations in eastern Transjordan and, prize of prizes, a complete Upper Acheulean hand ax.

We drove fifteen miles southwest. Quarrie improvised a shelter from the cold wind in the lee of the Cadillac. Lights were dangerous, for they might attract raiders. Quarrie cooked, hidden by empty four-gallon gasoline cans. We hurried through fried sausage and bread, canned peaches and strong tea. The car was then reloaded and readied for escape, if necessary. It was bitterly cold as we huddled on a ground sheet. Hot tea an hour before dawn was most welcome. Two hours later we saw smoke rising from black tents and nearby mud-brick buildings. This was El Jafar, the permanent home of Sheik Mohammed abu Tayi of the Howeitat, and son of Auda, whose grave we had just seen. As we drove toward a long black tent upheld by eight poles, the number always being a criterion of wealth, Mohammed came to meet us, a tall, dignified young man, exactly my age, dressed in rich Bedouin robes. He greeted us cordially but with obvious suspicion. Flying Officer Silcox was in uniform so the tribesmen presumed we were a military mission; these always meant trouble to the Bedouin.

Outside the sheik's tent, tethered to the sloping flagpoles, were two large ostriches. A disapproving Bedouin eye discouraged me from taking their pictures, though Mohammed abu Tayi generously offered me one of these fine birds. Through Quarrie I refused as graciously as possible, secretly amused at the thought of arriving at Air Headquarters with an ostrich tied to the running board. Little did I realize the magnitude of such a gift; the Arabian ostrich, I learned later, is a *rara avis* indeed!

Reminders of Lawrence and Gertrude Bell went with me into the black tent, where members of the sheik's household scurried to prepare coffee and tea. As we sat leaning against camel saddles before the camel-dung fire, sipping coffee from handleless cups offered to us in turn by Mohammed and making stilted conversation, I remembered how those two had sat before this very fire; I remembered Miss Bell had written: ". . . when you have drunk the milk of the vaga over the camp fire of Abu Tayi you are baptised of the desert and there is no other salvation for you."

I was burning with questions about the Bedouin way of life, but I knew no Arabic. I studied the faces of the seated Bedouins. The hair and eyes were dark brown, the complexion weather-beaten, the nose thin, aquiline or straight. Their hands and feet were small, their eyes shining and keen. I thought, someday I must measure a good series of Bedouins.

Quarrie explained in Arabic that we were searching for ancient flint implements on the surface of the desert. Every eye was on him as he talked. No one believed a word. Why should the Royal Air Force send a man in uniform to hunt for old stones?

I knew Lawrence had often drunk coffee before this fire with Auda, Mohammed's distinguished warrior father, and I asked the question of the seated tribesmen, Did the Bedouin remember Lawrence of Arabia? But only one old Bedouin muttered in Arabic in a far corner of the tent, "He means Abu Fluss [the Father of Money]."

This referred, doubtless, to Lawrence's reputed arrival with two large bags of golden sovereigns—gift money, it was said, to win these Bedouins to the Allied cause in World War I.

Several years later, on one of my annual buying trips in Europe, I met Lawrence in England and told him this anecdote. I could see he did not like being remembered as the Father of Money. I felt a little ashamed, although he himself had asked whether the Arabs remembered him.

So, raking my memory, I told him that in Transjordan a whole folklore was rising around the Lawrence legend that would be remembered for many generations to come. Among the Bedouins, I said, as he well knew, there is complete awe of the foreigner who can enter the country and beat them at their own games.

Lawrence, I went on to say, had set the Arabs examples in their own fields, not only in desert military prowess but in deeds of daring, such as blowing up bridges against the advance of the enemy Turks, but mainly by the fantastic feats of riding endurance which were still remembered in Arabia and which he accomplished in competition with some of the best of the desert riders of his day.

As I described this to Lawrence he seemed very pleased.

Here was a man with a brilliant mind, small in stature but with a physical endurance almost unparalleled, who loved adulation as much as he hated it.

With great reluctance he had come to see me in a Plymouth hotel. The man who for a time had held the future of Arabia in his hands was working nearby as a mechanic in the Royal Air Force, under the name of "Aircraftsman T. E. Shaw." I wondered, as we talked, why a brilliant life had chosen obscurity.

Finally, turning his blazing blue-gray eyes on me, he began to talk of Arabia and his life there, of our work at Kish and, best of all, of himself. A boyish exuberance burned through his speech. He told of his disappointment in events in the Near East, of the promises he had made in the best of good faith, and of their disavowal at the Versailles Conference. Every wile and argument he knew had been used for the Arab cause. He had failed. He felt he had betrayed the Arabs and, while it was no fault of his that powers stronger than he had ruled otherwise, so far as the Bedouins and Arabs knew, his word had been broken. The Bedouins do not make excuses for broken promises or betrayal of trust.

After the Versailles Conference he had decided to retire and write, and the result had been *Revolt in the Desert* and *The Seven Pillars of Wisdom*. Now, he said, much as he wished it, he could not return to the Near East; since he had once been there as a great leader, to return in any other capacity would be unthinkable. He was, therefore, forced to stay away from that part of the world which he loved most. A curious irony of fate! But, he said, he had found his niche in the Royal Air Force. This required all his time, energy, and interest; his past and his private life were now his own.

Lawrence, in his neat blue uniform, stood with his back to the fire, talking so vividly of people he had known in the Near East— Sir Percy Cox, Sir Ronald Storrs, Gertrude Bell, Sir Leonard Woolley, with whom he had worked at Carchemish—that they seemed to be with us in the ugly little hotel room. I felt his pride that these great ones had been his associates and that they had all stood together in the campaign of World War I. Then, suddenly, he stopped and gave me a wise look.

"You know," he said, "it's more fun to make kings than to be one."

I presumed he was referring to King Faisal of Iraq, and probably King Abdullah of Transjordan. He had shaped their rise to power, but his had been the more thrilling life.

Lawrence asked me if I had noticed the camel brands, or *wasms*, hammered on the walls of Bayir Castle. I told him I had seen these myriad signs which had been crudely hammered there by Bedouins as they passed; the Arab equivalent of "Kilroy was here." Lawrence suggested that if I had an opportunity in the future I should make as complete a collection as possible of all these camel brands, which are found on wellheads, walls, and buildings throughout Transjordan and Iraq. He explained that many of the primitive Bedouin property marks were very similar in character to Himyaritic script, an early form of writing in South Arabia.

In the years to come I was able to make a collection of more than a thousand of these camel brands and to have one of Professor Enno Littmann's students, Dr. Hans Winkler, write the commentary as Lawrence had suggested so many years before. This study was published by the American Oriental Society in 1953. Thus writing may have developed from the property marks, hammered on stones in Southwestern Asia to designate either property or the fact that a tribe, or subtribe, had passed by a certain point on the desert. This doubtless led to tattooing, another interesting study.

I began to record tattooed designs on Arabs in 1925. The tattooing on the men is confined to the hands, wrists, and forearms, and occasionally the face. Whereas the women have elaborate designs on the body, especially around the navel, where rayed designs symbolize the sun. Winifred Smeaton (now Mrs. Homer Thomas) and I have recorded a large series of tattooed designs and information regarding this practice. This will form a large monograph entitled *Body-marking in Southwestern Asia*. I believe that property marks were hammered on rocks at a very early date, then came the brands on camels and sheep, and these were followed by simple tattooed designs on women. This developed into a caste system which was very important within the primitive tribal groups, for it indicated into which group a woman might marry. From these simple designs originated writing.

I want to give proper credit to Lawrence for making the original suggestion and recommending the compilation of all data regarding camel brands, tattooing, and scarification in Southwestern Asia, that night in Plymouth on the English coast.

It was approaching time for Lawrence to return to barracks. He put on his trench coat, and I accompanied him down the street about half a mile to a long narrow bridge, leading to a dark tunnel. As we stepped out of the hotel his gayness seemed to leave him and he was once again the aloof person who had met me on the station platform about seventy-two hours earlier. We walked along in step through the pouring rain, he saying nothing, I saying nothing. A small light was burning near the entrance to the tunnel, and beyond that was complete darkness. We were right on the Plymouth shore and could hear the beating of the waves on the ground below. The moment seemed inexpressibly lonely. Suddenly he stopped, put out his hand, and said abruptly, "Good-by, I've enjoyed seeing you. I hope we meet again." As he disappeared into the dark tunnel he turned and waved his hand. That was the last I saw of Colonel T. E. Lawrence, "Lawrence of Arabia."

Back in Amman, we told proudly of our visit to Mohammed and his Howeitat tribesmen, of our ten new prehistoric surface stations, displayed the hand ax from Bayir, and described breathtaking Petra, which we had visited on our way back, that "rose-red city half as old as time," truly a metropolis of the dead.

Several days later the Cadillac was permitted to join a convoy of four RAF trucks visiting desert landing grounds, and I did research along the way.

South of Qasr el Azraq, Group Captain Rees showed me low-piled basalt boulders arranged in two long lines radiating from an enclosure, easily visible from the air, some of them fifteen miles long. These he called "kites"; we now believe them to have been ancient gazelle traps. Later we climbed the three peaks of Jebel Qurna, collecting many worked flints. Nearby were stones bearing Safaitic inscriptions.

Next day, north of Landing Ground "K," I found many types of flint implements, including hammerstones, scrapers, knives, and hundreds of rejects and flakes. Suddenly I saw a T-shaped flint implement, a type brand new in this region, which showed an excellent flint-flaking technique. Within an hour we had a small series.

Another interesting discovery was a limestone block obviously used formerly as an anvil, for beside it were two flint hammerstones and flint flakes. On the summit of the northern peak, Umm Wual (The Mother of Ibexes), I found Mousterian implements bearing a magnificent desert varnish and chocolate patina, and one of the men picked up a beautiful small hand ax.

Standing on top of Umm Wual, we could look south toward Tell el Hibr, little dreaming that where we stood we were already in Saudi Arabia, for there were no marked boundaries.

Quarrie chased a large desert lizard (*Varanus* sp.) under an immovable basalt boulder, and in a small cairn we found three small snakes, which were quickly embalmed in formalin. At Field Museum, Karl Schmidt identified these as a new species of horned viper which was named *Pseudocerastes fieldi*. Karl explained, "The more poisonous the snake, the greater the honor to have it named for you." I could only hope that the horned viper would always recognize me as a blood brother!

Before leaving the RAF convoy a signal was sent: "Cadillac proceeding alone and overloaded toward Rutba. Please send help if does not arrive by nightfall. Field." But we arrived safely at Baghdad, bringing with us more than a thousand pounds of flints, basalt boulders with inscriptions, and limestone blocks bearing camel brands.

Baghdad was as dirty and noisy as ever. I found waiting a list of supplies and equipment needed at Kish, which took two days to assemble. By that time the car had been overhauled and pronounced desert-shape, and with the entire back and both running boards loaded I set off for Kish on a December morning. I had been longing for two years to go back.

It was fun to meet my fat and genial friend the Hilla barber again and this time to be able to speak enough Arabic to carry on a broken conversation.

The track winding alongside the main canal which flows eastward to Kish was tantalizingly familiar. As the top of the red mound of the ziggurat came into sight, my heart started to pound.

154

It was very exciting to be going back, this time not as a paying student guest but as a staff member of the Field Museum-Oxford University Expedition. Still I knew I would miss Buxton—not only his delightful company, but his expert knowledge. From now on I would have to make decisions myself, for I knew that neither the new director at Kish nor his assistant was interested in skeletal material. The responsibility of salvaging any bones that might be found during the coming winter months, plus their preservation, packing, and shipping, would all be mine.

Then across the canal I saw Kish again, the temple tower of Tell Inghara standing clear in the afternoon light, the mounds on the plain made by the trial trenches. There by the tell was the outer wall of what would later prove to be the Temple of Nabonidus. The broken outlines of a once great city were before me, more sharply outlined than when I had last seen Kish in December 1925.

I turned left past Mound "W" where Buxton and I had found our first burial and drove over the familiar plain to the camp. The last hurdle was the small irrigation canal. The camp was only a quarter of a mile away. The rickety bridge was of palm branches crossed with piles of camel's-thorn and plastered over with mud. I was not at all certain the heavily burdened car could cross. As I hesitated, a white-robed figure came running madly across the sand. It was Mahdi, our camp guard, come to welcome me like the inevitable long-lost brother. I interrupted his kissing of my hand to thank him and assure him how glad I was to see him, but would he please step aside so I could try to drive the car over the bridge, if the bridge would hold? Mahdi said that of course the bridge would hold because his friends had made it. This was not entirely logical, since Mahdi had absolutely no mechanical sense; in fact he had amazingly little sense on any subject. He stood smiling, his crossed bandoliers of bullets shining in the sunset, while I clung to the wheel and shot forward and crossed the bridge with a lurch and a prayer. Mahdi jumped onto the loaded running board, took off his headdress—a rare occurrence—and began to wave it while shouting at the top of his voice. This was not entirely in my honor but rather to show his prestige to the other camp Arabs and anyone else who might be within sight and sound.

No dog came running to meet us, and I was disappointed to learn that Samsiluna, the mongrel dog that had been my friend, was dead.

The camp under the ziggurat had grown to impressive size. The white tent was gone, and several new mud huts stood in its place. The courtyard was now surrounded on three sides by these connecting huts. In the door of the cook hut stood Shemu, hand high in salute, still wearing his caracul hat, which had changed from black to gray in the last two years. There was a beaming smile on his face, and I could see that he was genuinely glad to see me. Juad, the other camp guard, came running forward to cover my hand with kisses.

Around the corner of the courtyard came Mr. Louis Charles Watelin, the new director, who had replaced Mr. Mackay, now working for Sir John Marshall in the Indus Valley of northwestern India. Mr. Watelin was six feet tall, smartly dressed, and wore goggles on his hat which gave the effect of two pairs of eyes, both of which were smiling as he welcomed me back to Kish.

Close at his heels came Eric Schroeder, the young English archaeologist, assistant to Watelin. They had arrived several days before. I was delighted to find that someone about my own age was to be in camp that winter because during the long months there is considerable loneliness, and one feels extremely far away from home and friends.

Within a few minutes many willing hands had stripped the crowded Cadillac of packages and cartons, and the car was put away in a reed-mat shelter which served as a garage; not burglar-proof in any sense, but capable of keeping out some of the terrible dust which blows over the plain. Mr. Watelin assigned to me the same mud hut that had been mine during my first visit to Kish.

It was exciting to be back again, to wander about the camp and see the old friends and faces, and to find how many of them I remembered. Dinner in the partly underground dining room was about the same: Shemu's food tasted—or was as tasteless—as ever. But his smile was as broad, and his Elizabethan expletives spluttered happily.

During supper, at the request of Watelin and Eric, I gave a

brief résumé of the results of our archaeological survey of the North Arabian Desert.

Then Watelin told stories while the familiar beaked coffeepot went the rounds. He was, I learned in the days to come, a charming person, rarely ill-tempered, and outwardly patient when the real treasure he was seeking did not come to light. He was an engineer by profession and far more interested in the engineering problems involved and the large buildings excavated than in the small objects of material culture. He told us how he had worked at Susa in southwestern Iran (Persia) with the great Jacques de Morgan, and described in detail the finding there of the great Stele of Naramsin, one of the most magnificent sculptures ever excavated, depicting the king trampling on his enemies; this is now in the Louvre. It was clear that everything else that had been excavated under Watelin's direction seemed insignificant by comparison, and he hoped that here at Kish we would find some great stone monument comparable to that famous stele.

Eric Schroeder was very quiet. He listened to my desert stories and Watelin's adventures with burning interest, even as I had listened to Buxton, Mackay, and Langdon at this very table, only two years before.

How often, since then, I had prayed that circumstances would return me to Kish, and here I was crossing the courtyard to sleep in the same hard bed, in the same tiny mud hut beneath the dark, towering mound of Tell el Uhaimir.

After breakfast the Cadillac started off at the first touch, with Watelin and Eric and boxes and other paraphernalia crowded in the back seat. We drove to Mound "W" where the crowd of workmen awaited the signal to begin. I was delighted to see familiar faces, for Buxton and I had spent much of our precious three weeks in these trenches and had come to know some of the workmen well. They came up to shake hands and seemed pleased to see me again. They were sure, they said happily, they would find plenty of skeletons to keep me busy.

I told them they would receive extra baksheesh for any human or animal bones. It was important to get this into their heads, because if a skeleton was found and baksheesh was not given in proportion to some of the rarer smaller objects, then they would hurry to remove the skeleton rather carelessly in order to clear more earth and find more objects. But if they were paid as much for a tomb group as for a series of small objects, then they could have their money and do no work—an ideal combination.

We continued over to Tell Inghara, where *Rais* Hassan Jedur was waiting with his men for the signal to begin work. I was very happy to see Hassan once again. He looked the same, and the firmness of his handclasp and the warmth of his smile increased my feeling of coming home to friends. Since our last meeting he had worked with Langdon at Jemdet Nasr. Much had happened at Kish and vicinity since I had been away.

Watelin asked me to accompany him to the summit of Tell Inghara to survey the work in progress. He explained that he had decided to concentrate for the next four seasons on the area lying west of the larger ziggurat. The earth was to be removed stratum by stratum, with the intention of continuing down to virgin soil in an attempt to reveal the cultures and physical characters of the earliest inhabitants of Kish.

To clarify and describe the sequences of cultures, we must follow the course of Watelin's procedure as though it had taken place in one continuous section.

On the top of the mound pottery fragments and other Arab remains were found. Soon after the trenches had begun to pierce the mound, late Neo-Babylonian (550 B.C.) remains were unearthed. Almost immediately beneath this stratum the walls of a magnificent Babylonian temple came to light. This building, one of the most beautiful ever excavated in Mesopotamia, was begun by Nebuchadnezzar and continued by Nabonidus, father-in-law of Belshazzar, he who saw "the handwriting on the wall." The walls of this temple, standing eighteen feet high and five feet thick, were in as good repair as the day they were constructed by that royal builder some twenty-five centuries before. Many of the rooms, probably for the use of priests, contained bricks piled against the inner walls. Watelin concluded that this great edifice was never completed. We may picture some story of this kind: Nebuchadnezzar, the great builder, whose rectangular seal is stamped on the bricks of many buildings, decided to build at Kish the largest and most beautiful temple of his reign. Work was begun on a large scale. However, he died before it could be finished and Nabonidus ordered the work continued. The building was nearing completion when raiders poured down on the fertile Mesopotamian plain.

Watelin had continued the trenches down toward virgin soil. The outer walls of a large palace were exposed due west of the larger ziggurat. From cylinder seals and inscriptions Langdon concluded that this palace was constructed about the time of Sargon I. Below the palace walls a peculiar stratum of red-colored earth was found. As the uncovered area increased, Watelin observed that the red earth covered the entire city of this particular date. This span of earth was entirely devoid of archaeological objects except for sun-dried bricks which lay at every conceivable angle. The period of this red-earth stratum may be estimated because a beautiful, inscribed lapsis-lazuli cylinder seal, found in a rich grave immediately above this band, gives the date of the grave as being about 2950 B.C. We can, therefore, state that all the objects beneath this red-earth stratum belong to the period before 3000 B.C.

Far to the left the trenches sunk by Mackay when Buxton, Langdon, and I were there in December 1925 ran like huge mole tunnels out on the level plain. Nearer lay the large, flat surface of the temenos wall, which Mackay had uncovered so patiently at the foot of the ziggurat. Coming nearer, and at an angle, were the first parts of the great hole that was to become the famous "Y" trench. Watelin selected this section, which was just south of the Temple of Nabonidus and just west of the outer walls of the base of the ziggurat of Tell Inghara, as the most likely point at which to find his dreamed-of objective—the royal tombs of Kish.

He explained his decision to remove all the earth out of "Y" trench down to virgin soil, or at least to the present water-table level. In this way he would have uncovered a representative section of the city. A trench of this character had never before been attempted in Iraq.

Right in front of us below was the section known as "Z" trenches, numbering from 1 to 6. Watelin explained to me that he was going to clear off all the "Z" trenches, uncovering the top of the red-earth stratum, cut through that, and continue down as deep as possible. This was the plan for the coming weeks and months ahead. I explained to him my great desire to find some human skeletal remains, particularly crania from beneath the red-earth stratum. Watelin told me that he would give me every facility, and that at any point where I wanted the work stopped in order to excavate skeletal material, this would be done. Naturally I was very grateful.

To the right of us lay the top of the walls of the Temple of Nabonidus. Over the top of the walls could be seen the mound known as "PCB," so called from the plano-convex bricks in the walls. Almost straight in front rose Tell el Uhaimir, and midway between where we were sitting and the red mound overshadowing the camp was the work proceeding at Mound "W." In the distance we could hear the men chanting as they worked. Above them rose a cloud of dust like a small sandstorm.

In order to remove some of the debris from the upper levels of Mound "W" and "Z" trenches, Watelin had installed eight Decauville light railway trucks, lent to the Expedition by the Royal Air Force. As each section was cleared the light railway track was moved and a new trench begun. Eric and I found that we were to be the mechanics in charge of maintenance. I had never seen a light railway before except in the movies. The installation was difficult, for many of the rails and fishplates were rusted and it was hard to remove the bolts and tighten them. Eric and I devised a scheme after we had knocked most of the skin off our knuckles, because, strangely enough, it was impossible to find any of the Arabs out of the two hundred workmen there who could really help us.

We decided that the next time the line had to be moved we would cut the track into sections and have it moved by the two hundred Arabs. Watelin gave his approval but did not think the idea too sound because he was afraid they might buckle the line. Next day Eric and I cut the track into four parts, each about a hundred and fifty feet long. I called Hassan Jedur to explain the procedure and told him to order the Arabs to co-operate and not to do any silly tricks with the track, because if anything went wrong we would be unable to replace it. Hassan Jedur lined up the men, each of whom lifted a section. As soon as the track was off the ground the Arabs became tremendously excited. They began to sing and dance and shout, and no words from us or threats from Hassan Jedur could restrain their childish exuberance. This was something on which we had not counted. I ran to the front of the line to try to control the Arabs in the vanguard. Eric tried to restrain those enthusiasts who were screaming to the ones in front to hurry up. Hassan Jedur was in the middle, swearing at the top of his lungs. Finally we managed to get the sections of track into the proper alignment and the first cars rolled over the bumpy track.

On another occasion, after we had laid the track Watelin decided that it should be moved to another angle. This seemed a fairly simple procedure; all the Arabs had to do was to line up on one side and walk slowly forward, carrying the track to its correct place. However, we had again not counted on their excitement. The moment they lifted it off the ground there were wild screams, yells, shouts, and the center bearers rushed forward, buckling the precious track into a big curve. We screamed and shouted and made them put it down on the ground. When I looked at it, it was in the shape of an S-shaped snake. Fortunately Watelin was not there. Eric and I decided that we would have to invent some new method of moving the track. We therefore had the men all kneel on the ground in a long line, since, kneeling, they would be unable to make these wild rushing swoops. It was a wonderful sight in the afternoon sun to see two hundred Arabs creeping solemnly on their knees, not in religious fervor, but moving a Decauville track to its proper alignment.

Back at camp, at Watelin's suggestion, I was constructing a new room for myself. This was to be the end of the U-shaped series of buildings forming the courtyard of our camp. Since I had never seen a mud hut constructed before, I had to rely almost entirely on the knowledge and skill of the local Arab master mason and his four assistants, aged eight to twelve. Two little barefoot boys stamped knee-deep in a pit filled with wet clay and chopped straw. Coconut-sized mud balls were carried on the upturned palm of each hand by the other two lads. The master mason caught each mud ball and slapped it into place, using water as a binder. The walls went up straight without any kind of plummet. Split palm beams were set in place across the walls. Reed mats were tied down. More mud balls were thrown up to the master mason which he stamped on the roof with his bare feet. The windows were the usual bottles held in place with mud. Two days later I moved into my new home. All went well until the next rainstorm. I was awakened with mud in my eye. Streams of muddy water poured down through the reed mats. The floor became a pool of mud. Sleep was hardly possible that night.

The master mason was neither surprised nor ashamed. The roof was mended and I lived well enough in my house that might have been built for Abraham five thousand years before.

In similar houses the Arabs around us lived almost as Abraham lived. On this visit I became better acquainted with the Kish country and its people. The leading sheik in the region was *Hajji* Miniehil, whose village lay about two miles west of our camp. The men of this village were extremely friendly because the Expedition was their only source of revenue; the majority of our workmen came from there.

Whenever we visited the village the dogs began to bark madly and the children swarmed out, eager to see the foreigners. They were ragged and unwashed, for their parents had no conception of sanitary conditions. If a child cut himself someone rubbed dirt into the gash, calling on "Allah, the Merciful, the Compassionate," to heal the wound. Since the ground around these villages was polluted by animals and infested with insects and germs, there was a high mortality rate among these people. Many of the children suffered from eye sores which later developed into cataracts and eventually blindness.

On the outskirts of the village we nearly always met a woman fetching water from a well, carrying a child in one arm and a heavy bucket on the other. As we approached she would cover the lower part of her face with her kerchief, following the Mohammedan custom of veiling the face in the presence of men. But at the entrance of the low mud-brick-walled courtyard young girls crowded around, many of them wearing golden nose rings as well as bracelets and anklets of silver.

Within the courtyard, horses, sheep, and chickens wandered

between the low camel's-thorn fences which surrounded the mud huts. There were always Arab women, dressed in long dark blue cotton garments, squatting before the hole in the ground that was their primitive oven, kneading and shaping the *chupatties* which, with dates, formed the staple diet of these Arabs.

The large mud hut in the center belonged to *Hajji* Miniehil and we were always welcome there.

One evening the sheik invited Eric and me to witness the dances of a famous local dancing girl who was only twelve years old. The evening began as usual; as we entered the hut, all the men stood up in our honor. The sheik stepped forward with the usual greeting and we muttered the customary Arabic saluation and seated ourselves next to the sheik in the circle around the charcoal fire. There were numerous inquiries as to our health and fervent prayers to Allah that we might remain healthy and beget many sons.

There were no chimneys in these huts and the air was heavy with smoke. Coffee was served in tiny handleless cups, and as in the black tents of the Bedouins, it was good manners to make as much noise as possible while drinking. The old men of the tribe, squatting on the floor around the hearth, formed a picture from the Bible. The sheik was a dignified and somber figure, much revered, as he had recently returned from the pilgrimage to Mecca.

The girl came in, accompanied by three men who played various native instruments during her dances—several drums and a one-stringed instrument resembling the Bedouin *rababa*. During the dance she knelt before one of the audience. He spat on a coin and stuck it on her face. As the dancing continued and the men became more excited, she collected other coins. She would then attempt to stand up and continue the hoochy-kootchy without letting the coins drop to the floor. This feat was applauded wildly. The dance continued for about an hour, and the girl was intoxicated with the sums of money she received. She stopped her dance before the eldest son of Sheik Miniehil, begging him to give her a large coin. He took out some money and put it in her hand. However, she did not think this was sufficient, and with a wild cry she threw it angrily into his face. The young man picked up a camel stick that was lying beside him; he struck her

163

several times as she lay groveling before him on the floor. Complete confusion ensued. The sheik had the greatest difficulty in restoring order. The girl refused to dance again, and lay sobbing and muttering on the floor. It did not seem wise for Eric and me to remain any longer.

Early each Friday—the Mohammedan day of rest—Eric and I mounted two local horses borrowed from the sheik. Accompanied by Mahdi, our ineffectual but always fierce-looking armed guard, he and I rode out into the desert. We would take with us saddlebags with a picnic lunch, and our cameras. These were the days Eric and I enjoyed the most. Here we were free. We could ride wherever we wanted between the Euphrates and the Tigris. We could turn our horses eastward from Tell Inghara and ride out across the plain to mounds which probably had never before been seen by archaeological eyes.

One Friday Watelin rode with us. Some miles east we found an unknown city with hundreds and hundreds of potsherds, small figurines, and a host of other archaeological objects covering the surface of the ground. This site should be excavated, although its distance from permanent water would make it almost as hard as that of Jemdet Nasr. However, it is always probable and possible that a new site may yield very rich treasures.

On some of these trips into the desert Eric and I would amuse ourselves by wearing Arab costumes. We did this partly to entertain ourselves and partly to fool Bedouins or Arabs riding at a great distance from us.

Once we were riding about ten miles east of Kish. It was high noon. The sun was very bright and waves of mirage floated on the sky line everywhere around us. We had taken the Arab precaution of wrapping our *kaffiyehs* around our heads to keep out the glare and the burning heat. Suddenly in the distance there were seven little puffs of sand. Just below the sky line were seven gazelles, about two hundred yards away. I raised my rifle, but Mahdi grabbed the gun and pushed it out of the line of sight. I was furious. I shouted at Mahdi. Mahdi, his eyes blazing, bared his right forearm. On the inside was tattooed a small stylized gazelle. He touched the gazelle with his left forefinger. Then, putting his two forefingers together, he said, "*Haram* [It is forbidden]." These signs and gestures meant that he was in some way a blood brother of the gazelle and that I must not shoot at it. This all happened very fast but by then the gazelles were practically out of range. I fired a shot in the general direction of the fleeing gazelles; I wanted a specimen for the museum study collection in Chicago. I've never seen such a look of horror, anger, fury in the eyes of an Arab. Mahdi, who had been so subservient, so quiet, so gentle, who had kissed my hand, the typical Arab Fellah Milquetoast! Here he was, his eyes flashing, his upper lip and mustache quivering in anger. I had obviously touched him very deeply.

If only at that moment I had known what an important incident this was, I would have questioned and cross-questioned Mahdi. It was not until some years later, when I made some studies on body-marking, including tattooing throughout Southwestern Asia, that I realized the significance of this event. It looks as though this was an example of primitive totemism, a custom long suspected in Arabia by Robertson Smith and others. Mahdi certainly indicated forcibly that he did not want me to shoot at the gazelle. He had a gazelle tattooed on his arm. He had made the sign of "blood brother" or extreme friendship by putting his two forefingers together. All of this showed he had for the gazelle some feeling of special relationship.

Later, when I had made exhaustive studies on the subject of tattooing, I would realize what a golden opportunity was missed when I failed to question Mahdi that day.

While the excavation of Mound "W" continued in the Babylonian levels, the main concentration of our efforts was in the "Z" trenches and the red-earth stratum. The latter was finally cleared over the entire area that was to be "Y" trench. Then in Mound "W" three pairs of golden earrings were unearthed. They were found in Babylonian graves in the period of Nebuchadnezzar, and had probably been worn by ladies at his court. Two pairs of these earrings are made of gold wire, while the lower parts of the third pair are formed by large, thin, semicircular beads. The most important pair is large and intricately designed, nearly two inches long, fashioned of lunate ornaments and seed pearls, probably from Bahrain. This is one of the most beautiful objects found in Mesopotamia. Although twenty-five hundred years old, these earrings are modern in concept and design; one of them remains in the Iraq Museum, Baghdad, the other in Field Museum, Chicago.

As the work progressed, "Y" trench yielded many important archaeological objects, throwing a new flood of light on the early history of Kish. The Arab workmen brought to light numerous graves containing human skeletons, pottery and stone vessels, shell lamps, and copper objects. There was a total absence of gold and semiprecious stones. The bodies found were not orientated in any particular manner and there were traces of mass burials in several graves. Some bodies had been wrapped in rush mats which left imprints on the surrounding earth. The human bones were almost decomposed, owing to the dampness of the soil near the present water level. The majority of the ancient population was long-headed, and I was able to salvage some skulls by applying wax to replace the natural gelatin, which had long since disappeared.

One of the most interesting objects from a grave in "Y" trench is a copper frog with eyes of inlaid limestone supporting a copper rod which rises from the middle of its back. The rod terminates in five petals, shaped like lotus leaves, which originally must have contained either the rushes to be burned as a rushlight or a stone vessel as an offering to one of their gods. This example of the high artistic attainments of the inhabitants of Kish in the middle of the fourth millennium before the Christian Era is now in Hall K in Field Museum.

The most sensational discovery of the 1927–28 season was excavated a few feet above water level. At a depth of forty-three feet below the summit of the mound, Ali Daud, one of our best pickmen, who was working in the lower levels of "Y" trench, shouted that he had found something. Watelin, Eric, and I descended into the trench. Ali proudly held up a copper nail with a large head. Watelin told him to proceed very cautiously. Ali had found the nail below an artificial staircase cut into the earth so that the basket-boys could carry the earth from the lower levels to the dump above. Soon he found a handful of copper nails. Watelin now told him to stop work and remove the stairway. An hour later the staircase had been removed. Ali knelt, took out his curved dagger (*khanjar*) from his belt, and began to remove the earth very slowly and carefully. We saw him uncover a small section, perhaps three inches square, which was obviously the face of some object, before he stepped back to allow Watelin to take his place. Watelin laid his small rucksack on the ground beside him, took out a series of scalpels and brushes, and began to flake away the earth from a flat surface. After about an hour, which Eric and I spent kneeling on the ground behind him watching intently what he was uncovering, we suddenly saw five copper nails arranged in a semicircle. Watelin looked up and said quietly, "This is a chariot wheel." Our faces whitened with excitement as we realized the significance of the find—a wheeled vehicle used before the Flood of Noah! Slowly the wheel was uncovered with the copper nails still in place around the rim. The center part had been cut through by Ali Daud who, as ill luck would have it, had come on the wheel exactly end on. The single copper nails were in the rim. The handful of nails had supported the axle. Only one third of the wheel remained.

Watelin told Ali to leave it in place and to continue working toward where the matching wheel must lie.

Later that afternoon, as we crouched impatiently, the second wheel began to be exposed.

As I sat watching in this trench on that beautiful afternoon I tried to visualize the ancient scene. But before my mind could cope with that I realized this was a discovery of major importance and a cable would mean a world scoop.

Watelin gave me permission and, sitting in the trench with a pad on my right knee, I composed a sixty-five-word cable to DeWitt Mackenzie, manager of the Associated Press in London. Before leaving England I had told him that should any sensational discoveries be made I would send him a cable concluding with the identifying code word "Baggrave."

At the end of the message describing the discovery of the oldest wheeled vehicle in the world I added, "Chicago papers please copy." In this way we would have the most rapid and efficient world coverage. As soon as Watelin had read the message I sent one of the workmen to the Kish camp to tell Juad to come on his

Arab pony as I had a message for him to take to Hilla. Juad, very proud to be on a special mission, galloped off with his robes flying in the direction of the setting sun silhouetting the mounds of Babylon, eight miles away. He carried the message to the station-master at Hilla. It was filed by an East Indian telegraph operator to his colleague in Baghdad. From there by radio to Cairo, from Cairo again by radio to England, where it was sent to the Associated Press office in Fleet Street, London. A few minutes later the message was across the Atlantic in the New York office of the Associated Press. As a result of the difference in time between Kish and Chicago, the Chicago *Daily News* printed the story of the discovery of the oldest wheeled vehicle in the world by the Field Museum-Oxford University Joint Expedition the same day I had written it in a trench in central Iraq many thousands of miles to the east. The evening papers in London also carried the story. Langdon was delighted. He longed, as we well knew, to be with us at Kish where he had sacrificed so much of his time and health, even, as we would shortly learn, his life.

There did not seem to be much point in attempting to preserve the fragments of our wheels. We took a number of photographs and measurements. However, since we were going to excavate a great deal more earth from the same level, we hoped to find another more complete chariot.

About a week later, while excavating the large tombs, traces of another wooden wheel came to light. After very careful work a four-wheeled chariot was unearthed. Each wheel, composed of wooden panels fitted together, was held in place by a rim composed of a hard white china-like substance. Around the entire rim were about fifty copper nails. The hub unfortunately collapsed upon exposure to the atmosphere. All four wheels were oval because of the pressure of the superimposed earth. Since it is difficult to understand how the copper nails could have ridden even on round wheels over such rough surface as the alluvial plains in the Kish area, I have always thought that the china-like substance was some adhesive which held a leather tire in place. Something must have protected the copper heads of the nails from being knocked to pieces by the small pebbles which cover that part of the plain. Our interest was particularly aroused by human and animal skeletons found in the tomb. A human skeleton guarded the entrance and animal skeletons lay between the shafts—horses, or asses, anyhow members of the Equid family. Evidently the driver stood at the back of the chariot, holding the reins that ran through a copper rein-ring. We were lucky enough to excavate three of these copper rein-rings; two are now in Field Museum.

One of the rein-rings was ornamented with a three-inch-high deer with a halter tied around the right foreleg. According to Dr. Laufer, this is one of the earliest examples of a domesticated deer, and he has suggested that in Central Asia the deer may well have been tamed before the horse.

A copper saw found beside the left front wheel of the chariot started our imaginations working. After many discussions with Watelin and Eric the following concept of the story of this tomb came to me one afternoon as I sat on the top of Tell Inghara watching the workmen driving deeper and deeper into "Y" trench.

The scene that passed through my mind took place more than fifty centuries ago. One of the rich noblemen at Kish ordered a chariot to carry him to and from the Great Temple. The cedar for the wheels was brought from Lebanon across the great North Arabian Desert to Baghdad and shipped down the river Euphrates to Kish. The crowd ran out to watch the passing of this noble lord as he drove from his large house, which was surrounded by waving palm trees, on the banks of the gently flowing Euphrates, and through the streets to the great Temple of Harsagkalemma, dedicated to the Earth Goddess.

The scene changes. The nobleman is dead. The same crowd which so often had gazed upon him in life in awe and wonder now follows him to the tomb. The chariot, drawn by prancing animals draped in black, carries the nobleman to his last resting place, down into the tomb. The servants, including the personal bodyguard, follow in silence. The carpenter, saw in hand, halts beside the chariot. The priests file down the slope and stand around the tomb. Many thousands of mourners attend the rites. There is a dead silence at the conclusion of the last prayer. The animals in harness at the head of the chariot proudly raise their heads. Each priest draws a long copper-bladed knife from its

169

sheath. He lifts it in his right hand. Suddenly the chief priest shouts, "Kill." The servants and the animals are all struck down. The body of one of the guards is left lying outside the inner door of the tomb, which is quickly covered with mud bricks.

More than five thousand years later this tomb was uncovered by us. The body of the watchman was found outside the bricked-up entrance of the tomb. The chariot occupied the central portion. In the shafts lay the skeletons of the animals. Around the chariot were the bones of the servants. Near the front wheel the carpenter and his saw were found. Beside him was one of the guards with his copper dagger still lying close to his right hand. Several other human skeletons were included in the tomb, as well as numerous pottery vessels.

Primitive belief in a life after death is undisputed. A nobleman would require his servants and his chariot, his most prized possessions, in the next world, there to serve him for all time.

At first it seemed impossible to preserve the delicate chariot fragments, still more impossible to pack them for shipment to Chicago.

I drove the Cadillac to Baghdad, where I purchased several large gallon containers of oak varnish and a series of different-sized paintbrushes. I also had a talk with Mr. R. S. Cooke, the new director of antiquities. He promised an export permit so that in Chicago we could attempt a reconstruction of the wheels, which would require expert care not available in Iraq.

Back at Kish, sixteen coats of oak varnish applied with a light brush formed a hard outer coating on the surface of our wheels. We decided to attempt to remove each wheel by enclosing it in a wooden box filled with plaster to prevent movement during transportation to Chicago. Sixteen days later four wheels were boxed and moved to camp. Four guards remained each night in the trench. We were afraid that passing jackals or foxes might be attracted by the smell of the oak varnish and come to root around the precious wheels. Since we could not persuade one or two, or even three, guards to stay, because they were afraid, we were forced to bribe four who were friends, all armed, to remain. Many photographs, motion pictures, and measurements were taken of the chariot, which is still the oldest wheeled vehicle in the world; there are others of the same period from Ur of the Chaldees, but none older.

In the division of objects at the close of the season, the four chariot wheels were among those specimens allotted to Field Museum. They were shipped to Chicago via Basra. When unpacked, the wheels had suffered considerably during their trip from Baghdad. Two of them, partially restored, are on exhibition in the Kish Hall (Hall K) in Field Museum, where they have been seen by millions of visitors.

Among the other discoveries of interest was a small, unpainted jar found one meter below the red-earth stratum. As I was cleaning it out my left palm became black. I spread the contents on a newspaper. Here were some seeds preserved by charring. Subsequent identification by Dr. H. V. Harlan, of the Department of Agriculture, reported on November 8, 1929, "I am able to make only a partial determination of the samples which you recently forwarded. All three samples contain seeds of six-rowed hulled barley. This does not preclude the possibility of their being hullless or two-rowed barley. I could, however, find no kernels which could be identified as either. The grain seems to be slightly smaller than that coming from the Egyptian excavations, and I think it is safe to say that it represents different varieties."

Dr. Laufer commented as follows: "Botanical investigation disclosed the fact that this barley is of the six-rowed variety, and this as far as is known here is the first actually brought to light in Mesopotamia. Barley seeds of the four-rowed variety were formerly discovered at Nippur. The six-rowed type is the characteristic prehistoric barley which was known to the Indo-European nations. Numerous examples of this have been found in the Swiss lake dwellings. It was this species which was taken along by the Anglo-Saxons on their migration from their original homes to the British Isles, then cultivated by them in England. In view of the discovery of the six-rowed barley at Kish, the conclusion is now warranted that this cereal, so important in the development of agriculture, was first brought into cultivation at a prehistoric date

171

in Mesopotamia, where the wild species also occurred, and that the cultivated species was diffused from that center to all other countries of the Near East, Egypt and Europe."

The great day finally came when Watelin decided to cut through the red-earth stratum in "Y" trench to the levels below. This was just before Christmas, 1927. Since I was writing a personal note to Professor Langdon at Oxford, I told him that we were now in a flood level, expecting to find the Flood of Noah at any minute and shortly thereafter the Ark! A report came from a Paris lab. that the red-earth stratum was a water-borne deposit. Watelin was thus able to establish that this was the deposit laid down by the Flood of Noah. On the floor of one of the small rooms just beneath the red-earth stratum we discovered bones of small fishes drowned in the Flood. The material consisted of fragments varying in thickness from about one to two inches, broken out of a stratum of hard clay. On one flat surface were numerous spines and bones of small fish. In some of the clay fragments the fish remains were exceedingly numerous, forming a compact layer about a half inch thick and distinguishable from the rest of the clay by the dark brown color. The number of fish in this small body of water indicated that they had died from some catastrophe. There were vertebrae, fins, spines, and small bones bearing teeth found in the throats of some fishes. Conspicuous among the remains were the pharyngeal bones of fishes belonging to *Cyprinidae*, a family of many genera, of which the carp, goldfish, and minnows may be mentioned as examples. According to Dr. Louis Hussakof of the American Museum of Natural History, the commonest genera were the small carp, *Barbus* and *Capoeta*.

As we stood in the small excavated room it was fairly easy to reconstruct the scene. These small fish, which had been swimming in the flooded waters of the Twin Rivers, were caught suddenly by a lowering of the level, and when the water evaporated, their bones were preserved in this clay stratum for us to find some five thousand years later. The small minnows and allied species which swim today in the larger canals and also in the Tigris and Euphrates belong to very similar species.

Here indeed was a story that made Ripley's "Believe It or Not" —fish meeting their death in the Flood of Noah!

This winter season of 1927–28 produced many of the most important objects found during the thirteen winters of excavation at Kish. At Oxford Langdon was receiving tablets from Mound "W" and also from the lower levels beneath the red-earth stratum in "Y" trench. I had as many skeletons to excavate as I could possibly handle—sometimes more.

The most important finds were: the oldest piece of writing; the oldest wheeled vehicles; the verification of the Flood; the oldest specimens of wheat and barley; and large tomb groups containing a few golden objects, many stone and copper bowls, and a few painted vessels, similar to those from Jemdet Nasr, in addition to thousands of unpainted pots ranging from Sumerian to Babylonian times. These specimens are now in the Iraq Museum in Baghdad, the Ashmolean Museum at Oxford, and in Kish Hall in Field Museum.

Back in January 1926, when we made the important discoveries at Jemdet Nasr, I had determined to continue work someday at that low mound.

During the previous winter in Chicago I had given several illustrated lectures on Kish and Jemdet Nasr. One lecture seemed particularly poor. Several slides got mixed up. However, at the end Mr. Henry J. Patten came up to say how much he had enjoyed my talk, and a few days later he sent Field Museum his check for five hundred dollars, "toward future excavation at Jemdet Nasr."

The Kish season was drawing to an end. It seemed to me this was our chance to start work on the ancient site of Jemdet Nasr.

THE low, historic mound of Jemdet Nasr lies northeast of Kish and eighteen miles away.

The inaccessibility of this ancient site, the hazard from marauding Bedouins, and the reluctance of our workmen to go so far from their village, all combined to make work there a difficult project. Langdon had found it so—even dangerous.

In the early winter of 1926, shortly after Buxton and I left Kish, Langdon had started excavations at Jemdet Nasr with the devoted Hassan Jedur as foreman. Mahdi, the timid, went along as protection from the lawless Bedouin raiders who roam the Jazira. A small reed-mat hut was constructed to house twenty men. Every morning Langdon drove out in the old Ford with dates and unleavened cakes and cans of water for the men, who each day welcomed the professor by kissing his feet and giving loud-voiced thanks to Allah for his safe arrival.

Work commenced at the eastern end of the mound, which later proved to be about 1000 feet long and 300 feet wide and 10 feet high. Almost immediately small rooms were uncovered. Several complete painted pots as well as hundreds of fragments were found. Later Langdon discovered an important series of tablets and archaic cylinder seals, a find similar to his discovery of the Kish "library" at Mound "W."

Langdon continued work until the end of March under the most trying conditions. One afternoon came a cloudburst. The men became panicky and Hassan Jedur told Langdon he could not make them stay any longer. Abandoning the Ford, they all started back through the deep mud to Kish. Night found them still stumbling through the mud; it was the next afternoon before they limped into camp. Langdon was shuddering with chill and exhaustion. Mackay sent for a car from Hilla to take him to the

175

Baghdad Hospital, where he arrived delirious with fever. Several weeks later he returned to Oxford. From there he wrote me often of his interest in all we were doing at Kish, particularly at Jemdet Nasr, but he never really recovered. He was to die a few years after this—a martyr to Jemdet Nasr. But he had made one of the most important discoveries in Mesopotamia. In his report on the cuneiform texts published at Oxford in 1928, he added these deductions:

All antiquities found at Jemdet Nasr belonged to the period about 3500 B.C., when it was destroyed by fire. These included monochrome and polychrome pottery with geometrical designs, comparable to Susa II, pressed and rolled stone seals, copper and stone implements. The tablets were not inscribed with a stylus with a narrow, triangular head but by a sharp, pointed instrument. The language was Sumerian. From the few gods which are known in the archaic period, this would suggest an early stage of religious belief, very close to monotheism, or belief in the existence of a single God (An, the Heaven god). In his opinion the history of the oldest religion of man is a rapid decline from monotheism to extreme polytheism, to a widely spread belief in evil spirits. It is in a very true sense the history of the fall of man.

The painted pottery found with these tablets indicates an intimate relationship with the types associated with the Proto-Elamite tablets from Susa. The painted pottery consisted for the most part of checkered or lozenge-shaped patterns. The seals are exactly the same type as those of Susa, the designs usually taking the form of simple crosses or groups of dots. The roll cylinder seals are of various shades of marble, limestone, shell, and alabaster; precious stones were never utilized. These reveal the same animal-flower motifs as in Elam: fish swimming in rows, goats, and geometrical designs repeated.

It was Langdon's conclusion that the Sumerian civilization entered the Mesopotamian Valley from Elam in this area, and then spread southward to the shore of the Persian Gulf. Moreover, this culture was connected with that of the Indus Valley in India, and particularly with Mohenjo-Daro in Sind, and Harappa in the Punjab.

Langdon's report had made me the more determined to con-

176

tinue work at Jemdet Nasr in the hope of finding some human skeletal fragments. Buxton and I had found none that first trip, and none had been found by Langdon. But I was convinced that with a little luck and perseverance some might be found.

So very difficult was the project that I proposed to Watelin that the five hundred dollars earmarked for work at Jemdet Nasr be spent in ten days with 180 men and boys, instead of using Langdon's method of 20 men for fifty days.

So that March of 1928 work was stopped early at Kish and we moved to Jemdet Nasr, set up some reed-mat huts, and began to sink trenches into the mound. Immediately we found pottery, some unbroken, but blackened by the fire which had destroyed the city nearly six thousand years before. Tablets in pictographic linear script, several types of seals, many of them with stylized animals in procession, shell lamps, and other objects were unearthed rapidly, for there was no overburden here, no new city or cities had been superimposed on the old. Many of the room floors were only three feet below the surface. And it was in these that I excavated six skulls, some of them extremely fragmentary, but one almost intact. It lay less than three feet under the ground; no earth had crushed it. I measured it in place, and it gave the important indication that the first dwellers in Mesopotamia were longheaded.

The work was going with a swing and we were giving out a pack of baksheesh cards each day. On the tenth day I stood on the highest point of the mound directing the excavations. Watelin and Eric were cataloguing specimens in their huts. A man came up to me, muttering in Arabic. The man was not one of my friends, so I did not listen very receptively to his plea to stop work. Muttering angrily, "*Jerad, jerad, hawai,*" which I did not understand, he walked away. Then my friend Rathi el Abud came. He said quietly that he thought we should stop work at once. "But why?" I demanded, since it was only three fifteen and this was to be our last day. I wanted to get every ounce of work out of the men, find every object we could find; as if, even then, I knew in my bones that we would never return to Jemdet Nasr. . . .

I told him he had better get back to work. "*Jerad!*" he insisted several times. Then, seeing I did not understand he walked over to a patch of camel's-thorn, pounced on something, brought it to me in his hand.

"*Jerad!*" he said in triumph. "Oh," I said, "a locust. Well, I don't think much of that."

He pointed gravely upward. I looked up and saw the sky had darkened as if covered with great wings. The men were looking up and muttering anxiously.

I had never seen a plague of locusts such as the Bible describes so graphically. But I had heard of modern plagues, of trains being stopped in their tracks and villages demolished, and I realized we had better hurry back to camp before the pests covered the desert in such numbers that we could not find our way. Already the locusts were upon us. I hated to lose all those man-hours of work, but there was no help for it, so I threw my arms in the air, shouted, "*Bydos,*" and started for camp. The insects flew through the air in waves, landed, rose, and flew again.

All around us the desert was turning from green-gray to brown. Long before we reached camp the locusts were coming in such numbers and at such speed that the entire sky was dark; locusts filled the air as far as one could see. They crawled everywhere, they ate everything. They were crawling up my legs; up my arms, inside my shirt; over my hat, neck, hands—they were everywhere. I tried to walk with dignity, but the Arabs were rushing past, screaming and shouting, throwing their *abbas* in the air, catching locusts, playing with them and having a wonderful time.

I crawled into my section of the reed-mat hut to find the earth floor literally moving. A cup of tea was a feat, for if you opened your mouth a locust jumped in.

Outside the men were roasting locusts over a camel-dung fire. Hassan Jedur asked politely if we would care to taste them. Eric and I sat on the ground beside him and watched an Arab tear the wings from an insect and stuff it into the glowing embers. It tasted rather like fried shrimp. I ate two and expressed my delight, mentioning something about John the Baptist, but I could not make them understand whom I meant. Eric liked the treat

178

no better than I did, but we thought that at least we were following the Biblical injunction to "live on locusts."

The skies continued to blacken; not a scrap of vegetation was left anywhere. The ground was covered with their dead. It was easy for us to visualize the plague that had ravaged Egypt.

Hassan Jedur said that we had been wise to stop work when we did, although for his part he was sorry, for he had been convinced that we had been on the point of making some wonderful discovery that afternoon. It was seldom he spoke of hunches, and I was impressed. For I felt as he did, that we had been on the verge of some great find that day at Jemdet Nasr.

Watelin decided that because of the locusts and the general unrest of the men it would be foolish to attempt to work there any more. On the eleventh day we had everything packed and were ready to return to Kish. I left at dawn with the burdened Cadillac and made two round trips before dark. On the last trip I turned as the sun was beginning to throw a long shadow over the barren desert from the low mound of Jemdet Nasr. On that mound man had lived more than six thousand years before. In eleven days we had unraveled part of his story. We had found a great quantity of very valuable material from early Mesopotamia. We had unearthed a footnote to history.

The Jemdet Nasr period is now as well known as any of the archeological periods in Southeastern Asia, but the dark mound still keeps many of its secrets.

Back at Kish, a memory of the food we had eaten out of cans at Jemdet Nasr made even the cooking of that far from Blue Ribbon chef Shemu seem delicious.

The next four days were spent in preparing for the divisions of the objects excavated during the winter season. It was now mid-March. Mr. Cooke drove down from Baghdad to make his selections for the Iraq Museum. He used the same sporting system as had his predecessor, Gertrude Bell.

The proudest find—the prize of the year—was the copper frog from "Y" trench with the five-petaled stand on top. We all watched with hungry eyes while the coin spun on that table.

179

Watelin had said he was never lucky in such matters. But by great good fortune he won the toss, and our precious frog jumped from Kish to the shores of Lake Michigan. Mr. Cooke, in turn, chose some fine stone bowls for Iraq and some tomb groups—in all, a magnificent collection.

The Iraq authorities were not interested in my skeletal remains of humans or animals, so these were outside, all packed and ready for shipment to Chicago. Also, by our previous agreement in Baghdad, Mr. Cooke had agreed that if we were able to preserve the chariot wheels they could go to Chicago, so they, too, were waiting outside, encased in dental plaster and packed in large boxes.

We drank a toast to Iraq's government after the division was over, and to its representative, the director of antiquities. Watelin made a charming speech in which he thanked Mr. Cooke for the permission to excavate in Iraq and to take the representative series to Oxford and Chicago. The speech, in French, sparkled with wit. Mr. Cooke was delighted and said he would carry his words to the authorities in Baghdad. He left in time to return to Baghdad that night and we proceeded upon our arduous task of packing everything for final shipment to England and the United States in twenty-two large packing cases purchased from the Royal Air Force.

Three days later everything was ready. A large truck arrived from Hilla to take the cases to the railroad station, where a flat-car would carry our treasures to Baghdad. Since the heavy truck could not possibly cross the bridge of palm branches, we had to ferry each case over the bridge with the Cadillac from Kish camp to the truck. To have lost all our treasures in an irrigation canal within sight of the mound where most of it had been excavated would have been too much to bear.

Then it was time to leave Kish—to shake hands with Mahdi, Juad, Shemu, and the other members of the camp staff, and climb into the Cadillac, which was again heavily loaded, and drive over the shaky bridge. Across the canal I looked back, wondering when if ever I would see the red ziggurat again. I had grown to love this lonely section of Mesopotamia, where two fascinating winters had been spent excavating Kish and trying to reconstruct its past. Now the mounds were smoothed over, lest raiders should try to penetrate the earth for treasure during the long hot summer, and the mud huts were bricked up and boarded and the camp deserted of all but the last of the crew. Already Kish was slipping back into loneliness, holding its secrets. It holds them still, for the royal tombs have never been found. To the last, I saw Shemu before the cook tent, waving his caracul hat.

We reached Baghdad in time for supper, and next morning Watelin left for Beirut and on to his beloved France. Eric and I began preparations for the long-hoped-for archaeological survey of the North Arabian Desert, a continuation of the work begun two years before.

My spirits were high as we drove out of Baghdad. We had been given permission by the Iraq Petroleum Company to accompany their survey party, now encamped near Rutba. This was the only way we could travel off the desert tracks and really see the country. Mr. J. Skliros, general manager of IPC, had shown great interest in my work and offered the facilities of his company to assist in further exploration. This help, given again in 1934 and 1950, has been of inestimable value.

We were now four: Eric, who was to make the ground plans of buildings; S. Y. Showket, photographer and interpreter; and Ivan Vania, White Russian driver-mechanic.

Behind us lumbered a truck carrying the rest of our supplies. The driver was a fierce Turk. Beside him rode his timorous assistant, an Armenian.

Once across the Tigris, I fell asleep, for the rushing around in Baghdad had been exhausting. I awoke from a catnap in a suffocating heat of whirling sand. We were in a real sandstorm. The furnace-hot wind raised clouds of dust. At high noon visibility was nearly zero, certainly not ten feet. The shade temperature was well over 100 degrees. For a few minutes I watched Vania's course, but could not see any track ahead.

Since Vania was an old desert driver, I tried to relax. Finally I asked him where we were.

"We're in the Falluja Desert. I can't follow the track, because it is silted over. We'll be at Falluja Bridge in about an hour."

Minutes passed as we crawled through the whirling ocean of sand. Right on our tail glowed the truck headlights.

Vania shouted, "There's the track. I knew I could find it."

Unfortunately this proved to be the wheelmarks of our own truck. Making our own great circle, we were completely lost in the Falluja Desert.

Vania was ashamed, then angry. I took the wheel and tried to keep a straight course. The sandstorm was at its height. It was hard to see, even to breathe. The burning wind was almost unbearable. Suddenly a telephone pole loomed between the headlights. I pulled the emergency brake in time. Showket walked ahead to find the next pole, then waved his flashlight. By this slow method we passed ten poles in about one hour. I decided to halt until the sandstorm cleared.

The Armenian, his eyes bulging with terror, begged for any seat except that beside the Turk. I ordered them both to make tea, at that moment rather like a labor of Hercules. Sheltered between the two cars, a camel's-thorn fire was soon blazing. The hot tea was welcome, if sandy.

We spent a miserable night, Eric and I taking turns on guard. Finally at dawn the wind died away, the sand fluttered to the ground, and on our right, through the mist, loomed several low mud-brick houses.

"Showket, please ask where we are and the nearest way to Falluja."

As he banged on a door I shouted, "Wake them up. You know how Arabs sleep."

"Sorry, sir, I can't."

"Go round to the back. Hammer on the door."

Showket returned. "No one can wake these people. That's a tomb."

The Armenian snickered. The Turk glowered.

On the ground we saw narrow tracks. Old-fashioned carts bear the dead from the village to the cemetery. These wheelmarks led us into the village, where we were directed to Falluja, only a few miles away.

Late in the afternoon we swung into Rutba Fort, where E. S. Fraser of the Nairn-Overland Company welcomed us with a hot bath, good dinner, cold drinks, and clean sheets. Rutba always was a real oasis. We reveled in its comforts. On the desert the normal procedure is to remove pants and shoes, wriggle into the bedroll, clamp on a fur-lined flying helmet, and pull up the covers. Morning and evening face and hand washing only is allowed, so a hot bath is really appreciated.

After dinner Eric and I drove across the plain to a line of six white tents, where we met Major A. L. Holt, William E. Browne, and Henry Moon. I was delighted because this IPC survey party was to crisscross the area between Rutba and the great lava bed, the Harrat ar Rajil.

In addition to the police guard, the two other members of the survey party were Dr. Evert W. K. Andrau, a Dutch geologist with an uncanny desert sense, and Mr. A. Cottin, railway surveyor, a tall, morose Frenchman.

The reason for the British, Dutch, and French representatives was that the Iraq Petroleum Company is a joint venture of these three, plus Standard Oil of New Jersey. Later, the United States pipe-liners built the two transdesert lines, but sections of the lines were maintained by British, French, and Dutch representatives.

A few days' travel found us on the summit of the famed Jebel Enaze, focal point of Iraq, Jordan, and Saudi Arabia. Bill Browne and Hank Moon took astronomical observations to fix the position of the cairn we had built while supper was being prepared.

That night, in my waterproof bedroll, beside the cairn, I had trouble going to sleep, for it was exciting to be on this famous landmark. Eagerly I awaited the first delicate rays of the sun to crawl up over the sands of Saudi Arabia.

"*Chai hadha*," said someone in the bitterly cold predawn gloom. The stars still twinkled. I reached a hand from under the covers to grab the mug of hot, sweet tea. One swallow was like driving a ramrod down the spine. A second later I was wide awake. About three inches of tea leaves had brewed all night in a large dixie. The Royal Air Force calls this "gunfire."

While several Primus stoves hissed contentedly, the police made a huge thorn bonfire, for the wind was icy. As soon as there was enough light to see my feet I began to hunt for stone implements. Just as I expected, Paleolithic man had been on Jebel Enaze (Anaiza).

Driving north, we crossed the Rutba–Amman track near Landing Ground "O." Nearby an outcrop of Mahunsur limestone yielded fish scales, gasteropods, and lamellibranchs in quantity. Andrau was delighted.

After this halt Browne invited me to lead the convoy, indicating a compass course almost due north.

He said, "Try to keep a straight line. You see, the center of your wheel tracks will be the official international boundary between Iraq and Transjordan until we can get it aligned on our new map. This is one of our main objectives. Good luck."

All day long the old Cadillac moved steadily over flint, gravel, and sand. Panting like a stag at bay, she would demand water, more water for the steaming radiator, for we had to drive miles in low gear; she drank nine gallons that day.

We stopped for lunch seventy miles north on some low hills called Tellul Basatin (The Hill of Gardens) by our Bedouin guide. Following the spring rains, these slopes become delightful green pastures. I collected another fine series of flint implements and flakes. As we crossed the Nairn track from Damascus to Baghdad a cloud of dust no bigger than a man's fist whirled upward far to the east. The Nairn sixteen-wheeler, the largest bus ever built (and from the United States), ground to a halt. The passengers were astonished to meet our large convoy this far out "in the blue." After exchanging greetings we went our separate ways, the bus to Damascus and we through scattered blocks of basalt to below the shiny black peak of Jebel Tenf, the boundary between Iraq and Syria.

In the morning we crawled all over this former crater, stepping over basalt boulders. A good series of worked flints was found.

Our final traverse before crossing into Transjordan was west to the eastern edge of the great lava bed, the Harrat ar Rajil. Our principal objective was Qasr el Burqu, a Roman fortress built to protect their eastern flank from marauding Bedouins.

In my last conversation on January 11, 1926, with Gertrude Bell, as she lay on a deck chair in her garden in Baghdad, she had turned her head to say, "Someday you may have an opportunity to visit Burqu. That's a fascinating place. Go to Burqu if you ever get a chance." Those were almost the last words I was ever to hear from her lips, for Miss Bell died that year.

We drove west toward Burqu beside the Harrat ar Rajil. The shade temperature under the rear wheels of the Cadillac was 112 degrees Fahrenheit. Often we had to change tires—once six times within as many hours. In every direction the mirage made each bush, each pile of rocks, appear to float in a quivering ocean. A tuft of grass looked like a distant Empire State Building, each car a spire by Sir Christopher Wren. Since we were in a waterless and uninhabited country, keeping touch with the convoy was essential. However, we had a few unpleasant minutes after searching for flints in a small depression. The Cadillac refused to start. We were completely alone. I fired my rifle three times. Silence. Downwind came the distant rumble of a Graham truck. Silence. I ran to the top of the circular crest, armed with an empty gasoline can. Using this as a mirror, I attracted a driver's attention. We were soon back in our position in the convoy. Fourteen years later this signaling through mirage was to give me an idea for land-air-sea rescues during World War II.

Eric had been riding with Cottin so we could cover two parallel transverses. They had spotted an ostrich padding along in the dancing mirage and had chased the huge bird but heavy sand enabled it to outrun their car. This was the last ostrich ever seen so far north.

The convoy reached the eastern fringe of the basalt-boulder-covered Harrat ar Rajil. Bill reassembled the six vehicles. No sign of the high tower of Qasr el Burqu. According to the surveyors, we were within a mile of the Roman fortress. For two hours we cruised in line up and down. Fifteen miles north of the point indicated on the map, Bill located the ancient fortress. I could see why Burqu had haunted Gertrude Bell. We wound amid large rocks to beneath the castle keep. The main tower was thirty feet high. Eric and I explored the ruins until dark.

The tireless surveyors set up their instruments. From now on the exact location of Qasr el Burqu would be known.

We all slept soundly, very soundly, until the sun was up. I slipped out of bed and walked among the ruins.

Lizards darted for cover; they were purplish black, protective coloration for the volcanic country. In the flint-strewn desert they are either fawn or speckled.

After breakfast Showket began to photograph the castle, its rooms and doorways. Eric walked around deciding how to make the ground plan and I picked up a few worked flints. Vania worked on the Cadillac. The surveyors drove around hunting for the Roman source of water.

I copied a fine series of camel brands, graffiti, and mason's marks from the walls. Among these was a treelike design, the symbol tattooed between the breasts of the Ruwalla Bedouin girls.

One door lintel bore an Arabic inscription. Using dried camel dung for chalk, I filled in each letter so that it would be easier to photograph. Dated 81 A.H. (A.D. 700), this proved to be the sixth oldest Arabic inscription known.

A search began for more inscriptions. The ten police, the drivers and helpers scoured the walls inside and out. As enthusiasm faltered I offered three bottles of beer for an inscription, then six, finally a case. Under the spell of this incentive, a feverish hunt developed inside the fortress. Blocks of basalt were overturned. Peering into a grave still containing a Bedouin skeleton and his ragged clothes, I saw a Greek inscription face down. Six men removed this former door lintel, weighing 150 pounds, to a truck. Months later the basalt block reached Chicago. Photographs of the eroded inscription were sent to Greek specialists in the United States and Europe. Professor William K. Prentice of Princeton read it: " '[This] memorial of La-ismas and Amelath [his wife], ever to be remembered, was built by Sagios So . . .' It cannot well be earlier than the second century after Christ, nor much later than the first half of the third century."

Prentice concluded, "There is a something about this inscription which appeals strongly to the imagination. What sort of people were these who lived for a time in this grim, black, unspeakably barren military outpost, beyond the farthest frontier of civilization in that region? Unforgettable they are called by the companions who survived them. They are forgotten now among the living; even their names cannot be read with certainty."

186

As I sat alone in a small room in the ruins of Qasr el Burqu I remembered that man has long believed in a future life, certainly as far back as the Neanderthalers of five hundred centuries ago.

I spent the rest of the day helping Eric make the ground and elevation plans, calling out measurements from the steel tape.

The surveyors had located a large catchment basin faced with dressed basalt to the north of the castle. This had been Burqu's local water supply, now bone dry.

That night the Arab cook reported we were out of water. Bill removed from around his neck a key that unlocked a padlock on a 200-gallon metal container in one of the big trucks. The cook returned, with staring eyes. "It's empty, sir." A leak had emptied our precious main water reserve for the return trip to Rutba.

Bill's face was furrowed. He collected all the water available and each man was given a full canteen. That was all, except for a 25-gallon oil drum with water for the radiators and batteries. Before dawn the motors were humming, racing over the gravel plain. During the burning heat of the day we sipped at our canteens, making each mouthful last. Our throats burned. One of the police, his canteen empty long before noon, begged for water. Our Bedouin guide, with a pitying look, gave him a swallow.

We did not halt at noon. By midafternoon the water in our canteens was nearly gone. In searing wind our lips cracked, our tongues began to swell. . . .

Bill stopped the convoy. Behind us rolled a reddish-brown cloud of sand, a mile high and extending to both horizons.

As I watched it approach with the sun behind it, I realized this must have been the "pillar of fire" that guided the children of Israel through the desert.

The sandstorm, moving at thirty miles per hour, struck with great violence, enveloping everything in a whirling mass of sand. We covered our heads with our coats but the sand penetrated everywhere. Our eyes, ears, and mouths were filled with it. This storm lasted ten terrible minutes.

Not until long after dark did our thirsty convoy crawl through the main gate of Rutba Fort.

On one of these trips out of Rutba we were in the center of the great lava bed in a searing wind and our throats were parched. I added concentrated lemon juice from a bottle to our tepid water. I was about to pour out the half inch of juice that remained in the bottle but instead, on a sort of hunch, I corked it carefully and stuck it upright in the sands. A few days later a sentry at Qasr el Azraq saw through his Zeiss glasses a man stumbling over the desert, falling, crawling on. When we reached him he could not speak, for his tongue was swollen. He wrote on a piece of paper, "Send help to save pilgrims in lava bed." He was a driver of the bus to Damascus; it had wandered off the road and broken a crankcase in trackless waste. Twenty-three pilgrims were found huddled in the bus, awaiting death. They had drunk the water from the rusty radiator. The co-driver was found spread-eagled dead, on the sand.

When the surviving driver could tell his story, he said he had run for help, then crawled after a mirage of a car that led him on. Finally he fell, as he thought dying, in the waterless lava bed; his hand, as he pitched forward, closed around a bottle. He had managed to open it and moisten his thickened lips with lemon juice. This had given him the strength to struggle on until he stumbled into the range of our glasses. Twenty-four lives out of twenty-five had been saved by that half inch of liquid.

I FIRST heard of the coming World's Fair, which was to be held on the Chicago lake front in 1933, shortly after taking up my duties at Field Museum back in 1926. The Chicago *Tribune* had printed a glowing account of the Fair-to-be, and the general plans had been outlined. An island was to be filled in on the lake so that Field Museum, the Shedd Aquarium, the Adler Planetarium, as well as Soldier Field, would form the backdrop to the Fair. Our two Halls were to be open in time for the Exposition.

June 1, 1933, was the date set for the opening of the Hall of the Stone Age of the Old World and for the Hall of Races of Mankind—a date none of us working on the two Halls forgot for one moment, waking or sleeping. That date became like the sword of Damocles over our heads.

By the early spring of 1929 the blueprints had been drawn and redrawn to acceptable shape for the Hall of Races of Mankind. Comments and criticisms had been received from the leading physical anthropologists on every continent. We had collected a list of 164 racial types, stacks of photographs, and piles of notes and suggestions for exhibits. Blaschke was already at work on the Stone Age types, and Dr. Laufer and I were ready to begin.

Now came the question of an artist to portray the racial types for the Hall of Man. On several occasions I spoke to President Stanley Field of the desired results as "realistic portraits with an artistic flair." Finally he said he had no idea what I meant by this phrase. "Go over to the Art Institute," he said, "and pick out a 'realistic portrait with an artistic flair,' and I'll go and look at it."

I walked up the steps of the Art Institute with my usual wave to the lions that had welcomed me home to Chicago. All afternoon I walked through the rooms and passageways. There was no full-length figure, bust, or head in the entire institute that held the combination of inspiration and reality I wanted for the Races of Mankind.

I reported my failure. The museum president commented, "What does this memo mean? The Art Institute is one of the finest in the world. I'd like to know where there is a piece of sculpture such as you are looking for."

I answered quickly, "I'm really thinking of the Herbert Ward bronzes of African natives in the Smithsonian."

"All right, get Ward on the telephone."

"I can't. He's been dead for years."

After a moment's silence Stanley Field said, "Well, get me some pictures of his sculptures."

The pictures were found for him—Ward's "Sorcerer," "Fire-maker," and other incomparable life-sized bronzes of African natives. My telephone rang. "Now I understand perfectly what you mean by 'art and realism.' We'll have to find someone like Ward. Start looking."

At this point I did not think we could find one single artist with the talent and physical endurance to complete the 164 sculptures within the limited time. Our blueprints were in a final stage and the deadline hovered. My feeling was that to achieve a more or less uniform result we would have to select four artists, who used the same general technique, and send them on four separate quests, to the Americas, Europe, Africa, and Asia.

Marshall Field was in New York. He telegraphed from there that he would like to recommend the sculptor Malvina Hoffman, and suggested that I visit her studio there and give my opinion on her ability for this particular task.

Two days later I was in New York, standing in the Metropolitan Museum before Miss Hoffman's "Pavlova." The delicate mask of the great dancer with its pink and white flesh tints was amazingly lifelike. Here was the skill of a great artist, plus true realism—the effects I had tried to describe to Stanley Field.

I walked out of the museum and sat on a bench in Central Park. I thought of certain minor difficulties I was having with Blaschke. For example, a few nights before he had worked in the museum until nine, putting hair onto Monsieur Le Moustier's right thigh. Then he wrote a note to his wife and asked the guard at the front door for a stamp. The night guard refused him, since he was not allowed to touch the stamps in the counter drawer. The sculptor slapped his hat on his head with an angry "I'll not work any more for an institution that won't even allow me a stamp to send a letter to my wife."

Next morning he had not shown up for work. I telephoned and found him in a spluttering rage, but succeeded in bringing him back to work that afternoon, still furious.

And now we were considering a woman sculptor for the Races of Mankind!

It was very peaceful in the park, almost like the country. I thought over the problems that already faced us with the two Halls, and those that might be added if a woman were hired. I realized that on the selection of the artist depended the success or mediocrity of the Halls.

My two dreams were already demanding a high price in worry and strain.

Miss Hoffman was expecting me in her studio that afternoon but at no specific hour. I walked slowly down Fifth Avenue, stopping in a church for quiet meditation and guidance on the way. On east Thirty-fifth Street I stopped with a curious premonition outside No. 157.

The bell rang clearly. Malvina Hoffman, handsome, gray-haired, with finely chiseled features and wearing a green smock and black velvet tam, met me with a firm handshake.

She showed me around her studio. Two oversized heads of Nubians in black Belgian marble first caught my eye. Mentally I compared her work with that of my hero, Herbert Ward. Miss Hoffman was a very talented sculptor, capable of the most delicate realism combined with a strong dramatic sense. She had studied with the greatest—with Herbert Adams and Gutzon Borglum in New York, and in Paris with Auguste Rodin. She had received gold medals, awards, and foreign decorations.

Her sculpture lacked to some degree the powerful strokes of a man's. But on the other hand, among the racial portraits Dr. Laufer and I had in mind, only a few of the more primitive types such as the Sakai, Australian aboriginal, and Kalahari Bushman would require tremendous strength in their faces.

So, over a delectable cup of tea and thin sandwiches, I decided to be practical. I told her of the plan for the Hall of Races of Mankind in Field Museum.

"Our primary purpose," I explained, "is to show racial representatives of the main divisions of mankind, arranged by continents. The visitor should be able to walk around this hall in half an hour and obtain an impression of the principal racial groups of the world's two billion people. For these dramatic life-size, full-length figures, busts, and heads we require an artist of rare quality and ability who will be willing to work under the direction of the leading anthropologists."

Miss Hoffman nibbled a sandwich and asked how many figures we planned to have in the Hall. When I said the present list called for 164 figures, she nearly dropped her sandwich. No one, she explained, had ever talked to a sculptor in such figures!

I stressed the time limit (about fifty months remained), the need for traveling around the world, studying movies, stills, sketches, consulting with experts . . . Miss Hoffman said it was all terribly exciting and no one had ever attempted anything like it before. I asked her for an estimate of costs, and she replied faintly that she would have to do some figuring.

A few days later Malvina Hoffman came up the marble steps of Field Museum. It was the start of a long, hard trek for her.

She talked with Dr. Laufer, Stanley Field, and the director, S. C. Simms. Her attitude as the plan unfolded was that of a race horse at the post. Her eyes shone and the scope of the job fascinated her, especially when we described the central and dominating motif, the "Unity of Mankind," three idealized figures supporting the world. She would be given carte blanche for this triad and its setting. I could see an inner conflict raging, and later I heard that some of her friends had advised strongly "against prostituting your art. This will ruin you forever and ever as an artist."

That evening Stanley Field and Miss Hoffman dined with me and I asked her a question: "If Rodin were alive, what single piece of sculpture would you show him with pride?"

192

"I have done a life-size figure of a man in armor on horseback. I would like to show Rodin one of the legs and feet of that man."

"Yes, but no one can see them inside high boots."

"That doesn't matter. I am proud of them, although only the bronze founder and I saw them or will ever see them."

After dinner came the bomb. Regarding the cost of this huge project, Miss Hoffman proposed a six-figure sum of such proportions that it sounded like a national debt. Stanley Field, who was standing in front of the blazing fire, turned with the words, "Well, Miss Hoffman, that settles it. I certainly will not try to raise that sum." He strode toward the door.

Miss Hoffman replied, "Just a minute, Mr. Field. That figure is based on one full-length figure, bust, or head multiplied by the total numbers. A large order like this would reduce the amount very materially. Another way to reduce the expense is to cut down the types to about 100 instead of 164. I think that's enough for the public in any one Hall. You know, people tire easily."

"I agree with you about the number being too high. Henry, you and Dr. Laufer cut out some of the less important types. Work on it together tonight and let me have another list tomorrow noon."

That was a long night. A pot of coffee kept me awake. Writing out the list of selected racial types by continent, I began to arrange them in order of importance. In his apartment on the South Side Dr. Laufer was also revising his list. We conferred by telephone at midnight, at two o'clock, at six and eight. In his office at nine we checked and rechecked the full-length figures and busts. By ten o'clock I was almost cross-eyed, but we had reduced the total to 100 with the greatest difficulty, for it was hard to throw out many of the types, especially among the myriad of groups in Asia. The revised number included thirty full-length figures, a great reduction from the original list.

In the Drake Hotel Miss Hoffman was revising her estimate. At noon Dr. Laufer sent Stanley Field our new list, and Miss Hoffman turned in her figures. We had a very moderate lunch in the cafeteria. I was too tired and nervous to eat. At three o'clock on this cold February afternoon in 1930, Dr. Laufer called me to his office, where he was conversing with Miss Hoffman. We three were asked to appear in the president's office at three-fifteen. We were seated in huge brown leather chairs. My heart was thumping, not so much from gallons of coffee as from controlled excitement. Dr. Laufer was waxen with exhaustion. Neither of us had had a moment's sleep. Miss Hoffman looked haughty and extremely handsome. President Stanley Field paced up and down and pointing with his right forefinger, he asked, "Dr. Laufer, are you perfectly satisfied with this revised list?"

"Yes, Mr. Field. It is a good working list, but we must not be held to it, because circumstances may arise, especially in Asia, which may make it impossible to obtain a representative of some of these types. However, I'm satisfied, with those reservations."

"Thank you, Dr. Laufer. Henry, you've been working on this plan for a good long time now. You have received advice and suggestions from top anthropologists all over the world. In your considered opinion, is this the best possible plan you can produce?"

I told him yes, with certain reservations, and added that I had perfect faith in Miss Hoffman's ability.

"Thank you, Henry. Miss Hoffman, do you think that you will have the physical stamina and courage necessary to complete this assignment?"

"With God's help I will, Mr. Field."

"All right, my instructions from the Board of Trustees given at a meeting less than an hour ago are 'Full speed ahead.' The money is raised. We'll draw up a contract tomorrow. Good luck to the three of you!"

All three of us almost collapsed. The strain of the past few days and of the preceding sleepless night was suddenly released. We staggered to our feet and went upstairs to begin the great project.

We were at long last on our way.

All that winter of 1929-30 I worked on the two Exhibition Halls. These were two gigantic projects I was directing, with the deadline getting nearer every day. Many late nights were devoted to writing *The Arabs of Central Iraq, Their History, Ethnology and Physical Characters*, which would be published in

194

1935 and later be submitted as evidence in my supplication for the degree of Doctor of Science at Oxford.

By summer plans for both Halls were well under way. Joe Todd and his carpenters were building the dioramas and renovating a series of large upright cases. Blaschke was at work on the Stone Age figures in his studio at Cold Spring on Hudson. Miss Hoffman was in Paris, where she had a fine studio next to her house in the Rue de Vouillé. I was in Europe on the first of the annual summer pilgrimages to buy specimens for the Hall of Prehistoric Man and to select data for the Hall of Races of Mankind. For the next few years my thoughts would concern themselves with ancient and modern man as I raced to and fro, traveling every summer across the Atlantic with large letters of credit and returning home with weighted suitcases.

The summer buying tours for the two Halls provided many amusing and dramatic experiences.

I purchased prints for the Library of Racial Photographs, necessary for Miss Hoffman's studies as well as a permanent collection for students in the museum, by selecting prints from Ewing Galloway and Publishers Photo Service in New York, museum collections at Harvard, Yale, New York, Philadelphia, Washington, and in Europe from London, Paris, Rome, Vienna, Budapest, Prague, Brussels, Amsterdam, Berlin, Tübingen, Breslau, Hamburg, Copenhagen, Stockholm, and Oslo. I estimate that I looked through more than a million photographs to make the selection.

The main difficulty lay in obtaining photographs from the Soviet Union. The only ones I had found were very old prints from Bogoras, Hrdlička, and Laufer. In Vienna at the Anthropologisches Abteilung of the University, Professor Josef Weninger showed me a thousand full-plate glass negatives of the peoples of Russia taken under the direction of a German anthropologist during World War I, when about ten thousand Russian prisoners had been interned near Vienna. This anthropologist had been assigned to record anthropometric data and photograph each man front, side, and three-quarter. Here in the basement of No. 1 Van Swietengasse was treasure trove! I offered Weninger a thousand dollars for five hundred front and profile glossy contact prints of a carefully selected and well-balanced series representing all areas of the Soviet Union, aspecially the Caucasus, Central Asia, and Siberia. My offer was readily accepted because at that time the annual budget for operating this institute was less than a hundred dollars. The Library of Racial Photographs finished up with about twenty thousand excellent prints.

The most important item on my busy schedule was introducing Malvina to Sir Arthur Keith, that she might receive his assistance and guidance.

Sir Arthur had long been familiar with my dream of the Halls, and the project in faraway Chicago was dear to his heart. Several times he had said in his quiet Scotch way, "Well, dear boy, it's a grand scheme. But it will all depend on the artist."

I had introduced Blaschke to Sir Arthur. Their mutual liking had been instant. Now I was to bring another great artist to the world's greatest anthropologist—this one a woman.

The day I took Malvina to the College of Surgeons, the two shook hands while sizing each other up, for I had told each a good deal about the other. The conversation was stilted. Sir Arthur repeated several times that accuracy was paramount, realism necessary, and vitality essential—a difficult trio indeed!

I muttered something about Malvina's multi-ton group dedicated to "The Friendship of English-speaking Peoples" on Bush House in London, her "Pavlova" in colored wax, and the sensitive marble portrait of Keats. Sir Arthur remained impassive, unmoved, unconvinced that this handsome American woman was the person to be entrusted with creating the Races of Mankind.

She caught his quizzical glance and with true feminine intuition offered to portray him, as a demonstration of her technical ability. Between us we persuaded Sir Arthur to pose for three sittings and he was delighted with the result. He offered to help Miss Hoffman in every way. In the years to come, no one gave better or sounder advice. Our gratitude is boundless. Apart from hours of consultation and almost continuous correspondence for five years, Sir Arthur helped me plan the locations of the studios around the world that Miss Hoffman was to use, and gave her about fifty letters of introduction to his colleagues in Europe, Africa, India,

196

and Australia—the finest open sesame to anthropological collaboration.

Now we were faced with a poser. My original plan had called for composition figures with hair and glass eyes—true realism, similar to the reconstructions of prehistoric men and women then being made by Frederick Blaschke for Hall C.

Dr. Laufer and I believed this would produce the result we wanted for the Races of Mankind. However, Miss Hoffman objected to an international Madame Tussaud's waxworks with nearly nude figures. Then came the practical side. How were we going to get the hair? We could buy hanks of head hair in Paris, but what about the body hair?

Sir Arthur and I talked over this problem time and time again. Finally we were won over to the bronzes, with a few stone heads to break the possible monotony. When I returned to Chicago, Dr. Laufer agreed and recommended that the change from composition to bronze be made, particularly after Miss Hoffman proposed to indicate skin-color differences by variations in patine. Stanley Field agreed and the bronzes were ordered at a greatly increased price. He was a super money-raiser. His genuine enthusiasm for both Halls was inspiring.

We were off on the right track at last.

During the summer of 1931 when I was in Europe a cable from the director asked if I knew Gretchen Green and whether I would recommend her as an assistant to Miss Hoffman on her forthcoming round-the-world trip. I cabled back that Gretchen would be an excellent assistant and super courier. A few weeks later in Chicago I gave Gretchen a copy of the 122 letters of introduction for Miss Hoffman, arranged by country.

Meanwhile we had decided to ship to strategic spots around the world wooden cases, each containing a complete unit of supplies necessary for the modeling and casting. This would obviate trailing thousands of miles the bulk and weight of equipment and also the risk of theft or loss.

Dr. Laufer and I prepared a list of subjects to be modeled near these centers, together with the names and addresses of the local leading physical anthropologist to whom Miss Hoffman had an introduction or even several letters. On a large map we drew large red circles to check our world-wide coverage of study centers. Beside each circle a list of racial types to be modeled in that area was written in blue.

On my desk lay a pile of receipts, acknowledging the safe arrival of the shipments to each of the base points of operation.

It was then decided to send Gretchen Green eastbound to make arrangements for studios with north lights, to talk with the key physical anthropologists regarding the recruitment of racial types for a certain date, and to call on the officials so that Malvina's path would be made as smooth as possible by careful planning. Gretchen took a copy of the map, a list of the subjects desired, the names of the anthropologists, and a flexible time schedule for each study center.

On this trip we were concerned mainly with the peoples of the Pacific area, the Far East, the East Indies, and India. Thanks to the Exposition Coloniale in Paris, many African types had been available. Gretchen had many friends in India, for she had lived there under the benign shadow of Rabindranath Tagore. Thus on this subcontinent her planning was especially successful. The Viceroy gave our project his blessing and offered every form of assistance. Gretchen continued eastward on her mission, making arrangements as she traveled, until she met Malvina in Peking. Then she turned around and accompanied the expedition back to India. Gretchen's contribution to the final result, though intangible, was nonetheless very considerable.

The story of this round-the-world expedition has been well told by Miss Hoffman in her book, *Heads and Tales*, in which she has described so vividly her trials and tribulations and her successes.

After the world tour Malvina worked in full swing in her Paris studio. The full-length figures were roughed out in clay on an armature by one of her assistants, while Malvina concentrated on modeling from life. In this way her time and energy were conserved, a very necessary procedure in this unique, gigantic, world-wide project.

A strange incident occurred in the Paris studio when Malvina was working on the slightly over life-size trinity for the central group, the Unity of Mankind. Malcolm Whitman, former Davis

198

Cup champion, and his wife were lunching with her. Suddenly Malvina turned to Malcolm and said, "Please go on upstairs and take your pants off. I'll be up in a minute."

Mrs. Whitman looked surprised, to put it mildly. Malvina used Malcolm's superb legs as models for the White Man. In addition to the modeled legs, casts were made in plaster for the record. As part of our regular procedure, casts of the face, hands, and legs were made of each full-length figure, and face masks of the busts and heads. This was to eliminate future criticism.

Many months later, after all the casts had been shipped to the museum, two cases of tools and casts of the central group arrived in the New York Customs. Malvina, accompanied by a friend, appeared before the inspector at 12:50 P.M. The first case was pried open. Inside were modeling tools. The second case contained some plaster casts, including those of Malcolm Whitman's legs; they were smashed to smithereens.

"That gives me the queerest sensation," said Malvina.

"I don't see why," her friend said, "he's right here in New York and you can make other casts any time you want. If it had been one of the jungle dwellers in Malaya or someone like that, it would be different."

"I still feel queer about it."

As Malvina entered her house the telephone was ringing. The call was to notify her that at exactly one o'clock Malcolm Whitman had pushed his nurse aside in a hospital, opened the window, and jumped to his death.

One summer's day in Paris I saw a fine *femme à plateau* at the Exposition Coloniale. She was an Ubangi woman from near Lake Chad in Central Africa, with the enormous lips produced by the successive insertion of wooden studs of increasing size. Marshal Lyautey, the commissioner, gave me permission to take the girl to the studio for Malvina to model. All Paris seemed out and in the streets as I guided the Ubangi beauty to the taxi and we drove across the Place de la Concorde to the Rue de Vouillé. With the top down, we caused a sensation at traffic lights. Like all beautiful women, my companion did not remain oblivious to this attention. Supporting her ten-inch wooden lip stud with her left

199

hand, she chattered like a magpie while she nudged me violently with her right elbow. Her eyes shone with pleasure at being the cynosure of the Champs Elysées and the Rue de Rivoli. Molyneux might have original designs for Parisiennes and foreigners, but my companion had the biggest lips in France!

At the studio Kiki, Malvina's fascinating Persian cat, who had long been used to seeing strange people, arched his back in true wonderment.

I never see the museum's bronze-lipped counterpart of the Ubangi beauty without remembering with mingled amusement and embarrassment my taxi ride with her through Paris. As the Abbé Breuil would say, "*Toujours les femmes!*"

THE rapid flight I had taken through the museums of Europe after leaving Heidelberg and before taking up my work at Chicago paid dividends on the buying trips for the two Halls. I had learned a great deal about collections and displays on that hectic journey, but above all I had made friends. Now that purchases were to be made, objects selected, and advice solicited, I knew just whom to ask and where to go. Despite the fact that articles must be carefully chosen and well authenticated, the spending spree I now launched upon was almost without parallel. I had many thousands of dollars to spend. Sir Arthur Keith in London and the Abbé Breuil in France gave their advice again and again. More people than can ever be named contributed their time and learning to the Halls of Man.

In Paris Pat Kelley guided me from bookseller to bookseller to buy books and pamphlets on French prehistory. Le François on the Boulevard St. Germain was the best. Here we bought many thousand publications to make Field Museum Library the best in the United States on this subject.

Through Pat I learned that the type collection from Solutré, for which the Solutrean period is named, belonged to the Catholic Church. I also learned that the roof of the church required attention. The estimate for these repairs was about a thousand dollars and I paid the contractor in advance. The grateful fathers sent the entire collection to Marshall Field and Company, Paris, from whence it was shipped to Chicago. It was very exciting to open this pig in a poke. There were many pieces of laurel-leaf blades (feuilles-de-laurier), several of which fitted together. In a torn sheet of Le Petit Parisien was wrapped a real prize, a Solutrean dagger with the most delicate retouching—the only one known.

The Abbé advised and helped with many purchases. With his aid I bought for Field Museum most of the material used in the Hall of Prehistoric Man, and the finest study collection of French archaeology outside of France.

Nowhere in France was it possible to obtain for the Hall any painted pebbles from Mas d'Azil in the Ariège. These *galets coloriés* of the Azilian Period are believed to be tokens, currency, games, or possibly the soul symbol, as among the Arunta of Central Australia. In any event it was absolutely essential to have a series for Hall C, particularly since the Azilian boar-hunting scene opposite was to be staged at the type locality, Mas d'Azil. With the Abbé's approval, I offered a thousand-franc note (forty dollars) for one Azilian painted pebble, but without success.

In despair I told my sad story to Monsieur R. Lantier at the National Museum, St. Germain-en-Laye. Some weeks later I signed a document accepting on behalf of the museum, on a ninety-nine-year loan, five Azilian painted pebbles from the National Collection of France—a most generous gesture. I hope my successor will return them in A.D. 2030 or renew the loan!

In Paris Louis Peyrille of Périgueux had arrived to offer me a collection containing a spatulate ivory point ornamented with incised fish and designs. The Abbé took one look and exclaimed, "That's a *churinga*. We have two fragments at St.-Germain. This is the first complete one ever found in France. I claim this in behalf of the French government."

Peyrille, being a good salesman, refused to sell the collection without this piece. Some hours later I bought the lot, knowing I must relinquish the prize specimen. A week later I walked into a huge mirrored room in the Beaux-Arts to present on a small red cushion the *churinga* to Monsieur Paul Léon in behalf of Field Museum. The director of the Beaux-Arts bowed low and made a most gracious reply. Then he smiled and said, "This is a *churinga*? I believe the Australian aboriginals still use them."

I explained, "They make *churingas* as 'bull-roarers,' believing them to be the voice of their god Daramulun. If a woman hears this sound, she is put to death at once. It is now certain that the Crô-Magnons used them, probably in their ceremonials. The humming noise must have been terrifying from deep inside a cave."

I added that I had been buying in behalf of Field Museum all over France, and had given my word that I would submit every good piece to a member of the Beaux-Arts before taking it out of France. Therefore this unique *churinga*, and any comparable object, would be presented to the French people. Monsieur Léon shook hands and thanked me profusely in behalf of the Beaux-Arts. This was the only piece out of more than 120,000 which the French government claimed, so rich is France in prehistory.

Casts of the well-known human remains from all over the world were purchased through Mr. F. O. Barlow of R. F. Damon and Company in London. When the Hall opened, Field Museum would have the most complete set in existence.

I received authorization from Field Museum to visit the Cueva d'Altamira near Santander in northern Spain with the Abbé, a delightful assignment, for I had never seen the Altamira cave, which was the greatest sanctuary of Palaeolithic art until the discovery in 1940 of Lascaux in the Dordogne.

This cave had been the Abbé Breuil's special study. He had won his spurs there, copying the marvelous ceiling painted by Crô-Magnon artists. It was, for me, the highlight of all our travels. Charles R. Knight was in Europe with his wife and daughter Lucy, vacationing after completing his series of giant murals, ranging from before the Carboniferous forest to the animals of the La Brea tar pit in Los Angeles. We joined forces so that Mr. Knight could do four paintings for the walls of Hall C. He was to describe our adventures charmingly in his book, *Prehistoric Man: The Great Adventurer*.

En route we visited Count Bégouen, on whose estate in the Ariège district of France are Tuc d'Audoubert and Trois Frères, two of the most famous prehistoric caves in France. In the first we went a short distance by rowboat, then scrambled over banks and through the "chimney," a narrow tunnel with two bends. Deep inside we walked in single file, stopping to see the naked footprints of the Magdalenians still preserved in the damp clay. Here indeed was the Track of Man. . . . In one corner a story was read to us by the Abbé from the prints; a mother Magdalenian, twenty thousand years before, had chased her child and slipped to her right knee. This was prehistoric spooring and just as clear as to my Masai lion hunter in Kenya. A little farther on the Abbé halted and put his acetylene lamp behind his back. All around was darkness. The Abbé began to whistle the "Marseillaise," then swung his lamp around to the wall. There in relief stood two small bisons of clay, the male following the female. Below were naked heel prints. We were in a Magdalenian sanctuary. Around these bisons the ancient hunters had celebrated a fertility dance, two hundred centuries (or eight hundred generations) before. . . .

No words can describe my emotion in this sanctuary. No famous works of art in thirty-seven countries have produced the sense of awe comparable to the Bisons of Clay.

It was impossible for Blaschke to make casts. The bisons were far too fragile. The Bégouens gave Blaschke the first and only permission to model them life-size. A week later the models were safely packed in a huge wooden case en route to Paris. He also modeled life-size the famous horses in the Cap Blanc rock shelter.

At the cave of Trois Frères, called after the three cave-exploring sons of Count Bégouen, we saw hundreds of prehistoric engravings and finally reached "The Sorcerer," a masked figure wearing reindeer antlers, painted high on the cave wall. It was easy to visualize a scene in which the young hunters were assembled in fear and trembling before a hunt. After weird incantations, the Sorcerer appeared through a hole high up in the cave to give the hunt his benediction.

This is not such a far cry from today. Today the hunt is blessed in France as are cattle and crops in many lands. Our troops are blessed before they go into battle. In his innermost feelings, man has remained unchanged through the years, through the centuries, through the millennia.

On another expedition the Abbé and I visited the Trombe family at Ganties-les-Bains near Montespan, France, where four years before Félix Trombe and Georges Dubuc had discovered a second prehistoric gallery in the famous Grotte de Ganties.

The Abbé and I arrived late one Saturday evening at the farmstead of the Trombes. Before retiring I heard a general discussion of the cave and the prehistoric galleries. It was on occasions such as this that I was made to feel the infinitesimal value of the French I had learned with such concentration in school. One frequently repeated reference to "Le Siphon" was particularly unintelligible.

Just before dawn the roosters began to crow with unbounded energy and a persistence which to some might seem admirable. To the accompaniment of these chanted odes to the rising sun, the Abbé dressed rapidly and proceeded with heavy tread downstairs and into the courtyard. A few minutes later the clatter of hoofs interrupted the crowing. This was the Abbé going to Mass. Breakfast was served at seven and, while we were feasting on fresh eggs and coffee, back came the Abbé, hungrier and more vociferous about it than any bear of fact or fable. At the moment my inadequate French was standing me in poorer stead than ever, for I had fancied one of the younger and less inhibited members of the Trombe family had commented upon my coffee, which I had doused liberally with milk, as *jus de chapeau.* The Abbé arrived in time to explain that this was a term for milk-weakened coffee, or the result obtained by pouring hot water through an old and greasy felt hat!

At eight o'clock the Abbé, who never explained any plans, announced firmly that he and I were leaving for the cave. I took my waterproof rucksack and cave clothing—consisting of khaki trousers, a sweater, and a pair of rope sneakers. We took the usual supply of newspapers, candles, knives, matches, notebooks, and pencils.

We entered a tunnel extending into outer darkness. Immediately the Abbé ordered me to undress, and set a rapid example. Within three minutes we were attired only in shoes and berets, in which all cave explorers (speleologists) carry matches and a candle and several balls of wadded newspaper to protect the head from stalactites which might otherwise cut the scalp. The Abbé was a figure of dignity in his birthday suit while on his head rested a bulging beret.

He grasped his thick walking stick firmly in one hand and

his flickering acetylene torch in the other. *"Allons, vite. Vite."*

The rock floor changed to a shallow but icy stream. It deepened until we were plunging through water up to our waists. By this time we were both gasping from the extreme cold of the water and the struggle to maintain our footing on the slippery, rocky bed of the stream.

Suddenly the Abbé shouted, *"Il faut plonger. Ici le Siphon,"* and plunged headfirst under the surface of the water. The lamp went out with a hiss. Eons seemed to pass before I heard him on the surface again, on the other side of the wall, swimming with elephantine snortings. He shouted to me to dive under and swim to him. I dove into the black icy water with little hope of surviving the ordeal. A few desperate strokes brought me under the stalactite curtain, which at this point extended under the surface of the stream, and up panting and terrified beside the Abbé, who was standing in water to his chin and shouting for matches. I fumbled with my stuffed beret and in the darkness and cold dropped the box of matches, which floated away. The Abbé located his own box; no flame ever glowed more benignly. The Abbé was beaming like a happy child. *"Le Siphon. Quelque chose, eh?"*

I was so relieved to be alive that I beamed back.

We clambered ungracefully onto a mudbank above the cave stream. A few feet ahead lay the objective of our visit—a small clay cave bear modeled by a Magdalenian artist some twenty thousand years ago. The head had fallen off. Around the vital places were pierced holes. An ivory *sagaie* (spear point) lay nearby. It was simple to reconstruct the scene: a young hunter standing in the torchlight, holding his spear, the priest encouraging him before the clay effigy, "As you strike this, so will you kill the great bear." And the warrior driving the ivory shaft into the model to secure the magic aid needed for the hunt.

We lay on the mudbank feasting our eyes on this solemn sanctuary.

The return trip was simple. We dried off in the hot sunshine and returned to an enormous lunch in the farmhouse. The Abbé, who likes to laugh over our many adventures together, is very fond of recalling "Le Siphon."

It is difficult for the uninitiated to understand the spell of caves. To the student of anthropology they can hold treasure trove in prehistory and occupy his thoughts asleep and awake. How many times does the hunter of prehistoric man dream at night of uncovering the treasures of the ages and wake as disappointed as a child to find these treasures unreal.

There is, for example, my friend Joseph Mandement, a French dreamer and discoverer who has devoted his life to prehistory. His methods are unusual. He puts his subconscious to work and his dreams guide him. One night in a dream that was more like a vision he imagined himself looking into the entrance of Bédeilhac cave in France. It was night. A circle of Magdalenian hunters sat around the campfire within. He noticed drawings of the chase on the ceiling. Apart from the others, farther back in the shadows, were two young lovers dressed in skins. In the dream he saw the boy lead the girl into a darker side tunnel, on the right side of the cave, and to a ledge inside the tunnel. He heard them whispering as the boy stroked the girl's long, thick, black hair. Suddenly there was a terrible roaring sound, the rock walls shattered, and a great rock crashed down, barring the side tunnel's entrance. Mandement was certain the young lovers died in one another's arms in the blocked-off passageway.

Convinced of the accuracy of his vision, he placed a description in a bank vault. Then he proceeded to the cave at Bédeilhac. It was just as he had seen it in his dream, but the right wall was apparently a solid wall of gray limestone. He tapped it with a pick and it gave back a hollow sound.

Feverish with expectancy, Mandement hired local workers and broke through the wall. There was the narrow passageway, unopened since the earthquake had sealed it millennia before. He crawled inside and flashed his light around. The place was as he had dreamed it. The ledge was where he had seen it in his dream. Only the ledge was empty!

Mandement explains this by saying that during the earthquake vision there was so much confusion that he did not see the young couple slip out just before the crevice was closed by the falling rock!

In his bitter disappointment he did not at first remember the animals he had seen painted on the ceiling in his dream. Then he led the party to the exact spot; deep inside Bédeilhac are the animals of the chase engraved by Magdalenian artists, just as his vision had shown.

My last night in Paris before the opening of the Halls was dramatic. I had driven across the city to say good-by to old Dr. Henri Martin, who had always been so kind and helpful. After contributing to his laboratory in the Charente, Field Museum had received a representative series of duplicate Mousterian implements from La Quina and Solutrean tools and debris from Le Roc, as well as the first set of casts of the frieze of animals from Le Roc for the Solutrean diorama. I thanked him for his generous assistance over the years and returned to the Hotel Prince de Galles after a long, exhausting day.

Less than an hour later, as I sank into a delicious hot bath, the phone rang. Dripping wet, I heard Dr. Henri Martin beg me to return to his house. I dressed quickly. A taxi sped, as only French taxis dare, through the wet night. The old doctor, in a wine-colored velvet smoking jacket, took me into his library and brought me a purple-tasseled cushion on which lay a tiny glass phial. He said gently, "I want to make you a present of the rarest piece in my private collection. This is a Neanderthal tooth from La Quina. Take it as a souvenir of an old man whom you will never see again."

He added, "This tooth was found while I was using my private funds for excavation, before I received government assistance. Do not mention it until after you hear of my death."

He pressed the fifty-thousand-year-old tooth into my hand. Tears were in our eyes as we said good-by for the last time.

Back in Chicago the heat was really on. Our deadline was approaching fast.

My education was greatly improved by frequent luncheons with the young architects of A Century of Progress. It was an exciting experience to see a World's Fair grow from its beginnings, to see plans for the great Hall of Science first drawn on the back of an envelope, then on a tablecloth, then as a blueprint, and finally as a scale model with its blazing panels of colors—all the work of Joseph Urban, the well-known architect and designer. I saw other buildings grow from primitive pencil sketches to ground-breaking ceremonies. The two street towers of the Sky-ride grew like Jack's beanstalk. Cables were strung along the lake front like a Meccano set. All Chicago waited expectantly for the opening of the Fair.

Inside the museum my two Halls were taking shape. Blaschke worked long hours in the basement setting up the figures and foregrounds. Corwin was painting the curved backgrounds.

Technical problems confronted us in the Hall of Races of Mankind: lighting, floor covering, walls. I suggested plywood to give a rich background tone to Malvina Hoffman's bronzes. The too eager salesman oversold his product to Stanley Field when he said rapturously, "Mr. Field, this will be the biggest plywood room in the world. The Lumbermen's Convention will like to visit here."

Stanley Field promptly decided on painted beaverboard.

Another salesman urged upon us his linoleum for the floor. The most used three feet of linoleum in the Middle West, he said, was made by his firm. I asked him the location of this test piece. "The entrance to the Ladies' Room in Marshall Field's," was his practical reply. He got the order.

The lighting problem was even more complicated. My friend Ken Curtis of Curtis Lighting supplied the answer. Mr. Stair, their chief engineer, had recently returned from lighting the Sistine Chapel on a highly competitive bid.

By hiding metal channels along the Hall, the source of light was invisible. For days I carried a light meter backward and forward across the Hall, until the reading was constant.

Malvina's bronzes began to arrive and were placed with care on their wooden pedestals. The physical anthropology exhibits were set in alcoves at the east end. After six years of being a dream, the Hall of Mankind began to be an actuality.

Downstairs, in the Hall of the Stone Age, Corwin's backgrounds were painted and dry. Blaschke was putting the finishing touches to the dioramas. The cases of archaeological specimens were in place. Knight's paintings were hung. The Cap Blanc girl was moved into a special case. Opposite were installed the "Bisons of Clay." Within the Hall rose another age—the dawn of pre-history.

May 30, 1933, was the opening day of A Century of Progress Exposition. It was our deadline too. On that day, to our own blaze of publicity, our two Halls were at last thrown open to the world.

THE opening day of the World's Fair was thrilling, particularly to those among us who had watched it grow from a penciled sketch to an actuality. At the opening exercises I sat on the platform between Arthur Brisbane and Will Rogers, who was in sparkling form. Just before Rufus Dawes began his address, Will turned to me.

"Hear you work in that marble mausoleum over there. Get any kick out of playing with mummies?"

"Sure," I answered as blandly. "They never say no."

Will moved his wad of gum thoughtfully, with a Bushman-like click.

All that day, and through the days to come, thousands of visitors surged through the main gates, midway between the Shedd Aquarium and Field Museum. Hundreds of thousands walked up the marble steps to visit the two Halls—the Hall of the Stone Age of the Old World and the Hall of Races of Mankind. That day a dizzying round began as I personally conducted special guests through the two Halls.

The Hall of Prehistoric Man was all I had hoped it would be, as I had dreamed it since my sixteenth year. Here within the space of a half hour, walking past the eight dramatic and colorful dioramas, a visitor might read in true-to-life chapters the past quarter of a million years of Man's history.

The study of prehistory was at this time less than one hundred years old. It had started in 1847, when Boucher de Perthes published an account of certain hand-shaped flints he had found in the alluvial deposits of the Somme in northern France. Now, from fragments of a skull, a tooth, a bit of bone, a flake of flint, science had reconstructed in authentic settings life-sized images of man in the slowly advancing major stages of his development.

The data for the figures Blaschke and I collected on the trip into western Europe, and the prehistoric sites portrayed are those we visited with the Abbé Breuil, Henri Barrèyre, the photographer, and the artist Pierre Gatier. The backgrounds are by Charles Abel Corwin of Field Museum. The scenes are made authentic by the cultural objects I collected during the Marshall Field Archaeological Expeditions to western Europe in the years 1927, 1928, 1930, and 1932.

Group I shows a typical Chellean scene in northern France, in the Palaeolithic or Old Stone Age (approximately 250,000 years ago). In the near distance is a river, where lurk elephants, a hippopotamus, a stag, and a pack of wolves. In the foreground, crouching over a fire under a ledge of rock, are two ancient hunters, naked, shaggy, powerful, slanted of shoulder and brow, ferocious of eye. One is chipping a flint hand ax in preparation for the hunt that is their defense and subsistence. Shaggy and powerful though they are, they seem small and weak compared to the great beasts hiding nearby. But they are already on their first step toward supremacy over the beasts: they have a weapon and fire.

The lighting on this scene gives the effect of moonlight, symbolizing the dimness of our knowledge of man in this earliest dawn of human development, the earliest we dared to attempt.

Group II shows the Devil's Tower rock shelter at Gibraltar, which I had first seen with Dorothy Garrod and the Abbé, and where Dorothy had found the Neanderthal child called Abel. One young man, holding a heavy club, is standing with his back to the shelter, looking out over the dark blue Mediterranean. Another squats over a fire at the entrance of the cave, where mussels are cooking. In the entrance is the mother, with a small child on her hip; another child is playing by the fire. This family lived about fifty thousand years ago.

It is the first family.

Another Neanderthal family group is in the Hall of Historical Geology (Hall 38) in the museum. The setting is in the upper rock shelter at Le Moustier.

Group III is a replica of the cave of Gargas in the Haute-Garonne in southwestern France, about thirty thousand years ago.

The cave is illuminated by a fire and by a sandstone lamp resting on a stone shelf. On the stone walls of the cave are seen the famous frieze of hands, the imprints outlined with powdered red ochre—some of the hands are mutilated—and before them stands an Aurignacian, kneeling with one hand firm against the wall, in the other the hollow reindeer bone pipe by means of which he is blowing the red dust around his splayed fingers, outlining the hand.

This is Crô-Magnon, the world's first artist.

Group IV is the Solutrean frieze of Le Roc in France, as it was approximately twenty thousand years ago. The background shows trees, the entrance to the cave, and the blocks, carved in bas-relief, of animals exactly as they were arranged by the Solutrean artists. In the foreground is the sculptor, a husky Mongoloid type resembling the modern Eskimo. He is carving a horse from a stone block and wears the intent expression all artists wear when they are at work they love. It is an interesting point that all the animals portrayed in this frieze are pregnant—fertility rites?

Group V is a reproduction of the Magdalenian frieze in the Cap Blanc rock shelter in the Dordogne, France. The Magdalenians probably invaded France from the east. They are members of the Crô-Magnon race but of different stock from their predecessors. They are medium in stature, well shaped, with pleasing features. Man is on his way in this period; the Magdalenian is an impressive person with a high sense of artistry. As this case shows, he has produced some of the finest examples of prehistoric art. Shown here is the famous frieze of horses. Below rests the Magdalenian teen-ager.

This diorama marks the end of the Palaeolithic period. Group VI pictures a scene from the Mesolithic, or transition, period, about ten thousand years ago.

This shows an Azilian boar hunt in France. The Azilians were the last of the hunting races roaming Europe. They have degenerated in art, have no engravings or sculptures to leave behind them, and their paintings are limited to the simple painted Azilian pebbles. But they have perfected hunting. The dogs shown, held on rawhide leashes by these stalwart men—who, wearing modern

213

clothes, would pass unnoticed on Fifth Avenue—are the first domesticated dogs. The Azilian tempers his art to the hunt. He has invented bone chisels, awls, and polishers, the stone anvil, the flint-tipped lance, and the barbed harpoon. The ice sheets have melted over Europe, the Arctic wastes and flora are replaced by verdure, birch and pine, and the red deer has taken the place of the cold-loving mammoth.

Group VII is an exact view of the Carnac alignment in France. The tall blocks of weathered granite run to meet the sun. About eight thousand years ago this was evidently a place of worship dedicated to the sun. Facing the sun at dawn on the Summer Solstice stands the priest, arms upraised, to greet the new day. This is the Neolithic or New Stone Age.

Neolithic man probably entered Europe from east of the Caspian Sea, bringing with him a new culture upon which our modern civilization rests. He has contributed agriculture and the domestication of animals; he has produced the first good pottery. He grinds his flints instead of chipping, he has invented the grindstone. He has built the first houses.

These are pits, circular or oval, with roofs, and a place for the fire. Before long this man will be making crude wooden houses, some with several rooms, and even several stories.

He buries his dead in burial chambers and raises stones above them.

The Swiss Lake Dwellers shown in Group VIII represent the latter part of the Neolithic period, about 5000 B.C., at Auvernier on Lake Neuchâtel, Switzerland.

The pile village against a background of lake and snowy Alps might be a modern fishing village. The well-built, good-looking men drawing their seine from the water have their prototypes today. These men have driven piles into the water to hold their homes, which are made of tree trunks, often ten to twelve feet in length, laid across the piles and fastened with wooden dowel pins. The huts are rectangular, thatched, wattled and plastered inside and out with clay.

These men raise cattle—cows, goats, sheep, and pigs; grow flax which is woven into thread and cloth for clothing and fishing nets, tan leather, and have perfected stone tools and made beautiful

implements and jewelry of copper and bronze. They raise cereals
—barley and wheat—and grow apples, cherries, berries, and
grapes. They have made knives and swords. They ride horses.

In this scene, as I wrote in a Field Museum leaflet, *Prehistoric
Man:* "The dawn of the historical period is at hand."

Twelve years after this opening day of the two Halls in Chicago I, along with the rest of our human world, felt the impact of
the first atomic bomb on Japan.

Before my eyes flashed the dioramas that told the agelong
story: man raising himself above the beasts, to fall again and
again, to rise again. Many times, during the last million years,
Man has been threatened with complete destruction.

Prehistoric man shows the fluctuating history of man. He
shows us that there is hope—there is always hope—for the future
of mankind.

To reassure ourselves we must look beyond these dioramas,
back to the dawn of time.

"And God said, Let the waters under the heaven be gathered
unto one place, and let the dry land appear: and it was so. . . .
And God said, Let the waters bring forth abundantly the moving creature that hath life . . . And God blessed them, saying,
Be fruitful, and multiply, and fill the waters in the seas . . ."

The earth cools and water forms.

Life evolved in the waters and on the land hundreds of million
of years before man appeared.

Within the apparent calm of the waters there is abundant life,
each species the prey of another; each with hope of survival, the
supreme impelling force. Only those ever on the alert will survive
—until their turn comes.

Thus has it been for eons. . . .

On the land and in the air there is also abundant life. Again,
only those ever on the alert will survive—even temporarily.

Thus has it been for eons. . . .

On the sand beside these waters lives a colony of horseshoe
crabs, one of Nature's most successful experiments. Having
evolved an almost perfect balance with their environment, the
horseshoe crabs have remained practically unchanged for hun-

dreds of millions of years. While dinosaurs, the largest creatures ever to roam the earth, flourished and became extinct, the humble horseshoe crab survived.

If the combined estimates of the age of life on the earth can be determined by a study of the crust, by the amount of salt in the sea, and by the disintegration of radioactive substances, this age can be placed at more than two thousand million years.

If a twenty-four-hour clock represents the period of life on the earth, meaning life in the primeval oceans, a period of approximately a thousand million years, then recorded history—i.e., six thousand years since writing was known—is less than one third of one second.

Man's past is a much longer story than the average person appreciates. In order to plan intelligently for the future, we should draw on experiences of the past. This is the time for man to look at himself, to examine the causes for war, and to attempt to eliminate them.

In these respects a brief outline of the Story of Man may shed some light on the true perspective of man's place in nature.

Man has overcome far more insuperable difficulties in his past million years than the turning of atomic power to construction rather than destruction.

Man's struggles and victories began several million years ago—and those struggles were against greater odds, those victories more inspiring, than any man has known since the time that records were first inscribed on pictographic tablets.

Let us review in outline the main features in the dramatic Story of Man during the past million years. It is naturally difficult to trace the unwritten records of mankind, since many of the details lie buried in the earth or are lost beyond recall.

During the past few centuries it was believed that the world was created in the year 4004 B.C., according to the chronology of Archbishop Ussher (1581–1656), and that man was the result of special creation.

"So God created Man in his own image, in the image of God created he him; male and female created he them. And God blessed them, and God said unto them, Be fruitful, and multiply, and replenish the earth, and subdue it. . . ."

In the first half of the twentieth century scientific workers proved that hundreds of millions of years passed before any animal that could definitely be recognized as human evolved upon the earth.

Study of both living and fossil forms reveals that a laborious evolutionary process from simple one-celled organisms to many-celled, from fish to amphibians, from reptiles to birds and mammals, was necessary to produce the as yet most advanced form— Man. Evolution can be either progressive or regressive, never static.

Branching off from the main primate stock several million years ago, our ancestors naturally possessed many physical characteristics in common with the anthropoid apes. As time passed the gap grew ever wider. Some of us may resent our common ancestry but the facts remain. As E. G. Conklin writes: "Some may *prefer* to believe that their ancestors came from the Garden of Eden rather than the zoological garden!"

We still do not know just when or where the first humans evolved, but as the data from every continent are pieced together, the picture becomes clearer.

We shall not concern ourselves here with a long discussion of the cradle of man. My own belief, based on the evidence available, is that there may well have been two cradles—one in Central Asia and one in Africa. It also seems probable that the nursery of *Homo sapiens* was Southwestern Asia, because in this area there was a favorable climate, and numerous species of plants and animals, later cultivated and domesticated, flourished.

We only know that somewhere several million years ago some of our ancestors were walking semi-upright on the ground. For the first time they were using their eyes, instead of their noses, to find food. Generations later their descendants had developed keen eyesight with the corresponding reduction in the sense of smell. Thus we surmise the brain enlarged and the facial region became smaller.

The adaptation of the foot to walking and the more upright posture also reduced their agility in the trees.

Survival became more and more dependent on memory, reason, and adaptability to environment. Although these powers now differentiated man from all living creatures, he was still more hunted than hunter.

One summer night lightning played over the forest. Later, from smoldering brush, the man-figure kindled his first fire.

This was his first defense against beast and cold.

1. PERIOD 1,000,000–50,000 YEARS AGO

The oldest traces of man have been excavated in China, Java, South Africa, and England. These four widely dispersed points lie on the periphery of the combined land masses of the Old World.

These traces, never consisting of more than fragmentary human remains, stone tools, animal bones, and the charcoal of hearth fires, are still too few to draw any but the crudest picture of the oldest members of the human race. However, we can be certain that they had struggles and depressions but always indomitable hope for the future.

As we pass through the millennia we come to a little surer ground because more data exist. Perhaps a few imaginary scenes based on some facts may help to clear the image of the past 250,000 years.

At this time in western Europe the climate was mild. The elephant, rhinoceros, and hippopotamus were the dominant forms of animal life. The human beings of that period must have been rugged, power-jawed, and ferocious in appearance. Small in numbers and physically weak in comparison with the animals that surrounded them, the earliest hunters were forced to use their ingenuity and their powers of reason to survive.

Their knowledge of fire enabled them to keep off marauding animals after dark. These Chelleans, as they have been named (from Chelles-sur-Marne in northeastern France), developed considerable skill in flaking flint into hand axes and other simple tools. Presumably they possessed wooden spears with fire-hardened points, although no traces remain. During this period, some quarter of a million years ago, geologists state that the Chelleans could have walked from France to England because the English Channel had not yet been cut by the sea. To attempt to describe their life

218

would be sheer imagination, but all that we do know points to a struggle for survival and little leisure time. . . .

Development during the following tens of thousands of years appears to have been extremely slow. About fifty thousand years ago Europe was suffering from the effects of a cold climate, far colder even than the dread winter of 1945–46 following World War II.

The mammoth, reindeer, and other cold-loving animals wandered over western Europe.

At this time Neanderthal man made his first appearance. He was about five feet four inches tall, thickset, with a large head and relatively short limbs. The head, thrown slightly forward, was carried in that position by strong neck muscles. To our eyes his face would have a fierce expression, emphasized by the enormous brow ridges, small, round eyes, and a broad, flat nose.

The lobe of his brain associated with the power of speech was little developed, as compared with that of his modern cousin. It is presumed that he was capable of using a simple vocabulary, perhaps similar to that of the Bushman of the Kalahari Desert in South Africa.

Traces of Neanderthal man range from Gibraltar eastward across Europe to Tashkent in Soviet Central Asia and his culture extended northeast to Siberia and on to China.

In western Europe it has been possible to make some detailed studies and thus to draw a few warranted deductions on his life and habits.

For example, Neanderthal man lived in caves or rock shelters for warmth and safety. A fire, built near the entrance, formed excellent protection against cave lions, bears, hyenas, and other animals. Neanderthal man was probably the first to seize a woman and protect her from animals and other men. This was the beginning of family life—a great step forward!

Prior to this time, it is believed, mankind lived in bands, mainly for protection, and through this the tribal system had long since developed—probably from the earliest times.

During this period in which the Neanderthalers lived in western Europe for some twenty to thirty thousand years, there was still little time for relaxation and the development of the long-latent artistic sense. However, stone and bone tools showed marked improvements in technique. A good quality flint was located and much practice was devoted to flint-knapping. A hunter found by trial and error that, although two flint hand axes might look the same, one achieved its purpose better than the other. In modern terms, one was luckier. The Neanderthal hunter, whose family depended for their existence on his prowess and success, attributed this luck to supernatural assistance. As do all of us, especially primitive peoples living close to nature, he had respect for the beneficent, fear for the malevolent.

There is also evidence that he believed in a life after death.

One Neanderthal ceremonial burial suggests a reverence for the dead and a belief in a future life, because a beautifully worked flint hand ax was found in the hand of a skeleton. Fresh meat had been placed inside the grave. In addition, the inside of the grave contained red ocher, presumably the symbol of blood life.

However, he may not always have reverenced the dead because in another locality charred human bones suggest cannibalism. On the other hand, he may have eaten part of a gallant enemy in order to acquire some of his strength and skill. In Africa natives eat lion meat to give them strength and courage.

The Neanderthal hunters developed the use of fire, probably even learning how to make it by striking flints, fashioned new types of flint and quartzite tools, organized family life, and buried their dead in the belief of a future existence.

Until the past decade it was thought that Neanderthal man died out, possibly because of an epidemic or malaria, without meeting those who followed him in western Europe. Recent evidence, however, from Palestine and Tashkent indicate a mixture between Neanderthal man and *Homo sapiens—Homo sapiens*, "the wise and human," surely the worst misnomer of all time!

Here is added confirmation that Nature moves slowly but steadily and that few if any complete breaks in continuity exist.

2. 50,000—4500 B.C.

We now follow the Story of Man through a long period of years.

During this time Neanderthal man seems to have dominated,

but toward the latter part a new racial type makes its first appearance—the Crô-Magnons. These fine-looking people were of splendid physique, tall and with a brain capacity equal to that of the average American or European.

If you were to stand in the lobby of the Hotel Plaza in New York when a Crô-Magnon couple came in, you might well comment on this good-looking couple with black hair, dark eyes, and a slightly Oriental appearance. These Aurignacians, as they are called, seem to have been very close to the main line of our ancestors. Evidence indicates that they swept into Europe from the plains of Asia.

When they lived in western Europe, a thousand generations ago, the climate was bitterly cold. The food supply was abundant and for the first time man now had some leisure. He had time to think. He had time to develop his powers of reason. He had time to express his long-dormant artistic sense. Here was the dawn of art, magic, and religion. He had time to reflect on himself. He had time to speculate on the controlling forces of nature, including supernatural powers. He had time to wonder about life after death.

Man now had abundant time on his hands to speculate about his past, present, and future.

Since the climate was so cold, the Crô-Magnons lived in caves, usually near the entrance. Deep in the dark recesses behind their home were the dark, mysterious passages from which strange sounds sometimes came.

Family life around the hearth was similar to that of modern primitive peoples living in the cold north. They dressed in skins and wore shoes. The girls wore necklaces of reindeer teeth, sea shells, or fish vertebrae. The more favored sported necklaces of mammoth ivory beads fashioned by the Cartier craftsman of his day.

The young braves wore trophies to add the strength of their quarry to their own. The chosen few were allowed to ornament their black hair with feathers. The son of the chief proudly wore a necklace of cave bear incisors with a huge cave-lion tooth as the central motif.

The beginnings of magic, religion, and art were interwoven.

Ancient and modern parallels sometimes render us interpretations.

In attempting to visualize the past, we often turn to the life and customs of contemporary primitive peoples, especially to those living under Stone Age conditions.

The Aurignacians buried their dead with their finest shell ornaments, their most useful tools and weapons, presumably to make an imposing picture in the next world. They were expert craftsmen and artists, both painters and engravers, with a remarkable eye for detail and a superb sense of proportion and rhythm.

During these relatively few thousand years the Crô-Magnon artists developed their technique from running the fingers along the soft clayey wall of a cave to naturalistic polychrome painting. The former, the oldest example of art, is called "macaroni" when performed by Aurignacian artists, finger painting when done by our children.

Toward the close of this period the climate grew still colder. Horses and wild reindeer were the chief sources of food supply.

Between the Aurignacian and Magdalenian periods the Solutreans seem to have forced their way across eastern Europe into France and Spain. They were short and stocky, with black hair and Mongoloid features, linking them with Asia. We know little about them but they developed the finest of all flint-flaking techniques with the possible exception of a few Ancient Egyptian or Danish craftsmen. The most spectacular and characteristic Solutrean tool is the laurel-leaf blade made by pressure flaking. At the type station of Solutré in France the bones of many thousands of horses were found. These were the principal source of food.

Leaving this minor intermediate period of the Old Stone Age, we come to the Magdalenians, who also seem to have come from Asia into Europe. They developed every form of art far beyond that of the Aurignacians. They also modeled in clay. These also had leisure—probably more than any other group of human beings in the history of mankind.

We may now be standing on the threshold of a similar Renaissance as a result of atomic energy.

This brings us to the end of the Old Stone Age. In passing, however, we must observe that since most of our information comes from western Europe we have made no attempt to trace man's development on each continent but rather to follow the broad lines which led to the formation of the North American peoples.

More or less contemporaneously with the Magdalenians in western Europe, the first waves of Asiatics were moving across Bering Strait, through Alaska, and into the United States. These first waves probably began about twenty-five thousand years ago.

To return to the sequence in western Europe, toward the close of the cold Magdalenian period the climate began to grow milder and to resemble that of today. But as we approach the historical period the data become numerous and opinions conflicting. We shall, therefore, try to steer a middle course since we are concerned primarily with the chronological outline rather than with the wealth of detail.

Between the Old Stone Age and the New Stone Age there is a transitional period lasting several thousand years. This is a period of decadence. All fine artistic expression has disappeared. There are no more beautiful engravings on bone and stone. The only Azilian art seems to be simple geometric designs painted with red ocher on river pebbles, designs which may represent conventionalized human forms, some kind of currency or tally, or something akin to the Australian *churinga* or bull-roarer.

However, we believe that the Azilians learned to domesticate the dog.

The domestication of animals had begun. . . .

In the next subperiod the Tardenoisian, there are not even any painted pebbles, only small, triangular flints to be set into wooden handles and crude harpoons.

The New Stone Age or Neolithic period followed this decadent transition period.

These people appear to have been true strangers and they developed many phases of a common culture, including:

1. The beginnings of agriculture.
2. The domestication of animals on a large scale.
3. The manufacture of pottery.
4. The grinding and polishing of stone implements.

The cultivation of plants and the domestication of animals not only made settled community life possible but also had a profound effect on modern man's distribution.

Neolithic man lived in limestone caves, circular pit houses, and on pile dwellings over lakes, particularly in Switzerland. Elaborate monuments were constructed to eulogize the dead.

We are more familiar with the use of metals—first copper, then bronze, iron, and steel—the age in which we used to live. . . .

3. 4500 B.C.—BIRTH OF CHRIST

During this period of forty-five hundred years civilization began. The main areas of concentration were the great river valleys of China, India, Mesopotamia, and Egypt in the Old World and, in the New World, Central America and Peru.

This was the age of construction by almost unlimited manpower. For example, the building of the Great Pyramid in Egypt, the temple tower (ziggurat) at Ur of the Chaldees (the home of Abraham in Mesopotamia), and the Maya temples, as well as vast irrigation schemes in Egypt, Mesopotamia, and China, indicate some of their structural achievements. During these two hundred generations two of the most significant inventions were made: the development of writing and the making of the first wheel.

At Kish in Mesopotamia the Field Museum-Oxford University Joint Expedition found one of the earliest fragments of writing—a small stone tablet bearing pictographs recording a deal in wheat some six thousand years ago. This simple stylized presentation of symbols indicates a long period of previous development. I believe that writing originated from property marks placed on boundary stones and wells, later marked on animals, then tattooed on women, and finally placed on wood and stone as records of transactions to establish claims.

Also at Kish, since almost all transportation is based on the wheel, our discovery of the oldest wheeled vehicle yet unearthed had been of the greatest importance.

Many more or less contemporaneous developments occurred on every continent except Australia, where the ancestors of the Arunta still lived in a Stone Age culture. Among the more significant were the making of fine pottery, the fashioning of copper and, later, bronze tools, the domestication of the horse, and the

224

beginnings of serious thought and deep mental application. For example, in Mesopotamia astronomical research was encouraged by Nebuchadnezzar about 550 B.C. Libraries of cuneiform tablets were organized. Scientific research had begun. Man was struggling to determine the course of Nature and her habits. This search for the plan of the universe led to speculation on every phase of the earth and undoubtedly to its basic component parts. One hundred generations later man split the atom. . . .

Communal living, with the benefits of agriculture and plentiful labor, gave leisure to the select groups of thinkers from the Nile to the Yangtze.

Thus inventions had given mankind time to think. . . .

At the close of our period flowered the great civilizations of Greece and Rome.

However, as through the million years before Nebuchadnezzar enjoyed the pleasures of the Hanging Gardens of Babylon and through the twenty-five hundred years since that time, man has craved power over man.

This same ambition, which made him lord of creation, became the burning passion for power through conquest. That is what puts the fear of the atomic guided missile deep into our souls. . . .

4. THE BIRTH OF CHRIST—THE INDUSTRIAL REVOLUTION

According to St. Matthew, "And Jacob begat Joseph the husband of Mary, of whom was born Jesus, who is called Christ. So all the generations from Abraham to David are fourteen generations; and from David until the carrying away into Babylon are fourteen generations; now the birth of Christ was on this wise. . . ."

The nineteen hundred years following the birth of Christ are better known to all of us than any other historical period, so we shall pass over them lightly. With technical development, and in spite of almost constant warfare, mankind never feared for the future because rapid communication of ideas was still impossible. Lack of modern mobility permitted uninterrupted leisure as it now does to many contemporary primitive peoples, who still have time to read quietly and to absorb knowledge—to think.

225

Out of this time for reflection has grown the last phase of our arbitrary divisions of time—the Industrial Revolution, in which technical knowledge outruns man's power to cope with it. The result has been two world wars.

This was our human story, as it was portrayed to the world that morning in 1933 in the Hall of Prehistoric Man. Millions of observers have looked at the dioramas since then. How many, I wonder, have asked the question that troubles me as I look at that glass-bound review of human history: "Whither now mankind?"

Crowds swarmed into both Halls that opening day, buying postcards and leaflets in stacks. I remember that in the Hall of Races of Mankind that first year 42,000 pictures of the Shilluk warrior were sold.

Here modern man met with his own image. Malvina Hoffman's sculptures portrayed in imperishable bronze the purest types of the races of mankind, from every part of the world.

In the center stood her heroic trio—yellow, black, and white—symbolizing the Unity of Mankind. Sir Arthur Keith wrote in his introduction to my Field Museum leaflet, *The Races of Mankind*: "To me every type is Nature's attempt to give the word a happier and better kind of humanity."

The one hundred full-length figures, busts, or heads were of men and women selected for Malvina Hoffman by leading anthropologists from five continents: Africa, Asia, America, Oceania, and Australia.

No one can see these bronzes and fail to be impressed by the innate dignity of man. The Shilluk warrior epitomizes the hunt. The tiny African Pygmies portray the seriousness of family life. Daboa, the African dancing girl, is a jungle Pavlova. The merchant from Lhasa, Tibet, wears the look of the philosopher.

Each race has its own distinction and its own dignity.

Two bronze busts illustrate neck and lip deformation. One, of a Padaung woman of Upper Burma, illustrates the curious method of stretching the neck by means of brass rings placed one above the other.

The other is my gay acquaintance of the Paris boulevards, the immense-lipped Ubangi beauty. The urge to touch her elongated lower lip has proven irresistible to many visitors; as a result it shines from constant touching, reminiscent of St. Peter's toe kissed by the faithful in Rome.

Another irresistible attraction in this Hall is the Afghan's navel. Many an otherwise well-behaved forefinger cannot resist the temptation to poke this fascinating belly button. A jar of patine is kept in the Hall, for it needs frequent retouching.

There is an exhibit of artificial cranial deformation. A number of peoples of the world—the Manchus, for example—prefer to have their children's heads round rather than long. For this reason the grandmother spends hours molding the head with her fingers, and a tight band is tied around the child's head at all times, especially before the closing of the fontanelle. In addition, the baby is tied into a cradle with a hard board as a pillow. This also flattens the back of the head, thereby making it rounder.

Some peoples prefer to have the forehead flat and the back round. Among the ancient dwellers in Peru this was considered a sign of beauty and the most amazing head deformations resulted. In Europe, in the vicinity of Toulouse and in certain districts of Holland, the head was molded to make it rounder. A year after the Fair opened I examined a series of deformed skulls in Tbilisi (formerly Tiflis). These researches in the Caucasus will be published during 1953 by the Peabody Museum at Harvard.

The eastern end of Hall 3 is devoted to a series of exhibits dealing with physical anthropology, illustrating the principal method used in classifying the races and subraces of mankind. Graphic charts show the world distribution by skin color, hair, head form. Another series indicates cranial forms, age changes, and racial differences of the skull; sexual and racial variations in the outlines and proportions of the body; variations in the shapes of the eyes, nose, chin, and lips; and age changes in dentition. An exhibit showing the uses of the hand and foot among various peoples was prepared by Dr. Laufer. In another wall case thirty-seven photographs of the more important racial types are arranged geographically, and their suggested basic relationships indicated. This is based on an exhibit by Dr. Viktor Lebzelter in Vienna.

Also in this exhibit section is a series of colored transparencies of racial types to supplement the bronzes and to indicate the true skin colors of the human races.

That opening night of the Fair we dined aboard the *Mizpah* with Gene McDonald. The yacht lay inside the concrete breakwater. From a deck chair I looked out over a modern fairyland. Rockets hissed skyward over the aquarium. Floodlights brightened the buildings of the Century of Progress. The reflections in the water, the jewel lighting along Michigan Avenue, made the setting unreal as a fantasy. As I watched, my mind went back over the past six years. During that time I had traveled the equivalent of four times around the world in search of background information, photographs, and prehistoric collections. Malvina had made her trip around the world to model the representatives of every continent.

Now this, too, seemed like a dream, but the two Halls opened that day were real!

I went home and to bed and slept fourteen hours.

DURING the succeeding months I was taking out-of-town and foreign visitors around the museum and the Fair, and my feet became permanently two sizes larger as a result of trudging museum floors by day and the fairgrounds by night.

Hot, crowded, dusty, and exhausting though it was, I never had a better summer.

Millions came to Chicago. Millions enjoyed the Fair. Each night for many nights in succession I had a group of visitors to dinner somewhere inside the fairgrounds. Afterward we would tour the Hall of Science, stop for a drink in the Belgian village, watch the Seminole Indian wrestle an alligator, look up the high ladder to see the high diver with a flaming torch on his back plunge into a small water tank, and stagger around the "Lost World." As a good-night tonic, there was the "Streets of Paris" with "Venus on the Half Shell" and other daring exhibits. One very interesting exhibit showed a cross section of a city dump. During the past hundred years the main things preserved were tin cans and glass. Almost everything else disappeared, so that we may well be judged by future generations on the basis of Coca-Cola bottles and cans that once held horse meat.

Each side show cost a quarter. Having a string of guests night after night became a financial problem. Finally I obtained free passes. The friendly nods from the barkers and girls often puzzled my family or friends.

Marconi visited the Fair. He pressed a silver telegraph key. A light flashed on Chicago on the map. The letter s flew east and on—around the world. The time was three minutes and some seconds. Wild applause broke out. Later I had a chance to remind him of the time when in 1917 he had predicted television to me in the Palazzo del Drago in Rome.

When George Gershwin came we gave a dinner for him. Afterward we went down to the Fair. He insisted on being taken to the top of the Sky Ride. From these towers, several hundred feet high, one could really get a magnificent view of the World's Fair with its strange panorama of lights, the lake front, and the city, all reflected in the water. George said softly, "This is one of the most wonderful sights in the world. I have only one regret. The man who created it in his mind and imagination is not here to see it." The architect, Joseph Urban, had died just before the light from Uranus turned on the lights for the Chicago Fair.

Among the unusual visitors were Morris Frank and Buddy I, his Seeing Eye dog. Special permission was granted Morris to touch and "see" Malvina's bronzes, and for Buddy to enter the museum, where dogs were as a rule forbidden. In the Hall of Races of Mankind Buddy I seemed confused by the lifelike bronzes. I led Morris over to the figure of Daboa, the African dancing girl. He ran his hands over her with a pleased look. In the same way he "saw" the beautiful Mangbattu woman from the Belgian Congo, the Basque from northern Spain, the "duck-billed" woman—my Ubangi friend—and the giraffe-necked woman from Upper Burma.

I think that of the twenty million visitors to the Hall of Races of Mankind since 1933, probably no one has derived more pleasure or saw more than sightless Morris Frank.

Another interesting museum visitor was Maurice Tillet, the wrestling champion known as "The Angel." He arrived with a letter of introduction from Dr. Hooton, who had been examining him at Harvard. Here was a clear case of acromegaly caused by hyperpituitarism. As an undergraduate at Oxford I had made a special study of this disease with Sir Arthur Keith at the Royal College of Surgeons.

Although in most recorded cases acromegalics died before the age of thirty, the Angel had just passed his thirty-second birthday and was still wrestling, and a champion.

Colonel Clifford Cilley Gregg, director of the museum, saw in the Angel a chance for publicity. The champion's excellent sense of humor was a little tried when he found himself, wearing only a reindeer skin and gripping a prehistoric stone ax, standing motionless within the Neanderthal family group. Then, while Pathé cameras ground, I directed his sudden coming to life and plunging forward out of the group with a wide-open yell while brandishing his mighty ax. This newsreel with shots of me measuring him appeared from coast to coast; we both thought it pretty silly.

But the measuring was serious. The next day was spent measuring, observing, and photographing the Angel. I called in two endocrine specialists from Northwestern University and the University of Chicago who also interrogated him and made a case examination of his physical condition. Both were amazed at his co-ordination.

His chest expansion was 7½ inches, one of the largest ever recorded, and certainly a record for my steel tape. The X rays of his head revealed that his pituitary gland, normally the size of a green pea, was as large as a golf ball. Under normal conditions he would have gone blind, and died, when very young. Fortunately in his, the only recorded case, Nature had made allowances for this growth and left a space for the unusual development of the ductless gland.

The Angel proved to be well educated. He was a graduate of the University of Toulouse and spoke, in addition to his mother tongue, Spanish, English, and a little Russian, for his father, a French geologist, had once worked in the Urals.

While I was measuring him, the Angel suddenly asked me, in French, how long I thought he would live. I knew there was no fooling him. The moment newspaper type began to quiver before his eyes, that would be the beginning of the end. I told him, on the basis of our examination, that he might very well live ten years, or even more. That has proved true.

Each Christmas I receive two cards from him, one his professional greeting in green ink, showing him screaming like a savage beast, the other that of a small angel carrying a candle.

One wintry afternoon the wind moaned over the lake and the stone balustrade outside my office windows was covered with snow. I felt irritable. Grabbing a pen, I let loose at the Sinclair

231

Oil Company, whose slogan, "Mellowed a hundred million years," beneath a curiously unrealistic dinosaur and a small human figure, had really got my goat. In my letter to Harry Sinclair I pointed out that any ten-year-old would know that dinosaurs became extinct long before man appeared on the earth and that such advertising tended to destroy the educational function of museums.

Two days later the long-distance operator called from New York. The Sinclair Oil Company was sending a man on the Century to see me. Now I was in deep! Their representative said that by one of those quirks of fate Mr. Sinclair read my letter, and next on the pile was one from the ten-year-old son of a Texan geologist, who substantiated my claims. My suggestions were to keep the excellent slogan, eliminate the little Mr. Milquetoast in the corner, and have relatively accurate dinosaur silhouettes in the ads. I was invited to direct the making of model dinosaurs. Again I was beyond my depth, although I had made some special studies on dinosaurs during the geology courses at Oxford. I recommended a team of specialists as consultants to Messmore and Damon, who eventually made the "Lost World" exhibits for the Chicago and San Francisco fairs. I collected data and photographs of scale models of dinosaurs and, under the direction of the team, work began that resulted in the nationwide ads of the now familiar dinosaur.

My second and last fling at advertising came as the result of a broadcast about the discovery of the Kish wheels on the National Farm and Home Hour. Mr. Alfred Sloan was planning a series of five double-page spreads in the *Post*, *Collier's*, and other magazines, for General Motors, which included such slogans as "The long, long trail from him to you." This would have five illustrations: man against the world, the first wheeled vehicle, Joan of Arc on horseback, a chariot race, and man over horses, i.e., the G.M. cars. Another slogan was "When a Nation sits on a throne," another "In tune with the Universe." I was invited by Mr. Sloan to direct the reconstruction of the first wheeled vehicle and to act as consultant on the series. I worked at night with an artist for a couple of weeks. The sketches were sent to New York, approved by Mr. Sloan, and appeared as part of a $250,000 advertising campaign.

Those who work in museums have strange experiences. One wintry night the guard making the rounds was startled by a blood curdling scream in the Egyptian Hall in the basement. He switched on the lights in the hall and blew his whistle for help. The guards came rushing downstairs. No one was in the hall.

They walked about flashing their lights into the sarcophagi. In one deep case, about 125 feet long, a line of mummies is chronologically arranged. A single door gives access. It is always locked; it was locked on this night. To prevent moths or other pests from destroying the mummies, this case is airtight and always kept poisoned.

One of the guards peered into this case. He shouted, "Look here, this mummy is off its base." One of the naked withered bodies had fallen from its base and was lying face down on the linoleum inside the poisoned case. I studied it carefully the next morning. The base extended at least four inches on each side of the dried skin and bones. No living person could have entered the poisoned case. No vibration in the building could have knocked it off the base without rending the walls, for the museum floats on an island of concrete, there being no hardpan on the filled-in land along the lake front.

There is still no explanation of the scream or of the fallen mummy. It is just one more example of things we cannot explain.

All in all, life that year in Chicago was gay. A great deal of work, and a lot of fun.

THE first season of the Chicago World's Fair terminated in the fall of 1933 and left millions who had enjoyed it clamoring for a repeat performance in 1934. I had not been on an expedition for what seemed a very long time, although the summer trips to Europe had helped break the work of planning and directing the two halls.

These had been exciting years, but after almost seven in succession without any field work, and particularly with no visit to the Near East, my desire to return to that area grew. I continued to work at night on *The Arabs of Central Iraq, Their History, Ethnology and Physical Characters* and also wrote several scientific articles on the excavations at Kish and on the Near East. But there were certain matters, such as the technique of collecting and recording and preparing for publication reports of this nature, that could not be learned from books—just as Uncle Barbour had always said.

Dr. Laufer agreed that it was time for me to return to collect more detailed material on Iraq. He was fully in sympathy with the anthropometric survey. We discussed in detail the collection of data regarding the land and the people—dealing with the geology, geography, hydrography, and meteorology. In addition, there must be a description of the land, the agriculture, and the economic resources, collections of flora and fauna, and of course a detailed study of the population and its distribution, both rural and urban. In short a full anthropogeographical study.

That is why April Fool's Day, 1934, found me unpacking my bags in the "new" wing of the Tigris Palace Hotel in Baghdad, with Chicago, family, friends, and the Fair thousands of miles away.

Richard Martin was my assistant. Dick had had considerable

experience in the Near East as a member of the Oriental Institute Expedition in Syria. He knew some Arabic, was an excellent draftsman and a first-class photographer.

Our hotel rooms were cluttered with equipment—cameras, film, and other photographing equipment, camping equipment, Zeiss glasses, botany presses, killing bottles for insects, milk cans, specimen labels, many small envelopes for the hair samples, a stamping machine, first-aid kit, extra bottles of quinine, and a large horse hypodermic with spare needles for injecting the bellies of snakes or large frogs.

It was delightful to be back in Baghdad again. I called on old friends, including the American Minister, Mr. Paul Knabenshue.

Later in the day I went to pay my respects to the Air Vice-Marshal and found that he had received letters both from my stepfather's friend Lord Londonderry and from the Air Ministry, asking him to assist us through his command. He had returned recently from a brief visit to the marshes east of Amara. He wanted to know if our plans included a study of the all but unknown Marsh Arabs because they appeared to be different from all the other Arabs or Bedouins. I had not planned to study the Muntafiq, since they lived in inaccessible marshes full of malarial mosquitoes. However, the AVM told me that east of Amara there was a wonderful character, the great Sheik Falih as Saihud, Paramount Sheik of the Al bu Muhammad who live in the great marsh known as the Hor al Hawiza which extends for about thirty miles from the edge of the Chahala toward the foothills of Iran. The Vice-Marshal seemed certain we could obtain permission to visit this sheik under police escort.

That evening I saw Winifred Smeaton. Her father was professor of chemistry at the University of Michigan. At this time she was teaching English to the two children of Ali Jaudat, then *Rais Diwan*, the King's Chamberlain, and one of the right-hand advisers of King Faisal of Iraq. Trained under Boas at Columbia, she was a competent physical anthropologist with a good knowledge of classical and colloquial Arabic. Ali Jaudat al Ayubi had very graciously granted her permission to accompany our expedition. We talked over the possibility of visiting the Marsh Arabs. She agreed to the plan and suggested that I meet Mrs.

236

rower, the wife of a British judge in Iraq, who had written
veral books on the land and people of Iraq. Most of the time
Mrs. Drower had used her maiden name, E. S. Stevens, and her
ook, *By Tigris and Euphrates,* is one of the standard works for
at region.

Mrs. Drower readily accepted my invitation to join us. It was
rranged that Miss Smeaton and Mrs. Drower would work among
e women of the Marsh Arabs.

Mr. C. Grice, who had long been adviser to the Minister of
e Interior, issued special instructions, including a permit which
ould entitle us to visit every Liwa in Iraq. Later on, I told him,
e wished to go to the northern areas. First, to the Shammar
edouins, whose Paramount Sheik, Ajil al Yawir, lived just west
Mosul on the main track between Tall Afar and Jebel Sinjar.
We would then like to make a study of some of the "Devil
Worshipers," the Yezidis, who live in the Jebel Sinjar area and
villages around their sanctuary at Sheikh Adi northeast of
osul. Then we would attempt to collect samples of the Kurds in
e four mountain passes of Zakho, Rowandiz, Sulaimaniya, and
qra.

I knew we were asking a great deal, because permission to go
t among the Devil-Worshipers had never before been granted
those who wished to photograph, take blood and hair samples,
amine the teeth, and measure and observe some of the wildest
ople in all of Southwestern Asia. This was a problem from
hich all other anthropologists had shied away and everyone I
lked to warned me against visiting these wild and fanatic people.
s a result, it naturally appealed to me more than any of the
hers, although I did not wish to appear too enthusiastic because
was afraid we might get turned down officially right at the
art.

The next few days were spent in assembling the equipment for
r trip to the marshes east of Amara. The Oriental Institute of
e University of Chicago, through my friend Professor James
. Breasted, had offered assistance. We were loaned a station
agon with Mihran as driver. We were also joined by Showket,
o had been with us on the North Arabian Desert expeditions of

237

1927 and 1928 and had proved his worth as photographer, inter
preter, and general assistant.

Our party was to consist of Dick, Miss Smeaton, Mrs. Drower
Showket, and Mihran. As a result of a story in the Baghda
Times, we were besieged by people applying for jobs, until I re
fused to see any more applicants.

Dick and I were in our hotel rooms checking through the lis
of supplies when in came a bright-faced young man of abou
twenty-five, dressed in a khaki shirt and faded khaki pants. H
said, "My name is Yusuf, sir. I'm sure you will want to take m
on your trip. I am an excellent houseboy." I said, "Yusuf, I hav
just said that I do not wish to take anyone." He opened his brow
eyes wide. "Oh, sir, that does not apply to me, because I am
perfect servant. I was with Captain Guest and he taught me how
to collect plants and insects and to look after him, to make hi
bed, cook, shine his shoes, and do all his personal valeting. Yo
see, I am an Assyrian, absolutely reliable and trustworthy, an
Captain Guest gave me a wonderful letter." He produced from
battered wallet a letter from an Englishman signed Evan Gues
who gave Yusuf a high recommendation.

I said, "But, Yusuf, we can't take you in the car; we don'
have enough room." To which he replied, "All right, sir, I'll hol
onto the running board."

He had such an honest and nice expression, and such a fin
recommendation, that I decided to take a chance on a week'
trial. Immediately he said, "Have you everything ready to put i
the station wagon, because I can start packing that."

He did such a good job of packing and loading the materia
in the car that when with a smile he said, "I think I've done i
pretty well, sir, because now there's room for me in the statio
wagon," it was more than I could resist. So I said, "All righ
Yusuf, you can ride with us, but I reserve the right to send yo
back to Baghdad at any time." I could see that even the shadov
of my doubt hurt his pride.

We drove down to Hilla, where I called on our fat barbe
I hated to pass by my Arab friends at Kish, but we continued o
to Basra and up the other side of Iraq past Al Qurna, where th
Tigris and Euphrates meet. At this point we were supposed t

238

be very close to the Garden of Eden. Black smoke rolled over Eden; we drove by several active brick kilns like those of Sumerian times and later, when Nebuchadnezzar had the large stamped bricks fired for his palaces and temples.

At Amara we were warned not to go west among the Muntafiq, because these Marsh Arabs might well be hostile. However, everyone agreed that to go east with Sheik Falih as Saihud was quite a different matter. The chief of police said he would send a message by two police on horseback at dawn the next morning to inform the sheik of our pending arrival and assign ten police to escort us.

We were joined in Amara by two other assistants. Albert Meymourian had been lent to the expedition from the Department of Agriculture. He was to collect insects. Khedoory Muallim was also lent to us by the Royal College of Medicine as a taxidermist, to prepare the skins of the birds we planned to shoot in the marshes.

That afternoon we drove along the Chahala and reached a bridge where we left the station wagon. Crossing the canal in a large, flat-bottomed boat, we found many willing Arab hands on the other side. These were some of Sheik Falih's people who had been instructed to await our arrival. We walked over to the large reed council house and the sheik stepped out to greet us. I tried to hide my astonishment, but he was the largest Arab I've ever seen, even larger than the barber at Hilla.

Sheik Falih as Saihud, Paramount Sheik of the Al bu Muhammad tribe of Marsh Arabs, must have weighted about 350 pounds. He was at least six feet tall, and very broad in proportion. He wore a white flowing cotton *dishidashe* and a flaming red beard, which we learned later was normally white but was dyed red to give him a virile and youthful appearance. He was very genial and friendly.

In the house were a few wooden seats; these were offered to us. The sheik himself sat on a raised wooden bench, rather like a primitive throne, with his legs crossed—a mammoth of a man. From this seat he ruled his people.

We were quite a crowd, our party and our ten police—a formidable array even for a great sheik to entertain. However, he did not bat an eye at this company that had suddenly de-

239

scended like vultures from the sky. We were to be his guests a
long as we wished to stay. With Showket's help, I explained th
main purpose of our visit; a series of measurements and photo
graphs and scientific observations on the Marsh Arabs, in orde
to include them in *The Anthropology of Iraq*. When I mentione
that I was writing a book he clapped his hands understandingly
A number of stalwart Arabs rushed out and struggled back wit
baskets brimming with a miscellaneous collection of about fiv
hundred books. These were spread in piles on the floor and w
all went down on hands and knees to look at the titles. They wer
all in English. I could not imagine why our host should have thi
medley of books and expressed some surprise over a legal tom
filled with cases of Brown vs. Brown. The sheik evidently coul
not tell whether mine was a question of amazement or astonish
ment at his scholarly attributes, so he said, "Well, of course,
can't read a word anyway, so you can be sure I appreciate thi
library." Then he guffawed.

Sheik Falih then granted us permission to conduct our anthro
pometric survey on his people, and said he would send Shei
Khazaal, his eldest son, with us to show that he approved of ou
work.

Arrangements had been made for us to live in a large wicker
work hut that stood close beside the canal. This was the firs
chance Yusuf had to show his real mettle. By the time we entere
it the camp cots were up, the mosquito bars in place, and the tw
camp cots and nets for the ladies were installed in a hut close by
I knew then and there that he was invaluable, and told him tha
he had a job with our expedition as long as we stayed in Iraq.

Dinner was the usual Arab feast served to us in Sheik Falih
hut. About 120 small dishes were placed on the ground in a long
narrow line about four feet wide. Around these we draped ou
selves on the floor on mats and cushions. Sheik Falih sat on a
enormous cushion. During the first course he leaned across th
table and inquired, "Do you like hunting?" I replied that we ha
brought some shotguns and ammunition in the hope that w
might be able to collect some of the wild fowl in the marshes fo
specimens. The latter part of the sentence did not interest hin
but the fact that I was interested in shooting appealed to hi

240

remendously. He enjoyed cruising about the marshes and always carried a gun, which had been given him by the British government through Sir Percy Cox. He promised to show the weapon to us after dinner.

In the midst of this rather quiet and peaceful scene, aside from the loud sipping and gulping of coffee (the sign of good manners in an Arab household), there was a sudden commotion outside. An Arab came in at unusually high speed for entering the presence of a sheik and whispered something into his ear. The sheik beamed with pleasure and let out a hearty roar. We looked at him rather anxiously and he said very modestly, I thought, for such a great man, "I have just become the father of my hundredth son." This was a reason for rejoicing, and I thought it an occasion I'd never have another opportunity to witness no matter how long I lived or how far I traveled. I sprang to my feet and with the aid of Showket made an impassioned speech of congratulation. Later, when it seemed a little less tactless, I asked the sheik how many daughters he had. He raised his right hand, as large as a ham. "Like the stars in the firmament and the sand on the seashore," he said, adding, "You see, I've had so many wives that I can't possibly remember them all. But I have kept track of my sons."

Then Sheik Falih remembered his gun. This proved to be an 8-gauge shotgun with a special barrel, the longest-barreled fowling piece I've ever seen. Along the barrel was chased in silver a dedication of gratitude from the British government to Sheik Falih for services rendered by him against the Turks during World War I. He said that in the morning he would show us one of his other treasures; only daylight would do it justice.

In our hut Yusuf had everything in perfect order. Setting a police guard outside each hut, we went to sleep. This was not because we were afraid of being attacked but to impress our hosts with our endorsement by the Iraq government.

The next morning I met the sheik's son, Sheik Khazaal, a nice-looking young man about thirty years of age, who was dressed in a very fancy blue and gold *zibun*, with a belt ornamented with two gold tassels. Sheik Khazaal appeared to be bright and energetic, and perfectly willing to help us, although even with

241

Showket's help I could give him no idea what we were trying to do.

A messenger came to say that we were now to see Sheik Falih's second proudest possession—a tricycle also presented to him by the British government "for services rendered." For the demonstration Sheik Falih changed into a most extraordinary costume which consisted of a Prince Albert coat over his white nightgown. On his head he wore a brown *sadara,* the small peakless hat reminiscent of the RAF forage cap. He seemed to think this was the proper costume for the occasion and, walking out in a most dignified manner, was helped onto his tricycle by four men, and sat there posing with his 8-gauge gun pointed into space. It was one of the most remarkable spectacles I've ever witnessed, and although we took several photographs I have never felt justified in using them. They would certainly make this great man appear entirely ridiculous, which was not in the least in character with him.

The sheik explained that he had heard of bicycles and had requested one from the British government. Feeling that he might have an accident on a two-wheeler, they had ordered a reinforced tricycle from Coventry.

Falih made no attempt to pedal the tricycle. After six men had lifted him off with considerable grunting and groaning on his part, the sheik went to his hut and reappeared in Arab robes, which suited him far, far better.

After this eye-opening demonstration we went down to the wharf and found, tied up along the canal, a series of fifty of the very fine handsome pointed *mashahuf,* reminiscent of Venetian gondolas. The Marsh Arabs go everywhere in these boats, which seat four or six persons in addition to the paddlers.

Sheik Khazaal, Showket, and I climbed into a *mashahuf* and two boatmen were soon propelling us out into midstream in the direction of a village. Before leaving I had suggested to Mrs. Drower and Miss Smeaton that they wander around the encampment close to Sheik Falih's house and make friends with the women. Yusuf was busy getting together some of the collecting material for our first trip into the marsh. Meymourian went out with a butterfly net and a cyanide killing bottle to hunt along the banks of the Chahala. Khedoory slept. This turned out to be more or less his constant occupation, for he had malaria.

With Sheik Khazaal as guide, we proceeded downstream to the opposite bank. We were astonished to find some cattle tied to stakes, eating rushes. Sheik Khazaal explained that most of the villages in the marsh were built on piles of reeds which accumulated mud. They could thus really be considered floating islands. Young Sheik Naji of the island seemed to know Sheik Khazaal very well. We were taken to a simple reed-mat hut overlooking the canal. Through Showket, I explained the purpose of our visit and asked his indulgence in allowing us to measure, observe, and photograph some of his tribe. The young sheik complied very willingly, and said that if we could come the next morning about nine o'clock he would line up thirty men so we could begin work. He showed us a reed-mat hut close to his own council house where we could work without interruption.

That afternoon I told Sheik Khazaal that I would like to accompany him in a *mashahuf* with his shotgun and my 12-gauge to see if we could pick off some of the marsh birds. We were out about an hour and a half, fired about fifty shells, and had a very delightful evening. This curried great favor with the Arabs. I was sure that the story of our going shooting with Sheik Khazaal would make us far more popular than we might otherwise have been. These Arabs, like all Arabs in the Near East, appreciate sportsmanship, hunting, skill with rifle or gun above anything else.

Back in camp, I watched Khedoory skin and prepare the birds for specimens, and found to my disappointment that he was almost entirely unskilled in this very delicate procedure. Bird-skinning is a real art. I can remember hearing stories about George K. Cherrie who, even when his hands shook, could skin a humming bird perfectly. However, I felt that if the skins were preserved, no matter how badly, they were probably worth the trouble of remaking when they reached Chicago. This proved to be the case. Although we do not have a very large collection, they are of great importance as coming from such an unusual and rarely collected district.

I found Yusuf with ten children surrounding him, begging him for money and shaking white cloth bags of animals almost in hi face. A table of packing cases was set up and we opened half dozen tin containers; into these were placed the animals. Showke would call out to me as a boy approached, "four beetles, tw scorpions, one lizard," for which I would hand out a couple o small coins. The animals were then put into the respective jar and when the job was over we had at least a hundred. The insect were given to Meymourian for killing, preserving, and packing We had brought boxes for packing specimens, paper, labels, an one of our ten-gallon heavy-duty export milk cans for formalir

That evening found us all pleased with out first day's sporadi collecting. The ladies had also had a very pleasant and talkativ day, and had been well received by the Arab women. Mr Drower had recorded certain speech differences used by th Marsh Arabs. Miss Smeaton was engaged with a woman tatto artist who traveled throughout the marshes, decorating the skin of the women. They were sure that if given more time they coul really produce some valuable new information.

The next day we returned to the small village, where Shei Naji received us. Again we were quite a party—four police, Dic Martin, Showket, Sheik Khazaal, and our equipment, includin the wooden stool for measuring the sitting height. Sheik Na brought into the hut fifteen Marsh Arabs from twenty to thirty five years of age. They were rather mystified by all this equip ment and showed both interest and repugnance. I asked Shei Khazaal and Sheik Naji to be seated so that they could see tha we did not hurt anyone. Then I scanned the faces of the grou squatting on the ground, looking at us none too pleasantly, unt I spotted a youth with four beautiful braids. He was smiling an obviously enjoying the whole procedure.

I asked him politely if he would submit to examination. With out giving him much chance to refuse, I took him by the arm, le him to the stool, sat him down, and recorded the observations o his hair—the form, quality, texture; his eye color; nasal profil number of teeth; occlusion; and general dental condition. Then took the calipers, measured his head, face, nose, and ears, aske him to stand up so I could measure his stature and finally h sitting height. The sequence was done rather deliberately in a unscientific manner, but one I thought would be most conducive to encouraging the others to submit. The first individual is always the hardest.

Collecting so much data in a relatively short time is always difficult. A Bedouin encampment or a village group soon becomes restless. A great deal of information can be obtained in the first flush of curiosity which the arrival of foreigners always arouses. This curiosity and interest turn first to slight distrust, then to resentment. It was good to have Dick along to share the task, for we had to work fast.

I asked the young man if I was hurting him. He smiled and said that he felt fine. The others giggled. He was then led out through a side door to where Dick was waiting to photograph him. The young Arab came back into the room full of smiles.

I asked him if I might take a hair sample, and since he did not refuse—in fact I don't think he knew what I was trying to do—I took the scissors and snipped a few strands from near the top of his head, taking great care not to interfere with his braids. This was put into an envelope, which was given the same number as his measurements, observations, and photographs.

Our study of the first Marsh Arab was completed. This was Individual No. 1 of the series which was later to prove, as the Air Vice-Marshal had predicted, one of the most interesting in all of Iraq.

Our work continued thus for about ten days, until we had a fine series of 221 men. We went from village to village, taking about thirty-five members from each group. After that number I found they became restless and I was afraid we would have some trouble, perhaps an incident, and then the whole thing would be stopped. There is always a very fine line between insistence and starting a riot. I must say that is part of the fun of the whole business for me, and just because it is so difficult I've always enjoyed it. Showket is an expert at handling Iraqis. Together we have had considerable experience. Thus, if I get a look from him indicating I'd better not go on I follow it very rigidly. His judgment in these matters has proved excellent.

While we were collecting our series, Freddie Smeaton was measuring some of the women. This was far more difficult. In

245

fact she was unable to persuade more than a few to submit. However, she and Mrs. Drower were collecting a pile of notes on the folklore, customs, language peculiarities, and the general living conditions of these Marsh Arabs. Albert Meymourian had made a large collection of insects. Khedoory continued to sleep a good part of the time. However, he sang rather well and in the evening he would entertain us with a song which, I think, he had written in collaboration with a famous singer in Baghdad. The opening words were *"Schlonech, Schlonech."* All of us learned the song and he taught it to most of the Arabs, who chanted it very happily in the evening. So he was useful after all.

Yusuf had the animal collection well organized, particularly as to lizards, snakes, frogs, toads, and turtles. He also had begun to collect herbarium specimens. We were all busy, enjoying ourselves, and hard at work.

It was now time for a little recreation. Sheik Falih planned a wild boar hunt. He warned us in advance that this was dangerous; the two ladies were not invited.

Just after breakfast we started out with fifteen boats. The sheik was in his own special *tarrada*, because, being so broad in the beam, and a great ruler, he had to have a boat incomparably stronger, greater, and richer than any other Arab's. His boat was at least thirty-six inches across and had the great distinction of a blue and white striped awning. Sheik Falih, robed in white, was magnificent. Sitting in the stern and paddled by eight men, he was able to outdistance everyone, and certainly looked every inch a king. Sheik Khazaal told me that he had picked two of the best boatmen for me. Both he and his father wanted me to have the first shot since I was the guest of honor.

We were out in an open space, perhaps a mile across, when from behind I could see the *tarrada* with Sheik Falih approaching. He passed us, the sheik sitting with his 8-gauge gun resting on his knee and the striped flaps of his awning folded back. He waved majestically.

We waited for the other boats to pull up into a line. Sheik Falih then announced that the hunt was to begin.

My two boatmen became wildly excited and started off the *mashahuf* with bold, strong strokes in the direction of the tall

246

reeds, which we all entered in an almost West Point line. We were to converge on the upland in a semicircle. We found a narrow lane, down which the boatmen guided the *mashahuf*. Suddenly, right ahead of me, I heard a snorting and stamping. I asked the boatmen if this was a *khanzir* (wild boar). They replied that it was much larger: it was a *gamuss*. Since I had no idea what animal this was, and Showket was nowhere near, I slid off the safety catch and waited as we approached this noise, which sounded like a herd of elephants just ahead.

The boatman behind me tapped me on the back, and I could see that he was terribly excited. My interpretation was that here was a large animal and that I must shoot it. He was using Marsh Arab patois. He might just as well have been speaking double Dutch, as far as I could understand. Suddenly the reeds parted. My finger was on the trigger. I almost fired. Right in front of me I saw the face and horns of a domesticated bull. He looked at me in equal astonishment and snorted. Never have I come closer to shooting the wrong animal. The boatman kept thumping me on the back, for he was terrified that I was going to kill one of their tame water buffaloes.

We turned out of this narrow lane and proceeded through the reeds. I knew that somewhere to my right, probably behind me, was Sheik Falih armed with his great 8-gauge gun with the long barrel, which might thunder into us at any moment. I did not dare stand up, for I was afraid I might capsize the skiff. This would be extremely ignominious and I would probably lose my gun. I crouched low and looked for the clearing, which I felt in my bones must be only a short way ahead.

After two or three minutes of gliding through the reeds the boat suddenly lurched forward and we plunged into a clearing. There, right in front of me, was an island. On top of the trampled reeds were lying two wild boar. They jumped up and plunged into the water with an explosive noise. The boatmen steadied the boat. I took a careful bead on the neck of the wild boar and fired a oo slug. The head of the boar plunged into the water, then came up again, and he churned on into the reeds. There was no time for a second shot.

Now there was tremendous excitement. To my amazement I

saw the towering figure of Sheik Falih standing up in his *tarrada*, supporting himself by means of the striped canopy as he swayed and lurched through the water. In his right hand he held upraised his great gun, and he was shouting orders. The boar was threshing in the reeds a hundred yards ahead. I was anxious to give it the coup-de-grâce but did not dare to go in front of Sheik Falih. From a standing position he raised his gun to fire one shot as the boar, in his death struggle, crossed a lane. My boatmen quickly paddled me over to him. The sheik put out his great hand, beamed with excitement, and shook hands with me. Here was a wonderful team, the foreigner and the sheik killing a magnificent specimen together.

All the boatmen crowded around the boar. Then, led by the stern paddler in my *mashahuf*, they began a chant about the fair-haired, blue-eyed foreigner who had shot the large wild boar with help of Sheik Falih as Saihud. There were just a few lines to this chant, but it was quickly taken up by all the Arabs, who stood up in their boats, their paddles in the air, chanting rhythmically. I was delighted to have made a lucky shot.

I had explained to Sheik Falih that we wanted the skin and skeleton of a boar for our collection. However, the pig is unclean in the eyes of Moslems and under no circumstances will they touch one. As we looked at the huge dead carcass floating beside the tall reeds, I could see that there was some doubt in Sheik Falih's eyes. There was dismay and consternation on the faces of the Arabs, but when Showket and Yusuf moved forward with a rope to tie its legs together, they just stood by and watched. There was some muttering that the beast was unclean and that it was a disgusting sight even for Christians, such as we were, to touch it. But Sheik Falih by this time had sat down in his majestic *tarrada*, and there was nothing they could do about it.

As the boats approached the village the men, women, and children came out to greet us. Sheik Falih asked us to slow down while he went ahead. He stepped ashore. The women and children were driven with sticks back into their huts. Yusuf and six Arabs towed the carcass to the far side of a small hut, standing by itself. Two police mounted guard. Everyone was told to keep away.

Yusuf worked all through the night and by dawn the borax-treated skin was pegged out on the ground, drying. The skull and bones were being cleaned. Later in the day we would be able to pack it in a wooden case, and our first large mammal specimen would be ready for its long journey to Chicago. After photographs and measurements, we estimated that it weighed about 300 pounds.

The next day an Arab brought in four shoats, sand-colored and with broad reddish stripes running along the full length of the back and sides. Yusuf made every effort to keep them alive, but they died on the third morning. Dick injected formalin with the horse hypodermic, sewed them into bags, and put them into the milk can. We now had a male, female, and four shoats. These proved to be among our most important zoological specimens. We still need a further series from the marshes in Iraq to determine whether these animals represent a new subspecies or were just local variants of *Sus scrofa attila*.

On our last afternoon among the Al bu Muhammad Marsh Arabs, Sheik Falih said he wanted to take us out for an evening flight of birds so he could show us something of the range of the magnificent 8-gauge gun given him by Sir Percy Cox. He accepted some shells very gratefully. Sheik Khazaal was in one boat, Showket and I in another, and Sheik Falih in his *tarrada*. He gave us a half hour's start and as we reached the center of a large area of open water surrounded by reed he came up quickly behind us. I shot at a large white pelican (*Pelecanus crispus*), firing six shots. We could hear the bullets pattering on its wings but it merely shook its head and kept on. Sheik Khazaal also opened fired on the same bird, which kept flying. Sheik Falih was about a quarter of a mile away on our right. He was undoubtedly watching what we were doing, although the sides of his canopy were down. Finally this magnificent bird settled on the water at what I estimated to be a hundred yards away from Sheik Falih. The sheik lifted up the left-hand side of his blue and white canopy and fired one shot. The bird fell on its side as if by royal command. The sheik pulled down his canopy and moved on across the open expanse. By this gesture he had scored off both Sheik Khazaal and

249

myself. I shouted a cheer, but there was no response. He just sailed away majestically into the distance.

The only person depressed by this successful shot was Khedoory, who was still sleeping. I gave him some aspirin and the enormous white pelican and suggested that he go to work. That evening he did not sing.

That evening Sheik Falih gave us a farewell banquet at which we sat around and listened to his stories. He was a delightful person, full of charm, with a really great presence. We thanked him in glowing phrases and promised to send some photographs of him and his family, especially of Sheik Khazaal, who was soon to be married.

Among the hundreds of animals collected at nearby Halfayah were sixty-six small pencil-thin snakes which were placed in a pottery vessel with a cheesecloth cover tied firmly in place. On the way back to Amara, I felt a tickle on my chest. When I opened my shirt a snake popped out into Mrs. Drower's lap; the floor of the car was moving with snakes. Everyone screamed. Mihran stopped the station wagon abruptly and we got out fast. Sixty-five snakes were collected and put into a bag, for the pot had smashed over a bump.

One snake was missing. Just as we were about to get back into the station wagon I felt a tickle on my leg, and, shaking my foot, again to my horror, I found another small snake wreathed around the top of my sock. Dick muttered, "That must be a garter snake."

Two Arab women passed by as we were hunting snakes all over the floor of the car. They showed no interest, only a just-those-crazy-foreigners-again look. . . .

In Amara we reorganized our equipment. The plants and insects from the marshes were labeled, catalogued, and packed into tin-lined cases, ready for shipment to Chicago. A tinsmith came to the hotel to solder them. In the meantime Showket had disappeared to his uncle's Abdul Kerim's photographic studio in Baghdad. During the next several days he and Dick Martin developed the negatives, which turned out well. The racial-type photographs, which were to be one of the main features of Part

I, No. 2, of *The Anthropology of Iraq,* proved to be splendid.

From the point of view of the anthropometric survey I was quite satisfied, because in the preceding years with Buxton, and in my own work in 1927–28, I had obtained a representative series from the central part of lower Iraq. Now in 1934 we had a series of the Marsh Arabs from the southeastern corner of Iraq. After we had left Iraq, Freddie Smeaton obtained a series from the hospital in An Nasiriya. Thus we had representative series from the lower part of Iraq, with the single exception of the Muntafiq Marsh Arabs. However, my feeling is that their measurements would not differ from the Al bu Muhammad east of Amara.

Mrs. Drower and Freddie required some time to write up their notes before we started off on another trip. Since I was anxious to cross the desert, following the IPC pipe lines in order to continue the archaeological survey of the North Arabian Desert, Dick, Showket, and I planned to drive to Haifa along the "H" line and then come back along the "T" line to Mosul, where we were to meet Freddie. We obtained permission to stay at the pipeline stations and to arrange to sign for any supplies we might wish to draw. I drove the secondhand Buick, purchased in Baghdad, Mihran the station wagon. By spreading the load on the two cars, since there were on the desert survey only Richard Martin, Showket, Yusuf, Mihran, and myself, we could ride very comfortably.

We drove through Ramadi to Rutba, now a fashionable trans-desert halt. In the morning I heard that there were several Sulubba tents pitched not far away. Since these were the very elusive Sulubba who claim to be descendants of the Crusaders, I was anxious to bring our series up to fifty males. This was difficult because there is usually only one Sulubba family attached to each of the great Bedouin encampments. Driving out to their camp, I was pleased to find there were eight males. I told them they would be paid for their trouble, and they agreed to submit more or less willingly. We set up the equipment right out in the open, for I knew that unless we went to work then and there they would disappear. We also photographed the women and some of the children. Within an hour we had added this small bag of Sulubba to our collection.

While driving across the plain to their tent we had passed a remarkably bad smell. The Sulubba told us that this was a pile of camels killed in reprisal as the result of a raid. We drove along following our noses, finally holding them. Here was a pile of thirty camels in the last stages of decay. However, through all this mass of putrefying flesh sprouted the skulls. I shocked Showket by saying that I wanted as many of the skulls salvaged as possible. We drove back to the Sulubba and explained to them that if they would clean these skulls, and pack them in boxes, I would pay them very liberally. The amount offered was out of all proportion to their normal way of life. They simply could not refuse this golden opportunity, crazy and smelly though it might be. Showket did not like the smell much more than I did, but under his direction four Sulubba scraped such flesh as remained from eighteen skulls and packed them in nine Standard Oil wooden boxes purchased in Rutba Fort. Showket said this was the best he could do. Mihran had a most disagreeable expression on his face and I could see he thought this was about the utter limit in stupidity and nonsense. The covers were nailed onto the boxes and I arranged with a passing truck driver on his way to Baghdad to deliver the cases to the Iraq Museum. These eighteen camel skulls comprise one of the best series from the Arabian Peninsula, though I'm sure Showket and Mihran would never believe it.

At Mosul Freddie was waiting, and with her was Mrs. M. Don Clawson, wife of the genial American dentist for the Iraq Petroleum Company, who was to accompany us in order to obtain teeth smears of the Shammar, for no data of this character were available on these Bedouins.

We were interested in the relationship between diet and disease and here was an opportunity for us to have a trained technician obtain the smears, which were to be sent for analysis to her husband at the American University in Beirut.

I sent a note to Major W. C. F. Wilson, the Political Officer, informing him we had arrived safely and that I would like to see him in the morning. That night we went to bed early, all except Yusuf, who never seemed to need any sleep.

The next morning I found Major and Mrs. Wilson as charming as I had remembered them. They had a very attractive Oriental house with large high ceilings and cool rooms. Over a second cup of coffee we talked about some of the events in the intervening years since we had seen each other. I then spread out the map of northern Iraq.

Before I began Major Wilson said, "I understand that you wish to visit the Shammar Bedouins. I think it would be a very useful piece of work for you to make a study of the physical characteristics of the Shammar. After all, this is the largest tribe in all North Arabia and you will find Sheik Ajil al Yawir a delightful host. I understand you also wish to do a series of Turkomans. That is also fairly simple. Also for your work on the Kurds, I'm entirely in sympathy with that and will see what can be done to help you."

Then his voice grew tense. "But in regard to your unmentioned, and to me the most interesting, project, I have to talk to you in two capacities. I am referring, of course, to your desire to measure, study, and photograph some of the Yezidis. These Devil Worshipers are, as you know, a very deeply religious, bitterly anti-Christian and often fanatical group. No one has ever attempted to measure, photograph, and study them in the manner you propose; it has always been considered too dangerous and difficult. As Political Adviser for the Mosul Liwa, I should be duty-bound to warn you against it, and almost to prevent you from attempting it. However, I realize that the Yezidis are one of the most important groups in all Southwestern Asia, and as your friend and adviser I urge you to do what you can to obtain a series of studies because I can realize at once their great importance and significance. But I not only warn you, I order you to be extremely careful."

I then broke the news that Freddie Smeaton was going to try to measure Yezidi women. He said that this would redouble his anxiety during our stay in Sinjar. I promised to telephone him, wherever we might be, every night.

In the morning the equipment was brought down to the cars. As usual a small crowd of onlookers outside the hotel watched the proceedings with avid interest. The collecting equipment was put in accessible positions in the station wagon. The two large milk cans were roped to the sides of the Buick.

We drove almost due west and toward sunset we approached the black tents of the northern Shammar on a beautiful grassy plain. This was Ain Tellawi, and it was easy to distinguish the great tent of Sheik Ajil with its twelve tentpoles—the largest black tent I had ever seen in North Arabia.

We drove up to the barking of dozens of savage-looking dogs and the stares of numerous men, women, and children. We got out of the car, and as my feet touched the ground I looked up. Before me stood one of the most magnificent Arabs I've ever seen. He was almost six feet tall, large in frame, but not fat. He had a short black beard and heavy black eyebrows. His dark brown eyes were kindly. Sheik Ajil al Yawir, Paramount Sheik of the northern Shammar, stepped forward and extended his right hand. I had never heard such a rich, beautiful voice. Here was a real sheik of the desert, the first I had ever seen. He radiated power, justice, and strength. He shook hands with Freddie, who talked to him in voluble Arabic, which pleased him after my halting efforts. He then ushered us into his tent. We sat in the usual circle around the glowing hearth. Coffeepots were arranged on the floor. On the fire stood a blackened, spouted vessel in which water was just coming to the boil.

As if from nowhere appeared a tall Bedouin. He was standing with his face turned away from me, looking toward the doorway, and immediately behind the sheik. As he turned his face I was a little astonished to see that he had a great deal of Negroid blood. This was Umbarak, the sheik's personal slave and bodyguard. He was a magnificent specimen with his ebony skin, finely chiseled features, and glistening white teeth. His broad nose and everted lips added a certain majestic and dignified quality to his face.

Umbarak was the chief of Sheik Ajil's household and head of his 150 Negro emissaries. We learned that these Negroes were the tax collectors and personal representatives of the sheik. If a member of his immediate family was not sent on a mission, the sheik sent one of these Negro members of his household and bodyguard. Umbarak made the coffee beside the sheik. The sheik himself filled the first handleless cup; this was then poured onto the ground as a tribute to an ancient custom. The sheik then drank a little himself, sipping it in the noisy Bedouin fashion; this is also an ancient custom, to show that there is no poison in the coffee-pot.

The sheik then stood up and, followed closely by Umbarak, strode out of the tent, asking us to see the quarters where he had installed us. We found three white Indian bell tents, thirty feet across, set up in our honor as guests of the sheik. We were welcome to stay as long as we wished. Then, putting his hand over his heart, he bowed and swept away.

The largest tent was assigned to Freddie and Mrs. Clawson. Dick and I took the next largest, the other being for Mihran and Showket. Two hours later everything was in good shape, the mosquito nets up, the beds made, and the equipment stored in its proper place. It was now time for the evening meal. We washed and changed clothes and made ourselves as presentable as possible. Another tent had been put between the sheik's and our tents as a dining room. On the floor were about two hundred small dishes. The sheik was washing his hands. A Negro stood beside a large spouted ewer of copper, holding a towel and a bar of Palmolive soap in his hand. Each guest was given the soap, and water from the ewer was poured over his hands as he rubbed them. Inside the tent, I sat on Sheik Ajil's right, Freddie on his left. Showket sat beside me so that we could carry on some kind of conversation with the sheik.

In the center of the floor, between piles of boiled rice, were broiled split chickens. The small dishes contained sour milk called *laban*, gravy of different kinds, and cucumbers. Umbarak leaned over my right shoulder, tore a chicken to pieces, and spread the white meat in strips on the rice before me. This is a signal mark of honor, done for the honored guest. Then, having seen that I had the best pieces of chicken, he walked behind the sheik and did the same thing for him. Sheik Ajil began to eat. We followed because we were hungry and we knew it was good manners to show appreciation of the food, both by eating large quantities rapidly and by making as much noise as possible. This includes belching either during or after the meal—a sure sign of stomach satisfaction. The correct method of eating rice is to grab a handful covered with gravy and squeeze it until it becomes about the size of a golf ball, then ram it noisily into the mouth with a sucking gesture. The chicken was delicious, the rice equally good. Despite the insistent urging of our host, the time arrived when we became incapable of swallowing even one more sliver of white meat. With profuse apology for lack of appetite, we struggled to our feet and washed our faces and hands, a very necessary performance. We then followed the sheik into his big black tent, where coffee and tea were again served.

After several rounds of coffee Freddie and Mrs. Clawson asked permission to be excused. Dick followed suit. The sheik, Showket, and I were left alone beside the glowing camel-dung fire in the black tent. Sheik Ajil, stirring the red embers, said, "Now will you please tell me the purpose of your visit and how best I can help you?"

I had found from experience that the best procedure was for me to have each sentence translated by Showket. First I apologized for my poor Arabic. Then I outlined my twenty-five-year project, to which the sheik muttered a faint "*Mashallah!*" I told him about the prehistoric dwellers in the North Arabian Desert. Sheik Ajil interrupted to ask if these were the Beni Hilal (Sons of the Moon), who are believed by Bedouins to be their oldest ancestors. I told him that the people who had used the stone implements in the high desert were the direct ancestors of the Beni Hilal. Since he had never heard that they might have even older ancestors, he was deeply interested. Then I came to our story, how we had returned to Iraq with the object of taking photographs, measurements, observations, hair samples, blood samples, and other anthropometric data so that we could establish the average type for the northern Shammar Bedouins.

With gallant Bedouin hospitality, Sheik Ajil invited us to be his guests for as long as we wished, even for the rest of our lives.

I had a burning desire to ask him for a list of the tribes and subtribes of the Shammar, but this did not seem the opportune moment, and since he had given his permission for the main purpose of our trip I thought I'd better leave well enough alone.

Sheik Ajil told us that for two days we could not leave the neighborhood of the camp, because he considered it wisest to send out Negro messengers to inform each group of surrounding Bedouin tents that we foreigners were his guests.

256

13. Dr. Hugo Obermaier, the author, and Abbé Henri Breuil outside famous Altamira Cave in northern Spain. ©c. n. h. m.

14. Limestone caves in the Laguna de la Janda in southern Spain. ©c. n. h. m.

15. Neanderthal family, about 50,000 years ago, at Devil's Tower rock shelter on Gibraltar. The dioramas on this page are in Hall C in Field Museum.

16. Aurignacian artist, about 30,000 years ago, blowing the powdered red ocher through leg bone of a reindeer in Gargas Cave, France.

© C. N. H. M.

© C. N. H. M.

17. Bronze statue by Malvina Hoffman of Shilluk warrior from the Upper White Nile. These figures are among the Races of Mankind in Field Museum.

18. Bronze statue by Malvina Hoffman of a graceful dancing girl of the Sara tribe from the Lake Chad District of French Equatorial Africa.

19. Skulls from beehive tomb in southwestern Sinai. From left to right, the author, Mrs. William Terry, and Wendell Phillips.

20. Author measuring skull from beehive tomb in Sinai with Mrs. William Terry as recorder. Our Bedouin guide is in center beside Walter Thompson. These crania proved to belong to the basic long-headed Mediterranean type.

21. Bedouin being measured by author in southwestern Sinai during University of California African Expedition. The Bedouins of Sinai belong to the basic Mediterranean stock. They were friendly but shy about being examined or photographed.

22. Author pointing to Nabataean inscription from the Roman period in Wadi Feiran, southwestern Sinai. University of California African Ex tion, 1947–48.

23. Brick pavement and large circular drain excavated in Babylonian leve Kish. This city drain of 550 B.C. was thirty feet deep and two feet wide

Bedouin parks camel and asks for cigarettes from members of the University of California African Expedition in Wadi Feiran, southwestern Sinai.

Fluted cone towers and other Yezidi tombs at Sheikh Adi, northeastern Iraq.

26. Hedgehog looking at his toy cousin used as a rattle by a Babylonian child about 550 B.C. Excavated at Kish by Field Museum-Oxford Expedition.

27. Copper frog with limestone eyes on copper rod bearing five lotus leaves around ceremonial stone bowl. This stood in a Sumerian temple alcove at Kish.

28. Modern lawn coaster. Note similarity to the ancient holder (27) from Kish.

He then offered to send a favorite nephew as our escort and guide. At this point conversation ended. Showket and I walked back to our tent, which was shining in the moonlight like a white pearl set in a black ocean. I reported to Dick and Freddie the result of our conversation. We were all delighted. We were now on the way to achieving one of the main objectives of our expedition.

The nephew, a handsome young man with a fine black beard, spoke a very clear Bedouin Arabic. The sheik introduced him while patting him affectionately on the shoulder. To ingratiate myself with this pleasant young man, and also to pass the time pleasantly, I suggested that he and I go out that afternoon to shoot sandgrouse. Just before sunset we drove back to camp with a dozen birds. Showket was waiting for me. Something was wrong. The sheik had left a request for me to come to his tent as soon as I returned. I found the great sheik pacing up and down. His favorite son Ahmed, aged six, was very sick. He begged me to give the boy some medicine out of the black metal Burroughs, Wellcome box emblazoned with the red cross. I refused politely, but asked to see him. We were led into a tent, past weeping, wailing women, to the bedside. Kneeling beside the pale figure with closed eyes was the mother, distraught with grief and kissing his waxlike hand.

Flies crawled on Ahmed's face, around his still mouth and closed eyelids. Sheik Ajil again begged for medicine. I explained that I was not qualified to render anything more than simple first aid.

The sheik, the most powerful man in all North Arabia, was now as worried as any ordinary father. He wanted to do anything that might save his son. I heard myself giving orders: clear the smallest guest tent; set up a camp bed with a mosquito bar; move Ahmed at once into this bed; place guards on each tent flap and admit no one but the sheik and myself.

Fifteen minutes later Ahmed was asleep in the quiet tent with no flies to bother him. His mother and the other women were wailing in the distance. Umbarak had to keep them back with a stick.

I took Ahmed's temperature twice. Both times it read 105 degrees. I had never seen that on a thermometer before. He was panting for breath and complained of shooting pains below his left shoulder blade. Beads of perspiration trickled down his burning forehead. His father held his clammy hand. Gone was the dignity of bearing, the power radiated by a great leader. Here was a father fearful of losing his son. I bathed Ahmed's forehead and wrists with water.

Sheik Ajil took me outside. "Please, please save my favorite son," he pleaded.

I had an idea. I asked the sheik to drive me to the nearest telephone—twenty miles across the desert—so that I could get advice from a British medical officer. The sheik ripped out some orders. Alone he said farewell to his dying boy.

Soon we were bumping along in an open car, Sheik Ajil at the wheel and I beside him. In the back were crowded six of the Negro bodyguard. Just before nine o'clock we drove through the unlighted streets of Tall Afar with its mud-brick houses silhouetted against the rising full moon. The telephone office was closed. Two men with rifles were dispatched to bring the frightened operator from his house nearby. His hand shook so that he could scarcely unlock the door. Exactly at nine o'clock a light flashed on the primitive switchboard. I asked for Dr. T. H. McLeod, a Scotch doctor whom I had never met. The operator replied, as in all small communities: "Dr. McLeod is not at home. He is dining out. I will connect you."

Dr. McLeod listened to my description of Ahmed's condition and tentative diagnosis that he had pneumonia in the left lung. His advice was to give him no medicine, keep him quiet, and wait his arrival at ten o'clock in the morning. He repeated this in Arabic to Sheik Ajil, who again pleaded for some medicine from my black box. Dr. McLeod was adamant.

We drove back in the full moonlight across the plain. Sheik Ajil looked deeply worried. Evidently he thought talk would relieve the strain and he broke the silence. He said slowly, in Arabic: "I understand that in America large companies are run either by a sheik and his son or by a council of sheiks. Which is the better system?"

He explained that he was going to buy a new car. He under-

258

stood that the people who made the Chevrolet were a council of sheiks, but that there was another company with a sheik and his son who made a rival car (the Ford). I replied that if the sheik were a great man like himself, then there was no question as to which was the best procedure. He seemed pleased with the reply; it was exactly what he wanted to hear.

As we neared the camp I could see he was becoming tenser. He gripped the wheel in a ferocious manner, stared straight ahead, and said nothing.

Showket came forward as the Chevrolet bumped to a stop. "The child is better." Sheik Ajil hurried to the tent. The child was breathing more easily. I put my hand on his forehead; it was clammy but cool. His temperature was subnormal. My look of relief must have been mirrored in my eyes. Yusuf and I changed the damp sheets and gave the boy a sponge bath. Sheik Ajil stood motionless and expressionless. He wanted to stay, but the quieter the boy remained, the better. As he took my right hand in both of his, I could see the deep gratitude in his eyes. A few minutes later one of the bodyguards appeared at the tent flap. Wrapping his *abba* around his head, he crouched on the ground, his camel stick in his right hand. I asked Showket to arrange with Yusuf to divide the night watch.

It was now nearly midnight. Even the dogs around the camp were quiet. The Shammar Bedouins were asleep. Their sheik was tossing on his bed, grateful to Allah, but still anxious. I sat on a packing case beside this young boy who might be destined one day to be the Paramount Sheik of the Northern Shammar, the successor to Sheik Ajil. Supposing the boy should have a relapse? The minutes dragged. The boy stirred restlessly and moaned for water. He tried to gulp it savagely but I only allowed him three sips and laid him down gently, and within a few seconds he was sound asleep.

I tried to read by the oil lamp. It was hard to concentrate, for the boy kept turning and moaning and groaning. Yusuf was asleep in a blanket. The sheik's bodyguard was also sound asleep, his knees up and his head resting on them. At that moment I felt very alone. The moon was now almost down, the camp silent. I think I must have dozed a little because I awoke with a start, wondering where I was, to hear the boy moaning and calling again for water.

Just before six o'clock Sheik Ajil came into the tent. He could see by my expression that the boy was no worse. Since he wanted to do something for his son, I suggested that he take the next watch. Yusuf, the miraculous, had ready a cup of steaming coffee, followed by breakfast.

News had spread quickly around the camp that the boy was better. There was a suppressed feeling of jubilation in the air. I suggested to the sheik that the boy's mother be allowed to sit beside him but not disturb him. Her veiled and blue-robed figure hurried toward the white tent.

About nine o'clock Dr. and Mrs. McLeod drove up. Never have complete strangers been more welcome. Dr. McLeod confirmed my diagnosis of pneumonia in the left lung. The crisis was over. He prescribed rest and no medicine. He told the sheik that unless there was a relapse, which would of course be Allah's will, the boy would within a week or two be able to begin to play with the other children.

Two evenings later the sheik said he would like to give me a present to remember this occasion. He would not hear of my refusal. He offered me a white riding camel, an Arab brood mare, or anything he owned. My request surprised him; a complete list of the tribes and subtribes of the Northern Shammar.

"You were told to ask that by a woman."

"Yes, she was white-haired with keen, blue eyes. Miss Gertrude Bell. It was just as you guessed."

"Bint Bell tried many times to wheedle that list out of me. So did Lawrence and many others."

Sheik Ajil had guessed correctly. Gertrude Bell had suggested that if the opportunity ever arose I should attempt to obtain the list. I waited. Sheik Ajil suddenly stood up and in a loud voice cried: "It shall be done. For you it shall be done." Then, saying good night rather brusquely, but with a smile, he walked out of the tent. During the rest of our visit no mention was made of this request.

During this time, under his patronage and with his young nephew beside me, we visited the nearby encampments of the Shammar. Each night when we returned to our tents my heart sang, for we were achieving our objective; we were on our way to obtaining the first Bedouin series. We had every reason to believe that the Shammar were of the purest Bedouin stock, and therefore most important for comparison with the Baij Bedouins living between the Tigris and Euphrates rivers.

When Sheik Ajil saw how well we were received among his people, he said he saw no reason why Freddie should not try to measure some of the women. I could hardly wait to tell Freddie, knowing how thrilled she would be. She obtained data on 129 Shammar tribeswomen, a real triumph.

Dick and I wound up with a net of 299 males, which was pretty close to our objective of 300. Many times at Harvard, and later when we were recalculating the figures, I wished we had reached 300, because it would have made it much easier for the statistical calculations.

In about two weeks we finished our series. There was never any question in our minds that we were overstaying our welcome, because Sheik Ajil was always so kind and friendly and hospitable. However, I felt it was time to move on.

We said good-by to Sheik Ajil, and as we drove away from Ain Tellawi, among those who shouted and cheered most loudly was his little son Ahmed, now completely recovered.

Four weeks later, outside the Tigris Palace Hotel in Baghdad, a young Bedouin with four shoulder-length braids beside his face squatted, waiting. He handed me a large envelope. Inside were two sheets with the tribal lists, in Arabic, that had been promised me by Sheik Ajil. This was published in 1951 by the Peabody Museum (Harvard) in *The Anthropology of Iraq*, Part II, No. 1, where our studies on the Shammar appeared.

As for Ahmed, that fine young Bedouin is now studying political economy in Ohio.

IT WAS not without apprehension that we drove into Balad Sinjar.

This large hill town with its 25,000 Devil Worshipers, the Yezidis, guards the western approach of Iraq, forty miles from the Syrian frontier. We had met ugly looks on our way, and in one village a Yezidi sheik told us with flashing eyes: "No person in my village shall be photographed or touched by Christians."

The main street wound between flat-roofed mud houses. The Iraqi flag was flying over a mud building, the office of the *Muttasarif*. Showket and I went in to pay our respects and to find out if there were any messages from Major Wilson. There were, but these did not make us any more welcome to the *muttasarif*.

Here was another official who could benefit but little by our visit, but should something go wrong he would be held responsible. The *muttasarif* listened, then he said angrily: "You know, I only have to serve less than another year in office before I am retired with a pension. I then have one great ambition—to go to Paris for one final fling before I die. Should any difficulties arise with you, I might not receive my pension. These Yezidis are difficult people. They hate Christians in such a way that it is hard for you to understand. I am very worried about your visit."

I asked him to send for the chief of the Yezidis, so that I could talk to him with Showket as interpreter. The *muttasarif* shrugged his shoulders, but he sent for the sheik. We waited over cups of coffee. Each minute went by slowly.

There was a rustling outside the door and in swept a tall, thin, hawk-nosed, keen-eyed Yezidi sheik, the head of all the Yezidis in Balad Sinjar. He was about six feet tall, but his white, conical hat made him look a giant. His long, stringy hair hung down beside his eyes, which were fiercely resentful. Looking at him in that darkened room, I had a feeling of awe. The sheik bowed his head slowly in my direction, and only slightly to the *muttasarif*. He then crossed his arms and fixed his glance firmly on me.

I was thankful then that Showket spoke Kurdish. I told him that this was probably the most difficult translating assignment he had ever had. Our success or failure among the Yezidis depended on our convincing this man that he should allow us to measure some of his people. The sheik was glaring maliciously at us as we talked in a language which he could not understand. I asked Showket if he was sure that the sheik understood his Kurdish translation, and he said, "Oh yes, but he just doesn't want to say anything. He thinks I'm a Christian, too, and that makes it doubly worse." Incidentally, Showket *was* a Christian; the sheik had guessed right.

I apologized through Showket for my lack of knowledge of Arabic, but I told the sheik firmly that I had come a long way and that I had admired his people from afar, that I wished to have the privilege of studying some of his men. A faint glint of kindliness passed across his face.

"How many of my men do you wish?"

"Fifty."

"When would you like them?"

"As soon as the sun comes up in the morning."

"Where?"

"At the schoolhouse just at the top of the hill."

He shook hands with me. As he grasped my hand firmly he said, "They will be there. I will be there." He bowed, put his right hand on his heart, bowed again to the *muttasarif*, and strode out of the door. I was speechless.

I sent Showket running after him to say that I would make a contribution of five Iraqi dinars to his church. In this part of the world it is always safe to make a contribution to a church, never to an individual. The *muttasarif's* expression was really extraordinary. He looked as though he had seen a ghost as he turned to me. "I have no idea what came over that man. It's incredible. Of course he was just saying that to be polite. These wild people are always being polite, even to the ones they detest the most, the

264

Christians. He said yes, but tomorrow morning no one will be there."

I did not believe that. When the man shook hands with me and put his hand on his heart, I had been convinced he was telling me the truth.

We were billeted in the mayor's headquarters, in two rooms about fifteen feet square on each side of a long passage which ended in a heavy door. Outside two police with fixed bayonets stood on duty. The two cars were placed in the courtyard where the soldiers were quartered.

While the unpacking was proceeding, Showket and I walked out in the street to talk to some of the Yezidis and see if they really were as unfriendly as people had led us to believe. We found the older people not very polite but the children, like all children in that part of the world, were friendly and anxious to make some money. I told the children with Showket's help that if they would collect some animals for us the next day we would pay them at sundown. We gave them a list of the animals: snakes, lizards, scorpions, beetles, bats, insects of all kinds, frogs, toads— in fact any animal that was alive. Word spread quickly through the town that we would pay for animals, particularly snakes.

I could feel tenseness in the air though I tried to tell myself this must be mental. I have rarely felt this sensation so acutely before or since. In our rooms the corned-beef hash and Boston beans were heating over the small Primus stove. Coffee was boiling on the other hissing Primus. The inevitable cans of Bartlett pears were opened. From the market Yusuf had bought some *chupatties*. It had been a long day and we had missed luncheon except for bread and dates as we drove along. We sat around a table in the little room, which served on other occasions as the mayor's council chamber.

During dinner there was a knock on the door and one of the sentries announced a visitor. I suggested that he come in immediately, since I did not want to offend anyone in this already unpleasant and hostile atmosphere. In came a bent old man, with his gnarled fingers grasping a stick. He looked up as he approached our Coleman lamps and I saw he had no nose, only two holes: an obvious case of syphilis. The old man said fiercely that he understood we wished to buy some snakes. As he spoke, he unwrapped his outer garment, lifted a horned viper from between his belt and skin, and threw it not too gently on the ground. He then reached in with his left hand and produced the mate. Writhing on the concrete floor were two horned vipers, each about four feet long. No deadlier animal exists in Southwestern Asia. I recognized the type at once because it was the same snake whose cousins I had found near Bayir Wells in 1928.

The physical features of the old man were far more repulsive than the worst of the horned vipers. His price was one dinar apiece, roughly ten dollars. That was more than I could stand. It would set a very bad precedent if we paid anything like that for a couple of snakes in Iraq. I told him I had never paid any price like that for a snake anywhere in the world. The old man was very angry. Without a word he put them back in their warm spot between his skin and his belt. Halfway to the door he turned and muttered something about the "dirty *Nasrani* [*Christians*]." As I returned to my cold beans, I knew that we had made a real enemy.

We were drinking coffee when there was more noise outside. The other sentry shouted that a second snake charmer had arrived to sell two fine snakes. This proved to be a tall, rather handsome-looking Yezidi, quite gracious in his manner, who produced two horned vipers similar to the first pair. He asked one dinar for both. Even though we were paying an unusually high price for them, I knew that Karl Schmidt would like a pair from a new area for comparison with those from Bayir Wells. I told the Yezidi that I would buy them providing he held them while Dick injected them with the hypodermic. This is always a difficult and dangerous job, particularly with such an animal as the horned viper. Dick put on his heavy leather gloves, got out the horse syringe and the formalin. The snake charmer held the snakes while they were injected with concentrated formalin. Then they were sewn up in cheesecloth, labeled, and dropped into a milk can standing just outside our door. In the can were the other specimens we had collected along the way.

The snake charmer was very polite and, when I handed him

the dinar, seemed quite pleased. He shook hands with me, bowing as he went out the door.

We prepared everything for the morning. I explained to everyone that we were on the most difficult assignment we had ever attempted, and if there were any unpleasantness of any kind we might have to stop work within a few seconds. The *muttasarif* had arranged for Freddie to visit some Yezidi women at seven o'clock in the morning. She planned to take her instruments in case she could persuade some of them to submit to measurement. Since there was no information at all on the physical characteristics of the Yezidi women, it was important to obtain even a small series. As I lay on an army cot, I felt that we had passed a fairly successful day, although I did not like to remember the incident of the noseless man. Dogs barked incessantly. Although there was not much sound of human activity in Balad Sinjar, there was a certain feeling of restlessness in the air. I felt it very strongly. I figured it was probably just my imagination and nerves because of terrible stories of uprisings I'd been told about the fanatical Devil Worshipers.

We had breakfast and were ready before sunrise. I had taken the precaution of asking the local doctor to meet us at the school at dawn with his blood-sampling equipment. It is always advisable to have a local doctor perform this very ticklish operation. Freddie was to be taken with an escort provided by the *muttasarif* to the Yezidi women. I arranged that she should send me a message every hour. I would try to send coffee and sandwiches to her during the day at intervals, but all of this was uncertain because of the difficulties under which we were working.

A gray light was just appearing in the east as our little cavalcade started slowly up the hill to the schoolhouse. The *muttasarif*, who knew these people far better than I, had been certain no one would be there. As we came to the top I could see a tall figure dressed in white, standing before the building. He stepped forward. This was the sheik of the Yezidis. Placing his right hand over his heart, he shook hands with me and said, "My men are ready." Behind him, ranged along the wall, were fifty wild-looking Yezidis. I could hardly believe my eyes. Getting ready was a matter of only three minutes. In another room Showket

267

was helping Dick set up the camera and sheet. The young doctor, who had been trained at the American University in Beirut, was there. I told him the only thing for him to do was to take a sample of the blood of each person and encourage him to enter the next room where his photograph would be taken. Yusuf was to take the hair samples.

I invited the sheik to sit on a chair to watch the first patient. He sat on the chair, but I could see he was not used to it and was very uncomfortable. However, I could not put him in the inferior position of sitting on the ground while Dick and I were on our feet. The Yezidis glared with a fine degree of hostility as I passed down the line. I picked the only one who gave me a faint smile, a young man who seemed to think it was quite amusing to be standing there in the early dawn to be mauled around by a "dirty Christian." I therefore took him by the hand and led him to the slaughter. He was fairly willing. I then asked the man at the head of the line, who also was not too unfriendly-looking, to step to the door so he could see exactly what I did to the first person. It is well for the individual to be studied next to see exactly what is going to happen; he is much less frightened and nervous. There were just the four of us in the room—the sheik, the young man I was measuring, the other Yezidi, and I.

The young man sat down. I then checked on the form the color of his skin, eyes, and hair, and other observations. I asked if he was tattooed. He replied with some horror that his body was pure, without marks. He was not very pleased when I lifted off the conical hat. I then put the calipers on his head length; he said it was not causing any pain. The sheik was fascinated. I took the measurements as carefully as I could. I also told him that I did not need his name, because I was interested in the average rather than the individual. Both he and the sheik seemed very relieved.

I had completed eleven of the fifty Yezidis when I heard a vague commotion outside.

I had a premonition that something bad was going to happen. I had that sinking feeling in the pit of the stomach as I stepped to the door to look across the small courtyard. The sheik was looking over my shoulder. There, right in front of us, were the two snake charmers. The Yezidi subjects were crowded around them.

It was quite clear what they were saying, although I could not understand Kurdish. The younger man, from whom I'd bought the two horned vipers the night before, was saying to the noseless old man something along these lines: "You know why the foreigner bought my snakes. He bought them because I'm a real snake charmer. He didn't buy your snakes because he knew you were just a fake. Why, you wouldn't even dare pick up this snake."

At this point the younger man took a horned viper from that favorite storage place between his skin and his belt, and threw it on the courtyard in front of the man with no nose. The old man bent down and, baring his left arm, seized the horned viper and let it twist around his forearm with the words, "I am not afraid of any snake. I am the greatest snake charmer in Balad Sinjar. Every snake is a blood brother to me."

The viper was coiling itself around his left forearm. I saw the horned viper sink its teeth into the old man's wrist. The old man was perfectly calm. As soon as the snake had finished chewing his wrist he relaxed his hold and gave him back, quite calmly, to the owner. Here was the crisis. I shouted to everyone to stop work and pack up as quickly as possible. There was scrambling inside, and within thirty seconds the suitcases were packed and everything ready to be moved. The doctor rushed out of his tiny room. I told him what had happened. The subject had disappeared. The sheik had disappeared. We were left there with the old man, who was taking it all very calmly. We rushed him against his will to the dispensary down the hill where the doctor kept his drugs and medicines. I knew that if this old man died I would be held responsible, since I had started the snake buying. A length of piano wire was pulled as tight as possible around the left upper arm. The old man looked very sick to me. His eyes were glazing but he kept repeating that no snake could hurt him because he was a blood brother to all of them. The doctor said resignedly that the old man had undoubtedly been bitten many times before, and must have built up some immunity. He could do nothing more except incise the wound. The old man had sucked the poison but it was clear that some had passed up his arm under the tourniquet. The glands of the armpit were swelling. The old man kept asking to be left alone, so we released him and went back to our quarters.

Here we found the *muttasarif*. Bad news travels fast, especially in the East. His eyes flashed with anger, for he had predicted something of this kind would happen. I went down with him to his office as calmly as possible, to report the incident by telephone to Major Wilson. I talked as coherently as I could but I'm sure there was a tremor in my voice because I was very upset and worried about what would happen next. Major Wilson was also worried. He said we should stay in our quarters until further notice and in any case to telephone him again that night. For our protection, and particularly because we had Freddie Smeaton with us, he would send two armored cars to wait about ten miles out of Balad Sinjar. A plane would stand by in Mosul airport. He said to remain calm and to leave Balad Sinjar as soon as possible, but under no circumstances should we attempt to drive hurriedly, for rocks would be thrown or bullets fired.

As I hung up, Showket came panting in to tell me that Freddie had returned to our quarters. It was a great relief to have her safe. We spent the rest of that day sitting around in our rooms, anxious as to what might happen. This uneasiness was everywhere in the air. We stayed indoors because every now and then a rock would sail into the compound. The *muttasarif* sent word that the story had spread all over Balad Sinjar and we were held responsible. That night while we were having supper and trying to be as unconcerned as possible under the circumstances—by this time we had ten sentries with fixed bayonets outside our door—a sentry announced that there was a young man to see us. He was about twenty-two and not at all attractive. His surly, sneering expression, added to his costume and shaggy wild hair, gave him the appearance of a good and true worshiper of Satan. The son of the noseless snake charmer, he wanted to know how much I was going to give him in gold for his father's life, for he was dying from snakebite. I said I could see no reason why we should give them any gold because the whole thing had happened not directly as my responsibility; we had only been incidental. He said he had never done any work in his life and never expected to, that he and his two brothers had always lived off the father's earnings as the

270

best snake charmer in all Balad Sinjar. I lost my temper and told him that I hoped he would leave at once because I thought it was time he did some work. In any event I was not going to give him any money for his father, to whom I sent my cordial and hopeful greetings.

He went out almost as angry as his father had been when he left twenty-four hours before. Somehow we got through that night and the next day. We did not dare leave. I telephoned Major Wilson night and morning. The armored cars were just outside Balad Sinjar. The airplane crew was standing by. However, I hoped nothing would happen to cause us to ask for armed force because this would undoubtedly lead to a serious incident. The next night there was another commotion outside the door. To my utter delight, in came the old man, assisted by one of his sons, not the one who had come the day before. The old man came with some hesitation to where I was standing. I shook hands with him. He said that he felt much better. From time to time, he said, since he was a young man, flies (by which he meant mosquitoes) had landed on him and bitten him. After that he would feel sick for a day or two. He was trying to describe malaria. He said he now felt much better, but the day before his head had been buzzing as a result of having been bitten by an insect. Neither of us made any reference to the snake.

I was never so glad to see anyone as I was this old noseless man. He looked as though he had been out on a real bender, but was otherwise none the worse for wear. After we had talked for a minute he lighted one of my cigarettes and said, "By the way, I have two fine snakes. Would you care to buy them? They are one dinar apiece."

Without too much show of excitement I replied, "Yes, I'll be very glad to buy them if you will help us kill them." His son held them while Dick injected their yellow bellies. I paid him the two dinars. Then, as a signal mark of favor, I said that I hoped he would do me the honor of driving beside me in my car next morning. His face lit up because, of course, he had never been in an automobile. I told him if he would come about eight o'clock in the morning I would give him a ride. He could sit beside me and wave to his friends as we drove along.

This had occurred to me as the best insurance that no one would stone us.

On the telephone Major Wilson confirmed this as a good idea. The *muttasarif* was far too angry to think anything I thought was a good idea. However, it looked as though we were going to leave, so that cheered him up.

The measurements in Balad Sinjar had been very few: eleven men, three women. We had some zoological and botanical specimens. One afternoon we had climbed up Jebel Sinjar to visit a small cave, where we had found some broken pottery and some late Roman lamps. Since this cave had been used by shepherds there was little of archaeological interest on the surface.

The cars were packed and we were ready, but there was no sign of the old man and his son. Major Wilson had arranged for us to meet the armored cars sometime before nine o'clock on the plain. By this time there was a crowd of fifty Devil Worshipers standing around the cars, looking far from friendly.

Just as we were giving up hope the noseless old man came around the corner, supported by his two sons. The Devil Worshipers were indeed surprised to see the old man turn up. He gave me a rather wan but certainly a pleasant smile and he shook hands. I helped him into the front seat with all the showmanship I could muster. The crowd milled around the car. I told Mihran to keep about thirty feet behind the Buick. The *muttasarif* arrived to see us off. I had taken the precaution of having the top put down, so that everyone could see the old man riding beside me. I then suggested that he could get a better view by sitting up on the back of the front seat. As soon as I got him into this position I started the motor. The crowd separated as we moved at five miles an hour through them; the station wagon followed. I told the old man he had better wave to his sons, because this was an experience few of them could ever hope to achieve. He waved to them and shouted. We were now surrounded by wild-looking Yezidis whose mood had changed from anger to wonder. The old man was waving like royalty and the crowd waved back as we crept toward the top of the hill and the city limits.

As we started to rise over the crest, another group came up the side street. They did not see the old man, and began to shout some

272

unpleasant remarks about Christians. The old man waved to them. They could not believe that the snake charmer they had known all their lives was riding in the car with the Christians. We continued very slowly on down the hill toward the last house. Just as we arrived there, some children tumbled out of another side street. They apparently did not know the old man or care; all they saw were the foreigners leaving. I saw them pick up stones. Accelerating in second gear, the Buick shot forward in a cloud of dust. The station wagon with Mihran at the wheel was close behind. However, a handful of rocks hit the back of the station wagon. We flew down the plain. About a quarter of a mile below the town, I got out and explained to the old man that one of the rituals of auto riding for the first time is that the car takes you only a certain distance and then you have to walk back on your feet, just to be sure that the car has carried you the distance in such a short time. The old man nodded his head knowingly and said of course he would like to walk back just to see how wonderful the car had been. As we shook hands, I gave him a small present of money. I looked back to see the old man walking slowly back toward the village. Running out to greet him was a crowd of boys and children, eager to hear his story.

Then at high speed we raced to the hill and over the plain. The two armored cars were waiting a half hour's drive away, their crews watching anxiously for us with field glasses. It was a great relief to see them and to speed on to the nearest telephone to let Major Wilson know we were safely out of Balad Sinjar.

Our next trip was to Aqra at the foothills of the mountains of Kurdistan. There we met the president of the Jaf, the great tribe which migrates across the Iranian-Iraq frontier to summer and winter quarters. In one of the wadis just below Aqra we found some stone implements indicating that prehistoric man in an early phase of culture had passed that way.

The drive from Mosul to the famous Ruwandiz gorge is the finest scenery in Iraq. The road, cut into the limestone, winds below towering cliffs with the stream bed far below; a dramatic contrast to the hot, dry, wind-swept Mesopotamian plain.

At Ruwandiz the *muttasarif* was expecting our arrival. There

273

was an invitation from the British vice-consul at nearby Diana-Ruwandiz to be his guests. He had a bungalow on a small, flat area surrounded by high mountains. The Ruwandiz area is magnificent, one of the most beautiful spots I have ever seen. We planned to measure and observe some of the people in that area, for our third sample in Kurdistan. We were now following the plan suggested by Sir Arthur Keith and Buxton. We measured a small series in Ruwandiz and Diana-Ruwandiz. However, I required about thirty moré Kurds because I felt that we should have a representative sample from this very important area. It was quite clear that this pass was one of the main lines of migration from Central Asia into the great North Arabian Desert. The *muttasarif* had us come to the prison next morning. Here, surrounded by barbed wire, we studied thirty Kurds, dressed in white, all wearing criminal insignia and some in chains.

Taking the stature of a man with a rifle and fixed bayonet behind his back was quite an unusual piece of anthropometric technique. I measured and observed them rapidly because there was no question of the subjects being unco-operative, although they glared at me in a savage manner. Later in Kirkuk prison I measured another series.

The chief of police told us about a huge cave, high on Jebel Baradost, a mountain towering above the gorge. With an escort of twelve armed Kurds, we walked for five hours up to the cave, whose entrance proved hard to find. On the lookout above I collected typologically Aurignacian stone implements. Inside the cave I spent five hours. In one narrow passage I found, under a layer of stalagmite, animal long bones split characteristically to remove the marrow, and some large teeth later identified as of *Sivatherium*, a huge giraffe thought to have become extinct before man roamed this region. I hoped to return to Jebel Baradost to sink some trial trenches inside the entrance.

We collected geological, zoological, and botanical specimens in this wonderful valley. It was hard for us to believe that the fertile plain surrounded by high mountains, and the great gorge so many miles from where we were, were really in Iraq. It seemed a land of enchantment, far away from the great alluvial plain which used to be called Mesopotamia.

At Sulaimaniya we obtained a small representative series of Kurds, but they were not too anxious to submit. While not openly hostile, there was a certain unfriendliness. Consequently, after we had done the best we could, we returned via Kirkuk to Baghdad.

Now I faced a sad task. I had received instructions from Dr. Laufer before leaving Chicago to return to Kish to salvage what could be taken away from the camp. No further funds were to be appropriated and it seemed doubtful that our excavations would ever be continued. Dick, Showket, and I drove down, with the Buick and the station wagon filled with packing cases, newspapers, and cotton wool. Once again the barber of Hilla, dressed in his form-fitting pale blue *zibun* with gold thread around the shoulders, was very pleased to see me. A three-ton truck joined us. We paused at Tell Inghara. It was indeed a sorry sight. It was July and the heat was oppressive. The wind was blowing and the dust was in a cloud over the trench, which had now become partly filled in. The Temple of Nabonidus was still standing, but the depth of "Y" trench was no longer discernible. The walls had collapsed and the leveling process had begun in earnest. We drove past Mound "W," where the trenches were almost obliterated, and across to the camp, which now looked very deserted. There was no sign of Mahdi or Juad to greet us, no Samsiluna to run out and bark, no Shemu and his caracul hat. In the sunlight on the southern slope of Tell el Uhaimir two foxes were playing. They felt perfectly safe—as indeed they were.

We opened the door of the Kish Museum. Before us were some pottery, a few skulls, and some objects which had not been packed at the conclusion of the previous season owing to a shortage of packing cases. Some of the Arabs from *Hajji* Miniehil's village saw us drive up and came running over the plain, hoping we were going to start work again.

Apart from the antiquities, which were my principal concern, the only other thing of any value was the equipment. We had about a hundred large shovels, which Watelin had imported from France, a few picks, and some tools for repairing the car and for general work around the camp. These were all packed into the station wagon and given later to the Oriental Institute Expedition in Baghdad in return for their many kindnesses.

By nightfall of the second day we were ready to abandon the camp. I felt very depressed because I had spent such pleasant times at Kish and had hoped that it might be possible to continue work there; my own hunch was that underneath the great Temple of Nabonidus lay the royal tombs, brimful of treasures, richer than those excavated by Sir Leonard Woolley at Ur of the Chaldees. I realized fully that this was a large engineering task, that many thousands of cubic feet of earth, including the massive Nebuchadnezzar bricks, would have to be moved onto the plain without finding one single object for science or exhibition. However, with a giant bulldozer we could soon reach the lower levels. As the years go by, I doubt if that dream will ever come true.

Finally everything of value had been salvaged. We gave *Hajji* Miniehil some of the chairs and tables. The day had been sad for us all and I was glad when it was over.

In Baghdad we prepared everything for shipment to Chicago. We had twenty-four gallons of animals packed tightly into cans, about ten thousand plants, several dozen bags of geological specimens and about an equal number of bags of archaeological objects from the desert, mainly consisting of flint implements and flakes. One entire side of the Iraq Museum courtyard was stacked with our efforts.

While we were packing the animals and dried skulls for shipment to Chicago, Dr. Walter P. Kennedy very kindly allowed us to use one of his rooms in the Royal College of Medicine. Here we had kept the animals in alcohol, and some of the dried skulls collected during the expedition, including the splendid series of evil-smelling camel skulls from near Rutba.

Winifred Smeaton was planning to attend the meeting of the British Association for the Advancement of Science in England during August. I was worried about the ten thousand negatives and all the original anthropometric forms we had in our hotel room in Baghdad. I asked Freddie if she would take these with her to London, where I could pick them up later. I called on Norman Nairn to explain to him the value of these two suitcases, and he assured me that they would receive special care and attention.

When she left Baghdad two days later I went down to the Nairn terminus with the two suitcases, saw them loaded onto the big bus, and said good-by to Freddie, asking her to leave them for me at Claridge's in London, marked "To Await Arrival." Early in the morning the big Nairn bus started for Damascus, carrying Freddie and the main records of all our work in Iraq. I hated to let those things out of my sight, but it seemed stupid, since I was going to Russia, to try to lug them across Iran and the Soviet Union to London. Crossing frontiers with negatives is not a simple matter.

I returned to the hotel to prepare to leave Iraq, two days from then. I was walking down the street from the Ottoman Bank to our hotel when an Englishman wearing a sun helmet and shorts stopped me on the street. He asked me whether I'd ever seen him before and whether I knew his name. I replied that I did not know him. He then said, "If you will make no attempt to find out who I am, I will tell you something of interest to you."

I nodded assent. He came very close and spoke in a low voice: "I have been interested in the work you are doing in Iraq. I recommend that you get all your specimens and records out of Iraq as fast as possible."

As I walked back to the hotel I quickened my step. I had no idea what this unknown friend meant, but if there really was some risk involved, I'd better act fast.

In the hotel I ran up the stairs. I explained to Dick and Showket that I felt we should get the things out at once, although I did not tell them my reason, because I was sure they would think I had been touched by the sun. I asked Showket to tell the station manager of the Iraq Railways that I needed a small boxcar on the train leaving at five o'clock that night for Basra.

I telephoned the chief of police to inform him that I was sending the results of our expedition to Basra that night and would appreciate it if he would send two police on the train to guard the specimens until they were put on board the boat. Showket found out that the next ship for the United States left on the second morning, which would just give us time. I telegraphed the chief of the port at Basra, asking him to reserve space for the shipment which would arrive the following night. I also told him I was

277

sending Showket with the train so he could supervise the loading onto the vessel. In the meantime Showket had located four carpenters and a dozen porters, unusually strong-backed Kurds, who could carry on their backs anything from a plank fifteen feet long to a piano. I called the Iraq Museum to tell them the cases had to leave that night for Basra. Within six hours we had all that material packed, labeled, addressed, and actually on the train, guarded by two soldiers and by Showket. I felt a great load off my mind.

That night we dined with the American Minister. The Knabenshues were delightful hosts. About midnight we said good night and drove back to the hotel. It was a stifling hot night. For sleeping there were two alternatives: in a room with the large punkah fan moving overhead, or the roof. Dick always slept in his room, but I preferred the roof. Yusuf spread his bedroll somewhere on the roof near my camp cot .

Suddenly I was awakened by Yusuf. "Hurry, quick, sir, Mr. Martin's room on fire." I rushed down the flight of stairs leading to the passageway. Smoke was pouring up this staircase. With Yusuf at my heels I ran to the end of the passageway. Dick's room was across this open space, which was glass-enclosed. The blue billowing smoke was choking and blinding—it was the burning panchromatic developer and other film equipment. By that time one of the hotel boys was there, and I told him to call the fire department and rouse the management—then I shouted in Yusuf's ear that I was going to find Dick. I told him that if I did not come out of the smoke within thirty seconds he must come in and pull me out. In moments of crisis Yusuf's eyes would shine and I knew that I could trust him even with my life. The smoke was almost choking me, even with a wet towel over my nose and mouth. I rushed forward to find Dick's room was a furnace. My first idea was to break through the door to see if he was inside. But I could hear nothing, which meant that he was either dead or not there. I ran back to Yusuf, to my bedroom. By this time there was a crowd of hotel boys standing at the entrance. I told them that they must form a chain, and on no account must anyone be left in there more than thirty seconds. They seemed to understand, and I rushed into the room and found Dick lying unconscious on his face on my bed. With the help of Yusuf and one of the hotel

278

boys we carried him down to the courtyard. I had to go back into my room. I went back with Yusuf. We picked up my brief case, found my passport, expedition papers, and a pile of receipts. I carried these to safety and put them on the step beside Dick, who was sitting up. I then went back for the fourth time. When I came out I was grabbed by one of the British authorities, who had turned up at the scene of the fire. He told me rather forcibly that I couldn't go back any more. I told him I was going right back again, and that neither he nor anyone else could stop me. He was not in the least angry, seeing my condition. He said calmly, "First I suggest that you look at what you brought out of the room the last time." I looked down, and to my amazement found that all I had salvaged from the inferno were my Zeiss glasses and a copy of *The New Yorker*.

After breakfast I had a splitting headache. My eyes were bloodshot. Dick was coughing badly, and his eyes were almost closed.

I was told that there were two men to see me. They said they owned the hotel and that Dick had started the fire by smoking in bed. They planned to sue me for the damages. This was indeed a blow, especially since we were planning to leave for Iran the next day. If we had to pay damages for the fire and water in the hotel, it would probably take up every available cent and we would be unable to go to Iran or to the Soviet Union—or even home to Chicago!

My head was splitting. Instead of fighting with the pair, I told them to bring their estimates later in the day. I went up to a room and lay with an ice pack over my eyes and forehead. An idea came. I got up, had a bath, shaved and dressed in clean white clothes, and drove to the power station of the city of Baghdad. Here I found a delightful red-faced Scot, mopping his brow as he worked. Of course he knew about the fire; everyone in Baghdad knew about the fire. I asked him if the engineer who had made the report to him that morning about the fire was present, as I had to talk to him right away. When he came I asked him if he would sign a statement, based on his examination, that the fire could have been started by faulty electric wiring.

He typed it, on the power company's stationery, and signed it. Armed with this most precious of documents, I returned to the hotel. We had finished luncheon when I was told the two men were outside, with two friends. As I came out on the balcony their eyes were shining with the certainty of triumph.

They had a sheet of paper on which were the estimates for restoring that section of the hotel, and assured me that one thousand pounds would cover the damages.

Instead of showing any dismay at the figure, I asked all four of them to sign the amount of damages, with their full names and addresses. They signed, with looks of triumph.

Then I told them I would not give them one cent, because my lawsuit would be for far more than this paltry sum; I would sue the four of them on the basis of their signatures on the document in front of me, not only for damages to all of our equipment, but also for endangering our lives with faulty wiring.

One demanded: "Do you have any authority for your statement that the wiring is faulty?" I produced the paper from my pocket. "Here is a statement signed by the engineer of the Light and Power Company of Baghdad, who made an inspection of the damage caused by your fire."

They returned presently with a magnificent document which absolved us from all and every shade of responsibility for the fire.

As I went up to my smoke-stained room that night I realized that this had been a pretty close call. Not only might the shipment have been ruined, but we might have lost all our photographic supplies and all our photographs and records. If I had not sent the two suitcases containing the ten thousand negatives and the forms and other data with Freddie to London, these would have been in Dick's room. They might not have been burned but in any case would have been ruined by the water, for his room was about eight inches deep in black, viscid liquid.

I went to sleep thanking our unknown benefactor in the street, whom I never saw again. I have no idea who he was. I do not know whether he had a hunch that something was going to happen, or whether he knew someone was going to try to smoke us out, literally. In any event the shipment sailed from Basra, the suitcases were on their way to London, our part in the 1934 anthropometric survey of Iraq was over, and we could leave for Iran.

AT THE END of July we started the long upward drive from Baghdad to the plateau of Iran (Persia). Four of us were crowded into the customarily overloaded car, Dick, Yusuf, and I, and with us, by special permission of the Director-General of Health in Baghdad, our good-humored and delightful friend, Dr. Walter P. Kennedy of the Royal College of Medicine.

Up to this year, 1934, there had been few if any recorded series of blood groups between the Jordan Valley and India. Sir Arthur Keith had suggested that we start the blood grouping in Iraq and Dr. Kennedy had begun this work that was to grow to such proportions within the next two decades.

This was an exciting and beautiful journey, for Persia is another of those magic-sounding names. We neared Teheran, and behind the ancient capital, like a tremendous painted backdrop, rose the chain of Elburz Mountains, dominated by the extinct, snow-capped volcano of 18,600-foot Mount Demavand.

I was armed with the usual letters and official requests to smooth our way. As a result, after a wait of only five days, a special permit, called a *javaz*, was issued by the authorities at Teheran, permitting the members of our expedition to travel to and from Shiraz, to conduct anthropometric studies whenever convenient, collect geographical, zoological, and botanical specimens, and take photographs.

We left Teheran through a beautiful city gate ornamented with blue and white tile, and took the main road to the south. Outside the city and covering many acres, brick kilns belched black smoke. Near these was a large cemetery where women clad in black or dark clothes were wailing over the graves. At intervals the dusty road was blocked by funeral processions, each followed by hosts of mourners. Long lines of camels with tinkling

281

bells padded to and from the great markets, and swarms of small donkeys plodded, all but hidden under bulky loads.

After a few miles we took a road to the left to the site of the ancient city of Rayy, the ancient Rhages, covering miles of the plain. This onetime capital of the great Parthian Empire was being excavated by the joint expedition of the University Museum of Philadelphia and the Boston Museum of Fine Arts, under the direction of Dr. Erich F. Schmidt.

Erich welcomed us to this ruined city that once had held a million souls. Rayy in its prime must have been splendid.

It was an inspiring experience to walk between mounds and outcropping walls, below the ruined but still impressive acropolis, and re-create in one's mind the Rayy that about A.D. 700 had been a world center of culture and commerce. In 1220 the invasion of the Mongols under Genghis Khan brought Rayy, after a magnificent struggle, to a dramatic end. Naizmudin, a Mohammedan author, a native of Rayy who escaped the Mongolian destruction of the city, wrote:

"Could there well be worse slaughter than there was in Rhei (Rayy), where I, wretched as I am, was born and bred, where the whole population of 500,000 souls was either butchered or carried into slavery?"

Years later, when I saw the ruins of Berlin, I remembered Rayy, another city razed because of the dictatorial ambitions of a single man.

Eight hours later we reached Isfahan, probably the Aspadana of Ptolemy, a city that had survived the pillage of Genghis Khan and the massacre of its population by Tamerlane. Shah Abbas made it the capital of the Persian Empire.

We drove through the great central square, known as the Maidan-i-Shah, flanked with buildings, its focal point the splendid, domed royal mosque, patterned brightly with tile. At either end of the Maidan are two marble columns which once served as goal posts for the game called *chugan*, originated by the Persians, which has become our polo.

Next morning I called on the governor and explained our intention of doing anthropometric work along the road between Isfahan and Shiraz. It was plain that the suggestion made him uneasy, and it occurred to me that he might object less if we worked in the ghetto. He seemed relieved and spoke to Mr. Joseph Cohen of the Alliance Israélite, who readily agreed to assist us.

According to tradition, the Isfahan ghetto has existed about twenty-five hundred years. The Jews claim that they founded Isfahan, that the city was built by captives brought there by Nebuchadnezzar after he had taken Jerusalem. It is related that the Jews brought earth and water from Jerusalem and made tests wherever they went; in only one place did the earth and water correspond to the samples from Jerusalem. They founded a colony and named it Al-Yehudiyah, later Isfahan.

Now, we were told, about four thousand Jews lived in the ghetto of Isfahan. At seven in the morning of August 20, 1934, we drove in an ancient carriage about a mile from the Maidan, then, turning off the wide main street, we passed under an arch and down a narrowing street to a dark, forbidding doorway.

We worked all that sweltering day in the *madresseh* (school), and between sunrise and sunset measured one hundred individuals. The racial characteristics of this secluded community in central Iran had persisted to a marked degree, although there was considerable variation. It was quite clear from the study, and particularly from the examination of the photographs later, that this group of Jews in Isfahan was homogeneous only in religion. I knew that the Jews are a people, not a race, for there are Caucasian, Negro, and Mongolian Jews.

We were delighted to have this good series for comparison with the Jews of Iraq, other parts of Southwestern Asia, and the Caucasus to the north.

But when I spoke of extending the survey the governor became evasive, saying he would have to take the matter up with the chief of police and other authorities. It was clear that he did not recommend our working on any other groups in Isfahan.

I began instead to collect useful plants and drugs for Dr. Laufer, and information concerning their uses in the treatment of diseases. This quest led me through the twisting lanes of Isfahan to the home of Mirza Muhammed Ali Khan, a ninety-five-year-old doctor I had met in the market one afternoon walking beside his small donkey, which was loaded down with herbs. His father, several uncles, and a grandfather had been medical practitioners. In his house were two large volumes of prescriptions handwritten by his grandfather a hundred years before. I longed to microfilm every page for study, but we were running short of film. With the aid of Juda Rabbi Hedvat I wrote down many of his prescriptions for headaches and other ills, and how the herbs should be prepared and applied. Since we were guests I could offer no gift, only thank him for his courtesy. A report by Dr. David Hooper, introducing these medical notes, was published by Field Museum.

I had hoped to be able to study some of the workmen attached to the Oriental Institute Expedition working at Persepolis. Walter Kennedy was returning to Baghdad, for he could not remain longer away from his job. This left us with a serious transportation problem. Then Katherine and Myron Smith, with whom we had been staying, generously offered to drive us in their station wagon to Persepolis.

We set out with Katherine and Myron on the front seat, Dick, Yusuf, and I on the jump seats, and stacked behind us, all our supplies and equipment with Mimi, the Smiths' Alsatian, on top, barking and happily slobbering down our necks. It was exceptionally hot. Fifteen miles out we passed a track leading between dog-toothed hills to the Bakhtiari country. I looked after it longingly. How I hated to pass that turn! Sixteen years later I was to visit the Bakhtiari tents and study them.

In the village of Mahyar we saw a tower with ibex horns circling the top as ornamentation, "to give the building strength"; we had seen similar decoration on the Yezidi buildings in Iraqi Kurdistan. We passed fine examples of the famous "pigeon towers," several stories high, built solely for these birds. About fifty miles south of Isfahan we left the Bakhtiari country for that of the Qashqai.

Here the station wagon burned out a bearing, with the result that we spent three fascinating days in the ancient town of Yezd-i-Khast, which perches on the summit of a great mound with its mud-brick houses, supported on stiltlike poles, silhouetted against the sky. It is typical of central Iran, with narrow, rambling streets, small roofed bazaars, and mud dwellings. And still, this humble

284

place may be the site of the fabulous gardens and summerhouses of Semiramis. . . .

The women wore black or blue and veiled their faces at our approach; some wore rings through the nasal alae. No houris here. The men wore white or striped robes falling to the ground and, by official ruling, the *pahlavi*, a black hat with a broad peak.

Despite the general reluctance of the people to submit to anthropometric study, we were able by means of friendly coercion and some bribery to measure and photograph forty-eight men, with Katherine acting as recorder.

It was impossible to obtain statistical information. When asked as to relatives, living or dead, many refused to answer. But when a hundred children swarmed around us begging money, I paid them to bring animals and the result was a splendid collection of lizards and frogs for Karl Schmidt in Chicago. He has published a report on them in the scientific papers of Field Museum.

We received assistance in every way from Ismail Javadi, chief of police, who enjoyed comfortable quarters in the upper rooms of an ancient caravansary. Dick made a ground-floor plan of this centuries-old "hotel" and took photographs of an inscription over the door which is plainly visible from the main road, in large Kufic letters carved into faïence mosaic. It still seems strange to me that no one else appears to have photographed and copied this inscription which, upon being published by Dr. Richard Ettinghausen, was hailed as a minor "scoop."

In Arabic, it reads:

"Allah who is blessed and exalted said: the holiness of Ali son of Abu Talib is my fortress; whoever enters my fortress is in safety from my [hell] fire."

It is signed by Muhammad Riza al Imami al Isfahani, the well-known calligrapher, who died in 1659 or 1660.

Early in the morning of August 24 Myron returned from Isfahan with the missing car part, having jolted there and back in a truck. Twelve hours later, hot, desert-worn, and disheveled, we drove through the sentries gate of Persepolis and pulled up outside the former harem. Here we were welcomed by Dr. Ernst Herzfeld, the director of the Oriental Institute Expedition from the University of Chicago. We were shown at once to cool rooms where each bed had mosquito netting hung from the ceiling; hot baths were run, and within an hour we were bathed and changed and felt almost human again. After a delicious dinner with the staff in the sumptuous dining room of the erstwhile harem, we went to our wonderful beds and slept until the sun was high over the plain.

That morning we walked around the ruins of Persepolis—also Takht-i-Jamshid—with Donald McCown, one of the members of the expedition. At Kish we had found almost no stone. Here everything was of stone: standing columns, some with their capitals still in place, and the magnificent double stairway discovered by Herzfeld, with its procession of figures carved in the black rock.

About three miles away, on the other side of the Pulvar River, carved into a perpendicular rock which rises 250 feet above the plain, we were shown the Tombs of the Kings, including that of Darius. Below the rock is a square tower, the so-called "Kaaba of Zoroaster," and two rude but impressive fire altars. Fragments of coarse pottery are strewn on these hills. Dominating one mound stands a solitary stone pillar, probably the symbol of some ancient phallic ritual. Not far away are the ruins of Pasargadae, with palaces and temples that belonged to Cyrus the Great; his great white stone temple-like tomb stands impressively nearby, with graffiti and inscriptions on every surface, and brass trinkets and offerings thereon.

Beyond this lies the great stone terrace or platform known as the Throne of Solomon, and below on the plain, to the south, the tall monolith bearing the famous trilingual inscription, "I am Cyrus, the King, the Achaemenian."

From Persepolis to Shiraz is about thirty miles. The first view of the capital, with its many minarets rising out of the valley, is breath-takingly beautiful. It is noted for its gardens and Mosque of Jomeh and the tomb of the two poets, Saadi and Hafiz. Here we were the guests of Bill Browne, whose survey party I had accompanied into the North Arabian Desert in 1928, and his charming wife Myra. We were quite a crowd to stay the night,

286

and Mrs. Smith was given the only guest room. The rest of us unrolled our beds on the porch.

In the morning we went sight-seeing. The Shiraz market place was the usual one, with dozens of small boys who spoke broken English trying to become our guides. One twelve-year-old, who seemed a little brighter than the others, asked me if I would like to see Siah Kuh. I knew this meant "Man Mountain," so I asked the youngster, Hafiz by name, to jump on the running board and guide us to Siah Kuh. He pointed the way into a narrow street, where an immense wicker chair stood before a house. Beside it, on the wall, was a mark that must have been nearly nine feet high. I asked where Siah Kuh was, since I had never seen a giant in this part of the world, and was interested in obtaining his measurements and photographs. Our guide and interpreter said this was impossible, the Man Mountain was far away. "Far away" may mean ten blocks, five miles, or five hundred miles, so I pressed the point. Hafiz smiled and shook his head. "He is very far away. He is in a country of which you have probably never heard. He is in a country called New York."

I learned later that Siah Kuh was traveling with a circus. Frequently, when attending circuses in the United States, I have made inquiries but have never been lucky enough to meet him. I would like to tell him I had seen his chair in a back street of Shiraz.

We visited the western shores of Daryacheh-i-Maharlu, about ten miles southeast of Shiraz. Around it, numerous low hills contained rock shelters eroded from the limestone. On several mounds we found plain and painted sherds similar to those excavated by Herzfeld at the "Neolithic" village near Persepolis and to pottery found by Sir Aurel Stein in southeastern Iran. The shore line was white and crystalline with salt; in places we drove between orchards of pomegranates tended by primitive-looking people who seemed darker in complexion and unlike those of Kinareh near Persepolis. We found rock shelters, dark with smoke from shepherds' fires, and hundreds of small flints, many of them microlithic. We all felt trial trenches should be sunk here. Someday . . .

Everywhere we were finding evidence to substantiate the

theory, shared with Sir Arthur Keith and the Abbé Breuil, that prehistoric man had passed through southern Iran, coming into Europe and Africa from Central Asia.

It was quite clear I had obtained only the smallest smattering of information regarding the physical characters of the modern inhabitants of Iran. However, it was a beginning and, when analyzed and studied, would serve as a good starting point for the real anthropometric survey. Actually this was just about what happened, and when my *Contributions to the Anthropology of Iran* was published by Field Museum in 1939, I had compiled everything available concerning the ancient and modern inhabitants of the area.

Our work in Iran was now at an end and, back in Persepolis, we put together the specimens we had collected, prepared them for shipment to Chicago, arranged our notes and accounts, and made final plans for the last leg of our trip, a visit to the Soviet Union.

Our shipment of specimens for Field Museum looked small indeed compared to the big pile now on the high seas between Basra and New York. However, we had collected some useful plants and drugs, a few animals, and our anthropometric and allied data. I was sure that Karl Schmidt would be delighted with the fine collection of lizards, snakes, scorpions, beetles, and other small animals which were eventually put into cases awaiting shipment to Chicago, and temporarily lodged in the Teheran Museum.

We found the American Minister in Teheran, Mr. William H. Hornibrook, leading a very discouraged life. It appeared that when offered the appointment to Iran he had thought glowingly of beautiful Persian gardens where, with his wife and attractive daughter, he could live in idyllic peace. However, termites had just been discovered in the rafters of the legation and as a result the American Minister was living in a kind of glorified outhouse which was far from comfortable.

Mr. Hornibrook, despite his worries under the flood of cables coming from Washington and the shattered peace of his Persian dream garden, was most kind and facilitated our work in every way. Thanks to a letter of introduction from him to the Soviet Minister in Shimran, the summer residence of most of the big shots in Teheran, after almost no delay at all (which I found later was pretty close to a miracle) the visas for entrance to the Soviet Union were duly applied to our passports.

Now came a sad moment—saying good-by to the faithful Yusuf. We had not been separated since that day in Baghdad when he asked for a job and I had nearly turned him away. It was impossible to tell him how grateful I was for all the work he had done, particularly all the work he had not been asked to do. He had been faithful, cheerful, understanding in every way.

Early one morning, for the last time he helped us load the taxi with our equipment, by then reduced to suitcases, bedrolls, and a duffel bag. Dick and I shook hands with him, patted him on the back, and tried to put into words our gratitude. It was the only time I had ever seen him break down. I had given him his bus ticket back to Baghdad and a present which I had suggested he use as vacation money before taking another job. I was sure his old place would be open with the Agricultural Experimental Station outside Baghdad. He promised to spend most of his Fridays, his only holidays, collecting zoological and botanical specimens to send me in Chicago.

Tears rolled down his cheeks as we drove away.

We corresponded over the years, though during the war I had no word from Yusuf. In 1946 I had a letter from him saying he had survived the war in Iraq. As I write this, in a cottage overlooking the Atlantic in York Harbor, Maine, Yusuf brings coffee at intervals and keeps the household serene. I have just bought him a lamp for his bed table. Its base is a large pink Kewpie doll, and Yusuf is delighted. Someday he will show his children in Baghdad this souvenir from America.

We reached Resht to find a strong wind blowing. The Soviet steamer to Baku was to sail at five. Dick and I were the only passengers. Our passports, particularly the Soviet visas, were carefully scrutinized by the Soviet authorities. Bells clanged, whistles blew, a few Persian onlookers waved from the shore. Propellers churned but the wind was so strong that we were unable to leave the dock.

Finally the ship worked slowly against the wind into the channel. At once she began to pitch and roll violently. I was about to be as violently seasick, so I told Dick I would probably not see him again during the voyage but would be grateful if he came below every few hours to see if I was still alive. He seemed disappointed I was to miss dinner; he was sure we would have caviar, since the Caspian is the home of caviar. . . . I rushed below to the cold, damp, dimly lit bunk area assigned to us and crawled weakly into my bedroll.

I have crossed the Atlantic thirty-eight times by boat and been in some pretty bad storms, but never have I experienced such pitching and tossing. Our cabin was a bunk area intended to hold perhaps thirty cots; in it my bedroll slid from wall to wall to bring me up against solid matter with a bang. My thoughts clung feebly to memories of service on the great liners, where one pushed a bell that brought a sympathetic nurse. Sometimes a sailor walked through the cabin. Sometimes Dick came down. I would wave, each time a little more feebly.

After many agonizing centuries, the pitching seemed to lessen. Were my senses of perception growing dimmer? I wondered. No, it was really true, and we must be inside the Baku breakwater. I staggered up on deck to find we were in calm water, approaching the port city. A group of Russians loitering on the dock pointed to us excitedly; evidently we looked different from most passengers who came to Baku.

Dick, relatively fresh and tidy, was standing in the bow. He told me happily of the wonderful night he had had: a comical man with a thick black beard had entertained him with songs and stories all through the night. They had shared several excellent bottles of vodka through the storm. "There's my friend now," said Dick, pointing to a wild-looking bearded man behind the wheel.

"That man," I pointed out bitterly, "is the captain of this ship. While he was entertaining you, we might all have sunk to the bottom."

Still in a huff, I tottered down the gangplank onto Soviet soil.

290

IN THE customs shed at Baku an almost microscopic survey was made of our passports. Our visit to the Soviet Union, I carefully explained, was solely for the purpose of visiting museums and proceeding via the Caucasus through Moscow to Leningrad. We were not ordinary tourists. We were to be given special facilities and the Soviet travel organization, Intourist, had been ordered to help us. We had each paid for thirty days' travel and accommodations in advance, second class, at eight dollars a day. Our Intourist guide, who had met us at the dock, looked like a competent schoolteacher.

The customs officer kept glancing at a letter in Russian on top of his desk; I could read the letterhead, "Akademiia Nauk, Moskva [Academy of Sciences, Moscow]." My statements through the Intourist interpreter and the letter appeared to check, for at length, with papers stamped, we were privileged to open our bags, whereupon our clothes, scientific instruments, cameras, and other equipment were laid bare along the counter. It is astonishing how much space one's luggage can cover if it is the only luggage in the customs shed and everyone wants to look at everything. At the end of an hour I appealed to our Intourist guide, who explained that every scientific object was being checked.

While Dick and I were trying to watch all these people milling over our possessions, to see that nothing disappeared, a short middle-aged man came up and welcomed us with a great flourish, telling us in French that he had been sent by the Academy of Sciences to meet us at the port of entry. He said that the official's listing of these strange objects they had never seen before would probably take many hours.

I still felt shaky and miserable from our night on the Caspian but I refused to leave our possessions and go to a hotel. Our official host, whose name I never learned, bowed formally and left us to the mercy of the customs officials.

It was clear that our arrival had provided them with delightful entertainment. At the end of five hours in the customs shed we had a crowd of about thirty Russians swarming around us, admiring our effects, trying on our clothes, exclaiming over the material, and handling our precious instruments with excited cries.

Suddenly they came upon a large black photograph album containing pictures of our reconstruction of Neanderthal man in Field Museum. The Russians pointed and stared at this frightening face, shown in close-up, and asked rather respectfully who he might be. I explained, through our guide, that he was one of many such characters in Chicago, that fun was fun but they were taking too long going through our things, and that the next time I came to Baku I would bring several of these tough babies along and that one alone—I pointed ominously to Monsieur Le Moustier's glowering features as reproduced by Blaschke—could take two customs officials and bang their heads together at the end of an hour of going through his things. At once the head official ordered our baggage closed, and five minutes later we were driving toward our hotel with our Intourist guide, who seemed quite pleased with our victory in the shed.

There were very few cars on the street, but many streetcars loaded with workers in characteristic Russian dress. They were quite different from any other people I had seen in the Near East or Europe. It was about four-forty in the afternoon when we entered the dining room, expecting by that time the noon meal would long be over; to our surprise, we found the guests were just starting their luncheon. Before each person was a large dish containing a mound of the most delicious caviar I have ever tasted.

This was followed by a thick vegetable soup, slices of white sturgeon, cold sliced lamb, green salad—which we did not dare to eat—and for dessert, a champagne glass full of ice cream, like a sherbet, with very good black coffee.

It developed that meal times, from our point of view, were irregular. Breakfast was served from ten to twelve, lunch from four to six, dinner from nine until perhaps midnight.

I still felt rather shaky, so I went upstairs for a few hours' sleep before joining Dick and our guide in a sight-seeing trip around Baku. When I awoke it was dark. As I switched on the light by my bed there was a knock on my door. In came the maid, a tall, gray-haired woman in a worn uniform, who furtively approached into the circle of lamplight and, by means of the universally known sign language, made it clear that she would give me fifty rubles for one American dollar. Instantly I knew she had waited outside my door for the light to flash on, and with this knowledge came a terrifying sense of being threatened such as I have never known before or since in any country. This was a trap, I was sure of it, and as calmly as I could I summoned Dick, and then, in turn, the hotel manager and our Intourist guide. The maid was arguing rapidly in Russian, but I had our guide explain, in as sound terms as I could summon, that I had never bought money on the black market and would never do so . . . that we were in the Soviet Union in the interest of science, and that we were the unofficial guests of the Academy of Sciences in Moscow.

When the manager, white with horror, left with the maid, I felt certain I had passed some sort of test. Subsequent experiences might tend to erase the memory of that incident, but a sense of fear remained with me through two visits to Russia. There was always the feeling that at any moment one might err and unwittingly fall into a trap without ever knowing how or why.

We found that Baku, for all its 600,000 inhabitants, had the feeling and appearance of a small town. Dick and I brought back from our evening's walk an impression of dimness, a dearth of lights, and an absence of gaiety. The appearance of the citizens was striking: the men dressed as a rule in white Russian blouses and black pants, some wearing the characteristic high boots; the girls usually in single-colored dresses and gay head scarves. A great deal of red was worn, and even the usual giggling of the young girls was subdued. The older people looked careworn, the women appearing older than they probably were and carrying heavy burdens. The three movie theaters we passed were almost like those we would see at home.

Dick is very tall and his curly hair, tending to stand on end, makes him appear taller, and two tame tourists in foreign clothing, as we were, being shown around the town by an Intourist guide, created a certain amount of interest. At times crowds gathered around us. I could feel hands touching my clothing. I carefully watched one man and saw he was not trying to pick my pockets but was merely feeling the quality of my coat. I learned that even their best cloth could not compare with our well-worn tweeds and gray flannels.

The following day we were taken by our guide to see the oil fields. In this area of smoke and oily pools were standing hundreds, if not thousands, of derricks which I had seen in photographs but never before in reality. We stopped beside a drill where a dozen men, covered with oil, were watching the moving arm. As we turned to leave, one of the workmen threw himself before me on the ground and, groveling, implored me in German to save his life; he was not in sympathy with the Soviet regime, he was in danger of death, would I save him. Something about the man made me certain this, too, was a put-up job—another test—so I drew my foot away and pretended I did not understand. When we got into the car our Intourist guide asked casually if I understood German. I explained that I had studied at Heidelberg, which she undoubtedly knew, but that I had pretended not to understand the man as I did not want to get mixed up in matters political. Her expression was knowing and I felt pretty sure I had scored another "A" for my dossier.

The car took us to the Azerbaidzhan State Museum, where the director was on the steps to greet us. We were shown interesting paintings, coins, pottery, and bronze objects from mounds mainly in the Gandzha district, and dioramas which reconstructed the life of the seminomadic and nomadic cattle breeders of Daghestan. There was a fine collection of pottery, including some from Rayy, eighth to fourteenth century.

We were disappointed to find there was no physical anthropologist with whom we could discuss the physical characters of the ancient and modern peoples of the Caucasus. We were also unable to learn of any series of human skulls; in fact our question seemed to disturb the director not a little.

Our guide went with us to a long and very dull motion picture, took us to visit homes of oil laborers, and finally put us aboard a comfortable train bound for Tbilisi, formerly Tiflis.

Gandzha and Tbilisi were different as cities but oddly alike as experiences. The Intourist guide who met us at the stations might have been the same guide, wearing the same inevitable mackintosh, blue beret, and flat-heeled shoes. We visited the Museum of Georgia and promised an exchange of publications. We were constantly frustrated by language difficulties and not being able to read the labels, and our guide did not understand the technical terms.

In fact I was beginning to feel frustrated in many ways. It had long been a dream of mine to visit the Caucasus, in order to link studies there with those in Southwestern Asia. Here we were caught up in a steady round of parks, museums, work projects, and sight-seeing tours, as prescribed by Intourist. We had seen a splendid one-ring circus and visited an amusement park of "Culture and Rest," where, feeling that the marksmanship reputation of the United States was at stake, we had shot down metal silhouettes of tanks with Japanese flags painted on their sides, and hurled baseballs at a six-foot face of Hitler, before admiring crowds. Such was "Culture and Rest" in Tbilisi, in September 1934.

The city itself was endlessly fascinating, and we left it with reluctance to continue the long trip toward Leningrad. A large bus appeared one morning at eight outside our hotel and we clambered aboard, storing our luggage in the back. For the first time we were on our own, with no interpreter to guide us. None of the eight other passengers in the bus spoke a language we could understand. However, we had our book of words and phrases, and Intourist had provided a picnic lunch. We settled down to enjoy magnificent scenery, very like the Alps, and ancient cities set with fortresses and cathedrals.

I looked down every branch road with longing. But we could not go anywhere without an Intourist guide and special arrangements. Furthermore, our funds were beginning to run out and we had no money for tempting side trips.

Since our arrival in Russia I had been fighting a mental battle with Intourist. I knew that when we arrived home everyone would say we had been led around the Soviet Union by the nose and shown only what the government wanted us to see. Then I remembered the stranger who had welcomed us to the Soviet Union in the customhouse shed in Baku, in the name of the Academy of Sciences. That decided me. Privately I declared war on "what you should see in Russia."

At Ordzhonikidze the bus deposited us at the Intourist Hotel, where we were met by Sam Wul, who had been to the United States. It was wonderful to find someone we could talk to without an interpreter. I told him we were not simple tourists but were on a scientific mission and wished to do some research work around Ordzhonikidze. He assured me I would find the people friendly and eager to help, and the next morning he went with me to Intourist, where they arranged for a hundred people to be brought to a local school on the following day.

About five minutes after eight we entered the school, I, as always, doubtful whether any of our "patients" would really be there. But as we stepped through the door I saw fifty North Osete youths lined up and before them at intervals, as on a regimental parade ground, stood five nurses. The general of this army was a stiffly starched senior nurse who greeted us with: "You are five minutes late. Is that American efficiency?"

She seemed to respect authority, so I rapped out orders; one nurse to help record stature; one for hair samples; one to record pulse rate and body weight, two to do the blood sampling.

We were off to a flying start, finished our series of fifty before lunch, and in the afternoon fifty North Osete girls submitted willingly but with girlish giggles to our efficient assistants. I have never worked under easier or better conditions.

The expeditious handling of the series made another day's stay in the region possible. I knew Intourist was arranging the usual tour. Now was my time to attempt a glance at the off-the-track life of Russia. The problem was what to see, and how.

Inspiration came while Dick and I were strolling in the square after dinner, listening to the brass band. I could hardly wait to get to the Intourist office and talk to the manager. I told him that while we were very grateful for his arrangements to see the

296

factories and schools, we preferred to ride horses in the mountains.

He was not surprised. Spreading out a map, he showed us a village about thirty miles away where horses were available.

Rather irritatingly, I'm afraid, I pointed to a village on the map, Kuban, equally far away, in exactly the opposite direction. "We want to go there."

"Impossible," he said flatly.

I reminded him of our first conversation when he had assured me all people of Georgia were friendly to foreigners and it was possible for us to go anywhere. And I repeated the *anywhere*.

The girl interpreter, Irina, who was also a guide, was also doubtful, but early next morning she set out with us in a large Lincoln furnished by Intourist.

She was in a gloomy state, and talked continuously with foreboding, saying that she knew no one in Kuban, and there were sure to be difficulties. . . .

In Kuban, a small village of clean stone and frame houses, we called first on the mayor. Our arrival in a large, well-polished car evidently struck him as being official. He seemed greatly relieved to learn that we were merely foreigners.

Irina explained the nature of our visit: that we wished to hire three horses and ride up toward the snow line.

As she translated, she smiled in triumph. "You see, there are no horses! It would have been much better to go the other way where everything would have been prepared."

I looked over the official desk, past the huge portrait of Stalin, and through the window saw three horses pulling a plow across a field. I pointed.

The mayor's eyes lit up. "You want horses that plow? Very well, if that is what you want. Meantime if you would come to my house . . ."

I felt like the Pied Piper as I walked across the village square to the mayor's nicely furnished farmhouse. The whole village was out looking us over.

In a short while we were sitting about in straight-backed chairs sipping glasses of tea. Naturally our inability to speak the language made the party anything but lively. In order to put some semblance of life into the group I asked, through the interpreter, "By the way, Mr. Mayor, does there happen to be a wedding here today?"

From the look on his face one might have thought I had tilted a Ouija board. He sprang to his feet and exclaimed: "How did you know? One of my young cousins is getting married tonight." I replied that I hadn't known, but that quite often there was a wedding in a village, and I was always interested. He missed the gist of this, but as I had always wanted to attend a Russian wedding, I added: "Will you do me a favor while we are out riding, and buy me a suitable gift so that we may present it to the bride on our return?"

He hesitated, then, stammering indecisively, said, "Of course . . . ah . . . h'mm . . . and you are all three invited."

Our three plow horses arrived. Irina mounted hers, looking worried because she had lost control of the expedition. I told her to follow us and she would be all right. As we rode our plodding mounts up a winding, rocky pass she held her horse back, obviously trying to slow us down.

Within an hour we had reached a beautiful grassy slope that extended five miles up to the snow line. Several villages were scattered over the valley. Irina suggested nervously that we stop at the nearest because "they will be more used to seeing foreigners." This made me certain that we were seeing a part of Russia as it actually was.

Only the stone frames of houses were standing. The doors sagged open along the dusty road. It was a ghost town.

I was the first to break the silence by urging my horse down the empty street and toward the nearest ridge. As I rode up the green slope I felt the bleak desolation closing in. In this land, so gifted with natural beauty, an unknown element kept human life away. However, mingled with this sense of foreboding was a delightful appreciation of cantering a plow horse in the Caucasus Mountains; this comedy helped balance the mystery.

Atop the crest I stopped and looked out over the magnificent panorama. On the other side of the green valley was a small cluster of stone houses with smoke rising from their chimneys.

Nearer was a smaller group of small stone beehive-looking build-ings.

I rode down to these and found that each had a small opening in the front, four feet up, and about three feet square.

Dismounting, I peered within, and was astonished, and more than a little elated, to see skeletons, some still partially clothed. My anthopological mind did handsprings at the sight of this treasure trove of bones and skulls.

Here was our chance to get measurements and photographs of some first-class skulls! While Dick was setting up his camera I climbed into a tomb. It would have taken a combination acrobat, juggler, and mountain climber to gain entrance in a dignified manner. Amid a crumbling of rock I arrived headfirst upon the deceased. No doubt they were as surprised as I. Dick shouted to me that he was ready. With my head framed in the opening of the tomb, I turned to Irina to give instructions. She was standing with a look of pale horror on her face and muttering something. The ghost town had shaken her and this added find of bones and skulls was the final touch. Her eyes were glazed and from her incoherent babble I managed to eke out something about the "Valley of the Dead."

I realized at this point that perhaps impatience was the better part of valor. I told the girl that, no matter what she might think, I wanted her to carry each skull to Dick, who would photograph it, then return it to me.

She turned even paler, but she obeyed. As she returned the skulls I replaced each on its stark bones. I used the stone slab of the entrance as a working table and within two hours I had taken about a dozen measurements on twenty-two skulls. This seemed a perfectly adequate small series.

In any event the wind was blowing hard in the valley. Dick was having trouble taking the photographs and I doubted that Irina would be willing to carry skulls much longer. I climbed out of the tomb, dusted myself off, remounted, and started down the valley toward the small village we had seen from the crest. I left Dick packing the camera and Irina pulling herself together, still muttering "*Cherepov.*"

By a small stream near the village I saw an old man in a large, floppy felt hat. In an attempt to be courteous I dismounted and went over to shake hands. My politeness was met with a cry of alarm and a string of Osete oaths. As he backed away he put both of his hands in the air and tried to shoo me away.

In order not to further incite the old Osete I waited anxiously for Irina to interpret. She arrived in a few minutes with Dick and the old man went up to her, gesticulating all the while, and I could see from the look on her face that he was saying something extremely unpleasant—undoubtedly about me.

Her look of consternation turned to one of dread. She looked up at me fearfully. "Do you know why he won't shake hands with you?"

I replied that I did not; that I thought he was a very rude old man and I wished she would tell him so.

She went on as if she had not heard me. "He says that the reason he will not shake hands is that he saw you climb out of that tomb. The last person he saw go into that tomb was his grand-father—his grandfather who had died of plague!"

My mind raced through the book I had once read on "What to do until the doctor comes," but I could remember nothing about first aid for the plague. I glanced at Dick and Irina. Their wind-burned complexions had faded to a yellow-white.

Remembering the germicidal soap and towel in my rucksack, I went down to the stream, squatted beside it in good Arab fashion, and washed my hands, again and again. After I had rubbed my hands almost raw, I gave the bar to Irina and suggested that she wash her hands. From the look on the girl's face it was obvious that as far as she was concerned this was the only sensible remark I'd made all day. I was somewhat relieved to notice that as soon as we had all washed our hands thoroughly the old man's hostility seemed to decline and he waved us a casual farewell as we headed for the village.

We dismounted in front of the largest hut and it was evident that the word had not reached them that we had been associating with victims of the plague. Soon the whole population was gathered around, staring at us. Irina explained that we were Americans who wished to ride in their valley and that she hoped we would be welcome.

At this remark the senior man in the group immediately stepped forward, shook us each by the hand, and invited us into his house. We had hardly been seated when a tray was carried into the room with hard-boiled eggs, bread, and tea. Our gracious host insisted that we go to see something of which he was very proud. Finally I understood that our host's wife was a schoolteacher and that he wanted us to pay a visit to the school.

Since this seemed to be a fine opportunity to look at a school far out in the Caucasus Mountains, we accepted readily. The small, whitewashed building, twenty-five feet square, looked like a rural schoolhouse anywhere, except that its outer wall was white and shone like a new pin in the bright sunlight.

There were seventeen students in the room, nine of whom were past middle age. The desire for education had evidently swept this village because later we were informed that when a child wished to insult another child's parents he would say, "Oh well, your mother and father can't even read and write."

The teacher immediately insisted that I address a few remarks to the class. As if the plague wasn't bad enough, I now carried the weight of the U.S.A. on my shoulders as I stood up and said a few words about bringing greetings from my village in the United States (i.e., Chicago) to the people of their village. I also added that I envied them their situation, surrounded by snow-capped mountain peaks in this beautiful green valley.

From the looks on their faces I gathered that they seemed pleased, although I had no idea what they actually heard after my remarks had been translated into Russian, then into Osete. They all smiled and later clapped, although I think the latter was at a signal from the teacher. I returned the smile, excused myself, and we remounted the horses.

At sunset we arrived back at Kuban. I paid the farmer for our horses, I surmise rather handsomely because he shook hands with me four times.

The mayor informed us that we had missed the wedding but were invited to the reception. Since I thought we would probably have to shake hands with the bride and groom and all the families, I hesitated to accept.

Dick, always cheerful, said it was nonsense to think we had the plague and we'd better go to the party, particularly since they were expecting us. "Very rude to back out at the last minute," he said. He might well have added that it was very rude to give the bride and groom the plague, for rat fleas might be in my clothes. But the decision had been made and we headed for the reception.

Halfway to the party a young man came up to me with an untidy package which he said was my present for the bride. I surreptitiously tore off a corner of the wrapper to see what it was, and found a hideous tablecloth of local make.

Sounds of revelry were coming from the bride's house, so, preceded by the mayor and surrounded by curious onlookers, we hurried on down the street. We were ushered into a room filled with people, and were soon engulfed by a swarm of celebrants who shook our hands and patted us on the back. One or two who hadn't shaved for at least a week tried to kiss me on both cheeks. It was all in the spirit of good fun, and we joined in the celebration.

The warm Russian liquor flowed fast and freely and was already working magic. From my point of view the reception was rather chaotic, despite the fact that I do not drink. The bridegroom was with us, the bride was in another room, the music was coming from yet another room, and there was constant shouting, chatter, cheering, and laughter. In a courtyard at the back, couples were dancing madly. The weird music was produced by some tired flutes, clarinets, a drum, and an Armenian stringed instrument called the *cannon*. The dissonance bounced from wall to wall.

At first Irina was appalled that we should be enjoying this kind of thing but after a couple of drinks she joined the party. Except for an occasional touch of her hand to her face to discover whether she had broken out, one would never have known that she was ill at ease.

We stayed about an hour in the midst of all this merriment and utter confusion, sitting on the floor most of the time, trying to make sense with the local residents with Irina interpreting.

In one of these conversations I found myself cornered by a burly Osete who accepted every sentence by pounding me on the back with gusto. Deciding to start the routine of leaving this festivity, I got up from the floor and asked the mayor if we could see the bride. Dick, Irina, and I were escorted to a small back room where a girl dressed in white welcomed us with maidenly downcast eyes.

Feeling somewhat like Piglet in *Winnie-the-Pooh,* who gave a burst balloon to Eeyore on his birthday, I shuffled across the room and presented the dilapidated package. She opened it, then raised her large dark brown eyes. As Dick said afterward, "There was much gratitude in that look."

It was quite clear by now that we were outstaying our welcome, so we shook hands with the bride and wished her Godspeed. Amid a pandemonium of back-slapping and arm-pumping, we pushed our way through the smoke, laughter, noise, and general shuffle to the door. Here we stopped to shake hands with the mayor and to thank him for his great hospitality.

Just before the car pulled away I told the mayor to look me up the next time he came to Chicago. Irina leaned out the front window to tell the mayor what I had said, waved her hand, and collapsed in the front seat.

Immediately upon reaching the hotel we scrambled to find the first-aid manual. The next morning, when we awoke, Dick and I greeted each other with, "How's the plague?" Then, after a thorough search for symptoms which never materialized, we had breakfast and checked out of the hotel. Many months later we found to our gratification that the skulls I had measured came from a group related to ancient Osetes, who are among the most interesting groups in the entire Caucasus region. We had thus obtained a small but valuable series of measurements of ancient and living Osetes, and a report on our researches in the Caucasus will be published during 1953 by the Peabody Museum at Harvard.

At Rostov, near the mouth of the Don, we were met by the usual Intourist "eager beaver," who swept us majestically out of the crowded station and by taxi to the Bolshaya Moskovskaga, the Intourist hotel. Before we were unpacked she had unrolled a long list of places we "must" see: museums, universities, projects, industries, mills, workers' homes, schools, collective farms . . . Fresh from my triumph over Intourist in the depths of the Caucasus Mountains, with its fine resultant tally of skulls, I assumed a rather lofty attitude toward such all-over sight-seeing.

She breezed into the hotel early the next day and led us out proudly to a shiny, new-looking black Lincoln. We drove rapidly through the street, gaining only brief impressions of a citizenry that seemed to lack the zeal and enthusiasm we had noticed in the other Russian cities. The sun was shining and the skies blue, but the faces we saw seemed depressed-looking, even the young ones. After some twenty minutes of riding, our car swept through the gates of the Rostov Agricultural Machinery Works. We were surrounded by huge sheds and vast concrete buildings typical of any great industrial plant. Smoke billowed, machines pounded, activity was in the air.

In the main office we were welcomed by the manager, who received us very kindly and was greatly impressed when we told him Dick and I had been through the International Harvester Plant in Chicago. Evidently this established us with him as agricultural experts, for he begged us to call his attention to any improvements we might be able to suggest during our tour of the plant. The good points were obvious, but he would appreciate "American criticism." He asked us to make these suggestions to the head of each division. Both Dick and I, we discovered later, privately made up our minds not to criticize anything.

We were taken into another building where tractor parts were checked before being taken into the assembly line. People were milling about, and the air was thick with smoke and dust. On the concrete floor were piled thousands of tractor parts. There was a general atmosphere of hard work, but not of order.

The atmosphere was so charged with smoke and dust that we were beginning to cough. The foreman proudly led us into a small room where, in eight small booths, workers were standing with their noses pressed into nozzles that were going full blast. This was air, the foreman explained with bursting pride, which drove fumes and dust from one's head. I suggested that it might improve the health of the workers more if exhaust fans were placed at various levels in the workrooms. At once the foreman shoved the blackboard under my nose and excitedly demanded that I make drawings. I explained that drawing the inner workings of ventilators was beyond me but I was sure some engineer could be found to make them. The foreman promised to have them made right away.

We walked out of doors and between high brick walls to a small, dark, ovenlike furnace room where we were astonished to find only women shoveling coal into three boilers. Their faces and arms were black and shining with coal dust and sweat, but as they worked they sang, and this seemed to give them the necessary rhythm that drove their long-handled shovels against the terrific heat. There was almost no light, only that of the flames and from two small bulbs high against the ceiling, and the room was coal-black and like the stokehold of an oceangoing liner before the conversion to oil.

The forewoman, who resembled a brawny blacksmith, stepped forward, planted her feet, in workmen's shoes, before us, folded her arms, and glared at the puny males who had invaded this Amazonian domain. Our guide said we might ask her any question, and our first, naturally, was why women were doing this very strenuous work. The forewoman glared at me while she answered, through our interpreter, with biting sarcasm:

"It is not yet obvious that women are equal to men, and this is our way of proving it. Throughout this factory you will find women doing the hardest labor. This is to prove our physical equality, so that wages will be the same and we can share and share alike with the men."

Then, with a sort of coyness astonishing in such a massive woman, she added with a secretive smile, "This will only have to continue a year or so. When the men of the Soviet Union understand that women are equal and must be paid equal sums for their work, then we will no longer have to do the hard, dangerous tasks."

We could remain in that hot, bad atmosphere only a few minutes, and the air outside, though it was acrid with smoke, tasted like a mountain breeze.

Back in the Administration Building, the manager had already heard of our criticism regarding the bad air and the exhaust fans. The idea was evidently new to him, and he seemed very pleased. He promised to investigate it at once.

We were taken to Zernograd, a collective farm about forty

miles from Rostov. Our guide had been changed, and this one was a young American. We were delighted to have someone with whom we could talk, for it is not always easy to understand an interpreter. He would not talk about himself, though we gathered he was from the Middle West. He was disappointed to learn that we were not to remain in the Soviet Union but were returning to Chicago. At the mention of Chicago his face lit up and his reserve broke; he asked about the lake-front development, the World's Fair, gang warfare, and particularly what had happened to "Scar-face" Al Capone. We could see from his eagerness that he had known Chicago well and held a warm feeling for it still, despite his frequent assurances that he loved living in the Ukraine. Sud-denly he drew himself up and changed the talk to collective farm-ing, as if we had struck a sentimental chord he did not want plucked again. He was sitting on the front seat next the driver and had to turn to talk to us, and we were certain by the move-ment of the driver's head that he understood English; all the In-tourist drivers are chosen with great care.

The buildings at the collective farm were concrete, rather like military barracks, and appeared forbidding against the gloomy "Black Earth" of the Ukraine. Our guide, who had been rattling away the No. 1 propaganda line as to how much better off the peasants were under the collective system, since the farm could withstand hazards and losses that would bankrupt an individual, led us through a large flat double row of sheds containing, he said, ten thousand milking cows, mostly Friesian, Holstein, and Hereford mixtures. He repeated this number several times as if it were too large for us to comprehend. He said there had been certain difficulties with this large herd because the farm was run on businesslike lines, on orders issued from Moscow. For example, Moscow had ordered these ten thousand cows placed in one herd. Within a short time the cows had eaten all the grass surrounding their milking shed, so they did not have time to forage sufficient grass between milkings. Here was another difficulty; Moscow had ordered the cows milked four times a day. The interpretation of a day was daylight. Consequently, during the winter months the cows were milked at increasingly shorter intervals. This was very bad for them, but those were the rules from Moscow.

We went back to one of the bleak main buildings where, in a bare-walled, rather depressing dining room, some of the workers were finishing their noonday meal. There were about twenty tables in the room. We sat down with our American guide and were served good, strong, black coffee. At one table sat a man and a girl who watched us with unusual intentness. It was plain that they understood what we were saying. They were familiar types, and I asked our guide who they were. He smiled and said we would probably like to meet them, since the man was from Iowa, the girl from Illinois. The man, about sixty, with iron-gray hair closely cropped, might have served as model for the perfect American Gothic farmer by Grant Wood. The girl was about twenty-five, tense and neurotic in appearance, with long, stringy brown hair and a petulant mouth.

Since we were interested in meeting these expatriate Americans, our guide went over, presented our compliments, and invited them to join us. We could see their indignant refusal; then, at that very moment, the manager appeared.

He strode over to them, and I think must have given them a peremptory order to join us at once, for they both came over quickly, the girl, glowering, in the lead. She introduced herself as "Miss Smith" and her companion as "Mr. Brown," obvious noms-de-Ukraine. She was boiling with animosity, and began firing questions: who were we, where did we come from, why were we here, how long did we plan to stay? Questions flowed in a torrent from her discontented mouth.

After we had answered them all, I said it was time to ask her a few questions.

She snapped, "I'm a worker on this farm, and that's all there is to it."

Leaving her to stew in her own sour juice, I turned to "Mr. Brown," who seemed an apologetic sort of person. He told us he had been a farmer in Iowa, and "not a particularly good farmer," because he had twice been bankrupt, and the local bank had refused to renew his loan the third time. Ten years before, he had come to the Ukraine and here, despite his failure as a farmer in Iowa, he was a success because he knew more about growing corn than any other person. As a "foreign expert" he had worked himself up to head of the corn-growing section of the Zernograd Collective Farm. In Russia, to sum it up, Mr. Brown was a success.

I could feel the girl beside me seething as he talked. We had ignored her completely and this, the good old silent treatment, was apparently the one thing she could not bear. When I finally turned to her, and asked her how long she had been on the farm, her answer was explosive, and as if she were addressing an audience of hundreds, words poured forth:

"I came here five years ago because I hated Winnetka! I couldn't stand the life there. My family and I could not get along. They gave me the usual things—the regular formal education—the regular "coming-out" party at the Blackstone Hotel. The ballroom was decorated with white gardenias, and I hate gardenias! I resented every penny spent on the party, and I told my family so. They said I was ungrateful and spoiled.

"I wanted a place where everyone was equal and opportunities were equal. Naturally I came to the Soviet Union. I have always been interested in agriculture. Once I took a summer course in agriculture. Now my only desire is to make good and to be allowed to climb on a tractor and drive it, churning up the rich, black earth. That is my ambition. That is why I am here."

She paused, out of breath. I told her pleasantly that I thought she had come unnecessarily far from Winnetka to drive a tractor, because there was a plant called the International Harvester in Chicago which made bigger and better tractors than any I had been shown in the Soviet Union. As for the rich, black earth, there was a great deal of that in Illinois and Indiana.

She almost spat at me. "You do not understand Communism and the spirit in which we work." Then, even more savagely: "It is your family and the McCormicks who deserve to be wiped out in the Middle West. I can assure you that when I return to Illinois to lead the Revolution you will be one of the first to be purged!"

As we drove away I happened to look through the rear window, to see the former Winnetka debutante shaking her fist after me. We learned later that this girl, who talked so loudly about Communism and the joys of farming, was invited every year by her mother to the Riviera for two or three months "to relax after her strenuous labors on the collective farm."

Kharkov was a busy industrial city and Dick and I did not find it too interesting. We were glad to be leaving for Kiev. Our guide persuaded us to make a slight detour to visit the great dam over the Dnieper. As we approached the huge concrete piers spanning the high rapids, the guide rattled off astronomical figures concerning this, the largest power plant in Europe. In the main building the generators were throbbing with energy. The eight huge turbines, at that time the largest in the world, were in a magnificently constructed, spotlessly clean rectangular building which was far and away the most efficient-looking building we had seen since entering the Soviet Union.

As we walked outside over the concrete span—one of the greatest achievements of the twentieth century—our guide lectured us in glowing terms on this "great Soviet achievement." I could not resist; I pointed to the sign towering in the sky, the familiar circle with the intertwined letters, "G.E." There was the symbol of the brains that had harnessed the Dnieper River.

We had no more time for sight-seeing because we had to take the train for Kiev. In the twilight, as the train moved northwest, we could see the peasants' huts, whitewashed or plastered with yellow clay, surrounded by small gardens. In each garden were sunflowers, the favorite flower, we were told, of the Ukraine.

The usual Intourist girl met us at Kiev, which has always been considered one of the most beautiful cities in Europe. The upper part stands on a high bluff above the Dnieper, overlooking densely wooded country. The wide streets and beautiful parks were shaded by poplars, chestnut trees, and sweet-smelling white acacia. Around the city were flourishing orchards—pear, peach, and apricot. The Byzantines called this city the "Second Constantinople."

By this time we could stand our ground, and dismayed our eager guide with the advance announcement that we would visit no factories or projects. Rather reluctantly she took us instead to the Academy of Sciences, where we were fortunate enough to meet a number of archaeologists and were shown a well-equipped laboratory where trained specialists were working on the problems of ancient Ukrainia, and the Laboratory of Physical Anthropology, where bones and skulls were being cleaned, repaired, and assembled. The archaeologists were extremely keen on their work, and anxious for news of recent discoveries in Iraq and Iran. It was difficult for them to obtain any foreign archaeological publications, but they had heard of our excavations at Kish and hung eagerly on my firsthand account of our discoveries there and at Jemdet Nasr.

The next day, our last in Kiev, we were guided through the ancient Pechersk or Lavra Monastery, high over the Dnieper River. The main church had been converted into a museum. Below, close to the river, in subterranean caves and catacombs, were the mummified bodies of the monks. One bishop lay in his robes of state, hands crossed upon his breast, his desiccated face still recognizable like that of Rameses II in the Cairo Museum.

Before the Revolution, for many centuries pilgrims had prayed before these niches.

In one dimly lit cavernous room lay a pyramid of human skulls. This was the shocking Anti-Religious Museum. Our girl guide was delighted to translate for us the labels identifying the "holy relics," which had been prayed before by pilgrims throughout the centuries. The largest label stated that the poor ignorant Russians who had worshiped here before the Revolution had believed implicitly that these bodies had been preserved by God because they were holy. This, the label explained, was untrue, because after the Revolution excavations in the catacombs had revealed not only the mummies of the religious leaders but also—and these were prominently shown—the mummies of rats and mice, all preserved by the atmosphere.

Thoughtlessly I remarked upon the poorness of the lighting. Our guide instantly darted off to return with the curator. He bowed formally; he had been told I thought some changes should be made in the Anti-Religious Museum! This was embarrassing, so I muttered something about hidden lights. Suddenly he asked if I could stay in Kiev a week or two to help with technical suggestions. My expenses would be paid by the government. This was the first and only job offered me by the Soviet Union. Dick was listening with the broadest grin on his face. I declined as graciously as possible.

The next morning found us unpacking our well-worn bags in the National Hotel, just a drive-and-a-mashie-shot from the Kremlin. Our first duty call was upon Ambassador William Bullitt, to thank him personally for the many ways in which he had eased our trip across Russia.

Back at the hotel Dick vanished into his bathroom and, in a continuous thirty-six-hour shift, succeeded in developing the five hundred negatives. Fortunately he had brought string and clips, and by stringing almost every inch of space over his tub he managed to handle five hundred prints at the same time. During this time he laid down for only one hour, but I think he drank a hundred cups of tea.

We had still another problem. On a small roll of drawing paper were the ground plans and drawings of buildings Dick had made in Iran, which should have been sealed at Baku upon our entering the Soviet Union. Amid the confusion of the comic-opera scene in the customs shed, Dick's drawings of ancient buildings had been overlooked. For example, I explained unhappily to a cold-eyed censor in Moscow, the ground plan of the caravansary at Yezd-i-Khast certainly looked like drawings of gun emplacements. I had to admit these sketches looked suspicious. He would simply have to take our word for it that they were only archaeological studies made in Iran.

He made me go through my story again before two colleagues, then he placed the drawing in a tube, closed it with a lead seal, and handed it to us with a smile. We could not have been happier, and settled down to enjoy the beauties of Moscow.

Thanks to Mr. Bullitt, we were invited on a personally conducted tour of the Kremlin, an invitation our dazzled Intourist guide at first refused to believe possible. Five golden domes crowned the cathedral which, built in 1479, combined elements of Byzantine, Roman, and contemporary Russian. Here the Russian czars and emperors had been crowned. In the Archangel Cathedral, built in 1505, were the tombs of the princes and czars. It seemed incongruous that I should be standing there surrounded by dead Romanoffs while in Chicago my friend Rostislav

"Oudka" Romanoff, son of the Grand Duke Alexander, was selling ties behind the counter of Marshall Field and Company!

We attended the Children's Theater, where the audience, like children everywhere, screamed, laughed, shrieked, or stared with rapturous attention. One evening we paid a trip to the famed Moscow subway. Our guide led us to a boarded area where a door was opened by a large and powerful woman who glared at us, then, changed by a few crisp words from our girl guide, bowed low before us with the most groveling respect. The Amazon ushered us down a well-lit shaft to see the people of Moscow working on their subway. About 120 feet below we could see men and women shoveling sand and gravel like demons possessed. The Amazon explained that they were all volunteers. Motioning us to wait, she hurried away, but our guide seemed nervous and forcibly urged us out of the door.

We protested this hasty exit, and she admitted that, while it was a great honor for us to have been permitted to see it, she had paid for that honor with a little white lie. She had told the Amazon that Dick and I had built the New York subway! The Amazon had left us to bring two of the Soviet subway specialists to meet the two New York subway specialists!

Most impressive of our Moscow experiences was the visit to Lenin's tomb, a massive, truncated pyramid of red granite against the Kremlin wall. As we came into Red Square we could see a long line of pilgrims four abreast outside the shrine, extending across the square almost to St. Basil's Cathedral. The guide marched us straight to the head of the line, where the first four pilgrims stepped back to allow us to precede them. I protested to our girl guide, but she told us that was the way Russians preferred to treat foreigners who were in the country for a short time and must never wait to see anything.

We walked slowly, almost shuffling down the steps, from the bright sunshine of the square into the darkness of the tomb. A solid throng pressed ahead and after us into the Soviet holy of holies. In a room about twenty feet square, within a glass case and illuminated by a fairly strong light, lay the embalmed remains of Lenin. His eyes were closed as if in a deep sleep. His face was very pale. His body was covered with a red cloth. Never have

I seen so perfect an embalming, so great an illusion of "He is not dead, but sleepeth." I glanced at the faces around and have never seen deeper reverence. I saw no tears, only sorrow and piety. Here were people moved beyond words. The radiating power and strength of the still little figure could be felt. I would see humans as greatly moved once again, in Washington following the death of President Roosevelt, but I have never seen a crowd so intensely moved in any house of worship of any faith.

From the center of the square our guide pointed out the recessed top of the tomb which serves as a tribunal from which Soviet leaders review marching masses on state occasions. I was to see Generalissimo Stalin standing there when, in 1945, I stood in this square after World War II, watching the Soviet Victory Parade.

Behind the tomb, at the base of the Kremlin wall, are the graves of heroes of the Russian Revolution. Among them, our guide pointed out with undue pride the grave of John Reed, the American Communist, and, set in niches in the Kremlin wall, the funeral urns containing the ashes of other honored dead, including those of "Big Bill" Haywood, leader of the American IWW, Charles Ruthenberg, leader of the Communist Party of America, and Paxton Hibben, revolutionary writer.

All night the train rolled slowly through pine forests reminiscent of Norway and Sweden. We were in Leningrad in time for breakfast. From the balcony of our room in the Hotel Astoria we looked out over the city square to the cathedral, St. Isaac's, which had four bell towers around its dome instead of the five cupolas characteristic of cathedrals in Russia.

We floored our Intourist guide on sight with an advance refusal to visit the usual, and had her take us instead to the State Hermitage, next to the Winter Palace of the czars, where we had the privilege of meeting the director, Academician Orbeli, and his assistant, Dr. Camilla Trever. When she met us she had in her hand her monograph on the terra cottas of Afrasiab, which she inscribed to me in appreciation of our visit. Orbeli presented us with other publications of the Hermitage.

The Anthropological and Ethnographical Museum was just

across the Neva. Inside the classical columned museum was the Academy of Sciences of the USSR. Here we met two Soviet archaeologists whose work was familiar to us, Zamiatnin and Ravdonikas. As we were walking through the exhibits we met a man whose appearance was Mongoloid; without thinking I muttered, "American Indian." Zamiatnin smiled and patted my shoulder. "You are right. We brought him here from your Northwest to catalogue our specimens from the Haida and Kwakiutl." We came to a table where a man was cataloguing Igorot material. This proved to be R. F. Barton, an American, whose work in the Philippines is an anthropological classic. He was delighted to see us and put away his papers to go with us through the archaeological collections, the main one being of Old and New Stone Age specimens from every part of their vast territory. The cases tended to be overcrowded and poorly lit, but "Come back in ten years," our guide urged us, "and you will see what improvements will have been made!" A little more than ten years later I was back and was amazed.

We took Barton with us to the Astoria for an excellent dinner. He told us he had been invited to Leningrad to catalogue their large Philippine collection, and that the work was almost finished. Later he was to return to the Philippines and complete his monograph on the Igorots.

Dick and I went to a special performance of *Ivan Susanin*. As we had grown to expect of the ballet in the Soviet Union, here was another superb performance. The people walking around the foyer between acts looked sadder and thinner and not so well dressed as those in the Bolshoi Theater in Moscow.

Our guide, yawning as she left us, reminded us that we had an early appointment at the Institute of Plant Industry to meet Nicolai Vavilov, one of the world authorities on wheat.

No sooner did we present our names at his office than his round, clean-shaven, smiling face appeared at the door. He was obviously a dynamic and forceful character and spoke almost faultless English. He showed us the room where the wheat and barley samples were stored in labeled cardboard boxes and told us with pride that there were 12,000 samples of barley and 18,000 samples of wheat in this great collection, "the largest in the

314

world." Then he said he would show us the rarest of all his specimens. He took a box from the files and, keeping the label turned from us, opened it as cautiously as if it contained live mice. "Here," he said triumphantly, "are the rarest grains of wheat in our national collection."

I looked down into a small glass jar and saw five of the thirty-two grains I had found in the fire-scarred jar, the oldest wheat from Mesopotamia. I read the label on the box: "Charred wheat from Kish, Iraq, excavated by Field Museum-Oxford University Joint Expedition, March 1928. By exchange."

In the Institute of the Peoples of the Far North we were shown rooms full of relics from Arctic expeditions similar to those in the Royal Geographical Society in London. We were also shown charts and maps illustrating the opening up of this region, and of achievements accomplished and planned. We were told of farms started, homes built, and animal husbandry fostered on the frozen Chernozem; years later, when I read of cucumbers growing in the Soviet Far North, I remembered the shining eyes of our guide as she translated the plans for developing this forbidding region. Up to this time my interest in the area had been limited to the discovery on the Lena River of mammoths whose flesh was still fresh enough for hunting dogs to eat; in fact, I recalled having heard of a dinner given by the French Academy of Sciences at which the professors dined on 2000-year-old eggs from China, followed by mammoth steaks cut from the 15,000-year-old monsters preserved in the frozen tundra near the Lena River in Siberia.

We visited the Natural History Museum to see the famous "Beresovska Mammoth" from the Lena River, in a kneeling position in a large glass case, with the skin and long red hair still preserved; one of the most interesting zoological specimens in the world.

One evening Vavilov took me to a good but simple dinner at the House for Scientists, a three-story building where the top scientists have a club. He asked me my impressions of the Soviet Union. I was naturally very guarded, because although Dick and I had traveled far, we had traveled the thirty-five hundred miles in about six weeks. So I told him how kind people had been to us everywhere, in the Caucasus, Baku, Tbilisi, Ordzhonidkze, Kiev,

Moscow, and now Leningrad. I told him Dick and I had agreed these weeks had been among the most interesting in our lives.

"What do you think of the regime?"

His question was unexpected. I repeated how kind everyone, including all the officials, had been to us. His eyes narrowed.

"Do you understand Communism?" he said tensely. "No, it is difficult for a foreigner to understand this system—the fact that we are living not so much for the present as for the future."

He paused, and suddenly raised his eyes to meet mine. "Well, I will give you an example; see if this makes Communism clearer to you. My predecessor as director of the Institute of Plant Industry was a good botanist. The government asked him to make a survey of a large area in Central Asia with a view to planting barley there. He and his staff analyzed and examined, and recommended a certain type of barley for that area. The barley was planted. It was good seed. It failed. It did not grow because that year there was a terrible drought. No barley could have grown that year. Now do you think that, since the barley crop was a failure, the Soviet government would shoot the scientist at this desk? No, that would be barbaric. They took him into the corridor outside his office and shot him there."

I am afraid my mouth as well as my eyes were open. The room we were in seemed far less comfortable and the food choked me. "No," I agreed slowly, "I am afraid I will never understand Communism."

He was a most charming and interesting host. A few years later I heard he had died "of a liver ailment" in Saratov.

There was a bad moment in the customs shed when Dick sailed. He was to go by steamer from Leningrad to London; I by train to Berlin, then to Paris, to visit Malvina Hoffman and pass on some of her sculptures for the Hall of Races of Mankind before they went to the foundry. We would meet in London. The shed was swarming with Soviet customs officers, young and fierce-looking with greatcoats to the ground. They were tall, handsome, and uncompromising. One officer pounced on the tube containing the precious drawings from Iran, which had been sealed with lead in Moscow. Without qualms Dick and I saw him try to peer into the tube, for after all, it had been sealed by the Soviet government! To our horror, however, he called for a knife. I could see Dick turn pale. Only bluff could work, and looking about, I saw an old-fashioned type of telephone sticking its giraffe's neck from the wall. In a loud voice I commanded our Intourist girl to get Rubinen, Litvinov's secretary, in Moscow. The knife blade was against the string; the name of Litvinov froze it there. The officer closed his knife slowly and put it away, then, lifting the tube as if he had never seen it before, he exclaimed in a very loud voice that owing to the poor light in the shed he had not been able to see the seal, but of course it was the seal of the Moscow Customs Office, and what need to open that within the Soviet Union!

Sometime in the night I was awakened at the frontier. My passport was examined and stamped and the usual routine questions asked.

As the train gathered speed crossing the Soviet frontier, I felt a great surge of relief—of freedom. Until that moment I had not realized the strain of being in a country where all are afraid of each other, of the dread GPU, of the informers, of the failure to produce and the consequent punishment, of the constant propaganda from all mass media, of *fear* everywhere. We had met fine and friendly people, but they moved in an enveloping nightmare. That night on the train I found myself relaxing in an intangible sense of relief such as I had never before known.

It was fine to see Paris again, and the Abbé Breuil and Malvina and Pat Kelley and all the other old friends. It was even better to arrive the next day in England and find Dick waiting disconsolately on board the Sovflot boat, sitting on the trunk containing our collections from the Soviet Union. We took the next train to Leicester and out to Baggrave, where everything was as it always had been. Here with the family we were able to relax and enjoy ourselves, as well as work on our notes and the accounts. That last tiresome task was my job, complicated beyond belief by all the frontiers we had crossed and the different monies we had used. Moreover, all Field Museum accounts had to be kept in great detail, down to the last tip.

It was wonderful to be at Baggrave again. We had traveled so far, seen so much, done so many things, talked to so many people, that it seemed we had been away for years. I went down to Oxford to go over the details with Buxton, Balfour, and Marett and plan the elaborate work of putting all the research together: cataloguing the specimens and photographs and preparing the final reports; compiling the final data, editing and proofreading and seeing it through the press. I thought then it might take five years; it was to take nineteen.

Finally, while in London, we collected at Claridge's the two priceless suitcases of photographs, films, and records which had been salvaged when Dick's room caught fire in Baghdad.

We arrived back in Chicago from the 1934 expedition to find a considerable change in the museum. Dr. Laufer was dead. The shocking news had reached me in Moscow. His office, the department library, the corridors, and even the storerooms seemed strangely empty without his all-pervading presence. I had known him as a friend, adviser, and relentless protagonist. Instead of the long talks with him in which I sat with pad and pencil on my knee, taking notes, making lists of references, I found myself alone. *"Rebus in arduis . . ."*

Now I had a serious decision to make and without the benefit of his advice.

Should I catalogue the huge collections I had bought all over western Europe during the preceding years or devote my main effort to completing the manuscripts for publication? I had the feeling that a second World War was coming. Walking one wintry afternoon beside Lake Michigan where the waves were breaking on Oak Street Beach, I decided that the most important thing was to have all the specimens catalogued and put away in perfect order because without numbers and information the specimens were valueless. All that information I was carrying in my head or in notes. In the evening and over week ends I would work on the publications. As a result, when World War II neared and I was ordered to Washington, all the collections were in perfect order and several of the manuscripts were ready for the printer.

The book upon which I had worked so many nights after my

museum labors, *The Arabs of Central Iraq, Their History, Ethnology and Physical Characters,* was published by Field Museum in 1935. This large monograph, looking like a copy of the Chicago Telephone Directory, contained anthropometric data and 1000 photographs of the Arabs of the Kish area. Sir Arthur Keith wrote a 40,000-word introduction. This monograph, together with a large album of photographs of the Hall of Races of Mankind and the Hall of the Stone Age of western Europe—to show my work in Field Museum—were forwarded to Oxford University with formal application "for permission to supplicate" for the degree of Doctor or Science. Such publications must include a "major contribution to knowledge." I had first discussed working for this degree sixteen years before with Mr. Henry Balfour.

A year later, during the three hours' discussion by the examiners at Oxford, Buxton, my tutor and companion at Kish, appeared in my behalf. There was considerable argument because I was under thirty-five and the degree had not been awarded to anyone so young for a long time. The second obstacle was that I was a foreigner. However, in due course I received a letter saying that the university authorities granted me permission to supplicate for the degree of Doctor of Science, on June 14, 1937.

I went to England for the ceremony. Mother came down from Baggrave. That was a beautiful sunshiny day at Oxford. Dean Henderson accompanied me to a courtyard outside the Sheldonian Theatre, where a scout from New College straightened my white bow tie and helped me put on the special robe. It turned out that I was taking the senior degree of the day.

The *March of Time* in London had sent down a cameraman to take pictures so that I had to take my hood on and off several times for the benefit of the photographer. Then came a small white-haired man, dressed in a fancy black academic robe and carrying a shining silver mace, who muttered, "Follow me."

Exactly in his footsteps I marched up to a huge door which was struck three times by the mace. As the door opened we entered the Sheldonian Theatre. We walked slowly between two lines of seats, stopping in the center, while two proctors in black gowns marched three times up and down the front. I had been told that this was part of an ancient custom to allow tradespeople,

319

if the supplicant had unpaid bills, to grab the gown of one of the proctors and request immediate payment. Fortunately no one grabbed. The little man with the mace stepped to the right and whispered to me to advance alone. On a small raised platform in the center of the hall, under a tier of seats, sat the vice-chancellor flanked by two university officials. All three were wearing their mortarboards with black tassels. The vice-chancellor began to read in Latin. All three of them raised their mortarboards rapidly at frequent intervals as he read. I learned afterward that this was because when either God or the university is mentioned they must raise their hats. At the end of what seemed an interminable reading, the vice-chancellor stood up, shook me by the hand—a signal honor—and said, "Let me be the first to congratulate you on your Doctorate of Science." As I walked away, I saw Mother with several friends. Dean Henderson met me at the door and told me that, according to New College custom, I must walk around the New College garden in my new robe. As we strolled together the dean looked very pleased. "You know," he confided, "you've been an agreeable surprise to me. I always thought you ran with a rather wild set during your undergraduate days."

FROM Chicago I drove into Washington on a wet night in February 1941. The streets glistened in the headlights. I felt this was the opening of a new chapter in my life.

Next morning at the Navy Department I was informed that my commission as lieutenant, signed by Acting Secretary James Forrestal, would be in order that afternoon after the oath ceremony. However, my orders were that I had already been assigned to other duties "on higher authority."

"I need a tame anthropologist on my staff," President Roosevelt had said. He had first approached me in the museum the year before with questions concerning the Near East. Now war was in the air and that area at boiling point. I was to do research as a specialist on the Near East.

That afternoon Archie MacLeish, Librarian of Congress, assigned me to Study Room 115 in the Library, where, until November 30, 1945, I familiarized myself with every source of data and the key personnel on Southwestern Asia, also called the Near East or the Middle East. This dealt primarily with the land and the people of each country from Suez to Afghanistan.

There could have been no finer place for research, with ready access to the Thomas Jefferson Reading Room and the almost boundless wealth of books, periodicals, maps, library facilities, and reference material in the Departments of State, Agriculture, and Commerce. Before long I had a fair working knowledge of sources and a card index of specialists on the Near East. This interesting assignment rounded out my limited studies on the area from Suez to the Caucasus.

My cousin Ronnie Tree soon arrived from England, where he was M.P. for Oxfordshire. After dinner one evening, while discussing my present non-museum assignment, I told Ronnie I had

321

heard that the BBC was monitoring world-wide broadcasts and that some of this material was to deal with the Near East. Next morning Duff Cooper, Minister of Information in London, received a cable from Ronnie, who was also then in the MOI, asking him to send me by sea-mail pouch, in care of the British Embassy, all BBC daily and weekly monitoring results. From that time on a messenger brought them regularly to Study Room 115. After submitting to the Department of State a sample abstract of Near East information arranged by country, I was instructed to produce a mimeographed weekly summary based on BBC monitoring.

Anne Fuller, who had worked part time in Field Museum, wrote from Harvard saying that, with the world falling apart, she simply could not continue to sort Near Eastern stone implements and pottery in the basement of the Peabody Museum. She volunteered for work in Washington. In response to my reply that she could assist me, but temporarily as a volunteer, Anne arrived in the Library of Congress. For some weeks she assisted with the compilation of the weekly summary on the Near East, now enlarged to include other unclassified sources and references to new books and articles.

She craved more work, so I suggested that she compile a small handbook for GIs arriving in Lebanon. "You've lived there," I said, "you know how strangers should behave." I felt our military and civilian personnel, abroad for the first time, would require instruction in behavior and knowledge of local manners and customs. Anne was well qualified, for she had spent a year like a "blushing Moslem maiden" in the village of Buarij, high on Mount Lebanon, while obtaining data for a sociological thesis for the University of Chicago. A couple of weeks later the rough draft was ready.

Notes on the location, climate, history, communications, etc., were arranged under headings. Guidance in manners was given, such as: when drinking coffee, never place the handleless cup on the ground; never turn the soles toward a person no matter how much the knees ache; never admire a child or horse, for the fear of the evil eye is always present; sacred Moslem buildings must always be respected; strict Moslems neither smoke nor drink

322

alcohol, so do not offer them; avoid high-pressure methods which simply do not work except in reverse. At the end of the handbook was a list of about three hundred English-Arabic useful words and phrases together with the local coinage in U.S. equivalents.

Sometimes a minor tragedy is a means of getting measures passed in Washington. Fortunately, while the desirability of circulating this type of handbook to all overseas personnel was under discussion, a U.S. sergeant fired a shot in India and its echo was heard in Washington. This nameless sergeant, driving his jeep through a narrow, crowded street, was exasperated by a white cow that remained apparently deaf to the strident screams of the horn. He drew his revolver. The crowd, wildly incensed at seeing their sacred cow shot by a foreigner, surrounded the jeep. A passing M.P. patrol rescued the sergeant in the nick of time.

The cable bearing details of this incident turned the Washington tide in favor of a series of GI handbooks based on the Fuller-Field sample. In final form, attractive little pamphlets for about thirty areas, illustrated with charming sketches, were printed by the million for our GIs going overseas. The sacred cow had not died in vain.

The continuity of the work on the Near East, now more topical than ever, was interrupted in the spring of 1942 by orders to fly at once to Trinidad. Our enlisted men were the source of trouble there. The governor, Sir Hubert Young, was launching protests against the "U.S. invasion." Reports had reached Washington of serious unrest. Trinidad was a vital link in the bauxite-producing chain, for her vessels from British Guiana transferred this precious-for-planes ore into deep-draft ships bound for United States ports.

President Roosevelt wanted a firsthand report from the British side. My qualifications were unique: I had never been in the Caribbean, hence would have an open mind, and Sir Hubert had attended Eton and had fought with T. E. Lawrence against the Turks in World War I. He had written a book called *The Arab at Home*. Since I was an Old Etonian and knew Lawrence and the Arabs, these should serve as an introduction.

323

Two days later, with Aspinall's *Pocket Guide to the West Indies* in my pocket, I left the Washington airport.

At Miami the high priority worked perfectly, for nearly a thousand persons awaited passage by air.

Next morning I called on the governor, an obvious martinet with a kindly twinkle, who appeared enchanted to pour out his troubles to keenly receptive American ears. The flood of people's names and places soon had my head whirling. They were as difficult to master as those of the animals and birds. I begged a brief respite to make myself informed on the colony, and drove in a taxi to the Government Press. No handbook on Trinidad and Tobago existed. I bought piles of maps and recent publications and, at two bookshops, eight books on Trinidad. Equipped with bottles of mucilage, a large pair of scissors, red and blue pencils, paper clips, two reams of bond paper, and a box of carbon, I returned at noon to the Queen's Park. Six bridge tables were set up in a line across the windows. The waiter, bringing lunch on a tray, thought a harmless lunatic was occupying the best room in the hotel overlooking the Savannah.

With ruthless vandalism for a booklover I cut the main sections out of each publication. Now came the more difficult part, the cutting, pasting, and linking of the items. That night at eight o'clock two native girls appeared, ready to type all night. By lunchtime the following day three copies of my *Handbook of Trinidad and Tobago* were finished, complete with table of contents and bibliography.

Sir Hubert was fuming in his book-lined study; his mustache bristled. He felt I had kept him waiting more than twenty-four hours. He soon found out that, with the map spread out, the handbook, and knowledge acquired during its compilation, I could now follow him with some degree of success. I longed to hear him talk about Auda abu Tayi and the Howeitat and the Beni Sukhur Bedouins of Transjordan, of his desert campaigns around El Jafar and Bayir Wells, of his house at Eton. Instead I heard myself saying, "Sir Hubert, my orders are to bring you greetings from President Roosevelt and to take back to him your complaints on Anglo-American relations within this colony, a situation which is of grave concern to him. With your permission, I am instructed to find out the prevailing attitude of the West Indians toward the United States, Britain, and India. We know the docks need protection; if you will furnish me with a list of fire-fighting equipment necessary, I will take it back to Washington. I have no authority to make any promises of any kind in behalf of the U. S. Government."

Sir Hubert relaxed. "The first thing for you to do is to read some of the exchanges of cables between Mr. Churchill and myself."

A big "Secret" label rested amiably on top of the file. I was fascinated by the length and essay style of these cables. This interchange of messages could well have been published as examples of first-class writing. Each comma and semicolon was written out. My confidence in the stability of Britain was increased by this display of perfection even in the face of possible destruction by the Nazis. I chuckled over many typical Churchillian phrases, but none were at the expense of the President, for whom he obviously held the highest esteem.

At the end of an hour's reading I had gathered that Mr. Churchill ordered the governor to co-operate with the U. S. Army and Navy authorities to the fullest possible extent, always within the bounds of common sense and realizing that this "U.S. invasion" was solely for the duration.

I then asked Sir Hubert for specific charges. The list was long and as it flowed forth in unchecked stream Sir Hubert's face became purple with rage. He cited the bad behavior of our enlisted personnel, accidents caused by reckless GI drivers, the buying of native girls for two or more cigarettes, the proposed extension of the navy base for a new hospital, the shooting of a native near Docksite (a water-front pub) by an American sailor, and a general disrespect shown his authority in the colony, "an unmitigated insult, sir, to His Majesty's representative."

But, on the other side of the ledger, "our boys" were being beaten and robbed. As I drove back to the Queen's Park, it seemed almost easier to measure and blood-group the wild-looking Yezidis in Iraq than to sort out in my mind the political disturbances hovering over the beautiful little "land of the hummingbird."

That night I dined with Sir Hubert and Lady Young, a handsome Englishwoman with a lovely complexion and an air of great serenity. Her eyes alone betrayed her anxiety for her husband's worries. But the conversation was light and gay and Sir Hubert told many amusing anecdotes. The other guests were Sir Edward Cunard, Sir Lennox O'Reilly, the brilliant K.C. whose five fingers were in every pie in the colony, and Colonel Muller, the pink-cheeked and young-looking chief of police, soon to be the son-in-law of Sir Lennox.

Sir Lennox had been brought up in Leicestershire, so much of our talk was of the county and the Quorn. We might have been dining in some country house in England, not on this troubled tropical island off the rim of South America.

Port-of-Spain reported few crimes before the war, but with the influx of British and foreign troops and merchant seamen the water front had become a dangerous area after dark. With a plain-clothes detective I pub-crawled the dock area and picked up any information to be had concerning the temptations and troubles that beset enlisted men in Port-of-Spain.

We drifted first into Docksite, the canteen frequented by merchant seamen who had survived Nazi torpedoes. There, amid thick blue smoke and clinking beer glasses, seamen joined us for a drink. Not liking beer, I managed to work my usual alibi of "sticking to Cokes for a change."

Over foaming glasses, the men talked of war and of sharks. They spoke graphically of their fear of sharks. Torpedoes, one said, were part of war, but not sharks. Another commented that the merchant seaman was the "forgotten man" in this war.

They were embittered men and ready for any diversion, for each visit here might be their last.

We went to several other dives. They were nearly all the same. In the dark streets we were accosted by girls; the price, five cigarettes. My companion told me that four hundred of these girls were owned by the East Indian, Boisie, who operated a string of houses in this area, where, in recent weeks, enlisted men had been drugged and robbed and sometimes beaten up and left in the gutter.

326

These were the conditions the President had asked me to investigate so I told my companion I wanted to meet Boisie.

Arrangements were made through a jewelry fence who, the next night, led me down a dark alley on the water front and up a flight of rickety stairs to a door with a small grille. Within, the permeating atmosphere was Oriental—brass dishes, trays, table coverings, draperies, all from India. A thick carpet masked the footfall of Boisie, who slipped into the room from a side door. He was short and small-boned, with café-au-lait skin and raven-black hair. Around his neck was knotted a red kerchief and against his bared chest hung a gold chain suspending a gold locket. He looked like a Caribbean pirate.

"What do you want?"

"I have been sent down from Washington to study Anglo-American relations in Trinidad."

"So what?"

"I know you control the gambling and the girls and I want to hear your side. Tell me, what are your problems with the American sailors and soldiers and merchant seamen?"

He was watching me keenly with his clear, dark eyes. Suddenly he laughed.

"I'll be damned. That's a new one."

I explained that I was not a detective but an anthropologist, a matter which took some explaining.

Suddenly I became the recipient of the outpoured troubles of the king of the Trinidad underworld. Boisie had his own complaints to launch against the Yankee enlisted men. They had money; they liked to drink, gamble, and make love; also they liked to fight. This annoyed the authorities. The authorities in turn annoyed Boisie. This very building, he said peevishly, had been one of his best clubs until yesterday. Then there had been trouble and the police closed it.

"The best way for you to understand the situation," Boisie concluded earnestly, "is to see some of my joints. Of course I have to depend on your not handing any information over to the police."

I promised earnestly, and found myself touring the town as the evening's companion to the leading procurer in Port-of-Spain.

Boisie knocked on grilled doors which flew open magically

before his bland countenance. We visited places where dice rolled on green tables, where whiskey glasses circled the cloth.

We climbed other stairs to inspect one of the bordellos. As soon as the girls saw Boisie they rushed for their medical certificates: temporary guarantees of purity. Boisie generously offered me (as an anthropologist) a choice of English, French, East Indian, Negro, Chinese, Portuguese, mulatto, or any other racial cross; tall, medium, short, thin, plump or fat, dancers, contortionists, blondes, brunettes, redheads, girls with hair straight, curly, or woolly, tattooed girls . . .

I appealed to Boisie's power sense by asking him to give the enlisted men a chance to survive a night's celebration in Port-of-Spain. On his own initiative, he promised to order his bouncers to treat United States citizens less roughly in future and to inflict severe corporal punishment on any of his employees who might employ the gentle pickpocket art on their transient guests.

I suggested that strong coffee and sandwiches be sold in the gambling dens. This would not be as profitable as liquor, but, I pointed out, it might reduce the quarrels that brought his places so much police attention. Boisie promised to try out this suggestion. He added wistfully that he wished he could meet Al Capone so that he "could learn a thing or two from the Big Man."

I walked back to the Queen's Park just before dawn feeling I had read a curious footnote to the long strange Story of Man.

The rest of my investigation was conducted along more conventional lines. At the U. S. Navy base, the commanding officer said that the protested hospital should be built on higher land to escape the mosquitoes, because malaria had become a far more serious factor than had been anticipated. The fire hazard in the port was obvious; on the dock I was shown barrels of oil stacked beside mountains of boards awaiting shipment, with oil and sawdust everywhere. I took notes on everything that could possibly interest the President.

Middie Train, son of my lifelong friends Admiral and Mrs. Russell Train, took two days' leave and drove me around the island. We talked with East Indians and Hindus and Chinese merchants. We saw small Hindu temples gleaming white in the sunshine, and Chinese stores. My greeting, *"How tien shi?"*

brought many smiles of pleasure. We stopped for a swim in the warm surf on Manzanilla Beach. Near Bonasse I was shown some stone and shell artifacts from a nearby mound. We passed Los Gallos, where Columbus met the native Indians and Sir Walter Raleigh cast anchorage on his second voyage.

At La Brea we stood on the shores of the famous hundred-acre Pitch Lake, source of 100,000 tons of asphalt annually. The absorption of the sun's rays makes this one of the hottest places in the world; the shade thermometer registered 120 degrees to our misty eyes. Middie muttered, "This is worse than Washington," and it was.

According to legend, this pitch lake had inundated the village of the Chaima Indians as punishment. They had offended the Good Spirit by destroying the hummingbirds, the animated souls of their deceased relatives.

Next morning I was flying northward to Washington. High above the ground I began to write notes for my report.

I took my memorandum with recommendations to the President over to Grace Tully. A few days later the full report was handed in. I was gratified by the actions taken.

It was after that I began to remember the talk in Trinidad with the merchant seamen who had been torpedoed and escaped later from sharks. Night after night I thought of these men in the water, holding onto rafts or upturned lifeboats or lying in rubber boats, with shark fins cutting through the water around them. I wrote the President a memorandum suggesting that we try to develop a shark repellent. I was instructed to discuss the matter with the chief, BuAer. Knowing very little about sharks and shark behavior I called my old friend, Harold Coolidge, Harvard zoologist and member of scientific expeditions to Alaska, Africa, Southeast Asia, and the Dutch East Indies.

Together we called on Rear Admiral Ralph Davison, acting chief of the Bureau of Aeronautics. He became immediately interested, mainly from the psychological point of view, and requested the Committee on Medical Research of the Office of Scientific Research and Development to investigate the possibility of finding a chemical repellent to protect men in shark-infested waters.

A round-table conference was held in the National Academy of Sciences. W. Douglas Burden, trustee of the American Museum of Natural History and one of the founders of Marineland, Florida, was invited to become Responsible Investigator of this research project.

The technical staff included: Stuart Springer, professional shark-catcher from Salerno, Florida; Arthur McBride and Arthur Schmidt of Marine Studios, Florida; Dr. David Todd, chemist at Harvard; Dr. A. P. Black, chemist at the University of Florida; Dr. French, consulting chemist; Dr. C. M. Breder, Jr., director, New York Aquarium; and Michael Lerner, big-game fisherman. The institutions co-operating included: the Oceanographic Institution, Woods Hole; Scripps Institution of Oceanography, La Jolla; University of Florida; and the American Museum of Natural History. Springer, McBride, and Todd were the major contributors.

Our greatest problem was to persuade BuMed that sharks attacked living people. One naval officer wrote, "We have no record of anyone who has taken an oath to the U. S. Navy ever having been bitten by a shark."

Harold quipped, "Perhaps they didn't have time to file their seven carbons for information and suitable action."

We started by testing 150 possible repellents one after another. Nothing worked. Meanwhile a massive study of shark lore, including many native beliefs, was compiled in the Library of Congress, in the Army Medical Library, and the Smithsonian Institution. The wearing of long black drawers, knocking stones together under water, and other bits of native folklore were tried.

Chemicals were combined and tests with sharks run off Florida, southern California, and Ecuador. The results were far from conclusive.

We were all discouraged. We had nothing to recommend to the Navy, Coast Guard, and Air Force and were about ready to quit. An informal conference was held in Washington to discuss whether we should continue the almost hopeless task or recommend to the Naval Research Laboratory that the search be abandoned. The discussion continued far into the night. Finally, as a last resort, we asked Springer to tell us in detail about professional shark-catching, hoping for a new clue.

He described setting the lines on chains attached to buoys across a channel. We were half asleep. Springer added as an afterthought: "You know, if a shark dies on the hook and remains there for several days because of a storm, we never throw it overboard anywhere near the fishing ground because a dead shark pollutes the water."

Suddenly we were wide awake. Here might be the answer. A message was relayed to Woods Hole. A small shark was killed, and every four hours as it decomposed, a piece of meat was tried as a repellent on the ravenous sharks in the big tank. Several days later the telephone jangled and a voice said: "We have *it!*"

Two chemicals and the decomposing shark were combined. Production began. The "shark repellent" in a waterproof belt container is now standard equipment for military personnel flying over water and in lifeboats and life rafts.

Something else haunted me from that conversation in the waterfront dive in Port-of-Spain. I could not forget the bitterness of the merchant seamen calling themselves "the really forgotten men." How about a Medal for Valor for the merchant seamen? There was no such medal. I handed Grace Tully a memorandum suggesting that one be struck to encourage their hazardous efforts.

Next afternoon back came the memorandum with "Take up with Admiral Land. F.D.R." Admiral "Jerry" Land grunted as he read and said gruffly, "That's a good idea. We had already thought of it. Now we'll get some action."

Paul Manship, whom I had known at the Art Institute in Chicago, designed the medal and some weeks later the ideal recipient's name was found. He was young, shy enough but not too shy, had a wife and young son, and was a real hero.

On the day before the presentation, General "Pa" Watson called me. "The President would like you to be at the presentation ceremony of the Merchant Seaman's Medal of Honor. Can you be in my office at 2:45 tomorrow afternoon?"

I assured the general I would be there. "One more thing. The President sends you the following message, 'In peace or at war, it is very rare to be present at the birth of a brain child.' That's why he wants you here."

Next afternoon we were in the White House, the commissioners led by Admiral Land, Edwin F. Cheney, Paul Manship, and myself. The hero was beginning to look a little green around the gills. As we advanced, he fell back, muttering, "I'd rather be torpedoed again than go through this."

All the time Harold Coolidge and I were working on the shark repellent we had discussed rescue equipment and were appalled at the completely out-of-date methods and general apathy toward new ideas and modern equipment. Our first interest was in sea rescues because of the torpedoings and plane ditchings. We proposed to Colonel William J. Donovan, then Coordinator of Information, that a Committee on Emergency Rescue Equipment should be established. Owing to the President's interest, we were sent over to the Joint Chiefs of Staff, where Directive No. 54 was drawn up to cover this new function. This JCS Directive was broad in scope, bristling with authority to investigate, encourage research, and make recommendations on a Joint Service basis.

Our organization was soon functioning with John Bader of the Quartermaster Corps of the Army, Earle Hiscock of the Coast Guard, and Lt. Nevett Bartow USNR, as key members. Liaison Officers were appointed in all branches of the Services. Naturally the Navy, especially BuAer and the Coast Guard, as well as the Army Air Force were most concerned. A co-ordinated effort to collect and exchange every type of information and equipment on land-air-sea rescue was begun. Harold and I were steamed up like the crusaders of old. With our JCS Directive and as civilians we were ordered to practice co-ordination with the minimum regard for "channels." We arranged meetings between all persons directly concerned with every form of rescue in the Army and Navy, especially the Coast Guard and Air Force.

One of our first activities was to interview survivors. I remember a Norwegian merchant seaman who had spent twenty days in the North Atlantic with five companions in a seven-man rubber boat. Shy at first, he warmed up during lunch and talked graphically. His main needs during the ordeal were more water and a way of catching fish. This led to the research on converting salt water to fresh and to the development of the fishing kits. He told us how he had jigged fish by unraveling a bandage from the Red Cross box and thereby making a line, using a safety pin for a hook. Here were two concrete suggestions. Three of our best big-game fishermen responded to the call to Washington: Gifford Pinchot, Mike Lerner, and Kip Farrington. At their own expense the two latter brought their captains from Miami. A representative of the Ashaway Line & Twine Company was asked to be present. Within a week two fishing kits had been developed, one weighing less than one pound for the fliers, the other somewhat heavier for lifeboats and rubber boats.

Hundreds of generations before ours, prehistoric man had invented the first bone fishhook. In some ways we had made progress.

We continued to collect stories from merchant seamen. Many wanted Bibles, some asked for popular songs and hymns. One incident captured attention. A huge lifeboat lay tossing in mid-Atlantic. On the fifth day the twenty men were cross and irritable. Survival seemed doubtful as the hours dragged on. One man suggested a song. With cracked lips they sang popular songs and then hymns, the second being "Nearer, my God, to Thee." At the beginning of the third verse an argument began as to the correct version. The mate tried to restore order. Suddenly the two turned on him and threw him overboard. He went down screaming. The tragedy aided our cause. Bibles, books of hymns, and popular songs on waterproof paper were soon ready for distribution.

Another problem was false teeth. It appears that many merchant seamen wear either an upper or lower set or both. At sea the dentures usually stand in a glass beside their bunks and are used only at meals. Many torpedoed seamen had to be outfitted with new teeth. We proposed a waterproof belt with pockets for passport, papers, Bible, money, and false teeth. These were very well received—and worn.

Then came the word of sinkings in the Caribbean between British Guiana and Miami. Men reported that in brilliant sunshine they screamed and waved their shirts at planes but were often not seen. This was hard to understand and I discussed it with many fliers. Finally one of them said, "Why don't you get into the pilot's seat and then I think you'll understand."

Once inside the plane at Gravelly Point outside Washington, it was clear to me that the pilot sees far ahead and does not look straight down. The men in the rubber boat did not have time to light the reddish-brown smoke signal and have it carried up to five thousand feet before the plane was past, at two or three hundred miles an hour. The fluorescin dye-marker caused a large patch of brilliant yellow-green in the water, but this is not visible from a high angle. Surely some method could be found. They were working on radio. The "Gibson Girl" was the final result, but not for some time. Then I remembered that near the Roman fortress of Qasr el Burqu in the North Arabian Desert I had signaled through mirage, using a flattened gasoline can. The heliograph had been known for many centuries. Could an unbreakable mirror with a focusing device be developed, so that a man could direct the path of the beam at an airplane? I had great confidence in the Bureau of Standards. Through my friend, Wayne Chatfield Taylor, Under-Secretary of Commerce, we were introduced to Dr. Lyman Briggs, who passed us on to Larry Young and his colleagues. Larry said, "I think it can be done, but it will require considerable research."

Within a year the emergency signaling mirror made by G.E. was tested and retested. We gave one to Brad Washburn during an Alaskan expedition. He flashed the mirror at a plane at five thousand feet and five miles away. The plane reported a party on the ice. Our mirror really worked!

When reports came in from Anzio that our ground troops were being strafed by our own planes we experimented with thin plastic filters over the mirror. At the Bureau of Standards several colored filters worked fairly well. However, from Anzio a cabled report stated that under battle conditions these gadgets would not work satisfactorily.

One of the problems was to write in less than a hundred words the instructions for focusing the signaling mirror, this caption to be stamped on the back. We all had a hand at it. Perhaps an M.I.T. graduate could have worked it out eventually, but certainly no average merchant seaman. Suddenly I remembered Phil Wylie of the facile pen. He offered his services for one day. After writing and rewriting the hundred words, he came up with a text about 5 P.M.

On Biscayne Boulevard Phil handed the mirror to his young daughter Karen. "Read the instructions and see if you can focus this mirror on that wall." Karen read the paper and about ninety seconds later had aimed it correctly. We have no record of the number of persons saved by the signaling mirrors, but grateful reports were received. The mirror in its third stage was developed too late for an armed services order. With one hand this mirror may be focused on a plane up to ten miles distant.

The late Frank Page, son of Mr. Walter Hines Page, came to us from Sosthenes Behn of the International Telephone and Telegraph Company, to offer help. We explained that our main problem in radio communication from a rubber boat was how to get the antenna up into the air and keep it flying. Balloons and kites had been tried, but proved of little use.

A week or so later Frank phoned from New York to say that he was sending down by messenger two Wheelwright kites for demonstration. These were box kites shot like a rocket up into the air. We assembled representatives from all interested service branches on a hillside near Alexandria. The first attempt was a near failure; the second kite soared majestically.

Eventually, after long trials and errors, we had the fishing kits, mirror, a radio antenna kite, drinking-water kits for Arctic and sunshine areas, handbooks and movies for survival techniques. Emergency Rescue Equipment was making progress. Lives were being saved on every continent and ocean. The JCS were pleased with our efforts.

By this time we all thought it was desirable to "test emergency rescue equipment for saving life following ship-sinking or plane crash in water." Dozens of new inventions had poured in to ERE. No recommendations could be made without proper test. The three services still worked most independently; if one approved, another often disdained it.

Our recommendation for joint tests off Miami received JCS approval and a nod from the President. On March 22 we arrived

335

at the Hotel Columbus to present a letter of introduction from Admiral Waesche to the captain of the port, U. S. Coast Guard, Miami. With us was a list of 250 items to be tested and categorized.

For twelve days tests were run by number, the first combined service tests leading to joint orders. The President had been particularly anxious to have this precedent established.

The first test was between fluorescent panels and standard signal flags. Then came tests of smoke signals, dye markers, signaling mirrors, rubber boats and lifeboats with colored panels for aircraft recognition, life preservers and waterproof suits, and many others.

One of the most enthusiastic members of the group, our friend George Wheelwright, "midwife of Polaroid," volunteered to try out the waterproof suits and life preservers. A ham operator in Dade County, or perhaps farther away, could have heard the following: "Are you ready for Test No. 65, a new type of life preserver?" "All ready. Throw George overboard." Then a splash, as George jumped off into Biscayne Bay. George was really magnificent.

The last trials were run as night operations, the purpose to determine the visibility of the life-preserver light and the effectiveness of retro-reflective buttons.

These tests of emergency rescue equipment off Miami proved very helpful in trying out 250 lifesaving and rescue devices, but were probably far more important in establishing the precedent for tests before representatives of Army, Navy, and Army Air Forces personnel which resulted in a joint order.

Our report with recommendations was sent to the President and to the Joint Chiefs of Staff.

In 1950, as I sat in the comfortable Pan American Clipper from La Guardia to Damascus, I read the list of emergency equipment carried. It was gratifying to see that ERE had worked to some degree on every item, now standard rescue equipment on commercial air lines.

As each improvement or new development was accepted we slept easier, knowing a little more had been sent out in the way of help to men adrift on the waters, lost in the jungles, or wandering in the icy wastes; men bleeding in shark-infested areas, men losing hope . . .

Some relief from the gloomier moments of World War II was obtained from the ever jangling telephone. Dialing a Navy extension, you would hear a baby voice answer, "Lighter-than-air." A deep-voiced woman in War Shipping Administration replied to the first ring, "We handle seamen."

One rainy afternoon I was sitting in my tiny Study Room 115 in the Library of Congress Annex. It had been a very depressing day. Memorandum writing seemed to have little point except for the "file and forget" department. My private telephone rang. An authoritative voice asked without preliminaries, "How about those shoes of Mrs. Roosevelt's?" Since this could only be Malvina Thompson calling Field's store, I replied flippantly. Many apologies from the White House.

Gretchen Green, author of *The Whole World and Company*, telephoned one morning at 3:30 A.M.

"Where can I find two hundred camels?"

I protested sleepily.

"Henry, I have an idea. The British troops in North Africa are having trouble with their feet. If I can get two hundred camels, we can load them with foot powder, follow the Army, and beat Rommel."

I told her to call Bill Mann at the zoo.

Another past-midnight long-distance call came from my old friend, Eleanor Parker, in Chicago.

"I've just had the most vivid dream: Nazis tunneling under the English Channel. I want Mr. Churchill to know right away."

"Send him an air-mail warning. You can never get him on the telephone."

In wartime, research and development boards are under great pressure. Word spread that our civilian group had time to listen to inventors, even crackpots. Some "inventors" look peculiar and behave even more strangely, but they may have useful ideas.

A brilliant mathematician in California showed one of our friends a sheet of paper covered with symbols and numbers. A few handwritten lines said that a rocket-driven plastic-encased

337

bomb dropped from a plane could penetrate better than a far heavier steel shell.

We were short of steel; this was the theoretical answer. I was sent to see an admiral who pounded the desk and said, "Rockets are for kids on the Fourth of July. We never use them." Within a couple of years a rocket program was in high gear, even in the Navy.

A translator who had some copy to deliver to me asked if her brother might join us at lunch in the Willard. During lunch the brother remarked that he was an inventor. "I've made a beautiful plastic mine but no one will let me demonstrate it." The last seven words could have covered the Washington Monument in those days. This particular inventor was caught in the battle between Big Steel and Big Plastics. The former had always made mines; the latter wanted new business. A few days later, through General Campbell, Chief of Ordnance, successful tests were run at nearby Aberdeen, Maryland. Millions of plastics mines were produced for the European Theater of Operations.

At teatime on another day, the telephone rang and a voice said, "I've got a new invention. May I come around and show it to you?"

In the garden he produced from his pocket a medicine bottle containing a clear liquid. "You remember reading about 'Molotov cocktails' being used in the Spanish War? Gasoline in a bottle was thrown at a tank. On contact the bottle broke and burning gas ran over the vehicle, but most of it ran off. I've invented a gas that will stick and burn. Watch this."

I found an old iron stove lid behind the woodpile. The inventor threw some of the thickened liquid onto this metal, then a match. The gas flamed so intensely that in an instant a hole was burned through the lid. This looked like a real invention, although he had the same story of office-to-office trudging and always refusal after refusal to run tests.

Next morning the inventor, Albert Herron, was on his way to Standard Oil of New Jersey armed with half a medicine bottle of this precious liquid. We now know this as napalm, one of the greatest weapons against the Japanese, against the Nazis, then against our enemies in Korea. Herron had an improved formula.

338

Three suggestions were vetoed personally by the President:

1. A chemist's suggestion for poisoning the fish around the southern tip of Japan from submarines. By broadcasting repeated warnings, panic, leading to surrender, would ensue.

2. A fire spray that could be fired from a thousand yards into a concrete pillbox. A tracer bullet would create a flash flame, burning the occupants.

3. A young former German, then in the U. S. Army, volunteered to attempt to assassinate Hitler. As a onetime guest at Berchtesgaden, the SS Guards might let him pass into Der Fuehrer's presence. He was quite willing to die for his new country.

The last reminds me of the time I asked Air Chief Marshal Sir Cyril Newall why the RAF did not try to finish Hitler and his top aides that lovely afternoon in the forest of Compiègne when France surrendered and Hitler danced his historic jig. My question was, "Why didn't the RAF bomb and set fire to the forest with every available plane?"

"We always respect the Chief of State," was the solemn reply.

I now launched upon one of the most fascinating experiences of my life: "M" Project.

The President was concerned with the future rehabilitation and resettlement of several million permanently displaced persons in Europe and Asia, who would be unable to return when the war ended. In the spring of 1940 a presidential representative had come to my office in Field Museum to ask, "If water control of the Tigris and Euphrates is established with irrigation projects, agricultural development, and public health measures, how many people can Iraq support? An Italian estimate is seventeen million people. What is your guess?"

"I think that is far too high a figure. My guess would be seven to eight million, about double the present population. But it would be very expensive."

Population pressures had often caused wars throughout history. New techniques were being developed in irrigation and flood control, in agriculture and insecticides, in eradicating malaria and other semi-tropical diseases.

339

It seemed as though a study of world-wide settlement possibilities should prove profitable as soon as the shooting was over. I sent a memorandum "For the President" to Grace Tully. Back came the word to discuss the project with Dr. Isaiah Bowman, president of Johns Hopkins University. Next morning in Baltimore, gracious, white-haired Dr. Bowman sat in his study listening to research very close to his heart. After a few minutes he folded his hands on the desk. "Your idea for this migration project is most necessary. As you know, my *Limits of Land Settlement* contains years of study along these lines. I am entirely in sympathy and I will help you in every way, but I cannot take on any further obligations."

"Thank you, Dr. Bowman. However, I would very much like to report to the President that you will assist me to direct 'M' Project. If approval is given, I will not bother you with any details. However, I would like to be able to turn to you for general guidance and friendly criticism, and to send you Copy No. 2 of our 'Studies on Migration and Settlement.' May I tell the President that you will accept?"

"Yes. I will."

On the way back to the capital I found myself whistling. Here was a research program into which I could put my heart. A few weeks later "M" Project was under way. In the Library of Congress three study rooms adjoining 115 were assigned to us for what was to prove a fascinating three-year assignment.

My directive was to prepare from all government and non-government sources a series of studies on settlement possibilities on every continent. As F.D.R. later told me, "I remember so well at the Paris Peace Conference, a question came up about some region. Next morning at noon a decision had to be taken. I want you to compile a series of world-wide studies region by region, so that before I have to take action there will be background material available in a clear and concise form. You do not have to worry about political, financial, or economic factors. I will call in State, Treasury, Agriculture, and Interior to help make the final decisions.

"Remember, Henry, this will be political dynamite. If you are

340

discovered by the press, I shall deny all knowledge of this project."

Then, as an aside to Grace Tully, the President added, "But, Grace, if Henry is thrown to the wolves, please try to pick up a few pieces for his family."

During the next thirty-six months I hired a revolving team of specialists—revolving in the sense that we concentrated on one continent after another, making analyses of world-wide migration and settlement. For example, during the studies of Central and South America, country by country I selected specialists on Latin America, all capable of reading Spanish and/or Portuguese. Each Study was mimeographed and distributed to a very limited list of government officials. Each copy was stamped "Confidential" and signed by me. Within a few weeks the flow of Studies began. Copy No. 1 was delivered by hand to the White House.

Dr. Bowman received Copy No. 2 in his office in the Department of State. My function was to select the areas for study, direct the researchers, edit the final draft to ensure uniformity of presentation, arrange for government mimeographing, and supervise dissemination. An FBI security check was made before each person was hired and an oath of secrecy taken. During these three years no leak occurred. Not one word got out in the press or radio until Ladislas Farago wrote an article entitled, "The Solution as F.D.R. Saw It," in *United Nations World*, June 1947. From this I shall quote or paraphrase, for "M" Project is still classified "Confidential."

Farago, as a member of Admiral Zacharias' team working on psychological warfare against the Japanese, had access to our Studies.

In general, this article is more or less correct, except for the imaginary figures for a visionary "International Settlement Authority."

The question was, "Where could the displaced millions be settled intelligently?" To answer this poser the staff of "M" Project studied and appraised dozens of previous resettlement attempts and the immigration laws of all countries and, wherever possible, their practical application. By the latter part of 1944 we had prepared world-wide Studies on areas with surplus population, their racial and religious composition, and their nationals' potential skill and adaptability as emigrants.

As a result, we found on paper many potential areas of settlement with an appraisal from economic, social, geographic, ecologic, demographic, and geopolitical angles. The last sentence was never written, i.e., "Therefore Ruritania can absorb 50,000 refugees from Germany."

Our research team was particularly qualified in reading many foreign languages. At all times this group used at least fifteen, several of them being fluent in five or more. This language facility enabled rapid cross-reference and checking on any area or settlement project from many angles. As the region of study changed, new specialists and consultants were hired. My two top-flight colleagues were Dr. Sergei Yakobson of the Library of Congress and Dr. Robert Strausz-Hupé of the University of Pennsylvania.

During the third year we were working on a dozen Studies at the same time, processing about eighty mimeographed pages every twenty-four hours.

As I look back on this work I cannot refrain from commenting on the amazing co-operation shown by all religious groups, who gave us free access to their files, reports, including their failure and their causes. In great part this was due to Sergei Yakobson's wide range of acquaintances, especially in New York.

After Roosevelt's death on April 12, 1945, President Truman expressed to me his verbal interest in "M" Project and ordered it continued temporarily. His Point 4 Program for undeveloped areas became the practical application of these and later worldwide researches.

As midnight struck on November 30, 1945, we had disseminated 665 Studies, making sixty-six volumes, each three inches thick, as well as many special maps and a large atlas showing world-wide population pressures plus lack of food, the result pointing decisively at World War III.

Early in October 1943 I received a telephone call from Grace Tully, who said that the President wanted me for the week end at Shangri-la. We were to bring country clothes, no dressing for dinner. Tell no one.

342

Under the White House portico Colonel Starling and Mike Reilly of the secret service greeted us.

We waited a few minutes in the long, carpeted hall. Along came the President in his wheel chair. He looked tired, gray, and careworn, but he greeted us with a charming smile.

Out in the sunshine were three cars. The President took the right-hand back seat next to Mrs. Wilson Brown. Mike Reilly sat beside the chauffeur. The large limousine crunched over the gravel, followed by an extra-long touring car with the top up and old-fashioned running boards. There were six men and the driver, all secret service.

The third car, another black limousine, carried the admiral, Grace, and myself with a secret service man beside the chauffeur.

The cavalcade moved out of the gate, leaving the old gray State Department building on the right, across to Virginia Avenue and out to Frederick. The three cars stopped at each traffic light. Sirens would have attracted too much attention. At each stop two secret service men jumped nimbly from the running boards and moved beside the presidential car, signaling to traffic. Their right hands never left their right pockets. I was astonished to see how few people recognized the President wearing his cape and gray felt hat. In Frederick some children stopped playing to wave. They received a wave back and a smile. "Young America, that's what we're fighting for," said F.D.R.

We began to climb up a winding gravel hill amid low trees. This was Catoctin Reservation, where Marines guarded their Commander in Chief. On a ridge overlooking the broad valley stood a one-story house with two wings. At the door stood smiling Filipino servants from the presidential yacht. Grace called out to me, "The Boss says to wear your oldest country clothes for lunch."

A few minutes later as we walked back toward the large central room we were amused to see the walls lined with framed anti-Roosevelt cartoons, including the one of the little girl reporting to her mother, "Wilfred is writing that bad word again," as she saw "Rooseve . . . !!" in the wet concrete.

Our host was wheeled into the room. He was wearing a dark blue turtle-neck sweater and old gray flannels. Already his spirits

343

had risen and he looked far less tired. During lunch he entertained us all with delightful stories and anecdotes about Campobello, the sea, and fishing. I told a couple of desert experiences and stories about the Devil Worshipers of Iraq. Over coffee F.D.R. asked me about the Caucasus, the Georgian Military Highway, and the attitude of the Russian people. He was particularly interested in the Park of Culture and Rest in Tbilisi where, back in 1934, the target at the coconut shy was Hitler's nose and, at the miniature shooting range, tank silhouettes bearing newly painted Japanese flags.

Before dinner we all met again. Our host mixed and shook the cocktails. He was in the best of spirits, having shaken off at least a decade. Conversation was general during dinner, followed by most amusing stories over coffee and cigars. F.D.R. smoked cigarettes from his long white holder, almost incessantly. We had to raise our voices, for he was growing deaf. His hand shook visibly as he lit his cigarette. After dinner we all sat around talking until early bedtime. During the last hour the President worked on his stamp collection. As he turned the pages of the album and checked stamp after stamp for perforation and watermark, I felt the world was shaking but this relaxing figure was the chief architect of its future.

F.D.R. said good night. "Henry, I hope I don't dream about one of those bearded Devil Worshipers chasing me with a long knife."

In the middle of the morning Grace brought a message from the Boss that we might like to go for a walk before lunch. If so, Grace was to arrange it. This required sending for Mike Reilly, who produced his golden-bordered pass with the words, "You take this. I'll tell the boys that you are going for a walk. Please do not leave the road and be back within an hour."

We walked along the gravel road in the warm sunshine. This was a frightening stroll, for the trees, bushes, and stumps we approached turned out to be camouflaged Marines holding fierce Doberman pinschers by thick leather leashes. The very woods of Catoctin were alive with guards and savage dogs. This was too nerve-racking, so we turned back. Twice a tree came to life with,

344

"Your pass, please," as a Marine challenged us. To my delight, Mike's pass worked. We returned unexercised and a little un-nerved by the Sunday morning stroll. Lunch was a particularly gay affair, F.D.R. being in super form, for a good night's sleep and the fresh air had done wonders. During dessert our host called attention to a large wheel above the table. Each spoke carried an electric light. Looking up with a wicked twinkle in his eye, he said, "When Winston was here the other day, I told him that wheel was off one of the gun carriages we used against the British. You know, Winston always loves history." The wheel was not nearly that ancient.

That evening cocktails again before dinner, another good meal with entertaining conversation. For thirty-four hours no mention had been made of the war or any unpleasantness. We were a small house party in a cabin in the woods, enjoying ourselves with relaxation through good conversation. The telephone never rang. There were no outside interruptions. After dinner this magic spell was broken. Admiral Wilson Brown said, "I'm sorry to dis-turb you, Mr. President, but there are some papers to be signed."

F.D.R. turned wearily to us and said, "Well, I reckon my vaca-tion is over. I've got to go to work again, but it certainly was fun while it lasted. Don't go away. I'll be through in a few minutes. Where are those papers, Wilson?"

In a corner beside a good light the President began to sign paper after paper. Fifteen minutes later the pile was low. In this small space we could not help hearing the conversation. We were em-barrassed but we could not leave as we heard the admiral say, "Mr. President, the next is a list of naval promotions to com-modore and rear admiral."

Down the list the pencil ran. A check was put against some names with, "There's a good man. It's about time he was pro-moted. . . . A fine officer. Has done a good job in the Pacific. . . . Another well-deserved promotion. I've followed his career since he left the Naval Academy. . . . You remember him, he won the Navy Cross a few weeks ago. . . . Humph. How did this name get on the list? I told you last month I wouldn't promote him to commodore. I'll cross him off. . . . Here you are, Wilson. They are all signed. Good job. Thank you."

This had broken the spell. Now we were guests of the President of the United States. There was a war on. He was our Commander in Chief.

After saying good night to the others he said, "Henry, I want to talk to you about 'M' Project. You know, I've a plan which I want to put into effect as soon as the shooting stops. This time we must not prop up Europe with billions of dollars. Six months after the Nazis surrender, there will be a great letdown, especially in England.

"I want to start two large reclamation projects, one in North Africa, the other in Australia. I want to make North Africa the granary of Europe, just as it was in Roman days. We can pump desalinated water from the Mediterranean for irrigation and build air-conditioned cities in the desert. Technicians will be recruited from among the displaced persons. Steel pipe and housing materials can be manufactured as each country converts from wartime production to peaceful economy. We'll transport the men and equipment in an international fleet. We'll pay high wages, probably with a withholding tax to force savings. This will encourage the technicians to bring their families. That will be one practical way to take up the slack and encourage migration and settlement. Although this will be expensive, it will be far better than the dole—just handing out billions for nothing.

"The North African project will have a counterpart in Australia to help Southeast Asia and the Pacific area. We may have others along the Khabur in Syria and in the Tigris-Euphrates Valley. By the way, we'll have to think of catchy names for the North African and Australian projects—just like two football teams. They'll have to work like rival teams. Let me know if you come up with any names for them.

"Your 'M' Project is producing just the background information I'll need. Keep it up."

Then, lowering his voice, F.D.R. changed the subject. "You know I'm going to see Marshal Stalin soon."

"I've read about a possible meeting in the papers recently."

"Yes, I'm going to meet him. I want you to collect some ammunition for me. At some point the marshal may taunt me with some crack about our Negro problem. I want to know how the

Soviets treat their minorities, their attitude toward Jews, and the results of the Birobidzhan experiment. I'll need that on Tuesday evening. Well, good people, I think I'll toddle off to bed."

The trusty Filipinos moved noiselessly across the room and wheeled him away.

I could not sleep for hours. (The meeting with Stalin at Teheran was in November 1943.) The vision of that man concerning the major postwar problem, even during the heat of our first world-wide conflict, was inspiring. At breakfast the President joined us for a second cup of coffee. One of the Washington papers carried the story of the location of Shangri-la. With a sigh the President looked around the simple cabin. "Wait until the secret service see this story about Shangri-la. They will have a fit and probably try to talk me into giving up week ends here." His voice was cheerful but his expression seemed very sad. Then, more cheerfully: "Have all our guests signed the Visitors' Book, Grace? All right, bring it out. This may be the last time we are aboard." The book was the "Log of the U.S.S. Shangri-la."

We signed after Admiral and Mrs. Wilson Brown on the page following Winston Churchill, Harry Hopkins, and the others in their party.

As the wheel chair moved over the coconut-fiber mats, the President looked back once more as if to say, "Good-by, Shangri-la." He never returned.

During the ride F.D.R. did not speak for almost half an hour. On the way back to Washington, he became more serious as the weight of office pressed on his strong shoulders. In the White House he smiled as he shook hands with us, saying, "That was a grand week end. We'll do it again."

Frances Perkins told me that the last time she saw the President she asked him, "What are you going to do after you are no longer President?" F.D.R. replied that he planned to devote the rest of his life to redeveloping that area from the Sahara to the Tigris-Euphrates Valley. He talked glowingly of irrigation projects, dams, hydroelectric systems, and a great agricultural renaissance. It was obvious from his talk that one of his keenest interests was this project, which he had discussed with me some months before at Shangri-la.

347

We never saw him again.

As I stood on Constitution Avenue watching the funeral cortège approaching, that final week end at Shangri-la swam through the mist. . . .

WASHINGTON was broiling that Saturday, late in May 1945. It was one of those days on which everything went wrong all day long. I could not dictate one letter that did not have to be rewritten. Nothing could be found in the files, telephones interrupted continually.

At five-thirty, with frayed nerves I drove home to Georgetown. As I started up the stairs the telephone was ringing. After such a tiresome and fruitless day this seemed to be a little too much. Swearing fairly distinctly, I grabbed the telephone and heard a voice say, "Would you like to go to Moscow?" Thinking this was a joke from one of my friends who had had an equally bad day, I replied, "Don't ask silly questions. I want a shower and that's all." The voice at the other end began again: "This is the Soviet Embassy speaking. We have just received a cable from the Academy of Sciences of the Soviet Union in Moscow, inviting you to attend as their guest the 220th Jubilee Session in Moscow and Leningrad, beginning on June 15."

I still thought it might be a gag until the doorbell rang and there was a messenger with a copy of the cable.

Here was one of the most exciting invitations of my life. The almost total failures of the day were lost in a moment. Within a week my passport was issued by the ever-efficient Mrs. Shipley, chief of the Passport Division, and then came the mad dash around Washington for visas.

By this time I had the names of some of the people who might be going: Nobel prize winner Irving Langmuir of the General Electric Company; Arnold Nadai of Westinghouse; Harlow Shapley of Harvard Observatory among others. I notified several scientific organizations of which I was a member that I was planning to make this trip and said that if they wished to send any greetings to the Academy of Sciences of the Soviet Union I would be very glad to be the bearer.

Luther Evans, Librarian of Congress, told me that he would be grateful if I would take to Moscow some presents from the Library of Congres as a gesture of friendship and good will and congratulations on their anniversary meeting. Just before I left, Dr. Evans sent me a package containing a specially bound and inscribed copy of the Declaration of Independence, another package of records of American folklore, and a pile of Library of Congress publications. The national archivist gave me the first copies to be released of the letters written by some of the earliest Russian travelers to our northwest coast. He also gave me the first of seventy-two reels of microfilm of this early Russian-American correspondence.

I received letters appointing me as their representative from the Smithsonian Institution, the American Anthropological Association, the Archaeological Institute of America, and the National Geographic Society. I purchased a number of books which I thought would be of value to the library of the Russian Academy. At the last minute Watson Davis of Science Service gave me a package of publications he thought would be of especial interest. By the time all of these were assembled they filled two large duffel bags, and each weighed approximately a hundred pounds.

In New York, as instructed, I went to the Harvard Club. At the far end of the great dark-paneled room were some of the members of the mission already gathered. In the morning we all trooped around to the Soviet Consulate and had our passports duly stamped with the mystic Soviet visa.

In the middle of the afternoon two members of the party, James W. McBain, professor of chemistry at Stanford University, and I. M. Kolthoff, professor of chemistry at the University of Minnesota, arrived looking considerably the worse for wear. They had flown part of the way across country in the Soviet plane that was to take us from New York City to Moscow via Siberia. Their tale was none too encouraging. It appeared that one of the doors did not meet as closely as it was designed to do and as a result there had been a fine fresh draft blowing in from one side all during the flight.

350

We were not any more encouraged by hearing that Soviet pilots seemed to fly by sight and instinct rather than by instrument. As we heard these stories we looked at one another a little anxiously.

Suddenly Shapley grabbed the sheet of paper with the names on it and began to count them slowly like any normal mortal not an astronomer. In a hushed voice he asked, "Did you say there were only twelve seats and one bunk? Because there are sixteen names on this sheet of paper and all are going!"

We all had a very bad night, and I for one was thinking that it was extremely unlikely that all of us would arrive in Russia without mishap. After all, Arthur Pope had a bad heart, Dr. James E. Church (an expert on the creep of snow, from Reno) was over seventy years of age, and Kolthoff, who has a bad leg, told me at breakfast that he was sure something would happen to him if he tried the trip across Siberia. I think the danger of someone getting sick along the way decided our next move. Shapley sat down to draft a telegram to Mr. Grew in Washington.

The telegram called attention to the fact that all of us were anxious to attend the celebration to which we had so generously been invited by the Academy of Sciences of the Soviet Union, but that we felt attention should be called to the overloading of the plane beyond normal risk. We also explained that the Soviet authorities in Washington had been informed that only ten U.S. scientists had accepted; they were not responsible for this overloading.

Within a very short time a message came back by telegram saying that President Truman would make other arrangements for our travel via Air Transport Command across the Atlantic, North Africa to Teheran. The Soviet government would be requested to have two planes ready for us at Teheran to take us via Baku to Moscow.

The Soviet Consulate in New York was very pleased at the new arrangements and Mr. Bazykin, cultural attaché in their embassy in Washington, also assured us that he felt we would have a much better trip.

Some of us were delegated to go out to the airport to bring back the few extra-hardy individuals who were already there waiting to climb aboard the Soviet ship. Here we found Dr. Church and Dr. Charles Kellogg of the Department of Agriculture.

At 4:30 A.M. on Sunday, June 10, we climbed into two Army buses which took us and our baggage to La Guardia Field.

It was a gloomy morning. About six-thirty we were in our places in the C-54-A four-motor Douglas plane. Since we did not have anything else to do, this seemed like a good occasion to begin the "short snorter" activities. Each of us dragged out a bill and began the feverish signing. I closed my eyes as we bumped and twisted in the air. When I opened them we were coming down at Santa Maria in the Azores.

Breakfast was welcome. Just as the last plate of ham and eggs was being passed by a sergeant I heard the colonel right behind me say to Shapley:

"Dr. Shapley, your plane will be refueled and ready to leave the runway at three-fifteen local time, that is one hour and a quarter from now. Will that be a convenient time for you gentlemen to leave?"

Dr. Shapley replied that we would all be ready.

The sergeant, handing me the ham and eggs, leaned over my shoulder and whispered, "Who are you guys anyway? I've seen all the big shots come through here, but never heard the old man say, 'Your plane will be ready, gentlemen!'" I explained that we were just some simple civilians going on a scientific mission to Moscow. Of course, traveling under a presidential directive helps.

At five-thirty the next morning, directly in the path of the sun appeared the silhouette of the great city of Cairo. Mosques and minarets dotted the distant horizon. A few minutes later, below us were the pyramid of Cheops and the silent Sphinx with its paws outstretched, calm, composed, and majestic in that golden early morning light. Almost immediately afterward we swept over the Nile. Buxton and I had been in Cairo for only a couple of days in 1925, twenty years before. However, this caused me to be looked upon as an authority by the rest of the party and I found myself automatically in charge. I suggested Shepheard's, the Pyramids, the Sphinx, and the treasures of Tutankhamen in the Cairo Museum.

352

That night my head had barely touched the pillow, or so it seemed, when it was time to get up. We dressed in the dark, shaved, and were driven to our plane.

The stars were still shining very brightly as we took off toward Palestine. At five-thirty we passed over the Suez Canal. We saw the light shining on the surface of the Bitter Lakes and I remembered the meeting between F.D.R. and Ibn Saud, lord of Arabia. It seemed unbelievable that Roosevelt was gone; he had died two months before. Only a few days before the Soviet invitation came, Germany had surrendered.

I had asked the pilot if I could have permission to sit in the co-pilot's seat during the flight from the northern corner of the Dead Sea to Baghdad. I explained to him that I had made an archaeological survey on the ground but had never had the privilege of seeing it from the air. In the co-pilot's seat, with a large-scale map before me, I made notes as we flew. I was still there when we came to the Dead Sea, turned eastward from the Mediterranean, and continued over the mountains of Judah and over Hebron, the birthplace of many Biblical characters, our shadow touching lightly the dome over the manger at Bethlehem. To the northwest, Jerusalem appeared like a small gray sentinel of stone against a drab olive-green background. I remembered having walked around this wall with Buxton in the Christmas season of 1925.

Jerusalem, called in Hebrew "Yerushalayim," the vision of peace, and in Arabic "El Quds," has long been the most venerated city of the world. Looking down, I knew there was little peace now behind those ancient walls.

To the south of Baghdad a violent dust storm was raging. There was no sense in our diverting our course to fly over Kish and Babylon and the Arch of Ctesiphon. It was indeed hard to pass over Baghdad; harder still to know that just beyond the swirling storm lay the ancient city of Kish, my desert home for months from 1925 to 1928.

Below us were sharp escarpments with occasional peaks and many sharp, knifelike ridges. Most of us were yawning frequently and breathing deeply; several were short of breath. There were patches of snow on the peaks all around us. To the south stood

353

the high mountains of Luristan, snow-covered, inviting yet forbidding. Hamadan, the ancient Ecbatana, lay on the plain just below. At eleven-fifteen our wheels touched the ground; we had reached Teheran.

Next morning a cold wind swept down over the airfield. Before us in the gray dawn squatted two C-47s bearing the Red Star insignia. Our beautiful and luxurious C-54-A had gone home. Seeing our obvious uneasiness, an American pilot walked up to us, grinning. "See those three black stripes beside the door? That means the plane was condemned as unsafe by the USAAF three years ago."

We trailed up the ramp like lambs going to the slaughter. The door slammed. The motors started. The C-47 took off without any more ado and with no pause whatever for warming the motors.

We were soon flying northwest over the Elburz Mountains. From this height we could see clearly the sand-colored plain to the south, the snowy crest, and the lush, green vegetation to the north leading down to the Caspian. We landed at an airport outside Baku. Here, where Dick and I had once fumed through a five-hour inspection, our baggage was examined perfunctorily by broad-beamed Soviet women in dark blue uniforms with trolley-conductor caps.

A Russian breakfast reception awaited us in a room nearby, where thirty members of the Azerbaidzhan Academy of Sciences greeted us. Breakfast consisted of mountains of Caspian caviar, carafes of vodka, and thick slices of cold sturgeon, all washed down with Caucasian wines or hot, sweetened black tea. Speeches were made but fortunately not interpreted or we would have been there all day. Just before dark we touched down at Moscow Airport.

Several members of the Academy of Sciences of the U.S.S.R. had come to meet the U.S. group, among them Frumkin and Kapitza. Several planes landed in the half hour we were standing there. These brought the British and French missions and there was a good deal of handshaking and exchange of greetings. I caught a glimpse of Julian Huxley as he stepped out of the British plane. We waved happily.

354

From my hotel room that night I could see the red star glowing over the Kremlin towers. Here we all were in the Hotel Moskva in Moscow, having left New York four days before. It was hard to realize that so much could be crowded into about a hundred hours. Even in my excitement at being back in Moscow with all the memories surging around me, I experienced once again that faint sense of dread and need for extra caution that had oppressed me on my first visit to Russia.

The following afternoon saw the start of the great celebration of the 220th Anniversary of the founding of the Academy of Sciences by Peter the Great. The Bolshoi Theater was filled to capacity with the thousand top-ranking Soviet scientists and their wives, and the invited scientists representing twenty-two countries. On the stage was a long table covered with a claret-red cloth; over it was a large floral motif, the central figure of which was the face of Stalin. Slogans of welcome were everywhere.

At the table's center sat President Komarov, Academician Orbeli, and General Bruevich, resplendent in uniform and dangling medals. They were flanked by ten high-ranking Soviet academicians, and behind this central group sat 250 members and corresponding members of the Academy.

This was the occasion for expressing publicly the gratitude of Stalin and Company to the Soviet scientists for super-Soviet hospitality and also an excellent opportunity for passing out Propaganda (with a capital P) to the foreigners.

Greetings from Stalin, Molotov, and other Party members were read in Russian and with no translations. Orbeli welcomed the foreigners from all over the world. This was greeted with thunderous applause. Fortunately Saryacheva, geologist and wife of Iablakov, assistant to Bruevich, Secretary of the Academy, sat on my left. She explained the proceedings in a whisper.

The presidential address by frail and sick V. L. Komarov, tracing the history of the Academy from Peter the Great to 1945, was read by Orbeli. Included in the address was this paragraph:

American natural science is likewise thoroughly instilled with progressive ideas. The first great American naturalist, Benjamin Franklin, who investigated atmospheric electricity

355

and built the lightning rod, was a fighter for freedom. As an example of the scientific ties between Russia and America, taken from the history of these countries, one may refer to the work of Lomonosov in physics, in which he revealed himself as a successor of Franklin. The Academy of Sciences is true to these traditions and is endeavoring to extend its connections with American science.

That evening there was a banquet in the Hotel Moskva with about a thousand guests. On my right was a Soviet colonel with whom I was unable to communicate freely although he seemed to be very willing to drink toasts to the United States and to the advancement of science. Next to him was Raabe, rector of the newly-created University of Lublin in Poland. After many toasts he invited me to accompany him to see his new university. He offered to take me on a private train to Lublin. However, when I jokingly asked him next day when the train would leave, he had forgotten the whole incident!

By eleven o'clock couples were dancing wildly. The orchestra never stopped for breath and the toasts became more and more frequent. Soviet hospitality was in full swing.

It continued in full swing during our Moscow visit. The city was tremendous and confusing, Soviet hospitality on the same scale. With a splitting headache I attended a session of the Presidium of the Academy of Sciences and even made an extemporaneous speech, on a minute's notice, which I had intended to write out in advance and then read at some later date. As it happened, I found myself facing four hundred members and guests of the Academy and, trying to marshal my thoughts, I described as best I could the various messages of greeting entrusted to me from the many groups and organizations in the United States to those in the Soviet Union, and wound up with a few comments on international co-operation, limiting myself to the practical application of these theories in the study of man. I looked forward, I said, to a time when we might hold an international conference to attempt to prepare an "Anthropologia Asiatica" in collaboration with all specialists on this subject around the world. At the conclusion I handed the specially bound copy of the Declaration of Independence to President Komarov with the words: "You and your colleagues will find this document of the greatest interest."

We were taken en masse to see the Victory Parade in Red Square, an awe-inspiring spectacle with infantry, cavalry, and mechanized troops of the Red Army jamming the surrounding streets as far as eye could see, and Stalin, a man of granite, despite the drenching rain and bitter cold wind, standing motionless with his right hand to his visor through the interminable hours of marching. The reverberation of motors, the thunder of wheels and cheering, the clouds of blue smoke and smell of oil and gasoline made a tremendous spectacle of power and mechanized might. A thrill ran through the multitudes as faded and battle-worn standards—captured German flags—were carried in triumph to a point opposite Lenin's tomb and hurled dramatically into the slime at Stalin's feet. One knew these people then; they were conquerors. Since I had seen them last they had become sure of their invincibility.

Several nights later word came that we were to dine in the Kremlin! At seven o'clock we were ushered upstairs to the magnificent St. George's Banquet Hall.

There was a ripple of excitement through the two thousand guests and wild clapping as Stalin appeared, flanked by Molotov and Voroshilov, and took his place at the center of the head table.

The orchestra played a national air which almost drowned the clapping. Stalin sat down, and Molotov stood in front of the microphone and made an address of welcome to the members and corresponding members of the Academy of Sciences and to the foreign guests. The passing of hors d'oeuvres with drinks lasted about two hours and during this time numerous speakers were introduced by Molotov.

Stalin appeared to be rather quiet and reserved. I could see him clearly all the time; I watched him closely. His apparent shyness and his sitting with downcast eyes for rather long periods of time seemed unusual for so strong a character.

Every move he made was watched by his guests, who seemed to be hypnotized because they were dining in the Kremlin with the Generalissimo. Probably every one of those present was re-

357

membering some relative purged in the march of Communism; to them all, Stalin was the epitome of awe—and of terror.

The quality and quantity of the food and drinks were beyond description and there was a continuous flow of both from seven until midnight. The stage show began at nine-fifteen immediately behind Stalin. At the end of each performance Stalin clapped, keeping his right hand still all the time. Upon rare occasions he would turn his head very slowly as though the axis and atlas were fused, and there would be a surge of excitement throughout the guests, who would immediately nudge each other and whisper.

While one of the performers, a young girl in a diaphanous pale blue creation, was dancing and pirouetting behind him, Stalin was engaged in talking to Molotov. The poor girl got through her act and went off stage without anything except perfunctory applause from the Generalissimo, who never once looked in her direction.

The woman next to me explained that this would be a very sad night indeed for this dancer, because here was the greatest moment of her life and she had failed to capture Stalin's attention even for a second.

When a ballet star appeared, Stalin turned very slowly and watched her performance. She received a tremendous ovation and my friend on my right said that this would greatly enhance the star's career. She added, "She will receive some unusual present in the morning, probably a new automobile or a new wardrobe."

The whole thing seemed very strange: that one casual glance from one man seemed able to make or break a career. The only real interest shown by Stalin was when the Red Army Band and entertainers arrived. At this point he turned his chair around and watched the performance, clapping and obviously enjoying the show.

His exit was impressive. By midnight we were back in the hotel —slightly dazed.

The foreign scientists were taken on a side trip to Leningrad in a special train. The mark of war on Moscow had been almost imperceptible, but Leningrad was a silent and almost deserted city, with gaping areas of rubble scarring its streets.

I remembered it as one of the most beautiful cities in the world.

358

Now the houses were scarred with rifle and machine-gun fire; 150,000 bombs and shells had fallen on the city. Of the 3,000,000 inhabitants of Leningrad in 1941, but 2,000,000 remained. One out of three had died, mainly of starvation. The people we met in the streets looked drawn and haggard, spiritless.

On a park bench near the Neva River I saw a woman with a fuzzy-faced dog in her lap. This was the only pet—beast or bird —seen by any of us in Leningrad and this dog, I learned, came from Moscow. All animals had starved to death or been eaten during the blockade.

The tragedy in the faces of all the survivors was apparent. Each smile was made with an effort and there were no signs of gaiety or laughter on the streets or among the crowds. Leningrad was indeed a city of triumph, but at a ghastly price.

The only time they seemed to be moved was when we asked about the blockade. Then their eyes would light up and they would describe how they had been surrounded on all sides except for one narrow strip, their life line to Lake Ladoga, which was mercifully frozen so that their few supplies could trickle through.

I talked to one woman who was wearing two medals—one for the defense of Leningrad. After thanking her for her translating I commented on the fact that I did not know the significance of this second medal. She replied that she did not deserve it. She said, "It is not I who deserve this medal, one of the highest which our country can bestow, but rather my eighteen-year-old son, my father and mother, and my two brothers, all of whom died during the blockade." She then broke into a fit of tears and sobbing. This tragedy must have been repeated time and time again. The stories of the courage of the defenders of Leningrad are still to be written for the outside world to appreciate and understand. . . .

The struggle for existence was probably nowhere keener in all history than in this great city situated on the Gulf of Finland. Everywhere we went, we saw hunger and courage and the indomitable will to survive.

In Leningrad, as in Moscow, my principal points of interest were the museums. In them I met old acquaintances and new colleagues, and some invited me to their homes, but I was never

359

without the sense that in offering their hospitality to an American archaeologist they were doing a daring and even dangerous thing.

My account of these weeks in the two great Russian cities can be only that of a reporter trying to describe what was seen and heard amid an all-enveloping aura of Soviet propaganda. It was everywhere. It surrounded us wherever we went. None of it touched the heart.

But the people of Russia did, as I went, alone or with others of our group, to movies, theaters, the ballet. The friendly curiosity of the Russians was discreet but openly expressed. Our clothes marked us, for our oldest and most worn were magnificent compared with theirs.

I was collecting exchange papers and books from our scientific hosts, proportionate in number to those I had brought with me from the United States. Everywhere in the museums was this eagerness to exchange anthropological and archaeological finds. In the Laboratory of Physical Anthropology in Leningrad, Tolstov presented me with casts of the skeleton from Kiik-Koba and the skull from Murzak-Koba, with a letter of transmittal for Field Museum of Natural History. Professor Ravdonikas gave me two copies of the limited edition describing his excavations and discoveries of the petroglyphs (rock paintings) at Lake Onega, together with prints of the latter and numerous reprints of his articles.

Wherever I went the men and women of science talked very freely about the difficulties they had experienced and said that it would be many years before Russia would have all the things that were necessary for their scientific researches.

In the Leningrad Museum I was shown famous archaeological treasures excavated during the past twenty-five years. It was a great thrill to examine many of the specimens which I had known only from rather poor photographs in Soviet publications.

Here was the skeleton from Kiik-Koba, the skull from Murzak-Koba and the wonderful prehistoric carvings on ivory and bone from Malta in Siberia, Zamiatnin described many of the objects and called attention to the special exhibits.

In the central part of the hall were reconstructions by Gerasimov, among them a full-length life-size reconstruction of the

Teshik-Tash child, which I examined with great care, since we had restored the Neanderthaloid child known as Gibraltar II in Field Museum of Natural History.

I did not think this child had been as well restored as that by Frederick Blaschke, although at fifty feet the general resemblance to our reconstruction was striking.

Gerasimov had been present at Tashkent when Tamerlane's tomb was opened, and had discovered then that Tamerlane (the lame) had actually been lame. He also had an opportunity to examine the skull in great detail and to make a cast of it. Over this cast he modeled plastilene, measuring the thickness by means of a pin. This was the same technique developed by Blaschke in our work. However, Gerasimov was able to find traces of some of the soft parts, and part of the beard was still adhering to the flesh. In this way he was able to make what appeared to be an excellent reconstruction of the great Mongol warrior who died in 1405.

I longed to show Gerasimov our reconstructions in Field Museum because I found it impossible, through an interpreter, to convey anything approximating a true picture of the nine dioramas.

A few days later, back in Moscow, the majority of the U.S. mission left in a Soviet plane for Alaska. I stayed on to obtain more details on recent archaeological finds and publications. I paid several visits to the Ethnographical Institute and talked with S. P. Tolstov and M. G. Levin, mainly on recent discoveries in Central Asia; I visited the Museum of Oriental Civilizations, where I examined objects from Termez and Afrasiab; several times I visited the Archaeological Museum and Institute of Moscow University. Director Zenkievich and his assistant, Roginskii, showed me around, and I found the exhibits there little changed since 1934. Victor Bunak introduced me to Oshanin, specialist in the study of the peoples of Soviet Central Asia. I was then led ceremoniously into a laboratory where their greatest treasure was brought out on a wooden tray. This was the original skull of the Neanderthaloid child from Teshik-Tash which I had just seen, reconstructed, in Leningrad.

While in Leningrad, in the Museum of Archaeology, one of the reporters asked me, "Have you seen the skull in Moscow?" Thinking he meant the Neanderthaloid child, I replied, "Not yet. I hope to spend several hours with the young man next week."

"Oh no," he said quickly, "I don't mean a prehistoric skull. I mean Hitler's. You know they have it at Moscow University."

Now, in the Moscow Museum, surrounded by thousands of human skulls on shelves, I asked casually to see Hitler's skull. There was a crushing silence, then considerable muttering. A translator said finally, "We could not have understood your request correctly."

I said, "I was told in Leningrad that you have Hitler's skull [I used the Russian form Gitler]. Please let me examine it, for I am familiar with his dentition."

More mutterings, and I was invited to lunch.

In Berlin a few weeks later I was told that the Russians had found a charred but intact skull in the bunker under the Reichstag; and that the bright girl assistant to Hitler's dentist had smuggled his dental chart out of the files, turned one copy over to the United States authorities, being paroled as a result, and had given the other to the Russians, just to be on the safe side. Thus they knew it was Hitler's skull—quite an anthropological prize!

The Moscow Radio Committee called to ask me to make a short-wave broadcast to Europe and the United States. They also planned to use it over their national hookup. I welcomed this opportunity to express our appreciation to our hosts for entertaining us so well.

After thanking our hosts, the Academy of Sciences, for inviting me to attend their Jubilee Session, I made one concrete suggestion: that a central microfilming laboratory and library be installed so that some of the rare historical documents, especially those in Central Asia and Siberia, might be microfilmed for safety, and distributed to several of the big libraries of the world, particularly to the Library of Congress. In this way they would make available to other scholars some of the priceless documents which now exist only in one copy in some far-off library or research center. I also told them that I felt that they were living in "a scientific vacuum." By this I meant that they did not have the benefit of reading the studies, monographs, and reports by other archaeologists outside the Soviet Union. In this way they were limited in their scope and particularly in drawing general conclusions. It was impossible to separate racially the peoples of the Soviet Union from the peoples of Asia and Europe. Naturally they had all agreed with me on this subject in the libraries and scientific institutes I had visited, but I thought that a concrete proposal to encourage the exchange of scientific publications should be mentioned in this brief broadcast for the man on the street.

AFTER the Moscow broadcast I began to worry about how I was going to get home. The Academy of Sciences had told me that within a few days I could fly to Berlin in a Soviet plane.

I decided to visit the embassy to see if there were any possibility of an American plane—the faintest of hopes. However, as I walked into the arch of the Chancery, right next to the Hotel National and with no idea where to plead my cause, I saw a U.S. colonel striding into his office. He read my travel orders and then, leaning confidentially across his desk, whispered that I might be able to travel to Berlin in Ambassador Averell Harriman's plane, which was scheduled to leave the next day with Ambassador Ed Pauley. The colonel said there was one extra seat and no baggage limit because most of the Reparations Commission were taking just one small suitcase apiece for the Potsdam Conference. This stopped my worry about the duffel bags stuffed with the heavy literature I had been given during my trip to Moscow and Leningrad. The colonel told me not to tell anyone but to come back next day at noon ready to leave.

That night my passport was returned with the Soviet exit visa and word came from the colonel that Ambassador Pauley had very graciously given me permission to accompany his party to the Potsdam Conference.

At the Intourist office in the hotel my passport was taken away from me again and I must say that I hated to see it go. I was not by any means sure that it would turn up at the right time, at the right place, at the proper airport. I was driven out in a jeep with my piles of duffel bags, which were put into a shed. There were a number of distinguished Soviet representatives at the gate to say farewell to Mr. Pauley and his staff, which included Dr.

Isador Lubin and members of the Reparations Commission. I saw Maisky laughing and chatting with Ambassador Pauley.

The large and magnificent plane by which we were standing was known as *Grandpappy*, formerly *Becky*. It was Mr. Averell Harriman's million-dollar plane and had five large windows at eye level.

We waited about twenty minutes, by which time I was becoming more and more doubtful of ever seeing my baggage or my passport again. Then a Soviet official came striding across from the hangar. In his hand was a sheaf of passports—American passports. He distributed fifteen to the members of the Reparations Commission and there was one left. To my delight, relief, pleasure, and surprise, it was mine. He handed it over with a formal bow. I put it in my pocket nonchalantly, but my heart was thumping hard. Amid smiles and some mild wise-cracking to the embassy representatives, Mr. Pauley walked up the short ladder into *Grandpappy* and we followed. We taxied to the end of the runway, fastened our safety belts, and flew almost due west over Poland.

Four hours later we were over Berlin. Mr. Pauley asked the pilot to circle the city so we could see the ruins. This was an extraordinary experience. As the sun sank low on the horizon, the tops of the buildings appeared like a sectional honeycomb. There were no roofs anywhere in the central part of the city, but the side walls were standing. Flying over the Sportspalast, I could not help thinking about the last time I had seen that huge stadium, in 1936 when Hitler was at his zenith. I remembered the opening day of the Olympic Games when several hundred white doves had flown in clouds above the stadium. These were to be the messengers of peace—the "peace" that Hitler was bringing to the world.

Now, looking down, I remembered this scene and a leader's madness that had brought so much suffering to the world. As these thoughts flashed through my mind *Grandpappy* alighted. Suddenly I realized that I would have to do something about getting taken over to Air Transport Command. We had landed at a secret airdrome where the members of the Potsdam Conference were foregathering for their meeting. Mr. Pauley got out, followed by Dr. Lubin and other members of his staff. I hung around, trying to be as inconspicuous as possible, while the officials got their baggage into a truck and climbed into other cars to drive to their destinations.

My pile of baggage looked immense. Even the Great Pyramid of Cheops did not seem much larger. Mr. Pauley and the other members of his commission each had small suitcases, and here was I, the unbidden guest, with more than all of them put together. I had 200 pounds of publications for U.S. libraries. Finally the zero hour came for me, left alone with three U. S. Army officers, a colonel, a major, and a captain. The colonel, whose eyebrows met in a vertical bush above his glabella (all of whom, if I were describing his characteristics on an anthropometric blank, I would write "eyebrow concurrency plus"), said to the major, who repeated to the captain, "Who's that guy there?" pointing at me. The captain replied to the major, who replied to the colonel (although they were all standing with shoulders practically touching), "I don't know, sir." The colonel told the major, who told the captain, "Find out who he is. Get him out of here." The captain came over to where I was standing.

"Please, sir, get into that car over there. Where is your baggage?"

I pointed.

"Is all that your baggage?"

"Yes, Captain."

"Please get into that car, which will take you to a hotel. We have orders that no one can remain here. We are expecting prominent visitors." I found out later that Mr. Churchill had landed about an hour before and they were awaiting President Truman.

I replied meekly but clearly, "I'm afraid I can't do as you suggest because I am not going to the Potsdam Conference." At this point the colonel, who was glaring ferociously in my direction, stepped forward and roared, "What did you say?" I repeated, "I am not going to the Potsdam Conference. Can you please send me to ATC Headquarters?" The colonel said, "But you must be going to the Potsdam Conference, because no one else is allowed to land here. Would you please tell me why you're not going to

367

the Conference?" I told him I had received no invitation, so he said, "How on earth did you get here then?" I pointed to the million-dollar Harriman plane. The colonel, at a loss, ordered the major, who ordered the captain, "Get him out of here!" The captain said he would do everything he could to turn me over to ATC as rapidly as possible. By this time it was nine-fifteen. The captain left me and returned in fifteen minutes, looking pale. He told me the airport where we were was outside of Berlin and in order to get me to ATC HQ at Tempelhof it would be necessary to pass through one corner of the Russian Zone. This naturally added a further complication because as a civilian I was not allowed to drive a jeep, and how was I going to get across? At this point I became tired.

Ten minutes later the captain returned with a solution. My baggage was loaded onto a small truck. We followed it outside the hangar, where a large four-motored plane was standing. The captain said, "We will fly you to Tempelhof. That will eliminate all our ground problems." The pilot climbed in. I climbed in—the sole passenger in the great many-seated plane. My baggage was put in the back. The captain shouted to the pilot, "Be sure if you crash that you come down in the American or British Zone, or we'll have an international incident on our hands," and we took off and flew over Berlin, landing at Tempelhof four minutes later. It had been a very pleasant flight.

An ATC captain took me upstairs, showed me a room where there was an Army cot, and suggested that I might like to go to sleep. However, the excitement of the day—flying from Moscow and being in Berlin once again—was too much for sleep. Looking out of the window at the great Tempelhof courtyard bathed in moonlight, I could see tons and tons of paper and rubbish on the ground. I had a burning desire to walk around. The captain gave me permission, providing I did not go near any of the main doors, where, he said, the sentries would shoot after a brief challenge.

The courtyard was part in shadow, part in moonlight. As I smoked my pipe and walked about this huge space I could see the central building, which I knew must have been Goering's headquarters. The great concrete semicircle stood charred and windowless. Here had been the center and the brains of the

368

Luftwaffe—that Luftwaffe which had almost destroyed England. Here, in these buildings, were planned the raids on London, those terrible Baedeker raids in which so much of England's ancient past had been ruined. In that now windowless room above me Goering had planned raid after raid—terror raid after terror raid, fire-bomb raid after fire-bomb raid.

As these thoughts passed though my mind, standing there in the moonlight in the shattered wreckage of Tempelhof on July 17, 1945, I was filled with tremendous emotion. I started to walk back through piles of documents thrown from windows. The flashlight showed that I was walking through a file of Luftwaffe papers, reports, documents, memoranda, books, periodicals, journals, weather records, weather reports, weather statistics—at least twenty tons of them. Halfway through the courtyard my foot struck hard against a firm object; to my surprise, it was a life-size bronze bust of Goering. A paper covered the face; it was a "top secret" German document for the invasion of Britain, the Dover–Calais section, containing data on the weather and tides and with excellent photographs of both shores.

Greatly excited, I ran up the stairs to the captain's room, where he and three others were playing cards on an upturned packing case. Seeing my shining eyes, the captain muttered, "Now what?" I told of my find and the captain said wearily, "Good heavens; this place is lousy with Goerings, they're only worth two cigarettes apiece. You'd better give up and go to bed." Crestfallen, I said good night and retired to the Army cot.

After a couple of hours of cat-napping it was breakfast time. The captain guided me to the mess. The second cup of coffee gave me courage. I told him I realized fully that the Potsdam Conference had begun and that special security measures were in force. However, despite all this, I had a great longing to visit Unter den Linden and see the Reichstag. The captain looked anxious. I asked if it were possible to walk through the streets for several hours by myself. This was forbidden. Suddenly a bright idea came. I had heard him say that they were short of German translators in his office. I volunteered to help him in that capacity for a couple of hours; if we both worked hard, we could get his morning's work done in about half the normal time, then perhaps he would drive me downtown in his jeep.

Fortunately I was of help to him because there was a stream of people coming for jobs, mainly waiters who wished to be employed in the officers' mess. The conversation, therefore, was not too great a strain on my German. Two hours later the captain looked up from his desk and told one of his assistants that he was going out in a jeep. As we swept away from the curb the captain's manner changed entirely.

We explored Berlin, the honeycomb city with its top cut off and ruin below. We drove down the Unter den Linden, once the greatest avenue in Germany, now a shabby street bordered with windowless walls. As we headed for the Reichstag we passed a heap of ruins where a sign hung crazily: "Hotel Adlon." I had stayed there many times.

In the gray and battered Reichstag I employed every trick of the archaeologist's I knew, hunting through the ruins for Hitler's body. The odor of decomposing human bodies was heavy. Perhaps, I thought, they were Hitler's and Eva Braun's. Or was the strange story I had heard in Leningrad true, and did the Russians actually have the Fuehrer's skull?

The captain was enjoying himself by this time. Back in Tempelhof he broached a plan of his own. He had found a secret passage near the airdrome where Goering had had his headquarters. There were underground rooms and who knew what hidden treasures!

"How would you like to hunt for a whole raft of Rembrandts?" he asked.

Armed with flashlights and pickax, we investigated Goering's subterranean hideaway. In one small room we found a wall where the brick looked new. Under our shoes the broken glass was three feet deep, but we stood on it, in the dust, taking turns at picking at the wall. For about an hour we worked, breaking at last through the bricks. Our imaginations ran riot; I pictured our flashlights turned through to reveal hundreds of old masters stacked in piles. We finally had a hole large enough to look through and saw, beyond, another brick wall. Later a torn blueprint showed we were in an unfinished underground tunnel.

We began to laugh. It had been a lot of fun.

370

The next morning after breakfast my baggage was all assembled and again it looked like a vast pile standing at the entrance to the building, as I stood awaiting transportation to the airdrome. At nine o'clock I was to be flown in a Ninth Air Force plane to Paris. At five minutes to nine a command car drove up and, just as my bags were being loaded into it by some brawny GIs, the colonel came down the stairs. He asked me if I would mind staying over twenty-four hours in order to prepare for him a memorandum on the contents of each of the four floors in the library section of the building; that he would appreciate it very much and would promise to get me in a plane to Paris the following morning. I jumped at this chance and my luggage was repiled close to the entrance.

Two of the floors required only about half an hour of examination. The one holding the individual records of the Luftwaffe personnel took longer. I found form No. 1 exactly where it should be and No. 889,000 at the far end of the room. Each of the piles of forms was about twelve inches thick and arranged in perfect chronological order right from the beginning. Another floor, the one below, contained wooden racks of photographs.

However, the other two floors were quite a different matter. Here were thousands and thousands of books and periodicals. These were the world's weather records, arranged geographically by continent. The Russians had removed everything on Asia.

By nightfall I handed the memorandum on the materials contained in the Luftwaffe Library to the commanding officer with the recommendation that Dr. Reichelderfer be invited to send a representative of the U. S. Weather Bureau to Tempelhof to select reference books and maps for their library in Washington.

I was told I looked rather pale, and no wonder. I had spent a day with the ghost of the Luftwaffe.

Next morning I left in a Ninth Air Force DC-3 for Paris. As we flew low I rubbed my eyes; here was a city with rooftops and no shell-scarred and fire-gutted buildings. The Eiffel Tower, Arc de Triomphe, and Napoleon's Tomb looked triumphant and peaceful. The ATC flew me on to London. Bond Street, the City, and many areas were deeply scarred, but Claridge's was unchanged. I took the train from St. Pancras to Leicester. On the platform Mother met me. I had not seen her since she walked up the New York gangplank of the *Queen Mary* to return to Leicestershire to run a mobile canteen all through the war. Four days later I was out over the Atlantic.

On that flying week end in Berlin, I only skimmed the rubble that had been Germany. Four years later I saw below the exposed surface to the horror that had been part of a once arrogant country.

During the war, as director of "M" Project for President Roosevelt, I had supervised analyses of world migration and settlement. Among the most successful is ORT (Organization for Rehabilitation through Training), a Jewish organization which trains craftsmen all over the world. In 1949 I was asked to make a survey of the ORT organization in the Munich area. In addition to listing refugee camps and several ORT schools between Munich and Berchtesgaden, I was also to spend several days in Switzerland in order to visit the main industrial ORT school at Asnières.

I arrived in Paris on July 5 to find everything vastly improved over 1945, and even 1947. Paris was beautiful as only she can be. Paris was gay. Paris was full of tourists. By night Paris was entertained by Josephine Baker, "Les Girls" at the Casino de Paris, and by the Existentialists near Les Deux Magots . . .

One afternoon I stopped, en route to the train, at the garden reception given by Ambassador and Mrs. David Bruce. At the Gare de l'Est, I boarded the long-famous Orient Express.

It entered Germany at Kehl, just as I had entered it twenty-three years before on that hurried jaunt through the European museums, but not, as then, after sitting up throughout the night.

In Munich, Dr. Oswald Dutch, former director of ORT for Germany and Austria, invited me to accompany a group to Berchtesgaden.

We drove through Reichenhall to the village of Berchtesgaden.

As we drove down the well-graded slope from Hitler's "Eagle's Nest" the busload was abnormally silent. Our thoughts required silence. . . .

372

The next morning in Munich Dr. Dutch gave me the following information about ORT activities in Germany:

During 1948 ORT attained its maximum influence, having eighty-four schools in the U.S. and British zones and Austria. The maximum number of students was 8400 in the U. S. Zone, 2600 in the British Zone, and 1500 in Austria—a total of 12,500 students. However, during 1948 about 8000 emigrated from Germany and Austria.

Out of 240,000 DPs in Germany, about 40,000 were rehabilitated, that is, persuaded after almost ten years to go to work again. Jacob Oleijski, a prisoner at Landsberg, started an ORT school there during August 1945. At first no one wanted to attend the school; later it became overcrowded. Oleijski became director of ORT work in Germany.

We visited the ORT school in Munich. The boys and girls seemed keen on their work and it was inspiring to watch them learning trades which would make them useful citizens wherever they might live.

After luncheon with some of the ORT staff in the Haus der Kunst, Schmidt, a driver assigned to me by ORT, drove me in Mrs. Dorothea Greene's car to Dachau. The guards directed us rather casually to the crematorium. The Nazi superscription on the barbed-wire gate read: "*Arbeit macht frei* [Work makes free]," somewhat of a travesty considering the forced labor endured here by 35,000 or more workers at a time when the only hope of freedom was by death or the all but impossible escape. Eight-foot barbed-wire fences . . . watchtowers manned by machine guns and searchlights . . . hungry German police dogs that roamed between the inner fences had made Dachau impenetrable.

We turned into a charming garden with attractive flower beds set in green grass, lovely trees, and a few low buildings, two of which had chimneys about thirty-five feet tall. This seemed like a quiet, restful place, hidden by a high wall from the bustle of the camp. Here, in the garden spot of Bavaria, it is recorded that 238,000 men, women, and children were tortured, gassed, and burned by the Nazis. . . .

A young, thin-lipped, closely cropped, Nazi-looking man

373

sauntered over and offered to act as our guide. He showed us the entrance platform where the prisoners were unloaded—always under cover of darkness.

We were silent while walking around the four ovens, where more than 200,000 people were exterminated by one of the master killers of all time. A few faded flowers above Oven No. 3 were a simple tribute to three girls, British FANYs who had been burned there. A small tablet over Oven No. 2 carried the surnames of ten Frenchmen.

Before leaving this small building, reeking of a sadism and human suffering almost unparalleled, our guide led us to a small room which was the Nazi torture chamber. Here had stood a whipping table to which the victim was strapped to receive blows from a leather whip like a sjambok. Here had been the thumb-screw, rack, and bastinado chair, as well as other, Nazi-invented, tortures.

Schmidt and I crept outside into the fresh air, our heads reeling with the vividly imagined scenes of cruelty. . . . Outside were memorabilia of other tortures—too terrible to be written here.

At the front of the building rose a wooden platform, formerly a gallows. A simple wooden cross, placed there by the U. S. Army, was a dignified memorial to the dead.

Schmidt and I walked across the quiet and peaceful garden. Here was a concrete wall against which the Nazis had revolver practice, with human targets; concrete stanchions where chained dogs had been able to reach living victims, a little at a time; a narrow trench where the brave Nazi had made their victims kneel so that they could shoot them from behind.

In the corner near the wall a mass grave, covered with growing flowers, contained several thousand bodies found upon arrival by our troops. A sign in English called attention to this hallowed ground.

By this time I was feeling sick and wanted to leave. Schmidt felt far worse—he was a Jew who had survived three concentration camps. Seven of his relatives had been burned in Auschwitz, where he had survived almost two years at forced labor.

Schmidt brushed his eyes with the back of his right hand and strode off toward the car.

374

At this moment up swept a shiny Chevrolet and from it stepped a man and two women. They proved to be a German from Munich with his wife, and his sister from Detroit, where she had gone forty-two years before.

Ten minutes later the three returned into the open air, the American woman obviously on the verge of tears. The German muttered something about his having no idea such things were done at Dachau, although he had lived in Munich all during World War II. His wife, a rather handsome, well-dressed woman in her late forties, felt she should say something to her sister-in-law, so she whispered quietly in German, "For the first time in my life, I am truly ashamed of being a German." Her husband glared at her. "If I ever hear you say anything like that again, I'll beat you within an inch of your life."

I could not resist asking him if what he had seen and must have imagined made him proud of being a German. He began to shout at me like a madman. Schmidt whispered in my right ear, "I'd love to knock him down."

I challenged this unrepentant German with the fact that he must have heard of the mass killings at Dachau and the famed children's "Death March," when 250 children were marched from Stuttgart to Dachau and many died on the way. He replied fiercely: "I knew nothing about all this. None of us in Munich heard of these cruelties at Dachau. Of course, we knew there was the labor camp but that's all."

Pointing to the crematorium, he added arrogantly: "This was the work of a few crazy people. Madmen always crop up during wars. In any case the dirtiest work was done by French prisoners."

I turned on my heel and walked away. Schmidt and I decided to leave Dachau before we came to blows with someone. As we drove away through garden countryside, I knew the ovens of Dachau would haunt me for the rest of my life.

After Dachau there were other camps. There were visits among the great areas of displaced and dispossessed. Everywhere I went I talked with survivors of one of the greatest mass murders in history and collected their stories in an attempt to penetrate the mentality capable of such concerted sadism.

There are prehistoric caves where charred human bones have

been found, broken for their marrow by other human hands. Man has been hunter and the hunted—through the millennia. But nothing like Dachau has ever before been done by man—not in all human history.

One of the saddest of the DP problems is the handling of the "Unaccompanied Children." Remembering the "Lost Children" (*Besprizornye*) of Russia following World War I, the staff of "M" Project had predicted that a similar group would be rounded up in Germany after the total surrender. I visited children's villages and schools and rehabilitation centers. IRO, JDC, and ORT activities were working miracles.

Homeless boys were taking courses in carpentry, electrotechnics, radio, auto mechanics, locksmithing, dental mechanics, shoemaking, tailoring; and the few girls were being given courses in home economics and cooking.

Among other places, I visited the Kalmyk camp at Pfannenhofen. This forlorn group, born on Soviet soil, had been captured by the Germans and taken to Germany, where they were grouped together until the middle of 1946 when, according to the Yalta Agreement, "everyone must be returned to the country of origin," and the U. S. Army forcibly repatriated them into the Soviet Zone despite heart-rending appeals from the Kalmyks, who had always been sworn enemies of the Soviets.

The Soviets immediately machine-gunned them. It happened that about 600 Kalmyks were not taken in the trucks on the first trip. When the U. S. Army found that the Kalmyks were being slaughtered by the Soviet troops, the officer in charge refused to deliver the survivors across the border. Hence the surviving Kalmyks were placed in Pfannenhofen Camp, where they had remained ever since. The number in the camp was 623, and at Schliessheim Camp there were about 200, making a total of 823 Kalmyks in Bavaria.

We were received by their khan and his camp advisers. A Russian-speaking interpreter had been summoned to assist me in talking to the Kalmyks. We walked in a group around the camp where almond-eyed Mongolians watched us curiously, for Pfannenhofen was not seen by many visitors.

The khan and his advisers explained to me that they were ex-

376

clusively farmers, preferring a continental, not tropical, climate. They wanted to stay together as a unit, since most are now related. Out of the total of 623 persons, about 300 were workers.

We looked at the vegetable garden, pigstys, and chickens. Everything was in good order and the khan assured me that his people were as contented as any minority group could be with no hope for the future except death. . . .

These people are Buddhists. They believe in an afterlife, a better hereafter. For these reasons they must be good and kind to all people.

In World War I they fought with the Cossacks against the Germans. In 1917 they joined the anti-Communists against Communism. Most of them were killed. Many times during the Soviet regime they rose against the government. The result of these reprisals was mass killing and deportation to Siberia. After their last rising, Moscow decided to exclude the Kalmyks from the Red Army and deported all to Siberia. They were allowed to take only what they could carry with them, as they had to go on foot. They went, carrying small children and old people on their backs.

In 1920 there were many Kalmyks in General Wrangel's army. When this army was dissolved, some went to Yugoslavia, Bulgaria, Czechoslovakia, France, and Poland. From these countries during World War II the Germans press-ganged them into Germany for forced labor. They cannot emigrate, as most countries refuse to admit them because they belong to the yellow race. General Popov, who in 1945 fled from Prague to Washington in an American plane, had recruited Kalmyks as early as 1918 for the fight against Communism.

Here were the pitiful remnants of a brave people. I am glad to say that part of this group were among the rescued. The Tolstoy Foundation is now caring for some of these Kalmyks in New Jersey.

Wherever I went in Bavaria I heard stories of horror, and it was with relief that I boarded the train for Zürich, where I described my vivid impression of Dachau to two friends at dinner. All that night again I could not sleep as the horrors raced through my mind. Since leaving the gas chamber at Dachau my burning

377

desire had been to inhale clean, fresh air. A friend suggested the highest hotel in Europe—Jungfraujoch, 10,371 feet above sea level. There the summit of the Jungfrau rises 600 feet above the hotel. Everything was covered with snow or ice. The views in every direction were superb, the air cold and fresh.

After dinner I persuaded the recorder of meteorological data to take me through a long tunnel and up by elevator to a square building wherein were housed the aneroid barometer and other instruments. While he was entering the figures in a large book I climbed to the rooftop where the scoops of the wind gauges chased each other madly. A ladder stretched upward. Rung after rung I climbed in this fresh, ice-cold breeze. Standing with my face above the highest rung, where the wind swept down from the peak of the Jungfrau, I was on the highest man-made point in Europe, above man and all his works, good or evil.

The recorder found me clutching the top of the ladder on the roof. I could not explain. From his eyes I read that most common world-wide phrase, "these crazy Americans . . ."

Ten days later, with Mr. and Mrs. Robert Woods Bliss, we set out from Paris in a rented Cadillac complete with chauffeur on a sight-seeing trip. The French countryside was refreshingly beautiful, but the scars were still there.

It was like old times, for we were on our way to see the Abbé Breuil.

The next morning we drove through the charming Dordogne to Montignac-sur-Vézère where the Abbé Breuil awaited us in Fernand Windels' garden. The latter is the author of *Lascaux, Chapelle Sixtine de la Préhistoire*. Luncheon was served on a hilltop overlooking the valley. Prehistoric man always chose beautiful locations for his sanctuaries. We were within a few hundred paces of Lascaux, the "Sistine Chapel" of twenty-five millennia ago.

The Abbé was in extra fine form. In his classical French he related the story of the discovery of Lascaux on September 12, 1940, by four local boys accompanied by their dog, Robot, who suddenly disappeared down a deep hole. Young Ravidat, following his dog, entered a cave. His flickering lamp revealed the magnificent painted animals on the walls. Robot had led this boy into the finest gallery of prehistoric art in France. Lascaux took its rightful place beside Altamira and Niaux, the most famous prehistoric sanctuaries of western Europe.

As I walked down the stone steps arm in arm with my friend and teacher, Abbé Breuil, my heart beat happily as I recalled the multitude of Palaeolithic wall paintings, engravings, and sculptures-in-the-round in France and Spain which I had visited since 1926 under his guidance; there had been Font de Gaume, Niaux, Cap Blanc, Les Combarelles, Le Roc, Bédeilhac in France; and Tajo de las Figuras, La Pileta, Pindal, Castillo, and Altamira in Spain.

And now out of the bright sunlight we entered the dark outer chamber, passed down some steps, and then below us appeared the great panorama of animals of Lascaux.

The realistic paintings appeared fresh and clear on the sanctuary walls. Here were bisons, stags, and horses, some in well-composed scenes. The Abbé, in his most charming and gracious manner, showed us around. We were speechless. We were spellbound. The Aurignacians were really great artists. . . . Man, who can do so much that is ugly, has done much that is beautiful.

Down a short, upright ladder we climbed to see a superb male bison wounded by an arrow. In a crude style, near the horns was a man with a bird's head. Close by the silhouette of a bird surmounted a pole. As we stood in this narrow corner the Abbé, smoking a Caporal, pointed out the details of the composition. He suggested that this might be one of the earliest known pictographs.

We wished him good Aurignacian-hunting and regained the entrance, our eyes shining with admiration for the accomplishments of these artists of long, long ago.

> Aux lords azuréens de l'ombreuse Vézère,
> Ce ruisselet plus grand que le Gange et l'Amour:
> Lecteurs, allons rêver d'un baiser de lumière
> Dans la caverne obscure ou tout art a pris jour.

At Toulouse we parted company with Robert and Mildred Bliss, who returned by way of Conques to Paris, and were joined by Mary Pitcairn, secretary to General Omar Bradley. George Bijou, an American we met in Paris, drove us across the Midi, the

Pyrenees on our left barely visible through the haze. Before sunset we halted at Mas d'Azil to visit the excavations of my old friend Joseph Mandement, whose visions guide his excavations. He led us up ladders and through tunnels to see fragments of prehistoric human skeletons, masses of cave bear bones, and a few stone implements. We stopped to look back at the magnificent entrance to this long and high subterranean cave cut through the rock by the river Arize. I was able to describe to the others how the Azilians had lived here, pointed out the location of the "painted pebbles," and recalled the wild boar hunt scene with dogs, reconstructed in Field Museum.

We continued westward to Château Les Espas to call on the aged Count Bégouen, who had been so generous and helpful during our work on the Hall of the Stone Age of the Old World. He was bedridden and as I left he bade me good-by—a gallant gentleman.

The next morning we drove through the northern foothills of the Pyrenees to St. Jean de Luz.

Three days later Walter and Simone Washington drove us to San Sebastian, a delightful seaside spot. I had known them in Mexico before his transfer to our embassy in Madrid. Their hospitality was wonderful and through them we met many charming Spaniards.

Luncheon on the beach. Swimming daily to and from the island. *Tir au pigeon*. Biarritz. By train to Madrid. The Goyas in El Prado. The El Grecos in Toledo. By train to Lisbon. El Estoril beach, where men must wear tops to their bathing suits; the casino where the many ex-kings play; dinner with Ambassador Lincoln MacVeagh.

On September 6 my trip to Europe was over. After dinner I climbed aboard a four-engined Pan American giant and headed for home. I settled back and let the memories run riot; there was so much that was wonderful to remember. But so much that was horrible, too. Dachau could not be forgotten.

I AWOKE on December 1, 1945, with a sense of relief. For the first time in my life I was free. There had been school, college, Field Museum, and the government. For nineteen years, since leaving Oxford, there had always been regular office hours.

On this glorious December morning I was free to devote full time to anthropogeographical research, free to concentrate on the revision and publication of eight manuscripts of 9000 typed pages on Southwestern Asia.

Sir Henry Wellcome had said, "Your life should be divided, like Gaul, into three parts: study and training in your profession; museum work and research; and publication. For until your published researches are catalogued in the main libraries of the world, your work remains incomplete. That is the final stage."

Several days later we drove up to Chakri, a charming low house amid pine trees in Thomasville, Georgia, the "City of Roses."

I began to work on the manuscripts. In the late afternoon I drove to Susina to hunt quail and turkey with Robb White. Sitting in these great woods waiting for the gobbler-who-never-came-to-dinner was peaceful; I often made notes on the manuscript upon which I was working, until dark. We fished in the ponds, hunted ducks at dawn, shot doves, and tramped the brush for quail, and rode horseback through the pine woods. This was freedom at last. No more memoranda to write, no single-paragraph summaries of long reports, no temperamental assistants, no civil service inquirers, no security measures—just work and fun by day and movies at night.

A few weeks later in the old Packard, I drove across Texas to Laredo, up the Pan American Highway to Mexico City and down to Cuernavaca. The house was in a garden compound with a fine view of the mountains and a swimming pool.

Cuernavaca is a charming spot, with cobbled side streets, luxuriant foliage, and gaudily dressed, taciturn Indians. This town is a curious mixture of the very rich North Americans in huge villas or vast caravansaries; politicos and foreigners week-ending from Mexico City; U.S. schoolteachers abroad for education plus thrills; and the full-time inhabitants, many of whom live off *turistas* with sales in the *zócalo* of silverwork, colorful native garments, and more than the usual junk. Then there is always the National Lottery—a weekly hope for getting-rich-quick.

I took Spanish lessons, went to the movies, rode horseback. I worked on the last three sections of *The Anthropology of Iraq*.

Years before I had read Robert Redfield's *Tepoztlán—a Mexican Village*, a basic study of folk life and a standard work. This village lies about fifteen minutes by car from Cuernavaca. Naturally we became interested in Tepoztlán, its history, its people, its religions, its customs.

Tepoztlán is a spooky place. As one drives from Cuernavaca, beyond lie distant mountain ranges usually overshadowed by huge banks of milky-white cumulus. The land on both sides is parched. Big black birds wheel in the sky. The people and animals look sleepy. Time moves in slow motion. These Indians live to a ripe old age. No ulcers. No nervous breakdowns. No juvenile delinquents. No teen-age hysteria . . .

Teocalli, the Ome Tochtli or Tepoztecatl temple, is dedicated to the god of drunkenness, in whose honor a splendid debauch takes place here annually. The patron of Tepoztlán is Tepoztecatl, to whom a miraculous birth and heroic adventures are attributed. In the few houses I visited the shrine dominated the main room. A carved, painted figure of Jesus Christ or the Virgin Mary was the central motif. Copal gum is burned in an incense holder; on feast days, candles. But despite the outward Catholic domination of the village, I felt that their innermost religious convictions lay in their pre-Christian gods, in worship in their pre-Columbian ruins, for above Tepoztlán there is an all-pervading strangeness, a feeling that any non-Indian is an intruder on their sanctity. By day all seems calm and serene, but at sundown there is a marked change.

382

Dr. Xavier Romero, in the Laboratory of Anthropology of the National Museum, revealed that anthropometric data on 125 women had been recently obtained in Tepoztlán by Dr. Johanna Faulhaber de Saenz. There were no data on the men.

After conferences with my friends from Chicago World's Fair days, Dr. Daniel Rubin de la Borbolla, director of the Museo Nacional and Don Pablo Martinez del Rio, I decided to try to persuade these forbidding-looking Indians to submit to the calipers and camera.

This proved to be no simple self-assignment. Permission was granted by the mayor. I began work with several local assistants.

We filled in the sociological data, interrogating each subject in Spanish. At the end of a week of hard work I had 125 individuals recorded and photographed. By this time any glimmer of local enthusiasm for this research project was gone. The last Indian had gone out the door muttering an unpleasant curse in Nahuatl, their own language. However, this series plus those on the women would make a useful little publication in 1953.

Having collected plants and drugs in Iran and Iraq, I hunted down the most fashionable *curandera*, herb doctor, in Tepoztlán. The main treatment is washing with certain herbs. As an internal remedy, powdered woodpecker's head is extremely efficacious. Fumigation with cigarette smoke is also recommended. This is one angle not yet discovered by our Big Four tobacco companies. Jane Russell fumigating herself in tobacco smoke would make a good full-page ad.

After a dozen visits I had a collection of local herbs, with their names in Spanish and Nahuatl and their uses dictated by the *curandera*. Several recorders helped in this rather difficult job.

After six months of writing and revising the manuscript on *The Anthropology of Iraq*, I became restless to do some work in the state of Morelos. Don Pablo Martinez del Rio guided my reading on the ancient and modern inhabitants of Morelos. I dreamed of exploring the endless caves of Cacahuamilpa beyond Xochicalco, but without a well-equipped expedition this appeared foolhardy.

On February 22, 1947, I was in the Cuernavaca garden, analyzing the statistical data on the Kurds of northeastern Iraq. A knock on the gate, and an old Mexican shuffled across the lawn with a telegram. A prehistoric skeleton had been found near the road to the Pyramid of the Sun. Helmut de Terra invited me to come at once to Tepexpán.

The old Packard climbed up to Mexico City and over the road to San Juan Teotihuacán. Helmut led me down into the trench.

"This looks like the oldest American yet. You see, this is the Upper Pleistocene Becerra formation and this could not have been an intrusive burial."

"What's the age in round numbers?"

"About ten thousand years old. Twice as old as your Sumerians from Kish."

It was thrilling to stand there and reconstruct the past. Tepexpán man probably died elephant hunting on the swampy shore of Lake Tepexpán one hundred centuries ago.

Helmut and I searched the neighboring hills and ancient shore line for archaic stone implements and in particular for a stratified cave deposit or a surface campsite. We hunted for several days. Finally we located a tiny rock shelter near an ancient spring. White chalcedony flakes were picked up nearby. A trial trench proved unproductive. On the third day I was fortunate to find the central portion of a Folsom point of mottled chalcedony with the characteristic broad, longitudinal flake. Here was the first indication south of the Rio Grande that there was a cultural link between the oldest cultures of New Mexico and the Valley of Mexico. The Tepexpán hunters might well be connected culturally with the early dwellers of Folsom and Sandia. In 1952 other Folsom-like points were unearthed.

Back in the laboratory of the Museo Nacional, Dr. Xavier Romero showed me the skull and fragmentary skeleton. Examination revealed that this adult Mongoloid would have passed in the Tepoztlán plaza as one of the more primitive-looking Indians.

Months later Tepexpán man flew in a giant Clipper to Washington, where he was repaired and studied by Dr. Romero and Dr. T. Dale Stewart in the Smithsonian; a detailed report was published. His contribution to science concluded, he flew back to his exhibition case in Mexico City, the oldest American. . . .

Back in Cuernavaca I organized a search for caves and rock shelters suitable for trial trenches. This list of localities was forwarded to Dr. Daniel Rubin de la Borbolla together with bags of sherds and a few crude stone implements.

My report on the Indians of Tepoztlán was completed. It had been a delightful year in Mexico with many side trips. It was time to return to Thomasville. Back down the Pan American Highway I drove, across sweltering Texas, to pine-sheltered Chakri, Thomasville, arriving late in the spring of 1946.

Outside Chakri stood a house trailer. This was my office. Here, with a fan running, the radio quivering with hillbilly music from the local station, and an iced Coke, I was making the final revisions to the monograph on the archaeology of the North Arabian Desert, a study begun twenty-two years before. "New York is calling," came through an open window.

A cheery voice said, "This is Wendell Phillips. Do you want to join the University of California African Expedition as physical anthropologist?"

"Thank you, Wendell, but you know I'm interested in Asia, not Africa."

"Never mind that. Meet me at Tallahassee airport tomorrow morning."

Eight hours later I had agreed, especially after I learned that Professor William F. Albright of Johns Hopkins had signed up for the work in Egypt. Wendell promised me researches in the Faiyûm and in Sinai, which I have always considered to be culturally part of Asia, not Africa.

This was exciting. Another expedition ahead—my last had been in 1934, eons ago before World War II. Here would be an opportunity to do some anthropometric studies in the Faiyûm and on the Bedouins of Sinai as well as to search for Stone Age sites on the land bridge between Africa and Asia.

Wendell's plans were for a real expedition, on a grander scale than either the Citroën Trans-Asiatic Expedition (La Croisière Jaune) or Roy Chapman Andrews' expeditions to the Gobi Desert. An airplane, twenty-six cars, and thirty people seemed almost too unwieldy for practical results. There would be personnel problems: jealousy, feuds, and temperament.

Could this brash young supersalesman-dreamer organize and

carry through from Cairo to Cape Town this great expedition? Would the results be published by the University of California as a shelf of monographs and scientific papers? These were the thoughts racing through my head as, on a beautiful October afternoon, I studied maps of Egypt, the Sudan, and Kenya, while relaxing in a Pan American Clipper high over the Atlantic.

Late that night a Scotch express swept through the tunnel into Leicester station, where Mother met me. Here I spent a month awaiting Wendell's arrival and buying reference books on the Faiyûm and Sinai. This gave me a chance to study up on these two areas and to confer with experts and my old friend Sir Arthur Keith.

The Nazi bombing of the city of London had caused the total destruction of some five million books—hence it was especially hard to round up the books I wanted for my research.

Early in November Mother and I met Wendell at London airport. Driving on the left often made Wendell put his arm over his eyes as he awaited a head-on collision, on the way up to town. The bright red mailboxes, the tall helmeted bobbys, the pubs with Dickensian names, the crawling, snub-nosed taxis, the gold-braided doormen with flowing mustaches, the lunatic fringe around soapbox orators, and the newsboys calling out, "Evening piper, sir?"—all fascinated him.

Wendell was in buoyant spirits, "rarin' to get started in Egypt."

On November 9 we flew with Air France to Paris, and on over the Alps to Rome.

Professor Sergio Sergi came to call at our hotel, bringing news of the recently discovered Neanderthal skulls from Saccopastore. Late though it was, we drove to Città Università and climbed the stairs to his laboratory, where I studied with awe these precious skulls, perhaps fifty thousand years old—the oldest inhabitants of the boot of Europe, Italy.

The plane from London was overloaded, so no excess baggage could be carried. A duffel bag containing the precious reference books on Sinai and the Faiyûm was readdressed to Cairo. I have never seen it since that moment.

A heavily overladen Czech plane brought us to Lydda at sundown. I began to negotiate in Arabic for a taxi to Jerusalem. The price was fantastic. The Arab kept repeating, "You must have a big, new Chrysler."

"I don't see why. I have a ten-year-old Packard at home."

"That's the only car I'll let you take."

We paid in advance, grumbling, and glided off toward the Holy City in our Chrysler limousine at 35 mph. A pencil of light flashed from a hilltop onto the car. We were suddenly like goldfish in a bowl. The driver slowed to 20 mph. Another searchlight picked us out. "We must go steadily or they will machine-gun us." This drive was like a nightmare. Ten minutes later the lights went out as we entered Jerusalem. Immediately we were challenged by six Tommies, the young sergeant sporting a machine gun.

"Where are your passes?"

"We have none. We've just come from Lydda airport for one night in Jerusalem."

"Proceed slowly at your own risk. Halt at once if ordered, or you will be shot."

We crept through the dark streets, the only non-military vehicle.

Again we were stopped. A British sergeant ordered us to the nearest hotel, the Eden, just around the corner. The manager blinked as we came into the lobby, long after curfew. After supper Wendell and I began to struggle with our accounts, for by this time we had bills in English, French, Italian, and Greek currencies. As we sat side by side checking, a pattering sound came from outside. Wendell sprang up, put his head out of the circular window, and shouted, "Turn out the lights. Someone is shooting at us."

The manager came running in, grabbed Wendell unceremoniously by the legs, and slammed the window shut. "Come down into the basement at once. Don't you know how dangerous that is?"

"Sure, I was on Okinawa. Those are machine-gun bullets."

We were herded into a basement full of heavy columns; here were the other guests. In that hour 10,000 rounds were fired, many of them at the hotel. We were never told the reason. In the morning we called on Professor Millar Burrows, director of the American School of Oriental Research, bringing greetings from Professor Albright. Before luncheon we visited the Mosque of Omar; we were the only tourists. We drove to Bethlehem and Jericho, visited a collective farm beside the Dead Sea, and caught the plane at Lydda in time to land in Cairo before midnight.

Someone had built a large semi-tropical arch of clay as the gateway to Kom Oshim, a rectangular courtyard surrounded by one-story mud-brick buildings. Kom Oshim had been placed at the disposal of the University of California African Expedition by the Egyptian government as the base of operations for research in the Faiyûm area. Outside were lined up the fleet of Dodge power-wagons, jeeps, and trailers—the largest land expedition ever seen.

We met the other members of the staff: Bob Denison, palaeontologist, later to join Chicago Natural History Museum; Paul (P.E.P.) Deranyigala, director of Colombo Museums, a Cambridge boxing Blue and palaeontologist with a burning yen for fossil hippopotami; Harry Hoogstraal, zoologist from Chicago Natural History Museum and the finest of expedition members; Basil Cooke, palaeontologist from Johannesburg, also a good companion; Bill Terry, executive director, flier, and expert photographer; Gladys Terry, his wife, young, good-looking, our secretary-treasurer as well as a pilot and photographer; three Marines, Captain Grammar G. Edwards, known as the "Skipper," in charge of transportation; T/S Charles D. Evans, "Chuck" to all of us; and T/S James L. Houle. The youngest member was eighteen-year-old Dave Cohen from Minneapolis, who came along as a general handy man but was most interested in all kinds of hunting. Tolbah waited on table and looked after our rooms in a mild way. A good Arab servant, he remained cheerful all the time—a great asset.

Wendell and Bill Terry spent most of their time in Cairo with the Egyptian authorities, for permits are rarely issued promptly beside the Nile.

The days were warm and sunny, the nights cold in our mud huts, and laundry a constant problem. Every day 250 gallons of water were drawn in a trailer from the Auberge du Lac, a pleasant inn beside Lake Qârûn, where Roosevelt and Churchill had conferred during World War II. Arab women pounded our laundry with sticks in a nearby hut; quite a shirt-testing device.

In Cairo I requested permission to measure a series of Arabs in a village near Kom Oshim. With the encouragement of the late and charming Nokrashy Pasha, the Prime Minister, and Sanhouri Pasha, Minister of Education, as well as permission from the governor and chief of police of the Faiyûm, work began at nearby Tamiya.

Here I measured and observed 189 men. Bill and Gladys Terry took the front and profile photographs. At my request a mobile unit from the Department of Public Health, under the direction of Dr. Mohammed M. Sadr, conducted a medical and nutritional survey of Tamiya. Thus we made the first key study on the modern dwellers in the Faiyûm.

At Fidimin, in the center of the rich citrus belt, I measured 306 more.

Now I was really interested in the Faiyûm, its history and anthropogeography. In the evenings I read and made notes. At the Royal Egyptian Geographical Society I pored over thick tomes in English, French, German, and Italian to collect material on the Faiyûm and our next objective, Sinai. My disgust with British European Airways for having lost the duffel bag between Rome and Cairo could not be measured even in good old Anglo-Saxon phraseology.

The weeks passed swiftly, especially as we were planning our reconnaissance in Sinai. The principal objective of the Faiyûm work was to search for a highly elusive fossil primate whose skull is smaller than a child's hand.

Before World War I a German expedition had found lower jaws of *Parapithecus* and *Propliopithecus* in the lower Oligocene Qatrani beds in the desert north of the Faiyûm. Described by Schlosser in 1911, they were kept in Munich.

To find one of these fragile skulls beneath the surface of hundreds of square miles of sand is almost a hopeless task. We never found a trace. However, cases of fossil bones were packed for shipment. Far out in the desert two large whale skeletons were lying exposed in a semicircle. A fanciful thought: two whales chasing each other, turned to stone millions of years ago.

The cold gray dawn of my birthday, December 15, found me at the wheel of a Dodge power-wagon, a Leica camera around my neck. Shades of Wendell's promises in the piny woods of Georgia that I should not have to use a Leica or drive a truck! Beside me rode Dr. S. A. Huzayyin, prehistorian of Farouk I University in Alexandria and attached to the Expedition. Behind came Bill Terry, driving a 2½-ton International with Professor Albright and Ahmed Lutfi of the Department of Antiquities at his side. Thunderously the two trucks of the California African Expedition crossed the Suez Canal into Sinai, the land bridge between Africa and Asia. Here Moses and the Israelites had wandered for forty long years.

About sixty miles east of the Canal, on a hunch I turned the truck off the road near the low hills of Jebel Maghara. Tiny flint crescents, each with delicate retouches, lay in a small area. We were in a Mesolithic workshop. These lunates were probably tips for reed shafts serving as arrows, perhaps ten thousand years ago. Their cultural affinities linked to the Nile Valley rather than that of the Tigris-Euphrates.

The El Arish area proved a distinct disappointment, for sand covered all historical traces, thwarting the main purpose of Albright's visit to northern Sinai. However, our other efforts were amply repaid. At Er-Rawafi we found a Lower Palaeolithic station with hundreds of hand axes, scrapers, choppers, and flakes. This also must have been a workship, perhaps a thousand centuries before Christ. And southwest of El Arish we found a section of Roman pavement, a link in the ancient Roman empire.

Desiring to measure some Bedouins in Sinai, I drove to Magdhaba, a small police post beside the Wadi el Arish. Here were ten Terabin tribesmen. I started on a young man who appeared frightened and belligerent. The other Terabin glared fiercely, their heads wrapped in the white kerchiefs and their *agals* of twisted black camel's hair set at a rakish angle. I had recorded the subject's birthplace and asked the number of his brothers and sisters living and dead, when he sprang to his feet, his eyes blazing, and stalked away from the table. The seated Bedouins also rose up and walked away, muttering fiercely. No words of encouragement, no promises of baksheesh, and no apologies could stay

390

their flight from the anthropometer. I had failed miserably. Their cloaked backs disappeared into the stream bed of the Wadi el Arish and my heart sank as I lost forever and a day ten fine specimens of the Terabin of Sinai, simply by inquiring about sisters. Girls are so unimportant, the question was insulting.

Our last morning in El Arish I suddenly remembered that I had not bought any samples of wheat, barley, beans, and other locally grown products for the study of economic botany. Taking the Dodge and a native mechanic-driver, I set off for the market place. In a booth sat an aged Arab behind sacks of grain and many kinds of beans. Immediately a crowd gathered around me. This always happens east of Suez, so I was not concerned except that I stupidly had not brought a native with me. The glances were far from friendly. I asked the old merchant to sell me a double handful of each local product. He began to wrap small packages of wheat and barley and beans. His gnarled old fingers moved like cold molasses. The crowd around me must have numbered fifty by this time. For the first time in my life I was surrounded by unfriendly Arabs—and all alone.

I paid the merchant, gathered the packages under my arm, and forced my way politely through the crowd. As I began the long, long walk of a hundred yards to the truck a group of children began to dance in front of me, crying, *"Huwa Yahudi, huwa Yahudi* [He's a Jew]." Then the crowd began to cry, *"Yahudi Americani."* I realized that if I made a dash for the truck I would never reach it alive. To be killed by a mob for buying a few handfuls of seeds in El Arish would be really stupid! Action was necessary. I stopped, felt in my pockets for some matches, which were there, and said casually out loud in Arabic, "I need some matches and cigarettes. Where can I buy them?"

A small boy saw a chance for baksheesh and pulled me back through the astonished crowd to a booth, and as I stood there—even farther from the U.S. truck and safety—I felt someone squeeze my arm. This was Mohammed, our young police escort, with his rifle. Mohammed led me quietly through the crowd. A voice called out, "Mohammed, isn't the foreigner an American Jew?"

Mohammed addressed the crowd: "He is an American. He is

not a Jew. He is a friend of the Arabs. More than that, he is our guest, for he is the guest of the governor and I am his protector. Remember your manners, O men of El Arish."

With that we walked slowly across to the truck. The frightened Arab at the wheel had the motor running, the brake off. I climbed up beside him. Mohammed sat on the outer edge of the seat, resting his rifle in the air. The truck surged forward and we rounded a corner amid a volley of oaths and curses on all Christians and one in particular. I thanked Mohammed as best I could, pressing a month's salary into his hand. An hour later, as I drove south, I began to tremble; cold perspiration coursed down my face. Mohammed took these for malarial symptoms, so I pretended to swallow some quinine. That was a really close call, one of the closest I have ever had.

Crossing the Wadi Tangeriya, we passed a chain of low white mounds. We were indeed in the great wilderness of El Tih—not a living animal in sight and but few plants struggling for existence. This is the next stage to true desert in the fertility scale. The horror of this great loneliness was broken as a small gray-brown bird with bluish underwings flew from one barren rock to another the better to watch our thunderous oncoming. The Wilderness of Tih is the loneliest spot I have ever seen: nothing but low hills and sand everywhere; the wind blows constantly. At night the scratching of the sand could easily lead to madness.

Miracle of miracles, palm trees and buildings finally appeared. This was no mirage; it was Nekhl, former capital of Sinai, the only village in the center of the peninsula. This was the crossroad, for through Nekhl ran an ancient road linking Cairo and Mecca and Bir Hasaneh to El Arish.

I have enjoyed palm trees in many places but none more gladly than in the wilderness of Tih. No mirage could have had greater appeal. We drove past an old Turkish fort with crenelated battlements and a fine arch. A white minaret stood out clearly against the blue, blue sky.

Our arrival was like that of the circus at home. Every man and child crowded around us. With Huzayyin as pacifier and recorder, I began to measure some Bedouins and one Negro. The children were dispatched to catch small animals. Bill Terry began to photograph the men and children, who readily exchanged beetles for cash. One young man brought in a huge yellowish-green scorpion. I was glad to have it inside the jerry can, safe in the arms of formaldehyde before its long ride to California.

Inside the fort six splendid white male camels were chewing chopped straw from their mud-brick feed boxes on the ground. Dark-skinned, well-built Sudanese Camel Corps men were at their twilight tasks. One stood strumming on his guitarlike *simsimiya*, whose resonator was made from a Ford V-8 hubcap! With some encouragement he played an Arab tune with excellent rhythm.

From the platform outside the main gateway we saw the palm trees and buildings silhouetted against a very pink sky, with long, feathery streamers running toward the zenith. Such beauty, even in nature, rarely exists and in a moment is gone.

About sixty miles west of Nekhl we found some flint implements and Roman pottery. We were on an ancient overland route used by the Stone Age hunters and the Romans. Later we came to a signpost standing in solitary grandeur. On the triple-faced stone pedestal were the words beside arrows: Nekhl-Kuntilla-Aqaba; Kosseima-Jerusalem-El Arish; and Egypt-Suez.

We stopped to photograph a beautiful, spreading green tree beside a wadi bed. Under ordinary circumstances this tree would pass unnoticed but here it stood in all its simple beauty—our first link with water and civilization after many, many miles through the great wilderness of Tih.

In the distance the superstructure of a ship glided through a sea of sand. This was the Suez Canal—and civilization again.

We picnicked beside the canal, still benumbed from our mental exposure to the Wilderness of Tih. That night we camped in the lee of the eastern bank. At sunset I climbed alone to the top of the bank and sat there alone. Behind lay the wilderness of the Exodus. Ahead flickered the light of Suez town through its belt of palm trees. Southward extended the friendly arm of the Red Sea. Stars were coming out; stillness everywhere except for native dogs in the distance. The ship, almost touching on each side, came slowly nearer. As it passed, friendly shouts brought me back to reality. On her stern in the bright lights the name was visible and below was listed her home port—New York, an immensely distant place it seemed to me. It was Christmas Eve.

Selman, the one-eyed, one-armed ex-policeman, had proved himself invaluable. He remained with us all the time in southwestern Sinai. On Christmas Day I asked him to walk across to a Bedouin encampment on the plain to ask if they knew of any mounds covered with broken pottery between Abu Zeneimeh and the entrance to the Wadi Feiran. Selman returned to say that the Bedouins had described a small mound "covered with pottery" beside the road about four miles south of the resthouse.

Here we found Middle Kingdom sherds in profusion on the surface and in the upper levels of the Sinai Mining Company's light railway cut through the center of the mound (*tell*). We decided to abandon the trip to the Wadi Feiran and to make a few soundings in debris in an attempt to establish the age of occupation. Then, examining the map, Albright suggested that this might be the ancient Egyptian port for Serabit el Khadem and other turquoise mines. Here on this foreshore in a natural harbor landed the Egyptian ships laden with technicians and slaves for mine working.

Four days later several trial trenches had been sunk into this mound. Albright decided that the Bedouins had guided us to the port of Merkhah, where the ancient Egyptians had moored their vessels about 1500 B.C. in quest of turquoise from the mines in the Wadi Maghara and on top of Serabit el Khadem. I patted Selman on the back.

The discovery of Merkhah is important because during the past half century Sir Flinders Petrie and many others had searched in vain for this port, from which ancient Egyptian ships transported the miners who were engaged in mining turquoise at Serabit el Khadem about five miles, air-line distance, from the shore.

The most important part of the discovery was that observations revealed that the Red Sea had never reached the base of the mound nearest to the water. This point was less than six feet above present water level. Hence Albright deduced that the level of the Red Sea had remained relatively unchanged since the time

394

of Moses. Nelson Glueck at Ezion-Geber, Solomon's seaport on the Gulf of Aqaba, recorded that in this arm of the Red Sea the level had also remained little changed.

These two factors proved that the height of the waters of the Gulf of Suez at the time of the Exodus was approximately the same as in the middle of the twentieth century. Hence Moses did not have to "divide the waters" to cross the Red Sea, but probably led the Israelites through the "Sea of Reeds" far to the north of Suez. Once again, scientific research threw new light on the Bible.

Now Bill Terry announced that we were ready to start for St. Catherine's Monastery in the heart of the great mountain complex of southern Sinai. In the *National Geographic Magazine* for December 1948, I have described in detail our trip to this famous monastery built by the Emperor Justinian during the fourth century of our era.

Father Nile, one of the novitiates, acted as our host. He was a charming gentleman in his late fifties with a fine, white Darwinian beard. We learned that his mastery of five languages and his ability to read printing upside down almost as readily as right side up had made his services as censor of value to the Egyptian government during World War II.

On his short-wave radio Father Nile often listened to Lowell Thomas, so we decided to send him our greetings by letter from the foot of Mount Sinai. Lowell was delighted.

One afternoon in his monastic rooms, as he brewed a cup of tea, he told me part of his story. He had enjoyed fully the pleasures of the world; gambling, horse racing, and beautiful women.

During the previous summer in Alexandria, he had suffered a slight heart attack. Thoughts of being paralyzed and bedridden tortured him. In the dark watches of the night he had a vision. God told him sternly that he was a real sinner. Then St. Catherine appeared to beckon him to the foot of Mount Sinai. Father Nile assumed his present name (an ancient one at the monastery) and shortly thereafter sold his possessions, distributed his wealth to his children, and journeyed to the monastery, a humble but inspired novice.

Sitting in this small room under the lee of Mount Sinai, it was strange to hear a bearded monk talk about going to the races at the Gezira Sporting Club, the roulette wheels in Cairo, and the bathing beauties at Alexandria.

Suddenly he realized that the past was running through his thoughts and he turned the conversation to Moses and the route of the Exodus.

Next morning long before dawn Wendell and I stood barefoot in front of the Burning Bush while the monks chanted their daily ritual in Greek. Father Nile looked the image of a venerable patriarch. This service is a test of endurance. It begins at 4:30 A.M. and continues until nine o'clock. The older members (i.e., eighty plus) lean on T-shaped wooden sticks. The rest stand, singing or making responses. This is the coldest little chapel I have ever been in, but several cups of hot coffee revived us.

I measured 70 Jebeliyeh, believed to be direct descendants of the Wallachian and Bosnian serfs sent as protection to St. Catherine's by Justinian.

One afternoon we climbed to the peak of Mount Sinai, up thirty-five hundred steps cut by the monks. On a great rock we sat amid mountain peaks in "a sea of abomination and desolation." Here Moses passed forty days and nights alone when the Lord gave him the "tables of stone, and a law, and commandments which I have written; that thou mayest teach them" (Exodus 24:12). I was deeply moved by the loneliness, the beauty, and my own thoughts . . .

Next morning we bade our charming hosts farewell. A last look showed two white-bearded patriarchs silhouetted against the blue sky as they waved to us from the crenelated battlement.

Shortly afterward work in the Faiyûm was finished. Preparations were made to leave our base camp at Kom Oshim for the Sudan, Kenya, and eventually Cape Town.

While the fossils were being packed and the fleet of trucks loaded, I drove the professor and Wendell through Zagazig to Rameses, where we were overnight guests of the French expedition excavating this great city. Fallen columns were being set up as the work of reconstruction continued. This was where the Israelites slaved for the pharaoh. Closing my eyes, I could almost hear the chanting of the toiling Israelites, punctuated by the crack of the lash.

In the distance a village nestled on the shore of the shallow lake known in Hebrew as Yam Sûph—the Sea of Reeds. I asked one of the Arab foremen, "Do storms come up quickly on the lake?"

"Yes, they come up in a few hours, generally right after sunset."

"Can you tell when they are coming?"

"You can feel them in your bones."

I thought of the Israelites as Moses led them onto a path leading out into the Sea of Reeds, the long, winding column of men, women, and children hurrying in the dark.

The alarm was raised. The Egyptians gave chase in their chariots. Suddenly the storm broke. The waters rose and "the Lord overthrew the Egyptians in the midst of the sea . . . there remained not so much as one of them."

With Professor Albright we drove south to the sites of Succoth and Pithom, mentioned in the Exodus. This was a great experience for Wendell and me, for we could visualize the Israelites and their flight from Rameses.

Wendell returned to Cairo, and Bill, Gladys, and I took the long, dusty train ride to Aswan. We stood beside the 120-foot obelisk hewn out on three sides, weighing about 1000 tons. Our guide explained that copper tools made holes for sycamore wedges which split the granite when wetted. Rameses employed two thousand men for the transportation of these granite obelisks and blocks.

In the hotel bar an old-timer asked me if I knew the American gentleman who had lived for many years in a house nearby. He recalled a handsome, irascible guest who always wore a white suit, white tie, and panama hat, and carried a cherrywood cigarette holder. That was Uncle Barbour without a doubt! How I wished he would walk in the door then and there. . . .

Time was running short, as I had to be with Mother at Hungarton Church in Leicestershire to dedicate a stained-glass window as a memorial to my stepfather. Wendell encouraged me to fly from Khartoum to Nairobi to spend three weeks in Kenya. I was surprised to find that the capital of Kenya was too full, like wartime Washington. It was hard to find a hotel room.

The Kenya section of the Expedition was searching for

Miocene apes in the Lodwar area near the southwestern corner of Lake Rudolf. As my time was short, the governor, Sir Philip Mitchell, suggested that I concentrate on the nearby Masai.

Louis and Mary Leakey were kindness itself. He is director of the Coryndon Memorial Museum and I had known him since our undergraduate days when he was at Cambridge. He has devoted his life to research in East Africa and is a blood brother of the Kikuyu tribe. He drove me to visit the ancient obsidian mines and rock shelters near Lake Naivasha, to Olegorsailie, one of the famous "museums-on-the-spot." Thousands of large hand axes lie on the surface; the most extraordinary sight of its kind in the world.

On Easter morning Louis drove me past Mount Kilimanjaro (19,317 feet), whose snow-covered dome appeared above the clouds, to Arusha in Tanganyika. This town is midway from Cairo to Cape Town. Beside the road we passed two Masai youths, their faces painted white and each wearing fifty small bird skins as a halo hat; they were in the "neuter" stage of initiation.

We drove past giraffes, guinea fowl, Grant's gazelle, kongoni, zebra, and dozens of other animals and birds, and up a winding mountain road into the Serengeti National Park and to Ngorongoro Crater. Here we camped in native-type thatched, round huts, each with a bedroom and sitting room with a fireplace, for it is cold here at night at eight thousand feet above sea level. At sunset, with the Zeiss glasses, I crept down to the edge of this crater, at least ten miles in diameter. Thousands of animals browsed on the rich pasture. Leakey pointed out the types—almost every kind, except lion, elephant, and rhinoceros. This was certainly big-game Africa. I had no desire to shoot any of them. To watch these vast herds through the glasses in the setting sun was adventure enough.

Back in Nairobi I called on Game Warden Ritchie, who gave me permission to accompany J. H. ("Jock") Hunter, game conservationist, to Selengei in the Masai Reserve. Jock was leaving on a five-day trip to destroy hyenas, lions or leopards preying on Masai cattle. He has recently written the best seller *Hunter*.

At Kajiado I picked up Godfrey Njao, a Masai schoolteacher

with an excellent command of English and a deep interest in the history of his famous tribe; he proved a good interpreter.

Hunter pitched camp under the spreading branches of a flat-topped acacia tree near a water hole beside the Selengei River. As soon as night fell the plains became stilled. The air was soft and warm like southern Florida. Now and then a hyena called to his mate, a weird sound far more like an owl's hooting than that of a four-footed animal. This was really Africa—surrounded by game and the Masai tribe.

After a fine breakfast we visited another water hole. In the mud, Hunter pointed out the recent spoor of elephants, rhinos, and a huge male lion. Three Masai cattle keepers told fantastic tales of the ferocity of this lion, how he killed calves and even full-grown heifers. Hunter's eyes narrowed. "That's a marauder. We'll bait a trap for the next two nights." My heart began to race at the thought of a real lion hunt.

In the late afternoon Jock and I were driving in an open truck with half a dozen Wakamba clinging to the top of the cab. Quietly pulling the handbrake, Jock pointed to a zebra standing a hundred yards away. The slanting rays of the sun picked out the black and white stripes as the zebra stood against a deep green bush.

"Take your time, mon. Rest your elbow on the hood."

I fired my trusty 6.5-mm. Mannlicher. The zebra bent his right ear forward.

"Shoot again, mon. Shoot."

I fired again. The zebra bent his left ear forward. I fired twice more. The zebra walked slowly away. Never have I felt more ashamed.

Jock sprang from the truck, saying, "Your sights must be off. I'll sight it in for you."

"There's nothing the matter with the rifle. I just don't hold it straight."

Then ordering a Wakamba boy to blaze a tree eighty paces distant, Jock stood and fired five times in rapid succession. We walked across to the target. The five bullets were arranged in a neat, small circle.

Later I shot a running male Grant's gazelle while standing

beside the truck. That was better. By the time we returned to camp it was almost too late to poison the hyena bait, for according to Hunter, "it is dangerous to use strychnine in the dark." However, there was just enough light for Jock and the boys to spread a dozen pieces of meat near the water hole.

Jock entertained us around the campfire for a couple of hours after dinner, telling stories of his big-game experiences in Africa, of close shaves, how rhinos now hunt in packs like hyenas, and of the wicked water buffalo. With regard to the latter, Jock agreed with Carl Akeley, who always said that this was the most dangerous animal in Africa.

At daybreak Jock woke me to report the panting of a leopard outside his tent. There were the footprints in the soft earth. A leopard had indeed been roaming around, attracted no doubt by the aroma of the Grant's gazelle lying covered in the truck. Jock made plans to catch this thiever of Masai cattle with his "dumb-trap."

The Wakamba built a circular thorn fence about five feet high, leaving a narrow entrance between two upright wooden posts. A rifle was mounted so that the muzzle pointed down between the posts. The bait was placed opposite the entrance. The animal stalks his prey and presses with his head against the wire, which releases the trigger and fires the bullet into the back of his head.

During the morning there was a crash on the ground nearby. Rushing out of my tent, I saw a huge vulture crumpled on the ground. A Wakamba boy smiled and pointed to a high tree full of vultures. As we looked, another large bird fell dead. Jock explained that the hyenas regurgitate the strychnine-poisoned hunks of meat; these are eaten by the less discriminating vultures, which suddenly die. I hoped they would watch out where they fell, for to be hit by one of them falling from several thousand feet could be a fatal blow.

While we were at dinner the gun went off, and we ran to the trap. Here was no leopard but a large male hyena lying dead as mutton with a bullet through the brain. Mwika and his Wakamba boys quickly dragged the body into the bush and covered the blood with sand. Hunter reloaded the rifle, but it did not go off again that night.

In the morning five poisoned hyenas lay dead, but the leopard was a little too clever!

Just before noon up drove George Russell, William Snyder, and Arch Oboler, the latter of radio mystery-writing fame, in one of the Expedition's Dodge trucks. At Wendell's insistence I had arranged for Oboler to join us at Selengei to make movies and sound recordings of Masai life.

At nearby Mashuru we stopped outside the village of mud huts surrounded by a huge thorn fence. The men and boys were away tending their cattle. Godfrey and I were led into a tiny house by two old crones with shaven heads. It was almost dark inside and the thick blue smoke rising from the open hearth made my eyes burn. After some minutes I could make out our hostess seated on a wooden stool across the room. My seat was on tanned, shiny cattle skins, the male bed. Across the room, in an alcove, was the bed for the women and the adjoining guest bunk. Conversation was difficult, and the combination of smoke and strong human smell in a tiny sealed room was overpowering.

Hanging on the mud wall just inside the entrance were a calabash used for blood and milk, their principal diet, and donkey panniers.

The women wore metal arm bands, several kinds of earrings, bead or cowrie necklaces, anklets, and leg bracelets. None of the women or girls could be persuaded to submit to the calipers in private or in public, despite Godfrey's entreaties.

Outside, Oboler recorded on tape the chatter of the group of girls crowding around the truck. When he played it back to them, their eyes shone with amazement.

When several Masai elders returned they were naturally not a little disturbed to see the truck at the village entrance with their girls crowding around and giggling. Godfrey was wonderful. Calming them down, he suggested a song, first the girls, then the men. When their voices were played back they screamed and shouted like children.

The men wore copper earrings and each carried a large calabash for the blood and milk. Most of them had snuff holders. Both men and women spoke softly and the dogs barked rarely—quite a contrast from an Arab village or a Bedouin encampment.

The flies were appalling. Hundreds and hundreds covered the girls and children. The girls were far from overdressed; a Bikini would have looked as out of place as a snowsuit. With their completely shaven heads and below-par average of clothes, there was plenty of fly space. One well-built belle was particularly attractive to the local *Diptera*. We estimated there were five thousand flies on her body. Here was a chance for an experiment. Grabbing the DDT, I sprayed this beauty, front, side, and back. The smiling girl was enchanted with the oily film on her chocolate-brown skin.

I was instantly surrounded by a bevy of girls begging to be sprayed, but we had to leave. As we drove off, the proud, flyless Masai maiden waved ecstatically.

We drove to an East Indian trading post where two Masai elders guided us across a very rough area to a grazing herd of their cattle. A young steer, selected by the herdsman, was brought to the camera. We were now to witness the bloodletting ceremony. A healthy steer is bled every forty days. If blood is to be drawn for the young warrior (*muran*), no woman may watch.

A halter was drawn tightly around the neck. The elder plucked a leaf, moistened it with his spittle, and stuck it on the target spot. Then he drew his bow and shot the triangular metal-tipped arrow from about two feet away into the leaf. The arrow was plucked at once. The blood flowed into a brown calabash, ornamented with a ring of cowrie shells, and already one-third full of milk. After five minutes the bleeding was stopped by removing the halter and by applying earth and spittle to the wound.

The animal was loosed and, shaking its head sadly, it walked back to the herd.

One elder shook up the calabash and offered me this blood-and-milk cocktail. Flies were crawling all over the outside. I had seen the milk before the blood was added; it looked like café au lait with flies floating in it. I could not bring myself to take a swallow. Snyder muttered, "Sissy," to which I replied, "But I never drink cocktails." Fortunately our hosts were not offended.

This was my last night in the Masai Reserve among the big game. I had seen high in a tree across the river from our camp a wooden platform which, Hunter explained, had been put up by a

Hollywood movie crew to photograph animals at the water hole. I asked Jock if I might spend at least part of the night on this platform, my last chance in Africa.

"You certainly may. I don't think you will see much, but that's up to you. Mwika, send two boys to help carry the blankets."

Godfrey said, "I want to go. You may need me up there."

A few minutes later we four started across the broad, flat bed of the Selengei River. Up the tree climbed the Wakamba, carrying blankets, my 6.5 Mannlicher, and Zeiss glasses. They threw down a rope and up I went from bough to bough. The platform felt a mile in the air in the dark. It had not been used for some time so the wire supports were none too secure and the platform tilted. My blankets were spread out and I took my place in the center. Godfrey installed himself near the main trunk.

Down went the Wakamba into the night and back to camp. My flashlight beam picked out the gazelle carcass hung by the hind leg to a low tree. There was the bait. Now to await the lion or leopard.

Godfrey, being a Masai, made himself comfortable with his back against the tree trunk and one arm around a wire support for the platform. He was soon asleep, relaxed and safe.

I was in a far more precarious position, lying full length on the sloping wooden platform with my Zeiss glasses, loaded rifle, and flashlight.

An hour is a long time in such a situation. Godfrey was sleeping soundly. I could not get comfortable. First an elbow ached, then a knee, and then it came on to rain.

Suddenly a lion roared and I almost jumped out of my skin. Godfrey woke up and peered down below toward the bait. He had agreed to nudge me if he saw anything. I knew his Masai eyes and sixth sense could pierce the inky night. Ten minutes later he shook his head and whispered that the lion had passed to the right of us. Nothing else was heard.

After five hours I was cold, wet, and cramped all over. With the greatest difficulty Godfrey got me and the equipment down to the ground. He led the way, carrying an oil lantern. I had the Mannlicher in my right hand as we strode across the dry river bed. All of a sudden, quite close on the right, there was a thundering snort, followed by heavy footfalls. Throwing the flash beam in that direction, I was horrified to see the hindquarters of a huge bull elephant not a hundred feet away. He was taking a bath.

The light annoyed him and he turned on a dime and bellowed out something I did not catch, but I knew what he meant: "Scram, I'm in the tub."

Godfrey grabbed my arm. "This is very dangerous. We must run for our lives."

"Put down the lantern and we'll make a dash for it."

"But what will Mr. Hunter say if we lose the lantern?"

"Never mind now!"

Godfrey and I ran far to the left, making a big semicircle. Godfrey took the natural precaution of keeping on the side of me opposite the bull elephant, who was making terrible noises as he rushed toward us. We reached the bank and took shelter in some trees until all was quiet. Then we crept back into camp. In the morning we all went out to look at the elephant spoor. Even Jock Hunter said, "That was a fine male, probably a rogue elephant."

Next day we left Jock with deep regret and drove back to Kajiado, where I measured a good series of Masai. For me the expedition was over. Another day, and I was back in Cairo.

Ali Bey el Hamamsi, King's Chamberlain, drove me to the airport the following evening and we were airborne over North Africa, the Mediterranean, France, the Channel, London airport, then Leicester platform, where Mother was waiting, and finally, on the *Queen Mary*, to New York.

Two years later my "Contributions to the Anthropology of the Faiyûm, Sinai, Northern Sudan and Kenya" was published by the University of California.

In April 1950 I was appointed Research Fellow in Physical Anthropology at the Peabody Museum, Harvard.

My last expedition, as leader of the Peabody Museum Expedition in the spring and summer of 1950, was for the purpose of complementing previous studies made on earlier expeditions to Iraq and Iran and to hunt the desert areas once again, to follow the wanderings of Stone Age man, and to seek again for traces of the Beni Hilal, "Sons of the Moon," ancestors of the Bedouin.

It was important to find out the sequence of Stone Age cultures in Iran, the racial type or types of these Palaeolithic hunters and their distribution so that the lacunae could be filled.

After fifteen years' absence from Southwestern Asia I was naturally most anxious to return, especially to fill in some of the gaps which I knew existed.

For example, I had not searched for surface stone implements in northeastern Syria, in Luristan, or in northern Saudi Arabia—all regions where I was confident they lay ready to be picked up. Caves and rock shelters in Iraqi Kurdistan and Luristan should be searched and soundings made.

From the point of view of physical anthropology certain groups required a series of measurements, observations, and photographs; these were the Assyrians (males and females) and Shebeks in Iraq, the Bakhtiaris, Lurs, and Kurds in Iran, samples from the Persian Gulf area, and the Bedouins of Saudi Arabia. My objective was to record anthropometric data on at least a thousand individuals. More data on tribal folklore and customs should also be compiled.

It was planned to obtain zoological and botanical specimens as well as sand samples, especially from areas where I had not collected previously. In this part of the work I was to have the expert and tireless assistance of Yusuf Lazar—the same Yusuf who had been with me as animal and plant collector in Iraq and Iran during 1934.

The photographic work was to be in charge of Robb White. An expert shot, he was to collect specimens for the Museum of Comparative Zoology at Harvard. Furthermore, he bought a new red jeep to accompany my 1950 Plymouth, for in the desert it is unwise to drive around without two vehicles.

In Washington we had the fun and excitement of making lists, checking prices, and obtaining small discounts on the Expedition equipment. Finding an eight-gallon, heavy-duty milk can proved difficult. Telephone calls were made to Sears Roebuck in Washington, Baltimore, and Philadelpha At the latter depot a husky-voiced girl asked with entrancing appeal:

"Wouldn't you like a cream separator or some other milking equipment?"

"No, thanks. I'm going to put snakes in the milk can."

A gasp came from Philadelphia.

Friends waved to us on Dumbarton Avenue as we drove away. Next morning the cars were loaded aboard the American Export Liner *Exeter* due in Beirut three weeks later, while Robb and I flew from La Guardia direct to Shannon in a superb Pan American Stratocruiser in thirteen hours. Conversation with our across-the-street neighbor, Joe Alsop, high above the clouds shortened the trip appreciably.

We arrived in Beirut, to find the smiling Yusuf and the two cars and equipment awaiting us.

We were quite a cavalcade as we drove from Damascus toward Palmyra. With us, in his jeep station wagon, was Mr. James H. Keeley, U. S. Minister to Syria, who accompanied us part of the way. As we passed the last cultivated patch my heart began to sing, for once again, after so many years, I was out in the North Arabian Desert.

On our way through village after village, the very blond element in this population caught my eye. Many flaxen-haired, blue-eyed boys and girls watched us as we drove past, raising the customary triple clouds of dust. In some villages were redheads, among them a girl who looked like Linda Darnell in *Forever Amber*.

To the right, flints glistened in the sun. Within a minute I had found a flint flaked by human hand, then half a dozen more. This was a new locality for my map of Stone Age sites of Southwestern Asia—the map begun with Buxton in December 1925. It was thrilling to be doing this type of research once again after the thousands of hours of writing, statistical work, checking references, compiling bibliographies, editing, proofreading, and making indexes.

Palmyra was familiar, and Deir-ez-Zor with its roofed bazaar, and the Euphrates wide and turbulent as before—nothing had changed for me, nor had much of this country changed since Abraham's time.

It was good to visit in black tents again, to watch the long-handled coffee roaster being shaken over a blazing camel's-thorn fire, to hear the rhythmic pounding of the coffee beans in the

406

brass *delal* and drink the thick coffee from handleless cups. And to hear, on leaving the tents, the familiar murmurs in Arabic: "Go with God."

As we drove toward Baghdad I was pleased with the archaeological finds so far and with the results to date of the anthropometric survey, particularly the large group of Assyrians measured in the RAF base at Habbaniya.

I recalled my first glimpse of Baghdad in a December dawn, with Ernie Worrell at the wheel of the old Nairn Cadillac and Langdon and Buxton bumping in the back seat over the rough desert. Here we were, sailing along on a paved highway over the bridge at Al Falluja, past Aqar Quf, into Baghdad.

I remembered the questions I had asked and Buxton saying: "Why don't you spend the next twenty-five years trying to answer your own questions?"

Exactly twenty-five years before! Buxton, Langdon, and Watelin—all were dead. I was hunting the final words of the long answer.

Turning up Rashid Street, all seemed unfamiliar, for now it was clean, paved, and no *arabanas* clanged their strident bells unceasingly. Baghdad had changed. I missed the old bridge of boats across the Tigris: a romantic entrance to the city of Harun al Rashid. However, there was less noise and the smells were not so bad. For that, anyone would be grateful.

As the French say, I "descended" at the Zia Hotel, run delightfully by Michael Zia and called for an ice-cold lemonade served by a famed barman, Jesus by name.

A short trip to central Iraq had been planned; this we decided to make before starting for Teheran. The purposes of this trip were to show Babylon to Robb, visit Kish, search for a ruined city between Kish and the Euphrates, and visit the Nippur excavations.

Early one morning three of us started south in the two cars. Beside me sat Dr. Faraj Basmachi, representative of the Department of Antiquities, with a large-scale map of the area east of Kish. We paused briefly at Babylon, where an old friend, *Hajji* Umran, who had been one of our best foremen at the Kish excavations, guided us around the now desolate mounds.

As we passed the standing mud-brick walls, still ornamented with the animals in glazed tiles, I told Robb how Koldewey had worked here season after season to remove the treasures to Berlin, how in the Pergamon Museum the great Ishtar Gate had been reconstructed life-size, with many original titles in place, only to be shattered by bombs in World War II. Now the rumor was that the Russians had removed what could be salvaged to the Hermitage in Leningrad. Such has been the fate so far of these glazed tiles admired by the eyes of Nebuchadnezzar about 550 B.C.

We visited the little museum to see the reconstructions of Babylon in all its glory, for now the most vivid imagination is required to visualize the Hanging Gardens.

Arriving at Hilla was again like old times. My barber friend was fatter than before. His stories, definitely not for young ladies, still kept his audience in hysterical laughter.

We followed the small canals eastward until the red peak of Tell el Uhaimir loomed in the distance; it was good to see Kish again. A flat concrete bridge carried us across the widest canal toward the ziggurat of Harsagkalemma. We walked past the great temple of Nabonidus, whose thick outer walls were still standing, to "Y" trench, now but an abomination and desolation. The carefully exposed walls had fallen in, and in less than twenty years trenches had refilled and mounds were growing where we had worked.

It was with regret that I left again, for despite all our efforts we had never located the royal tombs, which I am still convinced lie beneath the temple of Nabonidus. . . .

At *Hajji* Miniehil's village nearby, where most of our best workmen had been recruited, I was instantly surrounded by old friends. The *hajji* was dead but his handsome son, Sheik Ralli, greeted me most warmly. We spent a very pleasant hour chatting about old times, old friends. Time and again they begged me to restart excavations at Kish. I could only tell them that I saw no hope of this, but how I wished they could all come to Hall K in Field Museum to see how Dick Martin and I had installed the objects they and their friends had so patiently dug up at Kish from 1922 to 1933. They all remembered the chariot wheels, the many stone bowls, the golden earrings.

408

Among the gladdest to see me again was old Mahdi, our faithful but none too brave guard at the Kish camp. As usual he begged me for a present, trying to kiss my hand as he uttered Moslem blessings on my head. I thought of a way to give him money. I asked Sheik Ralli to have the children collect lizards for the next two days; Mahdi could bring them in a bag on horseback to Hilla Resthouse, where I could pay him and the children. To give money without service rendered, except to the blind or crippled beggars, encourages the begging of baksheesh. Mahdi immediately recruited a hundred children with fine results, and I left the village delighted to have paid this brief call among old friends.

From Baghdad Robb, Yusuf, and I drove the two cars across the mountains to Teheran, where we were the guests of Max and Leila Thornburg. At last a burning desire was to be granted: I was to measure the Bakhtiaris, those wonderful migratory people of Iran. Our Ambassador, John C. Wiley, arranged a special permit signed by Chief of Staff General Ali Razmara. We were informed at army headquarters that the Persian army would transport us and our equipment away from the railway. This would save much time, effort, and expense, for which we were most grateful.

We were granted permission to collect surface archaeological material and to make soundings in caves or rock shelters in Khuzistan and Luristan. It was clearly understood that we were to record anthropometric data, take photographs, and collect zoological and botanical specimens—as I had done in northern and central Iran during 1934. Mr. Samadi of the Department of Iraq Antiquities went with us.

Colonel Rukni, officer commanding Dizful Camp, had us taken in an army truck through Dizful to Shalgahi, where lived Morteza Khuli Khan Samsam, eighty-year-old Paramount Chief of the Bakhtiaris, in a two-story brick house on the edge of a wadi overlooking a large garden. Our three white guest tents were pitched on the edge of the wadi.

Morteza Khuli Khan was a delightful and charming host. Dinner was served under an open archway on the second floor through which a cool breeze played. A little boy waved a straw *punkah* (fan). There were at least a hundred small dishes placed

409

in a rectangle on the heavily carpeted floor. Two roasted chickens with knives and forks were placed before Robb and me.

As among the Bedouins, it is good manners to enjoy eating noisily. Mealtime has no place for conversation save for the subject literally in hand, usually rice with gravy, meat, vegetables, etc. There was far too much food, but I doubt if any was wasted, for hours later the servants were still munching in the kitchen.

Here were strange contrasts: our host, the Paramount Chief of the Bakhtiaris, one of the richest men in Persia and the final word in tribal law and dispute, eating off the floor, possessing a private electric light plant, riding in a jeep. His sons were European-educated, and two of them flew their own Cesna planes from Teheran to Shalgahi.

Morteza Khuli Khan said we had come a little late, for the main migration into the cool mountains above the Dizful Plain had begun some days before and now there remained but a few black tents this side of the Karun River.

Next morning we drove to the west bank of the Karun, that river made famous in picture and print by the annual crossing of the Bakhtiari tribe with their animals and all their possessions. The movie *Grass*, made some twenty-five years ago on a shoestring by Merion C. Cooper of Cinerama fame and Ernest Schoedensack, still remains one of the most famous documentaries. Their book of the same title describes this hazardous and most strenuous of regular migrations.

Only a few Bakhtiari tents studded the grassy plain but for me it was a great thrill to be at long last among this tribe, which was very similar to the Bedouins of North Arabia. There were the same black tents, barking mongrel dogs, shy women and girls, and glasses of sweet tea beside the hearth. Apart from their clothes and their faces, there was a real resemblance in their way of life. After some hesitation on the part of the Bakhtiaris and considerable encouragement from their chief, I measured and described No. 1 of the Bakhtiari series. Kuresh Shahbaz acted as interpreter and recorder, Robb photographed each man from the front and in profile, and Yusuf collected animals and plants with the assistance of the "Field Irregulars," as Robb called the children.

Morteza Khuli Khan suggested that we should go to Mahor

Birinji, since there were at least a hundred tents still there. We set off in the two cars with Ali Khuli Khan, chief of the Chehar Lang. As we rounded a curve in Mahor Birinji, a broad valley, I saw to my great satisfaction many black tents.

The arrival of the chief caused wild excitement. The men began to dance and sing before him. Many kissed his hand. Like magic a black tent was raised atop a slope in the middle of the plain. This was to be our guesthouse. Pillows and a gaudy quilt were spread over rugs for the chief. We sat in a circle of fine Bakhtiari faces and had tea.

Finally the chief stated the anthropometric purpose of our visit. There was no enthusiasm among the assembled tribal elders. However, if the chief decrees, they must obey. After luncheon, in the heat of the afternoon we all went to work.

Before the chief lay down for his siesta I asked permission to encourage the Bakhtiari children to catch animals, with promises of small coins of which I had a thousand in a cloth bag. Permission was granted at once, but, we were told, there were no scorpions in this pleasant valley. Fifty small fry rushed off to turn over stones and chase lizards, followed by Yusuf, armed with collecting equipment and a small bag of coins. At the end of three days they had a large collection, including 953 scorpions, many of them pregnant.

As before, I measured and described each man. Shahbaz was recorder and Robb photographer. This time all went smoothly and the series began to acquire statistical significance.

After supper a delegation of musicians and male dancers came to serenade their chief. One dance consisted of a mimic battle between two men armed with wooden swords, another of capering madly around, waving a handkerchief overhead. Several invited me to dance with them and, waving a blue handkerchief, I joined in, much to the entertainment of the dancers and onlookers. The chief shook me by the hand while I was still dizzy.

All through the night the lu-lu-lu of the women and the haunting notes of the flageolet and drum rarely stopped. This was a great occasion, a wedding. The twelve-year-old bride was to be married next day to a twenty-two-year-old boy. According to Bakhtiari custom, the bride is never allowed a wink of sleep for twenty-four hours before the marriage ceremony. This was also hard on us, but we were most grateful for this wedding because it had delayed their migration to the mountains and many visitors came to pay their respects from far and near. By early afternoon of the next day I had studied ninety-three Bahktiaris. Although there were plenty of subjects around, none would volunteer. The chief, who had begun his opium smoking on an empty stomach at 6 A.M., now was sleeping soundly after his second pipe and we could not wake him. By the time the drug wore off, the wedding was on. The bride was escorted by the women of her subsection of the tribe, the bridegroom by his family and friends. They sang and danced to the queer music. As foreigners we were now *de trop* without any question. We packed up and prepared to return to Shalgahi; like Arabs, we silently stole away.

Our way led next to Khurrumabad in the center of Luristan. It was a rough ride even though I sat beside the Bakhtiari driver. For Samadi, Shahbaz, and Yusuf in the back of this covered wagon, it was far worse.

Luristan is one of the most scenic areas I have ever visited: high, rugged mountains, some snow-covered, luscious green valleys, and many rushing torrents. My eyes never tired of the changing panorama.

In one section the charcoal burners lived in houses resembling Neolithic *fonds-de-cabane*. We stopped from time to time to take photographs, examine the 'scree slopes of rock shelters near the road, or to collect plants.

We pulled into Khurramabad long after nightfall. General Azizi was awaiting us. We were shown to our quarters in the barracks, where an iron cot had been set up in my honor. At three-thirty in the morning I was awakened out of deep sleep by a full military band playing the first bars of "Over There." This continued for half an hour with the familiar strains echoing through the rocky cliffs.

My first thought was that this was the height of flattery to the visiting Yank until, after five or six repeats, I realized that it was band practice, but why in the inky blackness of the night no one could explain next day. Perhaps it was a subtle compliment after all.

412

During the next few days we found and investigated several rock shelters, always hoping to find *Homo Iranicus*, a true missing link in our knowledge of ancient man in Southwestern Asia.

Still no bones, but every flake and sherd was helping to piece out the story of ancient man in Southwestern Asia and his probable lines of migration across Persia (Iran).

We went in the general's command car to Dorud, measuring Lurs along the way. We stopped at a Dalwand graveyard to look at the Persian inscriptions on the small headstones. On each grave was carved either a fine-pronged comb for a man or a double-toothed comb for a woman.

The mountain scenery at sunset was superb. As we came into Dorud, snowcapped peaks lay to the south and east. Bright and early Captain Ispahanzizi collected recruits for study. Inside our little courtyard crowded Lurs and Bakhtiaris. We worked hard and steadily all day long, while Yusuf and fifty local "Field Irregulars" collected a fine series of animals.

By sundown we had the following totals for Khuzistan and Luristan: 171 Bakhtiaris (170 men and 1 woman); and 70 Lurs—a very satisfactory record.

That night on a train pulling toward Teheran, Samadi, Shahbaz, Yusuf, and I slept fitfully, with the floor piled high and fifteen pieces of luggage in the baggage car. We reinvaded our charming hosts, the Thornburgs, next morning.

Before leaving Iran, calls on the American Embassy and the Iranian authorities were in order. In the afternoon I called on Mr. Ebtehaj, director of the Bank Melli, whom we had met at Mrs. Gifford Pinchot's in Washington a few months before.

In his glamorous office he listened to a review of our work and expressed disappointment that we were scheduled to leave in thirty-six hours. Grabbing the telephone, he said, "I would like to have His Majesty hear your account. I must also try to get you an appointment with General Razmara. And the crown jewels. You really should see them."

Lights flashed on a small panel. Within five minutes Mr. Ebtehaj had arranged an audience for me with the Shah, an appointment with General Razmara, and a visit to the bank vault.

Mr. Ebtehaj conducted Robb and me down to the vault. There

we saw the brilliant crown jewels, now the property of the Bank Melli. Before our eyes lay piles of diamonds and emeralds, sapphires and rubies, golden boxes encrusted with gems, coronation crowns, swords in lavishly ornamented scabbards. For the first time the words "a king's ransom" had some meaning to me. Outside, the world looked drab indeed.

Late that afternoon I was ushered past a group of high-ranking Persian officers into a map-lined room. General Razmara, fifty-year-old St. Cyr graduate and then Chief of Staff, welcomed me with a firm handshake. The general, a very strong character, had an immense knowledge of his country. We talked for forty minutes about the tribes of Persia, a subject very close to his thoughts because he had published twenty-one volumes, one for each district of the country. In each volume there is a chapter on the land and the people. He gave me the five volumes which were of special interest, inscribing the Luristan book with his signature, and requested a copy of my report on the Bakhtiari and my two-volume *Contributions to the Anthropology of Iran.*

It pelted with rain next morning as I drove up in a battered taxi to the gates leading to the Marble Palace. The walls of the palace gleamed under coursing water. After a very careful examination of my passport, an armed sentry escorted me through the downpour into the palace. On the way upstairs were several flat-topped glass cases, one containing the golden foundation tablets from Persepolis.

The Shah, dressed in a brown suit, welcomed me to a red damask divan. He asked me to tell him what we had found. Opening a map with penciled lines and arrows, I first mentioned gratefully the assistance rendered by the Department of Antiquities, General Razmara and the army at Dizful and Khurramabad, and the Trans-Iranian State Railway; then I gave him this summing up:

In 1925, from western Transjordan to the Indus Valley, no evidence for Stone Age man and his cultures had been found. Very few anthropometric data were available. Now, a quarter of a century later, a chain of surface sites and some caves and rock shelters proved the existence of man in Palaeolithic phases of culture. Turning specifically to Iran, I outlined my theory that

414

ancient migrations to or from Central Asia naturally followed the shortest distance through Mazanderan between the high Elburz Mountains and the Caspian. However, this became undesirable because of the high infant mortality from malaria and other insect-borne diseases. As a result, the women refused to pass that way.

At this point that Shah interrupted to ask, "Do you think women have always been that powerful?"

"Yes, sir."

Continuing to point to the map, I indicated lines with arrows from the Meshed area east of the deserts of Dasht-i-Kavir and Dasht-i-Lut south toward Zahidan (Duzdab), then west and northwest through the valleys of Khuzistan, Luristan, and Kurdistan and west across the mountain passes of Sulaimaniya, Rowandiz, Aqra, and Zakho onto the Mesopotamian plain.

So much for the probable lines of migration. Stone implements had been found in 1934 by W. E. Browne, Anglo-Iranian geologist, and in the same year by Don McCown and myself in the Lake Niriz area of the Iranian Plateau. In 1949 Carl Coon had excavated three rock shelters, one at Behistun (Bisitun), one at the southeast corner of the Caspian, and the third between Meshed and Zahidan. Stone Age skeletons and cultures had been found.

Four days before, at Konji Cave near Khurramabad, Mr. Samadi and I had excavated flint implements, the first *in situ* from Luristan. I described the two other sites in this region.

The Shah asked, "Why don't you go back now and excavate Konji? We will give you every assistance."

"Unfortunately, sir, I cannot because I have arranged to work in a cave in Iraqi Kurdistan five days from now. We have a deadline. You see, my brother-in-law's wife is expecting a baby and Robb has to fly home to Thomasville. The power of women, sir."

The Shah smiled. He listened attentively to the story of our recent work on the Bakhtiaris and Lurs and invited me to return to continue these archaeological and anthropological researches in his country.

We drove from Teheran back to Baghdad.

Dr. Naji al Asil, director of antiquities, sent *Sayyid* Fuad Safar on our next adventure for this was now a joint expedition to explore caves in Kurdistan. To me, this part of the trip was the fulfillment of a fifteen-year-old dream, for in 1934 we had visited a cave high on Jebel Baradost and since then I had longed to explore this cave. I was certain we would find stone implements in the lower levels, and perhaps the greatest prize of all—a Stone Age skeleton.

The truck left first, piled high with our tents, cooking equipment, food, bedding, picks, and shovels. Coleman lanterns and gasoline, kerosene and cooking-oil drums, and other camping impedimenta were roped into the truck. The Plymouth was full to its top, the jeep overloaded. At Kirkuk Dennis Batten, amateur speleologist and professional road builder for the Iraq Petroleum Company, was granted leave of absence to accompany us for three weeks. The IPC pickup was burdened with caving equipment.

Shortly after noon we drove into Erbil, ancient Arbela near the site of Gaugamela where Darius was defeated in 331 B.C. This enormous mound deserves excavation.

Just off the main square stood the truck with the beaming driver and the dandified so-called cook who was to prove the only really helpless member of the Expedition. From across the street came Philippus Dinkha, whom I had known in Kurdistan in 1934. He has an excellent command of English and an intimate knowledge of Jebel Baradost, for it was he who had guided me before.

From a nearby coffee shop came five Shergatis. These are trained excavators, a technique passed on from father to son in this village. Andrae had trained a group of Shergatis at Ashur. Other expeditions learned of their skill and gradually Shergat became a famous village in Iraq. Thus, in 1950 at Nimrud, Nippur, and Khafaje, the only archaeological expeditions at work, the foreman and pickmen were mainly Shergatis. A few have learned to sort and repair pottery.

Since these five men had worked at Qalat Jarmo near Chemchemal with Bob Braidwood of the Oriental Institute, they were familiar with the excavation of flint implements. Eisa, their foreman, had an excellent knowledge of excavation techniques and some ability to sort pottery according to period.

416

Robb and I called on the *muttasarrif* of Erbil, who telephoned the *Qaimmaqam* at Ruwandiz of our impending arrival and requested him to give us a police escort.

The *muttasarrif* told of a human skeleton thirty feet long, with a head as big as a sack of wheat, which had lain years before in a stone coffin on a mountainside in Kurdistan. The locality—as with all such wonders—was vague.

Our cavalcade was increasing. Now we were five cars, for Philip and the five Shergatis followed in his bulging taxi.

Just before sunset the convoy entered that famous beauty spot of Iraq, the Ruwandiz Gorge. The towering cliffs, abundant vegetation, and river fed by waterfalls is breath-taking, especially after the miles and miles of sand and gravel. Just before dark we halted on a slope beside Havdian, the village from which the ascent to Jebel Baradost is made.

That night under the stars I could not sleep well. For fifteen years I had dreamed of digging in the cave 3,500 feet above us, on the high slopes of Jebel Baradost.

Before dawn the camp was astir. Assyrians and Kurds crowded around the loaded pack horses. I arranged for horses for Robb, Dennis, Fuad, and myself. For five hours, thirty-three men and twelve horses wound up the steep and rocky path. In many places we had to dismount because of the danger. In fact one baggage pony tumbled ahead of us. Fortunately it fell unhurt about ten feet onto a grassy ledge.

Ages later, for the steep paths were apparently never-ending, we reached the cave, a narrow slit in the mountain with a pile of snow beside the entrance.

The cave was not large. Water covered the lowest chamber floor. Though there was no sign of the 72-foot hole Philip and I remembered, Philip was certain that this was the right cave, the one to which he had led me in 1934.

Camp was pitched, the beds set up, and brushwood piled outside the entrance. The cooking fire was lit inside. An icy-cold wind whistled down off the snowy slopes. Three Assyrian sentries were posted, one in the valley below and two on the rocks above. We were taking no chances of attack, for with our sixteen rifles, a shotgun, ammunition, Zeiss glasses, camera and film, camping equipment, food and supplies, we were the greatest prize in that part of Kurdistan.

By nine o'clock we were in bed, 3,500 feet up on Jebel Baradost. I could not sleep for anxiety; Dennis and Robb had reported that the cave was small, not more than five minutes to the innermost wall.

Questions raced through my head. Were we at the right cave? Philip had assured me again at supper near the blazing fire that this was the cave to which he had led us in 1934. The Assyrians and Kurds of Havdian agreed that this was the best-known cave on the Baradost.

I was still wakeful when at dawn Philip brought us mugs of hot tea.

With strings and metal pegs I marked out the trench. At seven the five Shergatis and twelve Kurds began work with Eisa as *rais*.

Dennis, Robb, Fuad, Philip, and I explored the cave. A narrow tunnel, a small pitch, a stalagmite floor, and we were in the lowest part. On the left was a small hole with a twenty-foot drop to water. Someone had written "NBG" beside this, indicating that he had descended but found nothing. The lower part was covered with two feet of water right up to the wall. That was all.

Where was the seventy-two-foot hole in the middle of the floor, the hole remembered by Philip, Yusuf, Showket, and myself? Where was the long tunnel we had seen which led far into the earth at least thirty minutes from the entrance?

Down, down went the workmen, removing large limestone blocks fallen from the roof millennia ago. Dozens of cubic feet were flaked away by Shergati scalpels and sifted through their fingers. A few sherds and animal bones were found.

Five days after the first pick had resounded in the cave, bedrock was reached in a hole ten feet square at a depth of fourteen feet six inches. There was no trace anywhere of Palaeolithic occupancy. This was indeed a bitter disappointment—one of the greatest in my life.

Had a rockfall blocked the inner passage since we were last there? I do not know. It still puzzles me. We are certain this was the cave and can only surmise, although no evidence was found, that such a fall had taken place, sealing the wall.

However, the pottery was of great interest to Fuad Safar, and the identification of the fauna living in this region from five to seven thousand years ago will prove a valuable contribution.

Dennis and Robb had searched every spot up and down the valley. They reported that Pastun was large and airy, with a thick deposit inside the spacious entrance. We moved our camp thirty minutes away to a ledge outside Pastun.

This cave had a high, cathedral-like vault with a hole through which a beam of sunlight poured to give light and warmth to the excavators. I marked out a thirty-foot square with string and pegs. Four men also began a sounding at the entrance to a small recess, a likely place for ancient man to have buried his dead.

Dennis and Robb explored every foot of the cave, which went back about a thousand feet. Several galleries proved to be dead ends. The stalactites with enormous stalagmitic bases stood like sentinels arrayed.

Fuad and I supervised the two trenches hour after hour, day after day. In the two soundings pottery, a few flints, and many animal bones were found, as well as three canines of cave bear and a long necklace of red beads.

On the fifth afternoon bedrock was attained at fourteen feet in both trial trenches. Again we had failed to find the Beni Hilal or his Stone Age cultures. But Fuad was delighted with the early types of pottery, which indicated a long period of historical occupation. His analyses were published in *Sumer* (vol. 6, pp. 118–123), 1950.

Camp was struck at dawn and the great cavalcade started down to Havdian, which we reached at noon. While I purchased and catalogued medicinal herbs and their uses in the village, Dennis paid off the workmen with almost no squabbling.

We drove to Nimrud to visit my New College friend, Max Mallowan and his wife, known to detective-story fans as Agatha Christie. As luck would have it, this was the day set aside each year for the local officials from Mosul to visit the excavations, so we were really no nuisance.

Max guided about fifty people on an hour's tour. He led us to the rampart overlooking a broad grass-covered plain, the site of a very famous zoo where several thousand years ago tigers, elephants, and other animals fascinated the crowds.

In another area being excavated were large stone bulls, a room covered with cuneiform inscriptions, and work in progress again, under the eagle eyes of Shergatis.

In one passageway a saluki had been uncovered the previous day. He lay on his side as though dreaming of luscious gazelles. Was this a burial custom similar to that employed in the Babylonian levels of Mound "W" at Kish, where dogs were buried beside walls, presumably to bring good fortune?

Below the floor of another room the skeletons of two little boys lay side by side, their knees bent. I thought of the two little princes in the Tower of London; had this been murder millennia before Christ? This train of thought was probably stimulated by being with Agatha Christie. If only Hercule Poirot could have come around the corner twirling his long mustache. Undoubtedly he would have seen far more than I. . . . After a delicious buffet lunch I was led by Agatha into the laboratory to be presented with the skull of an equid glistening with preservative. Agatha swears that my last words to her after she and Max had lunched with Mother and me at Claridge's the year before were: "Please box me up a horse's skull if you can find one." Here was the result and a beauty—possibly the Man o' War of his day.

My work in Syria, Iraq, and Iran was finished. It was now time to go to the Persian Gulf area to make an archaeological and anthropological reconnaissance, and to await there the decision from Riyadh regarding my request through the Department of State for permission to follow the Arabian-American Oil Company's Trans-Arabian Pipe Line (Tapline) across Saudi Arabia.

The seven wooden cases of antiquities were inspected by the Department of Antiquities and the customs, banded with steel tape, and loaded into the groaning Plymouth. The documents were given to Yusuf, who was to drive the car to the U. S. Legation in Beirut, to await my arrival there on June 17.

On May 24 I took off in an Iraqi Airways plane for Basra. The British pilot swooped low over Baghdad so that we could see the vast extent of the area flooded by rains. Many villages were just out of the high water. In the distance we could see Al Qurna, where the Twin Rivers meet to flow into the Persian Gulf, the traditional site of the Garden of Eden.

Basra was hot, Kuwait hotter. Qatar and the Trucial Oman Coast were hotter still.

I was delightfully entertained in these places by members of the oil companies. I still hoped that Ibn Saud would issue the permit for me to enter Saudi Arabia and to follow the Tapline from Dhahran to Tell el Hibr. Request for special permission—for up until then no anthropologist had been allowed to work in Saudi Arabia—had long been in the works through my friends, George McGhee, Assistant Secretary of State, Rives Childs, ambassador in Jidda, Ned Crocker, ambassador in Baghdad, and Sheik Hafiz Wahba, Saudi Arabian ambassador in London. Six weeks before, through the Department of State, I had requested a visa to make this journey in order to measure Bedouins and collect surface stone implements and pottery and a few zoological and botanical specimens.

Up to this moment no reply had been received.

At Dubai on the old Pirate Coast, now the Trucial Oman Coast, I spent a delightful long week end. In the *suq* (market) I bought fifty locally used drugs, recording their medicinal properties and native names.

Edward Henderson and I bathed in the shallow, 88-degree water of a lagoon near Dubai, and a rich pearl merchant took me out by boat to watch the pearl fishing. No pearls could be bought: I was told the entire catch is kept for an American trader who comes each year.

Still no word had come through and the time was drawing short, for I had to catch the *Exeter* on June 20 from Beirut to Naples.

All hope seemed gone when at Dubai a cable was handed me, relayed from Riyadh–Jidda–Baghdad–Bahrain, saying that permission was granted for me to land at Al Khobar and proceed along the Tapline to Turaif from June 6 to 17. At last I was going to Saudi Arabia, and as the guest of Aramco!

A shining Aramco launch took me in two hours from Bahrain to my long-promised land. As we glided through the deep blue

water I kept assuring myself that typologically Palaeolithic implements were lying on the surface of the desert just waiting for me
to pick them up. Thus would be established important fragments
in the great mosaic of Stone Age sites in Southwestern Asia from
Suez to the Caucasus. I might even be able to visit the great Wadi
Sirhan, long an object of my dreams. Animals and plants must be
collected to add to our large series from the "Fertile Crescent" to
the north—an area extending now from the Faiyûm to Persepolis.

Finally we warped alongside the jetty at Al Khobar. I still had
no entry permit and no visa. I was terrified that I might be turned
back because cabled permission might be hard to prove.

Despite the internal panic, I stepped ashore happier than I have
ever been to step on any foreign soil. My pile of collecting equipment was laid in a long line on the dock. No one said anything
to me. I waited patiently for a time. Porters moved my baggage
down to the line of trucks and cars. Then Joe Volkmann of Tapline greeted me from an Aramco truck. Willing hands grabbed
my gear, which was examined by genial customs officials.

My passport was stamped. Then I was driving in Saudi Arabia
at long, long last. The sand was blowing across the paved road.
We passed a large mosque, built by Aramco workers, before
reaching rows of neat bungalows, where we pulled up in front of
a guesthouse, clean as a pin and air-conditioned—such luxury after
the hot and dusty outside! An iced Coke and a hot bath made it
seem more like a mirage.

After a delicious dinner in the guesthouse I walked down to
the movies, past a floodlit baseball diamond with the bleachers
half full. As I came out of the movie I heard my favorite tune,
"Stardust," rising from a nearby dance floor where couples were
gliding in the moonlight. Hoagy Carmichael would have been
proud to see these Americans in a modern desert-built city dancing to his rhythm near the red glow of the oil plant.

I talked with "Cottie" Seager and other geologists about flint
implements and was shown some interesting samples from central
Arabia, proving the existence of Stone Age man in widely diver-
gent areas. Even here in Saudi Arabia the pieces of the mosaic
begin to form a pattern.

Next morning Bill Beling drove me to Ain as Saih. The wind

was blowing hard, bringing sand with it. We stopped to look at some rock-cut tombs and a field of small tumuli, similar to those on Bahrain.

By this time we were in a raging ground sandstorm, although the sun was still shining. Stopping beside low mounds covered with thousands of potsherds and heaps of shells, for the next hour we collected a representative series of decorated and glazed sherds for the Peabody Museum. The driver was not a little amazed to see us running around in this howling sand, which filled eyes, ears, nose, and mouth, picking up "trash"! With the wind at 40 miles an hour and the shade temperature 110 degrees, conditions were not ideal for scientific research! The shell heaps were covered with oysters, the refuse of ancient pearl fishers or oyster frys.

As I stood there in this sand-swept region I remembered that into the Persian Gulf, long renowned for pearl fisheries, had come the ancient dwellers of Mesopotamia and Iran, later the Phoenicians and Arabs. Even Chinese junks sailed these waters.

Next morning as I stood on the concrete runway at Dhahran, waiting to climb aboard the company shuttle plane, passengers were filing into the *Flying Camel*, the huge Aramco ship bound for New York. We were off first, carrying pipe-liners, boxes of equipment, and mail, and flew north to Ras Mishaab, then west across a flat, unbroken wilderness to Al Qaisumah.

Mr. and Mrs. John C. Kelley were my hosts. I was delighted to find that they were entomologists with large collections from South America in their Texas home.

Mr. Kelley drove me to Hafar al Batin, which lies on one of the main lines of migration between Baghdad and Riyadh, capital of Saudi Arabia.

Approaching Hafar al Batin, we saw that the plain was strewn with 400 black Bedouin tents. Beyond lay the fort with its crenelated battlements and towers. Hundreds of camels, sheep, and goats were being watered from the many 100-foot wells. Our arrival in a cloud of flying dust disconcerted quite a few of the camels, their snorts expressing obvious distaste.

We stopped to drink a cup of bitter black coffee brewed for us by Sheik Ibn Museis of the Muteir tribe. Here we were again in the days of Abraham, so little has Bedouin life altered.

Sipping coffee and looking around the little circle squatting on the rug-covered ground, I observed that these Bedouins belong to basic Mediterranean stock. They have changed little in type, guarding their racial purity with the strictest of sanctions. The Bedouin women do not veil; their faces are ornamented with simple tattooed designs. The teeth of these Bedouins are remarkably good; they eat very little sugar and no canned food.

In the morning during the drive to Rafha along the 30-inch steel snake known as the Tapline, I had stopped occasionally to search for flint implements but to no avail. However, on a low hill near Rafha, where ancient men could camp secure from surprise attack, I found a few flint flakes obviously chipped by human hands.

This was my first link—the evidence thin but positive—in northern Saudi Arabia with the men of the Old Stone Age, whose handiwork I had been pursuing for a quarter of a century from southwestern Sinai to the Caucasus mountains.

We followed the Tapline to the next pumping station at Badanah.

Since no archaeological ruins have been reported in this area, I decided to collect some animals for the study collections at Harvard.

With an Al Murra tribesman at the wheel we drove to the Bedouin camp a few miles away. We were greeted by the usual array of fierce-looking, barking dogs, then by the sheik, who invited us into his tent.

While the coffee was being roasted, I asked permission for the children to collect animals. A band of thirty children were soon scurrying around hunting for small lizards, beetles, centipedes, and other harmless forms of life. Within a few minutes the animals began to appear as if by magic. The quiet flat plain resounded to the shrill cries of youthful excitement. By exchanging coins for specimens, within an hour we had several hundred lizards, beetles, and locusts.

There were at least nine species of lizard represented in this collection. To my delight Ken Curran, station manager at Badanah, had obtained for me another of the large lizards, the *Thubb*.

424

This live specimen hissed at all who peered into the cage; none ventured a finger past the wire netting. Everywhere we went it claimed attention. Since we could not feed it, it was embalmed in formalin for its transatlantic journey by ship.

These lizards were sent for identification to Chicago Natural History Museum, where Karl P. Schmidt, world authority on the reptiles and amphibians of Southwestern Asia, is identifying these and others collected by the Peabody Museum-Harvard Expedition from Syria, Iraq, Iran, Bahrain, Qatar, and on the Trucial Oman Coast, and preparing a report for publication.

Since Southwestern Asia forms the crossroad of three continents—Asia, Africa, and Europe—the fauna is of exceptional interest.

Continuing northwest, we were met by Don Holm, geologist, who guided me to several small ruins, including a newly discovered Roman fortress, the southeasternmost outpost of the Roman Empire, ten miles to the southwest of Turaif.

No one else has ever built like the Romans. Their superior handiwork remains a marvel of the centuries. We made a ground plan of the gate and courtyard and searched in vain for an inscription. Pottery was collected on the surface of the ground. Stretching for several acres were piles of basalt, meaningless without an aerial photograph.

This newly discovered Roman fortress must have formed a link in the chain of outposts protecting the town from the desert. To the northwest lies Qasr el Azraq; to the north, Qasr el Burqu, long described as "the easternmost outpost of the Roman Empire." Now Qasr ed Dauquera rightfully assumes this distinction.

Perhaps in the long-veiled Wadi Sirhan to the south lies another unknown Roman outpost. Future explorations alone will decide.

We drove across the hot, low-rolling gravel and sand-covered hills to the southwest, searching here and there for prehistoric stone implements, collecting plants, and chasing the elusive lizards.

Probably the quantities of hand-chipped flint we discovered on the slopes of the blacker-than-black Tell el Hibr near the Saudi Arabian border were used as the earliest articles of commerce. This flint, some of it honey-brown in color, is the best quality I have ever seen in this part of the world. Here the prehistoric flint knapper must have truly enjoyed his work.

There was a parallel case of flint figuring in trade in western Europe. Flint from the famous quarry at Le Grand-Pressigny in France has been found hundreds of miles away—presumably used in trade in Neolithic and later times.

Tell el Hibr thus forms an important link in the chain of evidence for the distribution of Palaeolithic man in Southwestern Asia.

Next afternoon a Tapline Navion carried me to Beirut. As we flew northwest we soon crossed the undemarcated boundary between Saudi Arabia and the Hashemite Kingdom of the Jordan. From two thousand feet I waved au revoir to the kingdom of Ibn Saud, grateful indeed to this monarch for allowing me to be the first anthropologist to make a reconnaissance survey in his country, so rich in the cultural history of mankind.

Leaving the high, forbidding mass of Jebel ed Druz on our right, we flew over Deraa in southern Syria, where the Israelites slew Og, King of Bashan. Ahead loomed Mount Hermon, an imposing mass.

The little Navion seemed to strain to fly higher but the altimeter read 8000 feet, 7500 feet, 6000 feet. To my untrained eye, it looked as if we were not going to make it, but we landed at Beirut exactly to the minute on time. The pilot, it developed, had a date at a christening.

The Expedition was finished except for the hard work of packing the specimens and getting them on board the *Exeter*, and then the thirty months of research to be done at home.

Yusuf had delivered the Plymouth, loaded to capacity with the specimens from Iraq and Iran, to Dick Sanger in the U.S. Legation at Beirut.

Three days later I sailed with the Plymouth and eighteen packing cases of specimens bound for Harvard.

The next expedition is always the most exciting. As I write this, my thoughts are on the next. I am not certain as yet where it will take me, but I hope to India. That will complete the studies made across and around the area that is the Nursery of Man.

426

MANY times along the 500,000 miles and twenty-eight years spent on the track of man's story I have asked, as have so many others before me:

"Whither mankind?"

We have studied him underground and in trees. We have seen him try to touch the stars. We have seen him in his sublimity; and lower than any slavering beast ever to walk the earth. We know races and civilizations have vanished and others risen. We see man now on the brink of one more abyss.

> But Thy most dreaded instrument,
> In working out a pure intent,
> Is Man arrayed for mutual slaughter. . . .

We must take the long view.

The past hundred and fifty years have witnessed more technical development than the preceding million years. Speed of communications—of man himself and of his ideas—has passed his ability either to comprehend or to adjust himself to it.

In an airplane he can fly so fast that when he banks he blacks out. Radio reaches him in the stratosphere, anywhere on the earth's surface, and as deep as he can travel beneath the ground or under the sea. Television brings him the inauguration of a President, the coronation of a queen, sporting events, and entertainment, as living pictures. Six generations of such rapid development have naturally never allowed time for sociological adjustments, nationally or internationally. The national maladjustments result in the hundreds of millions of ill-fed, ill-housed and ill-satisfied peoples; the international in wars.

During the past hundred and fifty years the population has more than doubled, the greatest increases in round millions being

427

in Asia (600–1300), Europe (190–400), North, Central, and South America (15–300), Africa (100–185), and the U.S.S.R. (100–200). On January 1, 1953, the world population was estimated at 2,410,-000,000 persons.

This enormous expansion of the peopling of the world is the direct result of improved health conditions, medical attention, and the reduction in infant mortality. The building of large cities with communal heat, light, and power, associated with transported food, makes it possible for these large communities to develop—all the result of the Industrial Revolution and the past hundred and fifty years of technical advances. For example, nearly 20 per cent of our people live in cities of more than 500,000 and less than 25 per cent remain rural.

Since we are only following here the main course of human development, there is no need to examine the birth and death rates of different areas or racial stocks. In general terms, however, France and England and Wales show trends of major decreases while the United States, India, China, and the Soviet Union show major increases.

The pursuit of agriculture varies greatly throughout the world: in the United States, less than 20 per cent of the population work on farms; in France, 35 per cent; in Japan, 48 per cent; and in the U.S.S.R., 60 per cent. In many areas there has been a flight from the land—i.e., urbanization—which decreases the birth rate.

Migration has played a dominant role in the present distribution of population.

Since the earliest tribal times, man has sought greener pastures, which may consist of a better food supply for either himself or his domesticated animals, the prospect of wealth, improved living conditions, freedom for self-expression or freedom from persecution—or just the desire for a change of scenery.

Hundreds of millions of people have moved backward and forward across the continents—always hopeful.

The pioneer spirit has led to the settling of areas never previously believed habitable.

Man is far more adaptable to environment than any other animal. His ideology is far less malleable. The tenacity with which he clings to basic beliefs is often inflexible.

428

The main concentrations of population occur in the river valleys of China and India, western Europe, and the eastern part of the United States.

The least inhabited are the Far North, Far South, jungles of South America, and the great deserts of Africa and Asia.

In the Soviet Union the Far North has been developed beyond all predictions. Hydroelectric developments have opened up vast new areas, especially along the Dnieper and Ufa rivers.

The settlement of the remaining pioneer areas are almost certainly doomed to failure unless there are adequate long-term financial resources, a driving religious urge which surmounts all normal discouragement, or a flight from persecution. The political problems are insolubly intertwined with population problems, though they are all too rarely so regarded, except in the rather obvious case of Israel.

The fact that the area from India to Japan and from the Urals to Java is increasing and will continue to increase in population during the next few decades, while Western Europe will correspondingly decrease, tends to throw some previously held concepts into the ashcan.

Medical research and rapid aerial communication improve health, tend to stem epidemics, and in peacetime can concentrate on the increase of the birth rate and increase of longevity—all of which work in favor of producing more adults, especially in those areas already overburdened.

The deaths resulting from World War I, including the heavy toll taken by influenza during 1918, are estimated at twenty to twenty-five million. A generation later World War II cost about the same number, possibly five million higher because of displaced persons in Europe and China. Thus we see that even with all the modern twentieth-century weapons of warfare only fifty millions have been killed as the result of two world-wide struggles.

To return to the future. According to recent estimates, the population of India is increasing at the rate of five millions per annum. This estimate is over and above all deaths. Hence each decade India will increase by fifty millions, a figure which is more than the total population of each country in western Europe, except Germany, in 1939.

National vitality can most easily be shown by the number of girls aged thirteen to eighteen, the potential mothers. In this category Russia stands far ahead of all other countries both in percentage and in actual numbers.

The present and the immediate future of mankind rest on world co-operation through the United Nations or some similar world council. Population policies and immigration rules must be reviewed and rewritten. Population pressure is a major cause of war. World War III would be truly cataclysmic. . . . What future, then, for Man?

He stands once again at the crossroads: forward to international collaboration, the development of atomic energy to yield leisure and the time to think; or backward to self-destruction and finally a reversion to barbarism. It is true that we are now living in the Phase of Insecurity. Any person, be he deaf, dumb, blind, and insane, can press a button at any point on the earth and kill you long before you can finish this sentence. The prophets of gloom muttered way back in 1944: "Remember, if you hear the rocket bomb, you are alive, because they travel faster than sound."

Unloosing atomic energy naturally creates a political vacuum into which we may all be sucked by a struggle for world conquest.

The same basic human traits exist today beneath the outward veneer. Hunger, thirst, sexual desire, urge for power, all forms of fear, especially the fear of the unknown, and insecurity dominate.

The struggle for existence is the theme for all forms of life—including Man.

Some "realists" suggest that we abandon our cities, which make the finest of targets for atom bombs or atomic missiles, and either become troglodytes or build ribbon towns to avoid becoming atomized.

Other "realists" propose that we revert by choice to tribal living in a Neolithic culture. Our Stone Age ancestors would be mildly amused at such proposals. Surely they faced far greater difficulties of survival than we do now.

Mankind now stands at the threshold of the use of atomic energy for constructive, not destructive, purposes. Herein lies the hope for the future.

Never before have so many persons engaged in war at one time as during 1941–45. No people wants World War III. For the first time, with the atomic cloud hanging over each one of us, the entire world really craves peace and security.

When in 1945, as a guest of the Academy of Sciences of the Soviet Union for their Jubilee Session, I visited Moscow and Leningrad for six weeks, I talked with the Russian anthropologists and archaeologists of their recent discoveries. Here was also the opportunity to look at the people on the subway, on the streets, on busses, in the theater, at the movies, and in the "Parks of Culture and Rest." Each day I made a point of looking carefully at three thousand or more faces, generally by riding up and down the subway escalators. These people did not want war. They wanted peace. They wanted to be left alone to recover their immense war losses. They radiated vitality, especially among the young. I believe that after their past twenty-five years of struggle and personal sacrifice they want peace as much as any other people in the world.

My impression was that they had matured considerably since I was there in 1934—there was about the same difference as between a fifteen-year-old child and a young man of twenty-five who has just won a fight to the death.

While they do not want to fight, they want security from attack. However, they will obey their country's call, even if it be to arms.

In Berlin, during July 1945, I saw the devastation caused by aerial bombing. Driving from Tempelhof to the Reichstag in a jeep made me realize for the first time what such devastation really means. Newsreels do not show the sleek, fat rats feasting on the dead, nor does the sickly smell of the bodies curl around the nostrils.

Flying over Stalingrad, talking with the survivors of the blockade of Leningrad, looking down over Cassel and the ruins on each side of the Rhine, seeing Paris with the shock of finding a city with the roofs intact, and then London with its bandaged wounded—all these made me realize the horror that is modern warfare. The final contrast was climaxed when the big C-54 landed at La Guardia. We were home to the only land of plenty

431

in the world. The lights, the buildings, the stores, the clothes, and above all the food, give one a queer feeling of pride mingled with shame, the shame of plenty in a world of want.

As we look around us we can see quite plainly that we have robbed the soil, cut down the trees, killed the game, and often changed the balance of nature. More harm has been done to the good earth during the past few hundred years than in the preceding thousands.

Man is tending to destroy himself by stealing from the thin soil, by reproducing the unfit in superior numbers, and by unchecked population increase. However, the causes and effects are now becoming apparent. As in the long past Man will readjust these when the necessity really arises. That time is close at hand.

Since it is a basic human trait that no one really likes to be helped and the creditor is first appreciated, then envied, and finally hated, we are on the road to being one of the most hated nations on earth.

Hatred, that "strong aversion or detestation coupled with ill will," is usually a symbol of fear mingled with jealously. The conflict between two systems of government may be resolved without armed conflict. In these dark days of the twilight zone, when security is but a meaningless word, the peoples of the world are turning to that inner light which has never shone more brilliantly than now in the middle of the twentieth century. More and more is our faith in the Supreme Being renewed, whether our leader be Jesus Christ, Mohammed, Buddha, Confucius, Lao-tse —or Lenin. As life on earth becomes harder the individual naturally turns to God and the belief in a life beyond the grave. In the Christian world there are signs of a stirring. Among the Moslems the Zionists have created new bonds. In the Soviet Union state-created fears encourage internal strength through religious conviction. The richly ornamented icons are in museums, but the people pray fervently to a wooden or tin cross, symbol of Christianity. In China the religion of Gautama Buddha teaches that right belief, right resolve, right word, right act, right life, right effort, right thinking, and right meditation lead to *nirvana*, immortality.

432

The religious leaders and philosophers—all products of leisure time—have given us the Guiding Light. Hard times, insecurity, and fear are removing the temporary film.

Mankind stands on the threshold of the use of a new power which will supersede all known forms of energy and which will bring in its wake a great step forward toward freedom from want and the corresponding leisure. This will be the greatest age of constructive thought and creative ability. In the long pre-history and history of mankind, lasting at least one million years, there has been one comparable period, namely when the ice began to melt in western Europe. At that time there was an abundant food supply so that Man could devote the greater part of his time to his latent creative ability.

The second half of the twentieth century will usher in this greatest of all mental developments as a result of the leisure time afforded by the release and control of atomic energy.

This will also give time for thought and reflection, not among the cloistered few, but for tens, perhaps even hundreds of millions, of people.

The dawn of the great Cultural Age of Man is at hand. . . .

Thus, as we stand back to take the long view of mankind we can trace the advent of life on the earth, the historical outline of the past million years before THE BOMB; we can look critically at the present and predict the uncertain future.

All growth and development follow cycles. Even climate follows cycles. Ice Age has been followed by an interglacial period, then another Ice Age. The pattern is regular, the period varies. Another Ice Age is due about a thousand generations hence. By that time Man will have learned to regulate human reproduction in relation to world capacity and with atomic energy he may counteract the creeping ice.

Man's ingenuity will overcome all physical difficulties except for the final collision of the earth, which will destroy all forms of life.

This will complete THE CYCLE.

EPILOGUE

Man has traveled a long, hard path during the million-year interval between two flashes of lightning—one made by nature in the dark, primeval forest, which gave him fire, the other man-made in the United States.

Within the waters and on the land there is even more abundant life, each the prey of another. Only Man, with his powers of reason, may rise above this tyrannical law of nature.

"And God blessed them, and God said unto them, Be fruitful, and multiply, and replenish the earth, and subdue it: and have dominion over the fish of the sea, and over the fowl of the air, and over every living thing that moveth upon the earth. . . ."

What is Past is Prologue.

434

Index

INDEX

Abdullah, King of Hashemite Kingdom of the Jordan, 151
Aboudi, Mohammed, 42
Abu Zeneimeh (Sinai), 394
Academy of Sciences (Kiev), 309–310
Academy of Sciences (Leningrad), 314
Academy of Sciences (Moscow), 291, 293, 354–356, 362, 365
Academy of Sciences (Paris), 315
Acromegaly, 36–37, 230
Adams, Herbert, 191
Adler Planetarium (Chicago), 189
Africa, 388–404
Ahmed ibn Ajil al Yawir, 257–261
Ahmed Lutfi, 390
Ain as Saih (Saudi Arabia), 422–423
Ajil al Yawir, Sheik, 237, 253–261
Akeley, Carl, 400
Albright, William F., 385, 390, 394, 396–397
Algeciras (Spain), 98, 105
Ali Bey el Hamamsi, 404
Ali Jaudat al Ayubi, 236
Ali Khuli Khan, 411
Al Khobar (Saudi Arabia), 422
Alliance Israélite (Isfahan), 283
Al Qaisumah (Saudi Arabia), 423
Al Qatrani (Jordan), 146, 147
Al Qurna (Iraq), 238, 241
Alsop, Joseph W., Jr., 406

Altamira Cave (Spain), 203
Amara (Iraq), 236, 250
American Anthropological Association, 350
American Museum of Natural History, 134–135, 172, 330
American Oriental Society, 152
American School of Oriental Research (Jerusalem), 387
American School of Prehistoric Research, 141
American University (Beirut), 252, 268
Amman (Jordan), 44, 153
Andrau, Evert W. K., 183, 184
Andrews, Roy Chapman, 385
"Angel, The." See "The Angel"
Anglo-Saxons, 17
Aqra (Iraq), 273
Arabian American Oil Company (Aramco), 421–422
Archaeological Institute of America, 350
Army Medical Library (Washington), 330
Arne, T. J., 121
Art Institute (Chicago), 125, 189
Ashmolean Museum (Oxford), 18, 87–88, 173
Associated Press of America, 167, 168
Aswan (Egypt), 397

437

Auda abu Tayi, 147–149, 324
Aurignacian cave art, 141; diorama, 212–213
Azerbaidzhan Academy of Sciences (Baku), 354
Azerbaidzhan State Museum (Baku), 294
Azilian diorama, 213–214; painted pebbles, 202; skulls (Bavaria), 118

Babylon (Iraq), 50, 62–63, 88–89
Badanah (Saudi Arabia), 424
Bader, John, 332
Baggrave Hall (Leicestershire), 14–19, 27, 123, 317
Baghdad, 46–49, 90, 154, 235–236, 276–280, 353
Baij Bedouins (Iraq), 261
Bakhtiari Tribe (Iran), 409–412
Baku, 290–294, 354
Balad Sinjar (Iraq), 262
Balboa Park Museum (San Diego), 133
Balfour, Henry, 30, 32, 34–35, 113, 318–319
Barlow, F. O., 138, 203
Barrèyre, Henri, 138–140, 212
Barton, R. F., 314
Bartow, Nevett, 332
Basmachi, Faraj, 407
Basra, 277
Batten, Dennis, 416–419
Bayer, Adolf, 118–119
Bayir Wells (Jordan), 147–149, 152–153, 266
Beatty, Earl, 14, 16, 21
Beatty, Ethel Field, 14
Bédeilhac Cave (Ariège), 207–208
Bedford, Duke of, 36
Bégouen, Count, 203, 380
Behn, Sosthenes, 335
Beirut (Lebanon), 426
Beling, Willard, 422
Bell, Gertrude, 47–49, 54, 87, 90, 95, 147, 149, 151, 179, 184–185, 260

Belshazzar, 158
Benedict XV, 20
Beni Hilal, 256, 404, 419
Berchtesgaden, 22, 372
Berlin, 120–121, 362, 366–371
Bethlehem, 44, 388
Bijou, George, 379
Black, A. P., 330
Black, Davidson, 134
Blackstone Hotel (Chicago), 308
Blaschke, Frederick C., 118, 137–138, 140, 142–143, 145, 189, 190, 195–197, 204, 212, 292, 361
Bliss, Mildred, 378, 379
Bliss, Robert Woods, 378, 379
Boas, Franz, 236
Bogoras, W. G., 195
Bonn, 115
Borbolla, Daniel Rubin de la, 383, 385
Borglum, Gutzon, 191
Boucher de Perthes, Jacques, 211
Bowman, Isaiah, 340–341
Braidwood, Robert J., 416
Breasted, James Henry, 41, 237
Breckinridge, Mary Marvin (Mrs. Jefferson Patterson), 127
Breder, C. M., Jr., 330
Breuil, Abbé Henri, 32, 97–111, 113, 135, 137–138, 140–142, 200–206, 212, 288, 317, 378–379
Briggs, Lyman J., 334
Brisbane, Arthur, 211
British Broadcasting Corporation, 322
British Guiana, 323
British Museum, 18
Brøndsted, Johannes, 122
Brooksby Hall (Leicestershire), 14
Brown, Wilson, 343, 345
Browne, Myra, 286
Browne, William E., 183, 187, 286, 415
Bruce, David K. E., 372
Brünn (Brno) (Moravia), 119

438

Brüx calvarium, 119
Buckingham, J. S., 53
Bullitt, William C., 311
Bunak, Victor, 361
Burden, W. Douglas, 329
Burkitt, Miles, 110
Burnaby, Algernon Edwyn, 14, 19
Burnaby, Minna Field, 14–16, 18–20, 27, 39, 98, 123, 372, 386, 404
Burrows, Millar, 387
Buxton, L. H. Dudley, 30, 32, 37–40, 42, 44, 45, 48–50, 52, 55, 57–58, 61, 63, 64, 66–70, 73, 74, 77, 82–86, 88, 89, 91, 92, 94–97, 104, 134, 137, 145, 155, 157, 158, 175, 177, 274, 318, 319, 352, 353, 405, 407

Cairo, 39–41, 352
Campbell, Levin H., Jr., 338
Cap Blanc rock shelter (France), 140; skeleton, 134–136
Capone, Alphonse, 127, 128, 306, 328
Carmichael, Hoagland (Hoagy) Howard, 422
Carnac (Brittany), 142
Carnarvon, Earl of, 43
Carter, Howard, 18, 42–43
Castanet, Marcel, 141
Caucasus, 290–303
Charnwood Forest (Leicestershire), 27
Chellean diorama, 212
Cheney, Edwin F., 332
Cherrie, George K., 243
Chicago, 14, 125–137, 188–195, 208–215, 318–319
Chicago Natural History Museum, 425. See Field Museum of Natural History
Chicago World's Fair, 188, 190, 208–211, 228, 229, 235
Childs, James Rives, 421
Chitty, George J., 25
Christie, Agatha (Mrs. Max Mallowan), 419, 420

Church, James E., 351, 352
Churchill, Winston Spencer, 325, 347, 388
Clawson, M. Don, 252
Clawson, Rue, 252, 255, 256
Cohen, David, 388
Cohen, Joseph, 283
Combe-Capelle skeleton (Dordogne), 120
Conklin, E. G., 217
Cooke, H. B. S., 388
Cooke, R. S., 47, 48, 170, 179
Coolidge, Harold Jefferson, Jr, 329, 332
Coon, Carleton S., 415
Cooper, Alfred Duff, 322
Cooper, Merion C., 410
Copenhagen, 122
Corwin, Charles Abel, 139, 143, 209, 212
Coryndon Memorial Museum (Nairobi), 398
Cottin, A., 183, 185
Cox, Sir Percy, 151, 241, 249
Crawley, Leonard, 112
Crocker, Edward S., 421
Crô-Magnon dioramas, 212–213; skulls, 119
Cuernavaca (Mexico), 381
Cueva del Arco (Spain), 103
Cueva de la Paja (Spain), 103
Cunard, Sir Edward, 326
Curran, Kenneth, 424
Curtis, Kenneth, 209

Dachau, 373–375
Damascus, 336
Davies, D. C., 125, 136
Davis, Watson, 350
Davison, Ralph, 329
Dawes, Rufus, 211
Debuc, Georges, 205
Declaration of Independence, 350, 356–357
De la Feld, Hubertus, 113

439

De Morgan, Jacques, 18
Denison, Robert H., 388
Deranyigala, P. E. P., 388
De Terra, Helmut, 384
Devil's Tower rock shelter (Gibraltar), 104–105, 142, 212
Dhahran (Saudi Arabia), 423
Dnieproges (Ukraine), 309
Domesday Book, 27
Donovan, William J., 332
Dorud (Iran), 412
Doughty, Charles M., 148
Douglas, A. J., 34
Douglas, Marjory Stoneman, 13
Dresden, 120
Drower, Lady, 237, 238, 242, 244, 246, 251
Drury, John, 128
Druze (Syria and Jordan), 45
Dubai (Persian Gulf), 421
Dubois, Eugène, 122
Dutch, Oswald, 372

Ebtehaj, Abol Hassan, 413
Edwards, Grammar G., 388
Eichstett, Egon von, 134
El Arish (Sinai), 390–392
El Jafar (Jordan), 149
Elliot-Smith, Sir Grafton, 137
Erbil (Iraq), 416
Es Salt (Jordan), 44
Eton College, 23–26
Ettinghausen, Richard, 285
Evans, Charles D., 388
Evans, Luther, 350
Evans, Sir Arthur, 18
Ezekiel, Moses, 20

Faisal I, King of Iraq, 151
Faiyûm (Egypt), 388–389
Falih as Saihud, Sheik, 236–237, 242, 246–250
Falluja Desert (Iraq), 181–182
Farago, Ladislas, 341
Farrington, Oliver C., 137

Farrington, Selwyn Kip, Jr., 333
Fidimìn (Faiyûm), 389
Field, Cyrus W., 15
Field, Marshall I, 125
Field, Marshall III, 23, 133, 143, 190
Field, Marshall and Company (Chicago), 209, 312; Paris, 135, 201
Field, Stanley, 77, 125, 132, 133, 135, 143, 189, 190, 192–194, 197, 209
Field Columbian Museum, now Chicago Natural History Museum, 132. See also Field Museum of Natural History
Field Museum of Natural History (now Chicago Natural History Museum), 15, 22, 38, 82, 83, 88, 95, 113, 118, 123, 126–143, 166, 171, 173, 189–215, 284, 285, 288, 292, 319, 339, 360, 361, 380, 381
Field Museum-Oxford University Joint Expedition to Kish (Iraq), 38, 44, 50–88, 154–181, 224, 314. See also Kish; Tell Inghara; Tell el Uhaimir
Fischer, Eugen, 134
Flood of Noah, 172, 173
Forbes Quarry (Gibraltar), 104
Ford, Frank, 20
Forrestal, James, 321
Frank, Morris, 230
Franklin, Benjamin, 355
Fraser, E. S., 182
Frumkin, A., 354
Fuller, Anne, 322
Fünen dagger (Denmark), 122

Ganties-les-Bains (Haute-Garonne), 204–206
Garden of Eden, 50, 239, 421
Gargas (Haute-Garonne), 141–142
Garrod, Dorothy, 35, 98–99, 104–111, 142, 212
Garrod, Sir Archibald, 35, 97, 98
Gatier, Pierre, 138–140, 212
Gaza, 119

Genouillac, Abbé H. de, 53
Geological Museum (Heidelberg), 115
Gerasimov, M. M., 360, 361
Gershwin, George, 230
Gibraltar, 98, 103–105
Glueck, Nelson, 395
Godfrey Njao, 397, 398, 401, 403, 404
Gorianovic-Kramberger, M., 119
Green, Gretchen, 197, 198, 337
Greene, Dorothea, 373
Gregg, Clifford Cilley, 230
Gregory, William K., 134
Grew, Joseph C., 351
Grice, C., 237
Grimaud, M., 135
Guest, Evan, 238

Haarlem, 122
Haddon, A. C., 134
Hafar al Batin (Saudi Arabia), 423
Hajji Miniehil, 162–164, 275, 276, 408
Halfayah (Iraq), 250
Hall of Prehistoric Man, 132, 134–143, 201–215
Hall of Races of Mankind, 132–134, 189–200, 209–210, 226–228
Hallström, Gustav, 121
Harlan, H. V., 171
Harrat ar Rajil (Jordan), 45, 183–185
Harriman, W. Averell, 365, 366
Hashemite Kingdom of the Jordan, 44
Hassan Jedur, 59–61, 65, 75, 85, 158, 160, 161, 175, 178, 179
Hauser, O., 120–121
Hearst, William Randolph, 29
Heidelberg, 113–118
Helena, Queen of Italy, 21–22
Henderson, Edward, 421
Hermitage Museum (Leningrad), 313
Herron, Albert, 338
Herzfeld, Ernest, 285–287

Higgins, Sir John, 49, 80, 90, 95
Hill, M. D., 25–27, 29, 30, 32, 88, 131
Hilla (Iraq), 49, 50, 76, 82, 86, 168, 238, 408
Hiscock, Earle, 332
Hitler, Adolf, 362, 366, 370
Hoffman, Malvina, 190–199, 209, 226, 228, 230, 316, 317
Holm, Don, 425
Holt, A. L. 183
Homo heidelbergensis, 115
Homo rhodesiensis, 36
Hoogstraal, Harry, 388
Hooper, David, 284
Hooton, Earnest A., 32, 320
Hopkins, Harry L., 347
Hornibrook, William H., 288
Houle, James L., 388
Hrdlička, Aleš, 133, 134, 195
Hungarton Church (Leicestershire), 397
Hunter, J. H., 398–402, 404
Hussakof, Louis, 172
Huxley, Julian, 32, 33, 35, 36, 354
Huxley, Thomas Henry, 25, 115
Huzayyin, S. A., 390, 392

Ibn Saud, H. M. ibn Abdel Aziz ibn Abdel Rahman Al Faisal Al Saud, 353, 426
Ingram, Sir Bruce, 43
Institute of Peoples of the Far North (Leningrad), 315
Institute of Plant Industry (Leningrad), 314
Insull, Samuel, 144
International Harvester Company (Chicago), 308
International Refugee Organization (IRO), 376
Iran (Persia), 281–289, 409–415
Iraq (Mesopotamia), 46–93, 154–183, 235–280, 407–409, 415–420
Iraq Museum (Baghdad), 47, 87, 90, 95, 166, 173, 179, 252

441

Iraq Petroleum Company, 181, 252, 416
Isfahan, 282–284
Ismail Javadi, 285

Jaf Tribe (Iran and Iraq), 273
James, Montagu Rhodes, 26
Jebel Baradost (Iraq), 274, 416, 418
Jebel Enaze (Anaiza), 183, 184
Jebel Qurna (Jordan), 153
Jebel Tenf (Syria), 184
Jebel Thlathakhwat (Jordan), 147
Jebel Umm Wual (Saudi Arabia), 154
Jemdet Nasr (Iraq), 79–83, 90, 158, 172–179
Jericho, 44, 388
Jerusalem, 43–44, 95–96, 145, 353, 386–387
Johansen, Friis, 122
Joint Chiefs of Staff, 332, 336
Joint Distribution Committee (JDC), 376
Juda Rabbi Hedvat, 284
Jungfrau, 378

Kajiado (Kenya), 398, 404
Kalmyks, 376–377
Kapitza, Peter, 354
Keeble, Sir Frederick, 33
Keeley, James H., 406
Keith, Sir Arthur, 32, 36, 37, 83, 134, 137–139, 196, 197, 201, 226, 230, 274, 281, 288, 319
Kelley, Alice Bowler, 141
Kelley, Harper, 141, 201, 317
Kelley, John C., 423
Kellogg, Charles E., 352
Kemeys, Paul, 125
Kennedy, Walter P., 276, 281, 284
Kenya Colony, 397–404
Kerim, Abdul, 250
Kharkov (Ukraine), 309
Khazaal ibn Falih as Saihud, Sheik, 240–244, 246, 249, 250

Khurrumabad (Iran), 412
Kiev (Ukraine), 309
Kiik-Koba skeleton (Crimea), 360
Kish (Iraq), 14, 38, 50–78, 83–88, 154–173, 179–181, 224–225, 275–276, 315, 407–409
Knabenshue, Paul, 236, 278
Knight, Charles R., 136, 203, 209
Knight, Lucy, 203
Koldewey, Robert, 59, 89, 408
Kolthoff, I. M., 350, 351
Komarov, V. L., 355, 357
Kom Oshim (Faiyûm), 388
Krapina Skeletons (Croatia now Yugoslavia), 119
Kremlin, 311, 312, 355, 357
Kuban (Caucasus), 297, 301
Kurds (Iraq), 273–275

La Brea (Trinidad), 328
La Chapelle-aux-Saints Skeleton (Corrèze), 118
Lake Naivasha (Kenya), 398
Land, Emery Scott, 331, 332
Langdon, Stephen L., 44, 45, 49, 50, 52–56, 58, 59, 61, 63, 64, 69, 78–81, 88, 97, 157–159, 168, 172, 173, 175–177, 407
Langmuir, Irving, 349
Lantier, Raymond, 202
La Pileta (Spain), 105–111
La Quina (Charente), 142, 208
Lascaux Cave (Dordogne), 378–379
Lathrop, Barbour, 13, 28–30, 38, 39, 65, 88, 96, 101, 118, 125, 234, 397
Laufer, Berthold, 125, 126, 130, 131, 133–135, 143, 169, 171, 189, 191–195, 197, 227, 234, 275, 283, 318
Lavra Monastery (Kiev), 310
Lawrence, T. E., 147–153, 260, 323
Lazar, Yusuf (Kazar, Uash), 238, 240, 243, 245, 248, 249, 251, 259, 260, 265, 278, 279, 281, 284, 289, 405, 409, 412, 413, 418, 420, 426
Leaf, George, 15

442

Leakey Louis B., 398
Leakey, Mary, 398
Lebzelter, Viktor, 227
Leicester Museum (England), 17
Leicestershire (England), 27–28
Le Moustier rock shelter (Dordogne), 139–140; skeleton, 120, 138, 139
Leningrad, 313–317, 357–362
Léon, Paul, 202, 203
Lerner, Michael, 330, 333
Le Roc (Charente), 142
Les Eyzies (Dordogne), 139
Levin, M. G., 361
Library of Congress, 321, 322, 330, 337, 350, 362
Lindsay, Florence Field, 125
Lindsay, Thomas P., 125
Littmann, Enno, 152
Londonderry, Marquess of, 236
Lubin, Isador, 366, 367
Luristan (Iran), 412–413
Luxor (Egypt), 41–43

MacCurdy, George Grant, 141
Mackay, Ernest, 50, 52, 54, 55, 57, 58, 60, 61, 63, 65, 66, 69–71, 73, 75–80, 85, 87–88, 156–158, 175
Mackenzie, De Witt, 167
MacLeish, Archibald, 321
MacVeagh, Lincoln, 380
Madame Tussaud's (London), 143, 197
Magdalenian diorama, 213; necklaces, 141
Mahor Birinji (Iran), 411
Malinowski, Bronislaw, 35
Mallowan, Max E. L., 419
Malmö (Sweden), 122
Mandement, Joseph, 207–208, 380
Mann, William M., 338
Manship, Paul, 331, 332
Marconi, Guglielmo, 21, 229
Marett, R. R., 30, 32, 35, 318
Marshall, Sir John, 156

Marsh Arabs (Iraq), 237–250
Martin, Henri, 142, 208
Martin, Richard A., 235–236, 238, 245, 249–251, 255–257, 261, 268, 271, 275, 277–281, 284, 285, 289–291, 293, 299–301, 303, 304, 310–312, 314–317, 354
Martinez del Rio, Pablo, 383
Masai (Kenya), 398, 402, 403
Mas d'Azil (Ariège), 142, 202, 380
Mashuru (Kenya), 401
McBain, James W., 350
McBride, Arthur, 330
McCown, Donald, 286, 415
McDonald, Eugene F., Jr., 228
McGhee, George C., 421
McLeod, T. H., 258, 260
Merchant Seamen's Medal of Honor, 331–332
Merkhah Port (Sinai), 394
Metropolitan Museum of Art, 190
Mexico, 380–385
Meymourian, Albert, 239, 242, 244, 245
Miami, 335–336
Ministry of Information (London), 322
Mirza Muhammed Ali Khan, 283
"Miss Crô-Magnon," 136, 143
Mitchell, Sir Philip, 398
Mohammed abu Tayi, 149
Mollison, Theodor, 118
"Monsieur Le Moustier," 143, 190, 292
Moon, Henry, 183
Moravske-Zemske Museum (Brünn), 119
Morgan, Jacques de, 157
Morteza Khuli Khan Samsam, 409, 410
Moscow, 310–313
Moses and the Exodus, 395, 397
Mount Kilimanjaro (Kenya), 398
Mount of Olives, 44
Muallim, Khedoory, 239, 243, 250
Munich, 118, 372

443

Münter, Heinrich, 114, 115
Musée de l'Histoire Naturelle (Paris), 107
Musée National (St. Germain-en-Laye), 140
Museum für Völkerkunde (Dresden), 120
Museum für Vorgeschichte (Munich), 118
Museum of Archaeology (Leningrad), 361
Museum of Comparative Zoology (Harvard), 405
Museum of Fine Arts (Boston), 282
Museum of Georgia (Tbilisi), 295
Museum of Oriental Civilizations (Moscow), 361

Nabonidus, 158–160
Nadai, Arnold, 349
Nairn, Norman, 276
Nairn Overland Desert Mail, 44, 146, 182
Naji al Asil, 415
National Academy of Sciences (Washington), 330
National Farm and Home Hour (NBC), 232
National Geographic Society, 350
National Museum (Copenhagen), 122
National Museum (Mexico City), 383
Natural History Museum (Leningrad), 315
Naval Research Laboratory (Bethesda, Maryland), 330
Neanderthal dioramas, 212; Man, 139–140; tooth, 208
Neander Valley, 115
Nebuchadnezzar, 54–56, 62–64, 69, 158, 225, 239
Nekhl (Sinai), 392–393
Neolithic diorama, 214
Newall, Sir Cyril, 339

New College (Oxford), 13, 30, 31, 318–319
New York Aquarium, 330
Ngoro-ngoro Crater (Tanganyika), 398
Nimrud (Iraq), 419
Nippur (Iraq), 171
Njao, Godfrey, 397, 398, 401, 403, 404
Nokrashy Pasha, 389
Norsk Folksmuseum (Oslo), 121
North Arabian Desert, 44–46, 91–95, 145–149, 153–154, 181–188, 251–252, 406–407
Northwestern University Crime Detection Laboratory (Chicago), 129

Oboler, Arch, 401
Oceanographic Institution (Woods Hole), 330
Ofnet skulls (Bavaria), 118
Oleijski, Jacob, 373
Oppert, Jules, 53
Orbeli, Josif Abgerovich, 313, 355
Ordzhonikidze (Dzaudzhikau), 296
O'Reilly, Sir Lennox, 326
Organization for Rehabilitation through Training (ORT), 372–376
Oriental Institute (University of Chicago), 41, 237, 276, 281, 285–286, 416
Osborn, Henry Fairfield, 134
Osetes (Caucasus), 296
Oshanin, L. V., 361
Oslo, 121
Ostia, excavations at, 22
Oxford, 13, 30–35, 37–38, 97–98, 319–320
Oxford University Anthropological Society, 35

Page, Frank, 335
Page, Thomas Nelson, 19–21
Palmyra (Syria), 406
Paris, 122, 138, 371
Parker, Eleanor, 337

444

Patten, Henry J., 173
Pauley, Edwin Wendell, 365, 366, 367
Peabody Museum (Harvard), 303, 322, 404, 423
Pekarna (Czechoslovakia), 119
Percival, John, 82
Pergamon Museum (Berlin), 89
Périgueux (Dordogne), 138
Perkins, Frances, 347
Persepolis (Iran), 285-286
Petra (Jordan), 153
Petrie, Sir Flinders, 394
Peyrille, Louis, 202
Peyrony, D., 140
Philippus Dinkha, 416-418
Phillips, Wendell, 385-388, 396, 397
Pinchot, Gifford, 333
Pinchot, Leila, 413
Pitcairn, Mary (Mrs. William Jackson), 379
Pithecanthropus erectus, 122
Pittard, Eugène, 134
Pitt-Rivers Museum (Oxford), 30, 32
Poirot, Hercule, 420
Pope, Arthur Upham, 351
Předmost (Czechoslovakia), 119
Prentice, William K., 186
Provinzial Museum (Bonn), 115
Pseudocerastes fieldi, 154
Pumpelly, Raphael, 18
Pyramid of Cheops, 40

Qasr ed Dauquera (Saudi Arabia), 426
Qasr el Azraq (Jordan), 45, 90, 95, 153, 188, 426
Qasr el Burqu (Jordan), 90, 184-187, 426
Quarrie, S. W., 146-150, 154
Quorn Hunt (Leicestershire), 14, 15

Rafha (Saudi Arabia), 424
Ramadi (Iraq), 92, 93, 251
Rameses (Egypt), 396
Ras Mishaab (Saudi Arabia), 423

Ravdonikas, V. I., 314, 360
Rawson, Frederick H., 144
Rayy (Iran), 282, 294
Razmara, Ali, 409, 413, 414
Redfield, Robert, 382
Rees, L. W. B., 146, 153
Regent's Park Zoological Garden (London), 34-35
Reichelderfer, F. W., 371
Reilly, Michael, 343, 344
Reza Pahlevi, Mohammed, Shah, 414-415
Rhine, J. B., 93
Rhodesian skull, 36, 37
Robertson Smith, W., 165
Robrieux, Georges, 135
Rodin, Auguste, 191-193
Rogers, Will, 211
Roginskii, IA.IA., 361
Romanoff, Rostislav, 312
Rome, 18-19, 386
Romero, Javier, 383, 384
Ronda (Spain), 111
Roosevelt, Franklin Delano, 313, 321, 323, 324, 327-329, 331, 332, 335, 336, 339-343, 345-347, 353, 372, 388
Rostov-on-Don, 303-306
Royal Anthropological Institute of Great Britain and Ireland (London), 35, 36
Royal College of Medicine (Baghdad), 239, 276
Royal College of Surgeons (London), 36, 37, 137, 196
Royal Geographical Society (London), 35, 315
Russell, George, 401
Russell, Sir Thomas Wentworth, 40
Rutba Wells (Iraq), 92, 93, 181-183, 187, 188, 251, 252
Ruwandiz Gorge (Iraq), 273-274, 417

Saccopastore skulls (Italy), 386
Sadr, Mohammed M., 389

445

Safar, Fuad, 415, 417, 419
Sanger, Richard, 426
Sanhouri Pasha, 389
Sargon of Agade, 159
Saudi Arabia, 421–426
Schaafhausen, Hermann, 115
Schmidt, Arthur, 330
Schmidt, Erich F., 282
Schmidt, Karl P., 154, 266, 285, 288, 425
Schoedensack, Ernest, 410
Schroeder, Eric, 156, 157, 160, 161, 164, 166, 167, 169, 177, 178, 181, 186, 187
Scripps Institution of Oceanography (La Jolla), 330
Seager, O. A., 422
"Sea of Reeds" (Egypt), 395, 397
Selengei (Kenya), 398, 403
Serabit el Khadem (Sinai), 394
Serengeti National Park (Tanganyika), 398
Sergi, Sergio, 386
Shahbaz, Kuresh, 410, 412
Shammar Bedouins (Iraq), 252–261
Shangri-la, 342–347
Shapley, Harlow, 349, 351, 352
Shedd Aquarium (Chicago), 189, 211
Shepheard's Hotel (Cairo), 41, 352
Shergatis (Iraq), 416
Shipley, Ruth B., 349
Shiraz (Iran), 286–287
Showket, S. Y., 181, 182, 186, 237, 240–245, 247–249, 251, 255, 258, 262–264, 267, 275, 277, 418
Simms, S. C., 143, 192
Sinai (Egypt), 390–397
Sinclair, Harry F., 232
Sinclair Oil Company, 231–232
Skliros, J., 181
Sloan, Alfred P., Jr., 232–233
Smeaton, Winifred (Mrs. Homer Thomas), 152, 236–238, 242, 251–257, 261, 267, 276, 277, 280
Smith, Katherine, 284, 285, 287

Smith, Myron Bement, 284, 285
Smithsonian Institution, 330, 350
Smith-Woodward, Sir Arthur, 36
Snyder, William, 401, 402
Sollas, William J., 32, 34
Solutré (France), 201
Solutrean diorama, 213
Spain, 98–103, 105–111
Spooner, Warden, 31
Sprague, Albert A., 125
Springer, Stuart, 330, 331
Staatlichen Museum (Berlin), 120
Stalin, Marshal, 346, 357, 358
Starling, Edward W., 343
State National Museum (Stockholm), 121
St. Catherine's Monastery (Sinai), 395–396
Stein, Sir Aurel, 287
Stevens, E. S. (Lady Drower), 237
Stewart, T. Dale, 384
Stock, Frederick, 133
Stockholm, 121
Storms, Walter, 128, 129
Storrs, Sir Ronald, 95, 96, 151
Strasbourg, 113
Strausz-Hupé, Robert, 342
Strawn, Silas H., 144
Sulaimaniya (Iraq), 275
Sulubba (Sleyb), 251–252
Sunningdale School (England), 18–19, 22
Swiss Lake Dweller diorama, 214–215

Tajo de las Figuras (Spain), 100–102
Tamerlane, 361
Tamiya (Faiyûm), 389
Tapatanilla-Taivilla (Spain), 99
Tapline (Trans-Arabian Pipe Line), 422, 423
Taylor, Wayne Chatfield, 334
Teheran, 281, 354, 409
Tell Bargouthiat (Iraq), 79–81, 83
Tell el Hibr (Saudi Arabia), 154, 421, 425

Tell el Uhaimir (Kish), 50, 53, 54, 56, 58, 62, 88, 157, 159, 275, 408

Tell Inghara (Kish), 57, 60, 62, 63, 65, 66, 73, 78, 79, 83, 88, 155, 169, 275

Tempelhof (Berlin), 368, 371

Tepexpán skeleton (Mexico), 384

Tepoztlán (Mexico), 382–383

Terry, Gladys, 388, 397

Terry, William B., 388, 390, 392, 395, 397

Teshik-Tash (Tashkent), 105, 361

"The Angel" (Maurice Tillet), 230–231

Thomas, Lowell, 395

Thomasville (Georgia), 381, 385

Thompson, Malvina, 337

Thornburg, Leila, 409

Thornburg, Max Weston, 409, 413

Tillet, Maurice, 230–231

Tobago, 324

Todd, David, 330

Todd, Joseph, 195

Todd, Leonard, 23, 25

Tolstov, S. P., 360, 361

Tolstoy Foundation, 377

Train, C. Russell, 328

Train, Middleton, 328, 329

Transjordan (Jordan), 44

Tree, Ronald, 321

Trever, Camilla, 313

Trinidad, 323–329

Trois Frères (Ariège), 203, 204

Trombe, Félix, 204

Trucial Oman Coast (Persian Gulf), 421

Truman, Harry S., 342, 351

Tuc d'Audoubert (Ariège), 203

Tully, Grace, 329, 331, 340–344, 347

Turaif (Saudi Arabia), 426

Tutankhamen, 41–43, 352

Ubangi woman, 199–200, 227, 230

Ukraine, 303–310

University Museum (Philadelphia), 90, 282

University of California African Expedition, 385, 388–404

University of Florida, 330

Urban, Joseph, 209, 230

Ur of the Chaldees (Iraq), 50, 89, 90, 171, 224, 276

U. S. Department of Agriculture, 171

Ussher, James, 216

U.S.S.R., 289–317, 354–366

Valley of the Kings (Egypt), 41–43

Vania, Ivan, 181, 182

Vavilov, Nicolai, 314, 315

"Venus of Willendorf" (Bavaria), 98, 119

Vienna, 118–119, 195

Virchow, Rudolf, 115

Volkmann, Joseph, 422

Von Eichstett, Egon, 118

Wadi Feiran (Sinai), 394

Wadi Hauran (Iraq), 93, 95

Wadi Sirhan (Saudi Arabia), 148, 426

Waesche, Russell, 336

Wahba, Sheik Hafiz, 421

Wakamba (Kenya), 399, 403

Walden, A. F., 32

Wales, Prince of, 16, 17, 40

Ward, Herbert, 190

Washington, 321–324, 330–335, 337–342, 347–349, 405–406

Washington, Walter L., 380

Watelin, Louis Charles, 156–161, 164, 167, 169, 172, 177, 181, 275, 407

Watson, Edwin M., 331

Weld, Herbert, 53

Wellcome, Sir Henry S., 28–30, 113, 381

Wellcome Historical Medical Museum (London), 28

Weninger, Josef, 195

Wheelwright, George, 336
White, Robb, 381, 405-411, 413, 415, 417-419
Wiley, John C., 409
Wilson, W. C. F., 252-253, 262, 270-273
Wilson, Woodrow, 25
Windels, Fernand, 378
Windsor, Duke of, 16, 17, 40
Winkler, Hans, 152
Wisternitz (Czechoslovakia), 119, 120
Wood, Grant, 307
Woolley, Sir Leonard, 89, 90, 151, 276
Worrell, Ernest, 44-46, 407
Wren, Sir Christopher, 185

Wylie, Karen, 335
Wylie, Philip, 335

Yakobson, Sergei, 342
Yezidis (Iraq), 237, 253, 262-273
Yezd-i-Khast (Iran), 284
York Harbor (Maine), 14, 289
Young, Sir Hubert, 323-326

Zacharias, E. M., 341
Zagreb (Agram), 119
Zamiatnin, S. N., 314, 360
Zernograd Collective Farm (Ukraine), 305-307
Zia, Michael, 407
Zia Hotel (Baghdad), 407
Ziza (Jordan), 146
Zoological Society (London), 35, 36